Researching Non-Formal Religious Education in Europe

A publication of the Comenius- Institute and the Department of
Religious Education, University of Tübingen

Friedrich Schweitzer, Wolfgang Ilg,
Peter Schreiner (eds.)

Researching
Non-Formal Religious Education
in Europe

Waxmann 2019
Münster · New York

Bibliographic information published by die Deutsche Nationalbibliothek

Die Deutsche Nationalbibliothek lists this publication in the
Deutsche Nationalbibliografie; detailed bibliographic data
are available in the internet at http://dnb.dnb.de.

Print-ISBN 978-3-8309-3856-9
E-Book-ISBN 978-3-8309-8856-4

© Waxmann Verlag GmbH, 2019
Steinfurter Straße 555, 48159 Münster, Germany

www.waxmann.com
info@waxmann.com

Cover Design: Pleßmann Design, Ascheberg, Germany
Typesetting: satz&sonders GmbH, Dülmen
Print: CPI books GmbH, Leck
Printed on age-resistant paper, acid-free as per ISO 9706

Printed in Germany

Table of Contents

Introduction

Friedrich Schweitzer, Wolfgang Ilg, Peter Schreiner

Arguably, the emergence or invention of school has been a very powerful factor in the development of human culture. School has become the symbol of education and learning which explains why it has also become a cultural universal. Increasingly, there are no societies left in the world which have not introduced schools and made it mandatory for all children and youth to attend school for many years. Yet at the same time, another even more powerful source of education still remains. As many people have testified for themselves and in their biographies, despite the influence of mandatory school attendance, life itself has been the most important educational influence. The many hours spent in school classrooms seem to fade once their influence is compared to the unplanned experiences that have come with life – good and bad experiences, sometimes beneficial for a person and sometimes devastating.

Human learning cannot be reduced to what happens in schools. Calling life an educator, however, is only possible figuratively and metaphorically. Moreover, life is beyond all intentional planning in this respect. It just happens. Nevertheless, there is an important insight to be gained from considering the limits of school-based learning compared to experiences outside of school. In spite of the monopolising tendencies of the equation between learning or education and school, there are other fields and opportunities which deserve new attention, for example, educational programs offered by non-state actors like the churches or other associations and institutions of civil society.

It is the intention of the present volume to strengthen the awareness of the importance and influence of learning and education beyond school. Moreover, it pursues the more specific question what this kind of education means in terms of religious education. Contrary to other fields, religious education has never been limited to school and to the school subject of Religious Education offered there. Educational programs outside of the school have continued to be offered to children and youth in many places, often in addition to Religious Education at school. But what can be said about the reality and influence of such programs? What research findings are available to answer this question?

1. The focus on non-formal religious education

So far, religious education research has clearly had its focus most of all on the context of school. This is true for most European countries where Religious Education as a school subject plays a major role and therefore seems to define the scope of the respective research as well. The situation in countries like France or,

beyond Europe, in the United States of America where there is no such subject offered in state schools, is naturally different but the research from such countries
is also comparatively limited once the fields of general research on youth and religion or on the psychology of religion are excluded which are more independent
of institutional presuppositions. Even if this has never been discussed explicitly,
research in religious education seems to equal school-oriented research, at least in
most cases.

In recent years, however, the awareness of the meaning and scope of education
outside of the school has clearly grown, in general as well as concerning religious
education. This new awareness applies to both the influence of the family and of
everyday processes of learning, for example, with electronic media on the one hand
and on the other hand, the importance of educational programs and experiences outside school which are often sponsored by non-state associations and organizations.
This new awareness implies that there is a certain imbalance between the importance of religious education outside of school and the lack of research on such areas,
especially concerning empirical research. With few exceptions, very little is known
about the processes and effects of non-formal religious education. Valid research
results which would allow for general insights into such effects have remained rare.
Research has not kept pace with the new awareness of the importance of non-formal
religious education.

In other words, the traditional focus on Religious Education at school should
no longer be the only guiding principle for religious education research if this research is meant to do justice to the reality of religious education in general. The
present volume makes this observation its starting point by putting the emphasis
on non-formal religious education. The understanding of the concept of non-formal
education is based on the threefold distinction between informal, non-formal and
formal education. This distinction will be discussed in more detail and in terms of
different national contexts in the chapters contained in this volume. In a preliminary
manner it can be stated that *formal education* means all kinds of educational processes that are based on formal educational institutions, i.e. in most cases school.
Formal education is compulsory, it is achievement-oriented and closely connected
to grades and degrees which may be of decisive influence on the future course of
life. Moreover, formal education is highly regulated by a binding curriculum and is
characterised by the dominance of professional teachers while the pupils are treated
as clients who have to comply with the expectations set by the teachers and the curriculum. Opposed to this, *informal learning and education* refers to all processes
of education and learning that occur without an institutional basis especially designed for educational purposes. While the family, for example, can be called an
institution it is obvious that its purpose cannot be reduced to education, in spite
of its enormous impact on all later education. Most of what can been said about
the characteristics of formal education does not apply to informal education which
operates without grades and certificates as well as without professional teachers.
Non-formal education stands between the two fields of formal and informal educa-

tion in that it depends on educational programs (as opposed to informal education) but is much less formalised than education in the context of school. Again, most of the characteristics of formal education do not apply in this case while its often intentional character distinguishes non-formal from informal education.

It has to be admitted, however, that the three concepts and the characterizations summarised here are somewhat vague. In many cases it remains ambiguous if a certain educational program or institution belongs to the one field or rather to another. Kindergartens, for example, clearly show traits that fit with both, formal education as well as non-formal education (which is why research on religious education in kindergartens has been included in this volume). There are clear cases like (Christian) youth work (non-formal education) and school (formal education) but in many other cases the distinction is blurred. This is why the editors of this volume decided to make the meaning of the three concepts – formal, informal and non-formal religious education – one of the topics which is treated in the different chapters of the book, rather than presupposing a clear-cut definition which may turn out to be not applicable in many cases. Some of the chapters include detailed discussions of this question as well as an analysis of existing publications (cf. especially Simojoki in this volume). A summary evaluation of what the concept of non-formal religious education should mean and what belongs to it and what not, will be attempted in the conclusions at the end of this volume.

2. The need for researching non-formal religious education

That an exclusive focus on Religious Education at school is too narrow and fails to do justice to the reality of the field of religious education in general can also be grasped from recent discussions in general education as well as in politics. The distinction and appreciation of three kinds of education – formal, informal and non-formal – is becoming a general standard in this field (cf. OECD 2010; as an example from Germany: Bundesministerium 2008). Yet especially with religious education this new understanding has not yet engendered sufficient research in order to arrive at well-grounded understandings and data-based evaluations in the non-formal sector.

In recent years, religious education has become a discipline that sees its task not only in using research results from other fields, for example, from theology and religious studies or from general education and psychology that traditionally have been the most important partner disciplines for religious education. More and more, religious education is willing and able to do its own research, in terms of historical, analytical and empirical research at different national and international levels. Special international research conferences like the Lund (Sweden) Conference (Larsson and Gustavsson 2004) as well as international associations like ISREV (International Seminar on Religious Education and Values) or ISERT (International

Society for Empirical Research in Theology) with their usually bi-annual meetings testify to this development. In 2016, a very successful symposium supported by the "German Research Foundation" (DFG) was held at Tübingen (Germany), "Researching Religious Education: Classroom Processes and Outcomes" (publication: Schweitzer and Boschki 2018).

As mentioned above, however, in most cases, be it in public debates or in with research consultations like the ones just mentioned, religious education is understood in terms of the school subject which goes by this name, at least in many European countries. This limited understanding does not do justice to the importance of other fields and contexts of religious education outside of school, like families or congregations. The international studies on confirmation work, for example, which were carried out in nine European countries showed that about 500000 young people take part in this program every year (cf. Schweitzer et al. 2015 and 2017; Simojoki et al. 2018). Consequently, there is a growing interest in the meaning and impact of non-school educational programs in the field of religious education, not only in the case of confirmation work but also other programs offered by the Churches or other religious organizations (cf. Ilg 2011). Without research, this interest will necessarily remain abstract and without empirical basis.

Due to a number of factors concerning the respective research traditions as well as the political and religious situation in these countries described in the chapters of this volume, Finland, Norway and Switzerland (Kanton of Zurich) have developed approaches for researching non-formal religious education which are of special interest in the present context. In Finland, such approaches can be viewed most appropriately in the context of advanced Finnish research traditions in religious education which have included empirical studies in many fields beyond school, among others concerning diaconal work and volunteerism in youth work or / and in confirmation work. In Norway and in Switzerland, similar approaches have been developed and used, at least in the first place, for evaluating the effects and the effectiveness of different projects and models of religious education in congregational contexts as part of general reform initiatives in these countries (in both countries, these initiatives respond to new needs after Religious Education at school lost its traditional denominational or confessional emphasis). It can be expected that the experiences in these countries will also be of interest for other countries where no such research traditions exist in the context of non-formal religious education.

In many European countries and beyond, there is also a growing interest in non-formal religious education in the context of non-Christian religions, especially Islam. In this case, however, negative views often seem to play a role in this context (cf. Ulfat in this volume). There is concern about possible fundamentalist influences transferred by religion teachers who are active in the context of mosques or similar Muslim institutions addressing young people. Yet very little empirical data is available concerning the actual effects of non-formal religious education in Islam. Again, the main focus of research on Muslim education has been on the school subject of Islamic Religious Education while the informal and the non-formal sectors have been widely neglected.

Sometimes the question is raised if it is even possible to do empirical research in the non-formal sector and to come up with valid results. This critical view is based on the lack of structure and institutionalization which, from the perspective of non-formal education, not only is characteristic of this field but has to be counted among its decisive strengths and advantages over other forms of education. The question of feasibility of research on non-formal religious education therefore is another focus in the present book. Due to its characteristic institutional shapes as well as to the organizational forms of non-formal religious education, research in this field requires methodologies and approaches which are designed to be sensitive to the special object of research in terms of presuppositions of non-formal religious education. It should indeed not be assumed that research procedures developed in the context of school can just be transferred to the non-formal sector without explicitly considering their suitability and without making changes and adaptations. This is why there is a strong emphasis on research designs and methods in all of the contributions to this volume. The aim must be to achieve valid research results based on methodologies which may be different from those used in the context of school but which are no less rigorous and trustworthy in terms of the results.

In sum, empirical research on non-formal religious education must be called a neglected field, at least in most countries. Although the importance of non-formal education in general has come to be acknowledged because of its individual as well as social and societal impact and in spite of the awareness of its public significance, research has been rather slow to develop in this area. The present volume is the first international publication with a clear focus on empirical research concerning non-formal religious education. It offers a forum for summarising the state of the art, for a critical review of existing research as well as of current research projects, for developing (methodological) criteria and perspectives for future research in this field as well as for bringing together insights on educating, teaching and learning in religious education that might be valid beyond particular countries. In this sense it may be viewed as an attempt to what recently has been called international knowledge transfer in religious education (Manifesto 2019).

The fact that empirical approaches to religious education have widely tended to neglect the non-formal sector, is also the reason for the emphasis on empirical research in the present volume. This emphasis does not imply, however, that research should be limited to just one approach. Other approaches, for example historical studies or hermeneutical-analytical studies can be of no less importance for advancing the work of non-formal religious education. Moreover, religious education should always be based on an interplay between, among others, theology, insights from the philosophy of education and empirical research (for a recent example cf. Simojoki et al. 2018). Yet in order to give this volume a clear focus, it was decided that empirical approaches should be the main topic to be addressed here.

3. Aims of the volume

The main aim of this volume is to bring together experiences and results of empirical research in the field of non-formal religious education in different European countries. There also is the hope that this endeavor can help to generate new research projects which could be carried out in international cooperation.

The focus of the different chapters is on two aspects:

– The reality of non-formal religious education as it can be grasped from empirical research.
– Research-based evaluation of presuppositions and effects of non-formal religious education.

Given the state of research in this field, the first question must concern the reality of non-formal religious education. This question is of special interest because it refers to the availability of such education as well as to its shape, its structures and its functioning in different countries. To say it again, very few data and empirical insights are available concerning all of these aspects so far.

However, since the availability of non-formal religious education can only be considered a presupposition for the actual educational work and its possible effects, the second question must also be asked: What can be said, based on research, concerning the effects of non-formal religious education?

One background of the present volume has been the successful research carried out on confirmation work in nine European countries over the last ten years. Since this research has been previously presented internationally (cf. the volumes in English: Schweitzer et al. 2010, 2015, 2017), it will not be the main focus of the present book but will be presented together with the research on other fields of non-formal religious education. All religious programs for children and youth offered by the Churches or different religious communities are of interest here – be it in the sense of traditional children and youth work or of other programs which have different names (Catholic First Communion groups, mini-confirmands, Sunday School, Islamic programs, interreligious project groups, etc.).

Moreover, one important realization of recent research in some of the countries refers to the pivotal role of young volunteers, both for the quality and attractiveness of programs of non-formal education but also as a starting point for voluntary commitment in church and society at large (cf. the reports from the different countries in Schweitzer et al. 2017). This is why this book also includes research on non-formal religious education in the context of training and working with young volunteers.

The different chapters include presentations on specific research projects carried out by the authors themselves as well as summary accounts of the pertinent research in different countries. The aim is to:

– consider the state of the art concerning research on non-formal religious education,
– to critically review existing research,

– to bring together insights into this field of research that might be of interest beyond particular countries,
– to develop (methodological) criteria and perspectives for future research in this field,
– to stimulate national and international research on non-formal religious education.

4. The background of the volume: Research on non-formal religious education at Tübingen University and at the Comenius Institute

Concerning Protestant religious education, it is probably fair to say that the Department of Religious Education at the Protestant Faculty of the University of Tübingen and the Comenius Institute in Münster have played a pioneering role in respect to researching religious education in the non-formal sector in Germany. While the Comenius Institute has pursued an interest in theoretical questions of religious education in congregational contexts for several decades, sometimes also with smaller empirical research projects, in recent years it has developed a focus on data-based reports on different fields of church-related educational programs (cf. Schreiner in this volume). These fields also include Religious Education at school and church-sponsored schools but, more importantly in the present context of non-formal religious education, the reports refer to Sunday School, kindergartens and adult education. Altogether, the expertise concerning research on non-formal religious education to be found with the Comenius Institute can be called unique for the context of Germany.

In the case of the Department of Religious Education at the University of Tübingen (Faculty of Protestant Theology), there has also been both a strong theoretical interest in religious education beyond the school as well as a clear research focus in this area (cf., for example, Nipkow 1990; Schweitzer 1996 and 2006, also Schweitzer in this volume). The research projects carried out in this context over the last 15 years examined confirmation work, religious education in kindergartens, Christian youth work, young volunteers, and faith-related programs in adult education (cf. the respective chapters in this volume). All of these projects included empirical studies which, in part, are described in this volume.

Given their previous work and experiences, the two institutions could serve as organizers of the present volume as well as contribute a number of chapters describing this work. Yet the volume is not limited to the Protestant tradition which is characteristic of them. Instead, from the beginning, it was considered important to include Roman Catholic research projects (cf. Altmeyer and Boschki; Könemann and Sajak in this volume) as well as other religious traditions which could be realised for Muslim religious education (cf. Ulfat in this volume).

5. How the volume developed

Beyond the general ideas and aims described so far in this introduction, the actual starting point for this volume was an international symposium on "Researching Non-Formal Religious Education in Europe" which took place at the University of Tübingen in March 2018. Yet the book is not simply intended to document the contributions and discussions of this symposium. Instead, the authors were asked to actually write their chapters after the symposium and to include the results of the symposium discussions about the initial presentations from the different countries. Moreover, additional authors were invited to contribute in order to broaden the scope of the volume, again in light of new insights from the symposium and other considerations. All manuscripts were carefully reviewed by the editors and were then revised by the authors.

The choice of authors for this volume is based on general criteria such as international scope (contributions from nine European countries), gender, religious background (Protestant, Catholic, Orthodox, Muslim) and pertinent research experience. Moreover, the special interest and expertise in research approaches concerning non-formal religious education in Finland, Norway and Switzerland also played a role. In general, the attempt was made to represent at least all major research projects in the field of non-formal religious education in Europe. While it is certainly not possible to claim exhaustive coverage in a field which, by its designation as non-formal itself, defies clearly defined boundaries, an attempt was made to include as many research approaches and results as possible. The editors are grateful to the colleagues in different countries who were willing to advise them with respective choices and invitations of contributions.

6. The breakdown of the volume

A volume on researching non-formal religious education in Europe could be organised in a number of different ways. It could try to make the different countries the organising principle. The chapters could also be grouped according to the different methodologies used by the respective research projects. Still another possibility would be to order the chapters in terms of the age groups involved in the different programs under study.

While all of these possibilities would have been real options, the final decision was for a rather simple and straightforward order of the chapters which may be most useful for different readers. The first part of the book brings together general descriptions and research overviews. All other parts are grouped according to the programs they refer to: kindergarten, Sunday School, First Communion preparation and confirmation work, young volunteers. The sequence of the different parts roughly corresponds to the increasing age of the participants in the different programs but there is no claim that this could be a sequence in any strict sense. Many of the programs address different age groups at the same time or as part of a diversified program.

It must also be emphasised that the somewhat institutional ordering of the different parts of the book should not be taken to mean that non-formal religious education is secretly governed by a formal structure. As a number of the chapters in this volume show the opposite is true today. The traditional structures which used to exert quite a bit of influence in the non-formal sector are actually losing importance more and more as most programs tend to become more flexible and sometimes also more permeable for each other. This situation implies that there may also be new potentials for cooperation between the different fields but the research results reported in this volume also indicate that each of the different programs continues to be interested in maintaining itself as a distinct field of work.

7. A note of thanks

The symposium mentioned above was sponsored by the German Research Foundation (DFG). Additional support came from the Association of Friends of the University of Tübingen, the Department of Religious Education at the Protestant Faculty of the University of Tübingen and the Comenius Institute in Münster. The editors are very grateful for this multiple support without which the present publication would not have been possible.

All texts in the book have also gone through an extensive process of language editing. We are grateful to Marianne Martin who, as a native speaker, was responsible for this sometimes quite demanding task.

The editors of this volume are also very grateful for the continued reliable cooperation with the Waxmann Publishing House. Just like many times before, this cooperation proved to be very helpful for making this volume available to an international readership.

References

Baumbast, S., Hofmann-van de Poll, F., and Lüders, C. (2014). *Non-formale und informelle Lernprozesse in der Kinder- und Jugendarbeit und ihre Nachweise (Expertise)*. München: Deutsches Jugendinstitut.

Bundesministerium für Bildung und Forschung (ed.) (2008). *Stand der Anerkennung non-formalen und informellen Lernens in Deutschland im Rahmen der OECD Aktivität "Recognition of non-formal and informal Learning"*. Bonn/Berlin: BMBF.

Chisholm, L. (2005). *Bridges for Recognition. Recognising Non-formal and Informal learning in the Youth Sector*. https://pjp-eu.coe.int/en/web/youth-partnership/home: Council of Europe.

Ilg, W. (2011): Non-formale Bildung braucht Forschung. In: H. Peters, S. Otto, W. Ilg and G. Kistner (eds.). *Evaluation von Kinderfreizeiten. Wissenschaftliche Grundlagen, Ergebnisse und Anleitung zur eigenen Durchführung.* Hannover: aej, 177–184.

Larsson, R., and Gustavsson, C. (eds.) (2004). *Towards a European Perspective on Religious Education. The RE Research Conference March 11–14, 2004, University of Lund.* Skelleftea: Artos & Norma.

Manifesto (2019). International Knowledge Transfer in Religious Education: A Manifesto for Discussion. Münster/Tübingen: Comenius Institute.

Nipkow, K.E. (1990). *Bildung als Lebensbegleitung und Erneuerung. Kirchliche Bildungsverantwortung in Gemeinde, Schule und Gesellschaft.* Gütersloh: Gütersloher Verlagshaus.

OECD (2010). *Recognition of Non-formal Learning: Outcomes, Policies and Practices.* http://www.oecd.org/education/innovation-education/recognisingnon-formalandinformallearningoutcomespoliciesandpractices.htm (accessed January 31, 2019)

Schweitzer, F. (1996). *Die Suche nach eigenem Glauben. Einführung in die Religionspädagogik des Jugendalters.* Gütersloh: Gütersloher Verlagshaus.

Schweitzer, F. (2006). *Religionspädagogik.* Gütersloh: Gütersloher Verlagshaus.

Schweitzer, F., and Boschki, R. (eds.) (2018). *Researching Religious Education. Classroom Processes and Outcomes.* Münster/New York: Waxmann.

Schweitzer, F., Ilg, W., and Simojoki, H. (eds.) (2010). *Confirmation Work in Europe: Empirical Results, Experiences and Challenges. A Comparative Study in Seven Countries.* Gütersloh: Gütersloher Verlagshaus.

Schweitzer, F., Niemelä, K., Schlag, T., and Simojoki, H. (eds.) (2015). *Youth, Religion and Confirmation Work in Europe. The Second Study.* Gütersloh: Gütersloher Verlagshaus.

Schweitzer, F., Schlag, T., Simojoki, H., Tervo-Niemelä, K., and Ilg, W. (eds.) (2017). *Confirmation, Faith, and Volunteerism. A Longitudinal Study on Protestant Adolescents in the Transition towards Adulthood. European Perspectives.* Gütersloh: Gütersloher Verlagshaus.

Simojoki, H., Ilg, W., Schlag, T. and Schweitzer, F. (2018). *Zukunftsfähige Konfirmandenarbeit. Empirische Erträge – theologische Orientierungen – Perspektiven für die Praxis.* Gütersloh: Gütersloher Verlagshaus.

I
General Studies and Overviews

Youth counts!

Mapping Christian youth work in Germany empirically and identifying presuppositions of educationally active congregations

Wolfgang Ilg

"You've got more inside the store than in the showcase" – this is a frequent response by people who get in contact with church-related youth work. Often, they are surprised by the wide ranging and lively appeal that the praxis of Christian youth work offers. Nevertheless, whoever wants to gain valid results on the reality of youth work will largely be disappointed: Only a few empirical research projects on the non-formal activities in the churches are available, many of them refer to the local level. Even more, not even the basic numbers of members and group leaders are accurately recorded. Hardly any reliable statistics exist concerning this field of work. To this day, it remains difficult to estimate the number of young people who participate in activities offered by the churches in Germany. That the church-related youth work shares this fate with other forms of youth work – in sports, music, or culture – can only be of small comfort (for an overview: Lindner 2009, Rauschenbach et al 2010; Oechler and Schmidt 2014; one of the few positive examples within the Protestant youth work is Fauser et al. 2006).

1. The (in)visibility of non-formal education within the Protestant Church in Germany

Non-formal learning has received increasing attention in Germany during the last years. Especially scholars from the influential German Youth Institute (Deutsches Jugendinstitut, DJI) have emphasised the meaning of non-formal learning for the acquisition of general skills that are relevant for mastering one's challenges in school as well as in everyday life (Rauschenbach 2009; Baumbast et al. 2014). While youth work and other non-formal educational settings benefited from an enhanced awareness, for example in the studies on all-day-schools and general youth research (e.g. BMFSFJ 2017), the Protestant Church still tends to neglect these fields when it comes to general studies about church membership.

In the most prominent studies commissioned by the Evangelical Church in Germany (EKD) concerning church membership ("Kirchenmitgliedschaftsuntersuchungen"), work with children and adolescents is only marginally considered. While the keyword "church service" is mentioned more than 500 times within 450 pages, the term "youth work" is hardly mentioned in the publication of the current study concerning church membership (Bedford-Strohm and Jung 2015; cf. Ilg

2017 for a more detailed analysis). In light of this, it is in no way surprising that in this study the reference to a "church for the elderly" is the guiding perspective throughout the publication. It seems to be a vicious circle: The church membership study does not ask about youth work – and ends up with the conclusion that youth activities are of small relevance for the church, both at the present and in the future.

Such empirical imbalances were the initiating reasons for two research projects commissioned by the regional Protestant Churches of Baden and Württemberg and carried out at the Faculty of Protestant Theology at the University of Tübingen between 2013 and 2016. The aim of the projects was to take a major step in mapping Christian youth work empirically (a quantitative study) and to identify presuppositions for attractive youth activities in the parishes and Christian youth associations (with a qualitative study).

In this chapter, both research projects will be introduced. In addition to the methodologies and selected findings, the focus of the chapter lies on the question of how the studies' findings could be presented in a way that ensures that not only other researchers benefit from them, but also local staff and voluntary workers.

2. Youth counts – the quantitative study

How could young people count in the church, if no one had ever even counted how many of them are active in the church? (cf. Lehmann and Ilg 2015, 218) This question led to the statistical project reported here. While reliable reports exist about (religious) education in schools at least to some degree, there was no overview on non-formal education in the church, especially concerning youth work or musical activities such as children's choirs. The case was even worse: There were numbers which were published regularly, but they were incomplete. Those official figures were based on numbers every minister has to report on a yearly basis – but often the ministers are not in charge of youth work, and no one else except the ministers is asked to fill in the forms (for a detailed analysis cf. Ilg et al. 2014, 246–255).

In light of this, a comprehensive statistic of all church youth activities was a real challenge. A pilot project collecting the statistics for Protestant youth work (only in Württemberg, and only focusing on youth work in a narrow sense) successfully collected reliable results (Frieß and Ilg 2008) and became a model for the new comprehensive statistics.

In the planning phase of the new statistics, officials from various church-related fields of work signalled that not only youth work as such, but also that other non-formal fields should be looked at statistically: confirmation work, Sunday School and musical activities. Two neighbouring Churches worked together; the Protestant Churches of Baden and of Württemberg, which led to the benefit that by means of adding the data for Baden and for Württemberg, the whole federal state of

Baden-Württemberg could be covered. The research project was commissioned by these two Churches and awarded to a research group at Tübingen University.[1]

2.1 Methods

The objective of the research project "Youth counts" was the statistical compilation of non-formal activities within the Protestant work with children and adolescents between 6 and 26 years of age in Baden-Württemberg. A comprehensive survey of 2500 responsible bodies (parishes as well as local or regional youth work organizations) was undertaken within the time period of the school year of 2012/13. It is important to mention, that not all of the church-related sectors were covered. For example, the Religious Education classes at school, Protestant schools, and diaconal work were not included. Those fields might be taken into account in the next statistical project, while "Youth counts" limited itself to those non-formal fields that are predominantly run by volunteers.

Besides information about the number of participants and staff involved in the different sectors, data concerning age and gender was collected. Furthermore, the frequency of the activities and additional relevant details for the different sectors were gathered, such as questions about inclusion or about the financing of school-related youth work.

The online-survey was carried out using a specially adjusted version of the software "LimeSurvey", supported by the IT service provider "SilverAge". 85 % of the contacted responsible bodies participated in the online-survey, which led to a very solid data basis for further projections. One of the reasons of the high participation rate of the responsible bodies was the telephone hotline provided. Questions from the local participants could be answered on the phone and those who had not yet responded could be reminded to complete the survey via phone calls – a total of 150 hours on the phone for 850 calls were invested here.

What kind of data was collected? This project did not ask the participants but rather the local responsible persons. The aim was simply to collect valid numbers about the offers, participants and workers. It was neither intended nor possible to measure effects or to analyse the contents of the activities.

2.2 Results

From the numerous data collected, some exemplary findings will be presented in the following. They all refer to the federal state of Baden-Württemberg which has about 11 million inhabitants, 3.5 millions of them are Protestant.

---

1   The research group consisted among others of Friedrich Schweitzer, Peter Lehmann, Mareike Möhle, Hanne Lamparter, Nadine Quattlender, Michael Pohlers and Wolfgang Ilg. Especially Hanne Lamparter and Benjamin Ahme were involved in preparing this article.

Figure 1: Participants in the regular group offers in Baden-Württemberg 2012/13

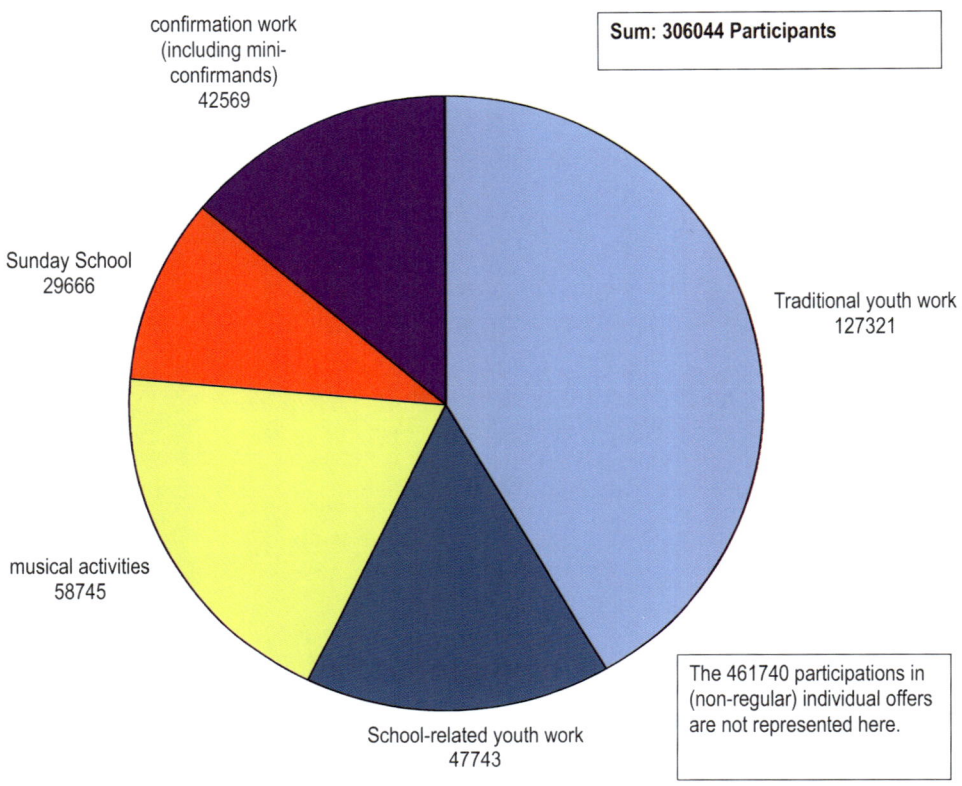

confirmation work
(including mini-
confirmands)
42569

Sum: 306044 Participants

Sunday School
29666

Traditional youth work
127321

musical activities
58745

School-related youth work
47743

The 461740 participations in
(non-regular) individual offers
are not represented here.

Number of participants

Within the period of the study, 306044 young people took part in one of the
15765 group offers in Baden-Württemberg. Figure 1 shows these results. This figure only depicts the youth groups taking place regularly, typically every week. 42%
of these groups are groups in the context of traditional youth work. 14% are made
up by confirmation work (where one has to keep in mind that only the cohort of the
13-year-old adolescents as well as, in some of the parishes, the mini-confirmands
are reached). 10% of the weekly meetings are children's church services or Sunday
School, 19% are groups related to music (e.g. children's choirs, brass bands). Altogether 15% are reached through activities of school-related youth work. Whereas
most of the other activities moderately decreased in numbers during the last years,
the number of school-related youth work activities has grown strongly throughout
the last years. This comparatively new field later gained the attention of a special
research project on its own (cf. Wolking in this volume).

In addition, there were 461740 participations at 11152 individual offers on the
year, such as summer camps, seminars, or sport tournaments. The term "individ-

Figure 2: Participation rates in the regular Protestant group work in relation to Protestant children and adolescents (Baden-Württemberg, in per cent)

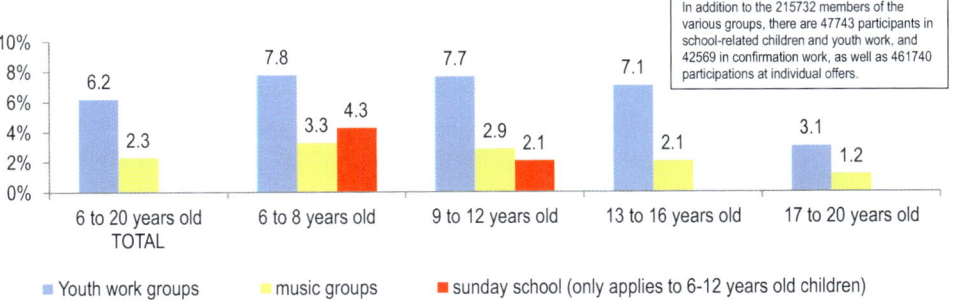

In addition to the 215732 members of the various groups, there are 47743 participants in school-related children and youth work, and 42569 in confirmation work, as well as 461740 participations at individual offers.

■ Youth work groups   ■ music groups   ■ sunday school (only applies to 6-12 years old children)

ual offers" is applied to all activities that did not take place on a regular basis, but occurred throughout the year.

Participation rates

Absolute numbers do not draw a vivid picture. What does it mean if 127321 young people take part in youth work groups regularly? A much more lucid question refers to the proportion of those who actually take part compared to all young people living in Baden-Württemberg.

When the number of participants in the children and youth work is related to the total number of *Protestant* 6- to 20-year-olds, this leads to a calculative participation rate of 18.5% of all Protestant children and adolescents within this cohort, as it is displayed in Figure 2. However, because of their concept, such offers are open to all young people regardless of their denomination. In Figure 3, the number of regular participants is related to data about the overall population (regardless of denomination). This leads to a total participation rate of 6.2% of all 6 to 20 years old in Baden-Württemberg. It has to be noted that only the participants at regular group activities are included here.

Figure 3: Participation rates in the regular Protestant group work in relation to all children and adolescents regardless of their denomination (Baden-Württemberg, in per cent)

In addition to the 215732 members of the various groups, there are 47743 participants in school-related children and youth work, and 42569 in confirmation work, as well as 461740 participations at individual offers.

■ Youth work groups   ■ music groups   ■ sunday school (only applies to 6-12 years old children)

Sunday School reaches (at its target age of 6–12 years) as many children as the music groups. A clear decrease of numbers for youth work and music groups is visible at the age of 17–20 years. A possible reason for this could be the adolescents' changing living conditions because of the graduation from school, the beginning of an apprenticeship, a new job, or studies at a university. However, at this age many persons become volunteers as well but are not represented in these statistics because it only refers to participants.

In sum: Protestant youth groups meeting on a regularly basis reach almost one fifth of the Protestants, which is about 6% of the total population to which Sunday School, musical activities, and many other fields have to be added. Compared to church services, with attendance rates of about 3–4% of the church members, it must be said clearly: The age group where the church sees the highest attendance of its activities is not the elderly, but youth!

Staff

In the two Protestant Churches, there are more than 70000 people working within one of the fields mentioned above – about 95% of them are volunteers. In comparison, during the period of the study there were about 97000 teachers working at public schools in Baden-Württemberg. This comparison shows just how many people are involved in children and adolescent activities in Baden-Württemberg's Protestant Churches. This means an average of 25 to 40 persons per parish.

These persons are qualified through training courses and accompanying support, for example, at courses for the youth-leader-certificate "Juleica": 36439 participated in training courses, 13665 persons in staff groups and in addition to that 2246 in trainee groups reflect the high intensity of staff training.

2.3 Dissemination strategy: making local data available

The objective of the study "Youth counts" was not only to collect data as precise as possible, but also to lay the foundations for the utilization of the data on the superordinate and the local level.

Main publication: The book "Youth counts"

The book "Youth counts" ("Jugend zählt") is the central publication of the data's overall analysis (Ilg et al. 2014). In this book, the data was edited in a standardised way and broken down into tables and figures for the different work fields. All figures in this text are taken from this book.

Table 1 shows the findings concerning the activities with children. The data is presented in three columns for the federal state Baden-Württemberg, the regional Church of Baden and the regional Church of Württemberg. Depending on

Table 1: Data presentation concerning work with children

	children's groups		
	Baden-Württemberg	Baden	Württemberg
Number of groups/offers	**3470**	787	2683
This exists in …% of all congregations	67 %	49 %	76 %
Total number of staff, thereof …	**13517**	**3177**	**10340**
female	64 %	67 %	64 %
male	36 %	33 %	36 %
younger than 16 years	12 %	12 %	11 %
16 to 17 years old	29 %	24 %	30 %
18 to 26 years old	31 %	30 %	31 %
older than 26 years	29 %	34 %	28 %
Total number of participants, thereof …	**47086**	**11844**	**35242**
female	57 %	56 %	57 %
male	43 %	44 %	43 %
younger than 6 years	9 %	10 %	9 %
6 to 8 years old	35 %	39 %	34 %
9 to 12 years old	47 %	44 %	48 %
13 to 16 years old	7 %	6 %	8 %
17 to 20 years old	0 %	1 %	0 %
21 to 26 years old	0 %	0 %	0 %
older than 26 years	1 %	0 %	1 %
Frequency			
weekly	82 %	74 %	85 %
every 14 days	9 %	11 %	9 %
monthly	5 %	9 %	4 %
more seldom	1 %	2 %	1 %
project-like	2 %	5 %	2 %
Group-structure			
number of participants per activity	13.6	15.0	13.1
number of staff per activity	3.9	4.0	3.9
child-staff-ratio	3.5	3.7	3.4
percentage of female-only groups	28 %	21 %	30 %
percentage of male-only groups	23 %	17 %	25 %

Reading example: 64 % of the total 13517 staff in children groups are women.

Figure 4: Proportion of parishes offering the mini-confirmands program in the church districts ("Konfi 3")

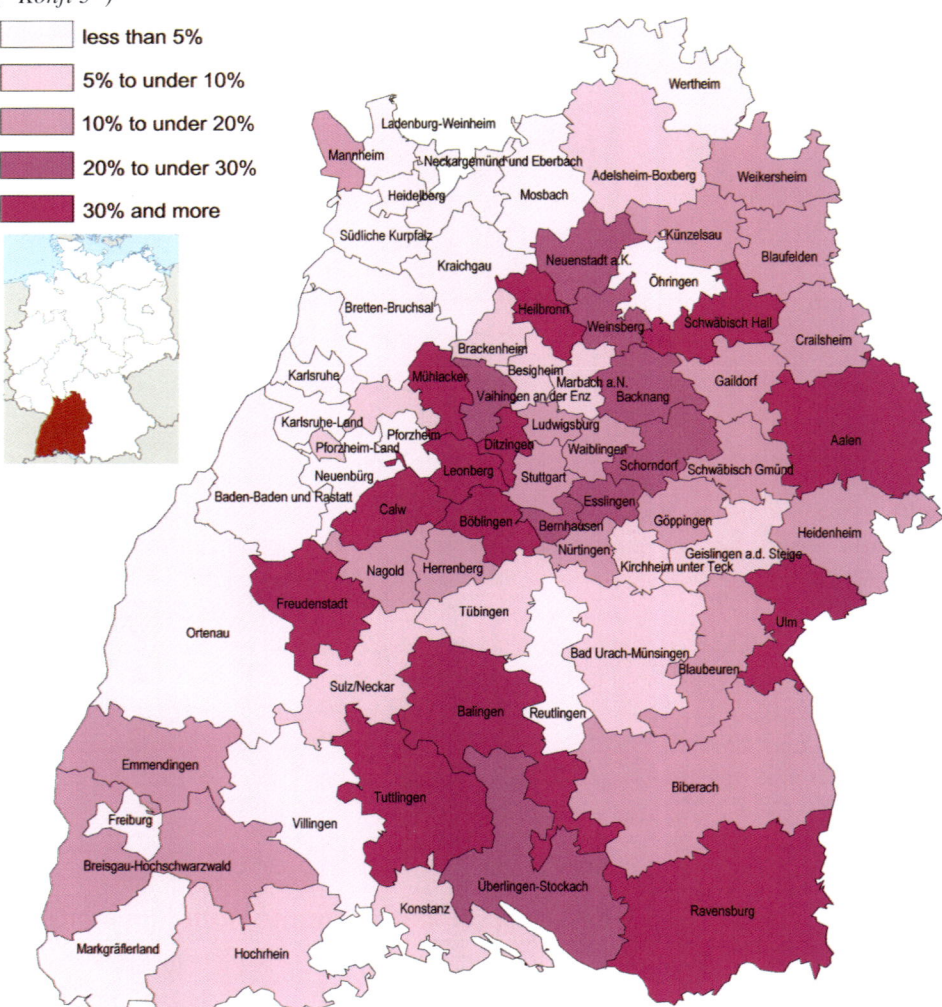

the regional affiliation and the thematic interest in one of the work fields, different conclusions that are relevant for practical applications can be drawn from the data. For example, from the perspective of public relations the number of over 47000 regularly participating children seems to be a remarkable figure. Those responsible for the training of the staff were surprised by the unexpectedly high number of adults in charge of youth and children's groups since their staff-magazines and training offers were mainly aimed at adolescent volunteers. Furthermore, those responsible for the development of new concepts noticed changes regarding the activities' frequencies: The traditional assumption, that such groups always meet on a weekly basis, was challenged by the fact, that 18 % of the groups meet only once or twice in a month. In the case of pedagogical questions regarding a kind of youth work that values interpersonal relationships, the ratio of the number of staff per child (1 to 3.5) was an important indicator of the high quality of individual mentoring, which could only be achieved because of the substantial commitment of volunteers. The data tables for all types of group offers in the book were used for discoveries like these, leading to possible conclusions for the praxis of youth work.

Figure 4 shows another way of presenting the data: Here one can see how many parishes have taken up the new way of confirmation work, called the "mini-confirmands" (Konfi 3). The parishes can decide whether they want to implement this new system or not. The map shows that it is actually implemented by 4 % (Baden) and 20 % (Württemberg), but the share of parishes varies according to the regional structure.

Providing data to local structures

In addition to the book as the main publication, further analyses were made and supplied to the local responsible persons. The production of several thousand individual analyses was performed by using computer programs (SPSS-Syntax) that applied the same type of analysis for different regional selections of data. Individual analyses for the number of groups, participants and staff were created for each church and administrative district and sent to them via E-Mail. These analyses followed the model of the book's structure in order to facilitate comparisons between the local and the statewide data. This way, comparisons to the overall picture were possible.

Additionally, the demographic data were edited individually for every parish. In total, several thousand graphics were generated automatically and sent to local officials of each parish and church district, both for the "Protestant demography" and for the "overall demography". This empowered the local agents to evaluate their situation individually and contextualise this with the overall data.

An important second effect of the data transmission was that the local agents were not only the "data suppliers" for an overarching research project, but also benefited from the findings of the project after its completion. This was an important experience that, most likely, will have a positive influence on the participation rate of future surveys.

Especially this strategy has received a lot of positive attention by practitioners in the local churches. Perhaps statistical researchers also could follow the New Testament advice of "It is more blessed to give than to receive" (Acts 20,35). In other words: It is not fair to always expect local experts to send out data while rarely thinking about how they could benefit from local evaluations of their data collections. Doing so has strongly improved the acceptance for statistics in the project "Youth Counts".

3. Youth in demand – the qualitative study

After its publication, the study "Youth Counts" was presented, among others, at the synods of both regional Churches. In the context of these presentations, a group of synod members showed a deeper interest in the subject. In January 2015, they proposed a motion with the title: "Extension of the youth study concerning the question whether there are shared characteristics between parishes whose work reaches an exceptional number of young people". In light of the data from "Youth Counts", the members of the synod recommended an in-depth follow-up study concerning parishes with a large and disproportionately well received range of activities. The leading question was: "Which factors contribute to the broad range of activities offered in this parish and why are they received so well?" This initiated the next study that will be described in the following.

The in-depth follow-up study "Youth in Demand" was conceptualised during spring 2015. Its implementation began in the summer of 2015 and lasted one year. The findings were presented and discussed in June 2016 at a study day in Karlsruhe with sixty experts for the work with children and adolescents. The impulses given at this meeting were included in the book which was published in fall 2016 (Pohlers et al. 2016).

Contrary to the quantitative study, the qualitative study did not aim for a complete and "objective" representation. Rather, local responsible agents were asked about their individual evaluation of – and perspectives on – the work with children and adolescents. Subjective perceptions and individual experiences are therefore paramount to this study. Its objective was not primarily to gain representative results or to test certain hypotheses, but to benefit from the rich pool of experiences, to reflect the current work, and to discover new potentials.

3.1 Methods

To find out why the work with children and adolescents succeeds in some places in a special way, interviews with employees and volunteers were conducted in 30 parishes. Furthermore, those responsible for the administration of the work with young people, Sunday School, musical activities, or confirmation work at the level of the regional Churches' management were also interviewed. The findings of "Youth Counts" fed into the selection of the parishes: The "most successful" fifth of the parishes were selected and accounted for the list of such parishes, from which a random sample received letters of invitation to participate in the interview study. Both the quantity of the activities (number of children reached, number of activities, both relative to the size of the congregation) and the range of activities were relevant for the selection of "successful parishes". Additionally, a preferably even distribution according to diverse criteria (Baden/Württemberg, rural/urban, small/mid-sized/large congregations) was looked after. About half of the parishes contacted agreed on an interview.

At 30 parishes, two rounds of interviews were conducted. One with three to six volunteers and another with the minister and other employees (where appropriate). Every interview was scheduled for one and a half hours. The interviews were semi-standardised, but started with an open introductory question, "What do you think are the factors contributing to the success of the work with young people in your parish?" The respondents were able to communicate "unfiltered expert knowledge". In the interviews with volunteers, the participants initially wrote down their responses on their own. In the second part, they were asked concretely and in a structured way about the role of the local presuppositions, the cooperation of employees and volunteers, financial resources, etc.

The interviews concluded with a question about their wishes for – and perspectives on – their work in the future. In total, 185 people were interviewed, 56 were employees and 129 volunteers. The interviews were recorded with digital recorders and subsequently fully transcribed, which resulted in 1500 pages of text. The analysis was made with the method of structured qualitative content analysis (Kuckartz 2014). With the help of the software MAXQDA, the texts were encoded and individual text passages were allocated to one of the thematic areas from a previously compiled system of categories. The accumulation of text passages was then content-wise combined and analysed, which was followed by a multistage discussion process within the team and with experts for the respective areas (also including a study day during the final stage of the research project). For the 200 pages report printed in the book, all of the personal data and geographical information were anonymised. After a comprehensive presentation of the findings from the interviews and numerous direct quotes, each of the chapters culminates in further reaching impulses derived from the findings.

3.2 Results

As expected, the content of the interviews proved to be multifaceted. They reflect the diversity and the different profiles of the selected parishes. Thus, as expected no universal remedy could be identified that would guarantee a successful work with children and adolescents. Anyhow, this was never the intention. In fact, impulses and suggestions are made, which need to be adjusted to the local presuppositions. In spite of the multitude of answers, it was possible to summarise success factors for the work with young people in the final chapter of the study.

Firstly, as it was said in many interviews, the activities must be centered about young people and their ideas. Not the institutional interest of the church, but the needs of young people are decisive and young people show a high appreciation of personal relationships. Secondly, the reference point for church youth work should be the Gospel of Jesus Christ, which is communicated in diverse and very different ways, explicitly and implicitly. Thirdly, the work of the church as a critical counterpart of the school should display its specific opportunities removed from the pressure of good grades, patronising instruction and imposed duties. The work with children and adolescents, fourthly, should confront the challenges of a culturally, ideologically and religiously plural society. With these general criteria in mind, twenty theses were formulated. They concretely tackle different aspects which – as the study showed – significantly contribute to the success of church-related work with children and adolescents. Three of the theses will be described as examples in the following section.

"Successful work has a different form in each congregation" (Thesis 1 and 4):

The work strongly depends on presuppositions like the surrounding social environment, the profile of the respective congregation, and the responsible persons. Each local surrounding features different opportunities and challenges. Congregations that are aware of this and correlate the content and organization of their work with the surrounding presuppositions provide an enormous contribution to the success of their work with children and adolescents.

"Youth work is work on relationships" (Thesis 7)

The interviewers often heard that relationships and friendships count more than large-scale initiatives and elaborate programs. Many young people yearn to experience themselves as a part of a community, have a sense of belonging and make new friends. Successful work with children and adolescents opens a space for encounters and personal relationships.

"Volunteers are the treasures of youth-active congregations" (Thesis 15)

Without volunteers, much of the work with children and adolescents would be impossible. Often, appreciation and support from the congregation for the work of volunteers has been identified as a factor for success. This appreciation can be uttered in the form of personal conversations, through public acknowledgment, or for example through the financing of ongoing training and seminars.

3.3 Dissemination strategy: the reflection sheet

The findings in the book offered an impulse for the (continuing) development of individual concepts and a profound reflection on the current practice. But practitioners, especially volunteers, are usually not willing to read 200 pages when it comes to results. So the project team decided to follow a double strategy.

In addition to the book, a short tool was developed for users with restricted time resources: In order to facilitate the access to the results for practitioners, a reflection sheet was designed, which is publicly available and can be downloaded from the internet (www.jugend-gefragt.de). This should promote the dissemination of the findings beyond the book and support the Protestant work with children and adolescents in the parishes. The reflection sheet contains three or four reflective questions for each of the 20 theses. The questions are supposed to encourage further contemplation, additional references to the respective chapters of the study facilitate the intake of the findings. In other words: The reflection sheet serves as an appetizer, inviting practitioners to select topics of special interest for their work, discuss concrete questions and take a deeper look into the book. Figure 5 provides an example of how the reflection sheet looks.

Thesis 6

Prerequisites like rooms or financial resources do not guarantee flourishing youth work, however, their absence can limit the opportunities massively. Offers for children and adolescents require their own equipment. It is part of the respectful contact to volunteers that parishes provide the necessary resources (rooms, work materials, petty cash for groups) in a straightforward manner. The reflection of possible new financial and other resources is part of the central tasks of managing committees.

Questions for reflection

– Which rooms and materials are especially valuable to us?
– How could we use cooperations to extend the present material pool for us and others?
– How long does it take until new volunteers receive a key to the parish hall?
– How large is the administrative burden for a group leader to account for new work materials of the value of 20 Euro?

Reading recommendations
  → Chapter 7 "Resources"
  → Chapter 6 "Cooperations"

Figure 5: Example of the reflection sheet

4. On the reception of the studies

Both Church synods, Baden and Württemberg, discussed the results of the research projects in their meetings. In the Württemberg Church, these discussions even led to a whole synod session with a special focus on children and adolescents – for the first time within 16 years!

In a similar way, the study's findings have been discussed locally at the level of parishes and church districts. However, very different experiences have been made.

While some church districts had very intensive discussions about their data (for example at many local synods with a special focus on "Youth Counts"), the study did not resonate in any conceivable way in other regions. It would be worth a study in its own right to survey the background and motivations for these different reactions to the study. The following factors seem to be especially significant and might be instructive for similar research projects:

– At grassroots level, there certainly is an interest in scientific findings. However, they must be delivered in "bite-sized pieces". In order for a study to be taken up at all, there needs to be a short version of it with central findings and "easily digestible" suggestions for direct application. If it is achieved that such a "teaser" quickens the appetite, a willingness to think about a study more deeply – and ask on which basis the findings were made – emerges. Research that aims at recognition on the local level should not consider itself too good to present its findings in a popular way. For the research projects mentioned above, these "teasers" consisted of a Powerpoint-presentation with the most important findings as well as the reflection sheet, both offered as downloads freely in the internet.
– An intensive tie to the local agents should not be established only at the end of the research project, but needs to be considered from the onset. Concerning the study "Youth in Demand", a study day meant an important intermediate step towards the completion of the final publication. Beyond questions regarding content, important impulses resulted from this study day. For example, the suggestion that the final publication should outline options of how to work with the study's findings in committees was very helpful. This resulted in printing a chapter in the results book suggesting ways of working with the data in local church boards or other committees: A support that seems to be "unscientific" – but had an enormous effect on the study's reception.
– Overall, it was important that, from the onset, the studies were designed not only to report their findings at the level of its complete dataset, but also to address each parish and church district with individual data and findings. This did not only improve the motivation to participate in the study considerably, but also added a genuine value for the local agents and was an incentive for them to work with the data. However, the data provided – each church district attained detailed analyses consisting of more than 100 PowerPoint slides – apparently demanded too much of many local agents, so that many exciting details were overlooked. It seems to be recommendable to limit the delivery of local results to an amount that can be processed also by people not familiar with statistics.

The question of how researchers can make sure that their findings are taken up at grassroots-level has to be considered increasingly by research projects. The planning of a study's reception should be an integral part of its conceptualization, so that the findings can have the impact they deserve, especially in the largely unexplored field of non-formal religious education.

References

Baumbast, St., Hofmann-van de Poll, F., and Lüders, C. (2014). *Non-formale und informelle Lernprozesse in der Kinder- und Jugendarbeit und ihre Nachweise.* München: Deutsches Jugendinstitut. https://www.dji.de/fileadmin/user_upload/bibs2014/DJI_Expertise_non-formales%20Lernen_final.pdf

Bedford-Strohm, H., and Jung, V. (eds.) (2015). *Vernetze Vielfalt: Kirche angesichts von Individualisierung und Säkularisierung. Die fünfte EKD-Erhebung über Kirchenmitgliedschaft.* Gütersloh: Gütersloher Verlagshaus.

BMFSFJ 2017 = Bundesministerium für Familie, Senioren, Frauen und Jugend (ed.) (2017). *15. Kinder- und Jugendbericht. Bericht über die Lebenssituation junger Menschen und die Leistungen der Kinder- und Jugendhilfe in Deutschland.* Berlin: BMFSFJ. https://www.bmfsfj.de/15-kjb

Fauser, K., Fischer, A., and Münchmeier, R. (2006). *Jugendliche als Akteure im Verband. Ergebnisse einer empirischen Untersuchung der Evangelischen Jugend.* Opladen/Farmington Hills: Verlag Barbara Budrich.

Frieß, B., and Ilg, W. (2008). *Evangelische Jugendarbeit in Zahlen. Die Statistik 2007 des Evangelischen Jugendwerks in Württemberg.* Stuttgart: buch+musik.

Ilg, W. (2017). Notwendige Horizonterweiterungen für die Kirchenmitgliedschaftsuntersuchungen. Möglichkeiten und Grenzen empirischer Annäherungen an gemeindepädagogische Arbeitsfelder am Beispiel der Kirchenmitgliedschaftsuntersuchungen und der Studien zur Konfirmandenarbeit. In: *Zeitschrift für Pädagogik und Theologie (ZPT)* 69(4), 317–329. DOI: https://doi.org/10.1515/zpt-2017-0036

Ilg, W., Heinzmann, G., and Cares, M. (eds.) (2014). *Jugend zählt! Ergebnisse, Herausforderungen und Perspektiven aus der Statistik 2013 zur Arbeit mit Kindern und Jugendlichen in den Evangelischen Landeskirchen in Baden und Württemberg.* Stuttgart: buch+musik.

Kuckartz, U. (2014). *Qualitative Inhaltsanalyse. Methoden, Praxis, Computerunterstützung.* Weinheim/Basel: Beltz Juventa.

Lehmann, P., and Ilg, W. (2015). Jugend zählt – vom Wert statistischer Daten. In: *deutsche jugend* 63, 209–218.

Lindner, W. (ed.) ([2]2009). *Kinder- und Jugendarbeit wirkt: Aktuelle und ausgewählte Evaluationsergebnisse der Kinder- und Jugendarbeit.* Wiesbaden: VS Verlag für Sozialwissenschaften.

Oechler, M., and Schmidt, H. (eds.) (2014). *Empirie der Kinder- und Jugendverbandsarbeit: Forschungsergebnisse und ihre Relevanz für die Entwicklung von Theorie, Praxis und Forschungsmethodik.* Wiesbaden: Springer.

Pohlers, M., Lamparter, H., Quattlender, N., Ilg, W., and Schweitzer, F. (2016). Jugendaktive Kirchengemeinden in Baden-Württemberg: Eine qualitative empirische Studie zur Arbeit mit Kindern und Jugendlichen. Die Vertiefungsstudie zu "Jugend zählt". In: W. Ilg and F. Schweitzer (eds.). *Jugend gefragt! Empirische Studien zur Realität evangelischer Arbeit mit Kindern und Jugendlichen in Baden-Württemberg.* Stuttgart: buch und musik, 37–231.

Rauschenbach, T. (2009). *Zukunftschance Bildung. Familie, Jugendhilfe und Schule in neuer Allianz.* Weinheim/München: Juventa.

Rauschenbach, T., Borrmann, S., Düx, W., Liebig, R., Pothmann, J., and Züchner, I. (2010). *Lage und Zukunft der Kinder- und Jugendarbeit in Baden-Württemberg. Eine Expertise.* Dortmund: Eigenverlag.

Catholic religious education in Germany

The sustainability of formal and non-formal learning

Judith Könemann, Clauß Peter Sajak

1. Starting point, concerns, and design of the study

A clear distinction can be made when it comes to religious education in Germany: There is, on the one hand, a formally organised religious education, which provides religious instruction that is oriented to and designed by a particular denomination as an ordinary subject at school. And, on the other hand, a non-formal religious education that is organised by churches and religious communities, and that includes the various sacramental catecheses, especially the field of church youth work and altar service as a part of youth work. In the wake of the Second Vatican Council, the ideas and goals of religious education were decisively shaped in the Catholic Church of the Federal Republic of Germany by the so-called "Würzburg Synod". This church assembly met in various sessions between 1971 and 1975, and set as its goal the implementation of the resolutions of the Second Vatican Council in the German church. Many of the documents approved by the Würzburg Synod are still very influential today. Thus, documents such as the resolution setting out its program, *Unsere Hoffnung* ("Our Hope"), the resolution *Ziele und Aufgaben kirchlicher Jugendarbeit* ("Goals and Tasks of Church Youth Work"), and the resolution on *Religionsunterricht in der Schule* ("Religious Education at School") still exert an influence today.

Finally, the Würzburg Synod also introduced a distinction that is characteristic of the German system of religious education: namely, between the formal place of learning of Religious Education, and the non-formal places of learning, such as catechesis and youth work. This distinction is due primarily to the fact that as part of the public education system, Religious Education cannot be justified only on theological and ecclesiastical grounds. Rather, it also has to be legitimised from a theologically independent perspective, one that is exclusively pedagogical and grounded in educational theory. Therefore, Religious Education is intended to facilitate meaningful and structured basic knowledge, "responsible thinking and behaviour with respect to religion and belief" (Resolution 2.5.1, 139), and an independent decision of faith. On the other hand, catechesis is intended to facilitate a more lively and independent interaction with the faith, and an experience of the communal dimension of the church, and especially its liturgical dimension. Because church youth work is seen as a further important place of learning, the Synod emphasises especially the importance of the relationship and social dimension of the "group" as a youth group. With its so-called "personnel", comprising not only the group leader but also the young people themselves, it is the place of learning of youth work that particularly emphasises the dimension of experience within the group as an independent form of expression of belief, and thus enables the development of attitudes and opinions that are often neglected in formal learning arrangements.

In contrast to Religious Education as a formal context of learning, the contexts of non-formal education have in recent years rarely been the subject of academic research, so that there is a certain need for research on the Catholic side. Below the level of academic debate, however, there is in the field of catechesis a real abundance of concepts and work materials that are used in catechetical procedures on the ground. To provide an overview of, and to sort out this multitude of concepts, which exist in very different states of abstraction, would be a research undertaking in itself.

The project presented here is concerned with catechesis and Religious Education as traditional contexts of learning in religious education. The background of the project is a discussion by the German Bishops' Conference concerning the following question: What long-term learning outcomes are achieved by processes of religious education at the different contexts of learning represented by *Religious Education at school*, *catechesis*, and *church youth work*? The initial question pursued here is therefore concerned with the sustainability and effectiveness of processes of religious education, and is closely linked to the issue of how the different contexts of learning relate to each other. Research has rarely dealt with the sustainability and effectiveness of processes of (religious) education, and when it has, it has tended to focus on the short-term effects of learning arrangements (e.g., Religion und Gesellschaft 2015; also see Altmeyer and Boschki in this volume). These issues gave rise to the idea of an exploratory study whose aim was to examine religious education with regard to sustainability and effectiveness, and thereby work out parameters that allow for the use of the concepts of sustainability and effectiveness in the field of (religious) education. The aim here is to use the findings of the exploratory study for a larger representative study.

The idea of the project rests on three pillars. First, the investigation of the goals that teachers and catechists actually pursue in Religious Education and catechesis. This raises the question of how far these goals are at all compatible or even overlap with the official magisterial goals for instruction and catechesis at the different contexts of learning. For this purpose, a detailed analysis was carried out of all Vatican and episcopal pronouncements on catechesis and Religious Education, which was then related to the findings of various empirical studies in research on religious education. Second, the current research literature in educational studies and the social sciences was examined in terms of its understanding of and criteria for effectiveness and sustainability – besides providing a survey of the state of research, this also yielded points of reference for viable criteria to study effectiveness and sustainability. Third, the qualitative and exploratory interview-based study aimed to investigate in a biographical-reconstructive manner the effectiveness and sustainability of processes of religious education in individual life contexts, which allowed the development of further points of reference and criteria for effectiveness and sustainability. It is above all this third pillar that is the focus here.

2. Methodological design of the study

Twelve structured, biographical-narrative interviews were conducted for this qualitative study. A first preliminary decision for the composition of the sampling was to select people for the investigation whose religious socialization through Religious Education and sacramental catechesis was on the one hand complete, but on the other hand, whose processes of religious education were not so long ago that the memories of them had been largely superimposed by other events in life. Thus, two groups of people came into focus for the study: firstly, pupils at the end of their time at school, who had at this point completed their formal religious socialization; and, secondly, young adults in employment or at the end of their studies, who were in, or about to begin, the process of making biographically significant decisions, e.g., the decision as to what shape their lives will take or career decisions (the transition between studies and career). The sample therefore comprised 16- to 18-year-olds and 26- to 28-year-olds. Since the question of sustainability and effectiveness is directed at all those who have undergone the processes of religious education mentioned, a second preliminary decision was made to select similar cases for the investigation, with this investigation then being based more on the so-called "normal case" as a sociological-heuristic and non-normative category, rather than on strongly contrasting individual cases which would simply have tended to emphasise the exceptions.

A further factor of selection in the sampling was to take into account different educational paths and attainments in order to ensure that the interviewees had the broadest possible range of social backgrounds. This also implied that the interviewees come from different family backgrounds since the educational path taken by children today is still relatively strongly influenced by the educational path taken by their parents, and is therefore dependent on social background. For the same reason, the career path was also important for the sampling. Thus, with regard to their educational path, the interviewees were assigned to the following four categories: pupils without A-levels as their goal, pupils with A-levels as their goal, career newcomers with vocational training, and career newcomers with a higher degree. Besides age in correspondence to religious socialization and the educational path or level of education acquired, the third criterion of selection was gender.

Finally, as the fourth criterion, the sampling selects four interview regions to take into account the religious-political or religious-demographic conditions in the Federal Republic of Germany. Münsterland was selected to represent a traditional Catholic area. A second region represented the situation of diaspora Catholics in a Protestant heartland: here, the Hanover/Brunswick area was selected as an urban and Protestant area in the northwest of Germany. As the third region, Greater Frankfurt/Mainz was chosen as an urban mixed-denominational, albeit rather Catholic, region. And, finally, the Magdeburg area was chosen as the fourth region to depict the situation of diaspora Catholics in a strongly de-churched area. In addition to these four criteria used for the composition of the sample, a further criterion was to study adolescents and young adults who, beyond Religious Education at school and catechesis, were not especially involved in religion or the church. However, this was possible to only a limited extent. Especially in the Magdeburg region, the willingness to participate in the study was very low and, in order to be able to cover this region at all, it was necessary to fall back on pupils and young adults who were involved in the church. However, the willingness to be interviewed was lower than had originally been assumed in the other regions as well, so that finding people to participate in the study was on the whole quite time-consuming and complicated. Thus, the sampling included more people involved in church or parish beyond the specific processes of religious education focused on than originally intended. The results presented below should therefore be read against this backdrop.

The interviewees were recruited according to a snowball system: for the search, colleagues from the investigators' work context were asked to act as disseminators, as were friends and acquaintances of the project group (also using social-media channels); and institutions were also approached. Through these initial personal contacts, a brief exposé outlining the concerns and aims of the research project, as well as its expectations, was given to the potential interviewees. The decisive criterion here was to pursue the snowball system so far that the interviewees were no longer acquainted with a person from the research team, and did not move in the same church or religious circles as a member of the research team.

In line with the interview guidelines developed, the interviewees were first asked about their experiences of Religious Education at school, preparation for Communion, and catechesis for Confirmation; what they remembered and how they felt about it; what importance religion had then and still has in their lives; and what is especially important to them. Second, they were asked various questions to gauge how they understand themselves in terms of their ideas on life and on their own personalities: What can you say about your current situation in life? What have been defining events in your life? How would you describe yourself as a person? What values are important to you personally? Which people have been particularly important to you, and why have they been important or even role models for you? At the end of the interview, the interviewees were asked a few questions about their social-structural data. The guidelines were tested in a few sample interviews before they took on their final form. The interviews were conducted in the environment of each interviewee, who also decided on the precise location of the interview. The interviews lasted between 45 and 90 minutes. The audio recordings were transcribed and the personal data anonymised. In addition, research protocols were prepared for each interview, recording anomalies, hypotheses, and the atmosphere in which the interview took place.

The interviews were transcribed in their entirety. The data analysis follows the multi-step method as developed by Schmidt (2012, 447–456). This facilitates the development of dimensions in line with the research assumptions that structure the material into evaluation categories. It also allows for the reconstruction of new categories through the open coding of individual passages that are in line with the object at hand. This method, developed by Schmidt from the work of Hopf (1996) and from Grounded Theory (Glaser and Strauss 1967; Strauss and Corbin 1996), makes texts accessible to interpretative analysis, without (as is the case, for example, in qualitative content analysis) having to leave the text as text itself (see Gläser and Laudel 2009, 47). On the one hand, the creation of the coding guidelines and the codebook, as well as the subsequent formation of categories used in the evaluation, took place *deductively*, i.e., with the help of empirically non-saturated, theoretical assumptions and everyday concepts (Kelle and Kluge 2010, 70), and on the basis of the so-called "concept of theoretical sensitivity" (Kruse 2015, 108–114). On the other hand, and in line with the open coding, the theoretical categories were based on the material, expanded, or modified *inductively*.

The interviews were then evaluated by means of this deductive and inductive coding system: categories from the concentrated codes were extracted, and then analysed comparatively. A coding schema and a codebook with a description of the code and examples were created across all categories and codes. One such example of a code is given below. Code: idea of belief. Subcode: importance of religion/belief. Example:

> *Yes, but not as much as it used to be. It has become less. But I was also an altar girl for 10 years. Maybe you then also had a different connection in school, because privately, you dealt with it more, then school lessons themselves were not so uninteresting any more. But now, for about the last five years, it has become a bit less.*

Besides the individual interpretations of the interviews, the categories were used to create a portrait and to sketch a biographical schema for each interview. The substantive categories, the portraits, and the biographical schemas were then used to capture and work out possible influences and effects regarding processes of religious learning and the general idea of belief held by the interviewees, correlations between the different categories and places of learning, and significant events in their biographies.

3. Sustainability of religious education – criteria

Before the results of the study are presented, it is necessary first of all to establish some initial indicators or factors so as to illustrate what is meant by the sustainability or effectiveness of religious education. A few comments are required here that deal with the first two parts of the study.

As already mentioned, the ideas and goals of religious education that the Catholic Church has in Germany have been decisively shaped by the Würzburg Synod. Thus, the Synod resolution "Religious Education at School" argued powerfully for the clear separation of tasks between Religious Education at school on the one hand, and catechesis on the other. According to this resolution and to all magisterial documents that have been issued ever since, Religious Education is intended above all to facilitate a meaningful and structured basic knowledge, an independent decision of faith, and the capacity for religious dialogue and judgment. Catechesis, on the other hand, is intended to facilitate a lively and independent exploration of faith and an experience of the communal dimension of the church.

This separation makes clear a distinction that may well only exist in the German-speaking context, i.e., in Germany, Austria and parts of Switzerland: while the formal place of learning represented by the school is expected to teach basic knowledge about the faith and the theological capacity of judgement, the catecheses offered in the parish aim to deepen the (cognitive) decision of faith through providing religious experiences and social events in the actual religious community. Such a "semantic split" in the didactics of religious education, a split that has its roots in the special status of Catholic Religious Education as an ordinary subject in the otherwise secular school, is not common in most other countries and cultures. In other areas, catechesis (which, for example, in the United States often takes place as Parish School of Religion or Confraternity of Christian Doctrine in the Catholic school of the parish) continues to be responsible for teaching knowledge about the faith, as well as for facilitating religious experiences.

This particular German construct and tradition is very clearly reflected in the goals of the teachers of religion who in recent years have been investigated in numerous empirical studies (Englert and Güth 1999; Feige et al. 2000, 2005 and 2006; Lück 2002 and 2003; Bucher and Miklas 2005; Jakobs et al. 2009). These studies show consistently that they primarily understand religious education in the context of Religious Education at school as the opportunity to help young people in life and to provide them with some kind of ethical orientation. Furthermore, they want to contribute to developing religious identity among pupils. The focus here is less of a denominational goal, and more based on the capacity for interreligious dialogue, which is intended to equip pupils for the social plurality of the modern world and its various challenges.

Finally, analysing the discourse in the social sciences on effectiveness and sustainability has shown that research on effectiveness appears above all in the field of the media and of media research; in contrast, there has been little or virtually no research on effectiveness and sustainability in the area of education, with the terminology generally being used here with little uniformity, and in an extremely diverse and heterogeneous way. Furthermore, the question of effectiveness is mostly related to short-term effectiveness. This also has to do with the fundamental difficulty of not being able to clearly differentiate sharply between the various factors of influence in educational processes.

This finding led in the study of sustainability/effectiveness conducted here to a working out of several indicators or factors of influences that could be used to formulate an initial working definition. First, traditional parameters in which the effectiveness of processes of religious learning and teaching have clearly lasted up to the present day. These parameters are, for example, religious practice, a civic involvement that is religiously motivated or has direct links to the church, a sense of belonging to a parish, and a certain degree of confidence in the church and its officials.

Second, the biographical-reconstructive interviews could be analysed inductively, which yielded further indicators that the interviewees had located as constituting religious learning experiences in their lives: for example, learning arrangements that had long remained in the memory; influential people at the various contexts of learning; the development of their own values and ideas on life and faith; the actual contents and themes of teaching that became important. Crucial for sustainability was above all that these learning arrangements, experiences and occurrences, as well as people, were remembered cognitively and/or affectively in a positive way.

One finding that can therefore be identified is that a cognitively and affectively positive memory of a process of religious learning, or of something from that process, will be considered sustainable, even where it is not possible to distinguish precisely between the different factors of influence that led to this memory.

4. Findings – the contexts of learning

Evaluating and interpreting the interviews provided a number of interesting observations on the traditional contexts of learning in Catholic socialization.

4.1 Context of learning: Religious Education at school

Religious Education at school was for most of the interviewees the first formal context of learning in religious education, and thus an important point in their religious socialization. As a rule, Religious Education begins in the first year of primary school and is, unlike preparation for the sacraments, compulsory for children of the Catholic faith. Preparation for First Communion and for Confirmation also differ from Religious Education in that they take place only over a limited period of time. Religious Education normally takes place from the first year of primary school to the end of secondary school, whereas preparation for Communion and Confirmation are very short-lived. This might account for the fact that there are no significant differences between older and younger interviewees in how they look back on and assess Religious Education.

How the interviewees remembered Religious Education was in most cases specific to the school year. Thus, as in other empirical studies (Bucher 2000; Kliemann and Rupp 2000), Religious Education at primary school was remembered particularly positively: it appeared in retrospect as lively, clear and holistic. There was, though, dissatisfaction with Religious Education in the first few years of secondary school (*Sekundarstufe I*), before a renewed interest in the later years of secondary school (*Sekundarstufe II*) – but only if it had relevance to life, was based on discussion, and was presented well. Example: "*Because you could focus on yourself there and find out what you yourself believe …*"

The interviewees mentioned a wide range of topics that they still remembered both positively and negatively. What stands out is that nearly all remembered topics that they could link to their own lives. "*Yes, at primary school we also had religion, that was, for example, very different there. You could, you then talked much more about personal things. That was more interesting than talking about history and stuff like that*". The link to life also had something to do with the favourite topics named by the interviewees. For example, the topics "*interreligious dialogue*" and "*other religions*" were remembered positively and particularly often: "*I find that really exciting, these religions, or these differences. I used to be really interested, also in things like Hinduism and stuff*".

Similarly, ethical and existential topics were also very popular among the interviewees – for example, current political themes, moral issues, and discussions on questions concerning the beginning and end of life (specifically: abortion, prenatal diagnosis, and euthanasia), as well as anthropological questions. Memory of these ethical and existential topics was accompanied by a methodological component. In particular, the interviewees recalled practical approaches, with discussions, exchanges and conversations about personal experiences and opinions being considered particularly important.

What is worth noting is that the interviewees who were involved on a voluntary basis in a parish and/or had a link to a specific church congregation wanted Religious Education to deal more with liturgical themes. They wanted to know more about liturgy and church services, etc., and they wanted to share their own experiences with other pupils. For example, a young woman told of her activity as an altar girl, something that she would like to talk about more often in Religious Education at school: "*Yes, I think, I'm proud of it, if I know something, because I'm an altar girl, in the religion lesson, if I can always use that. Yes, I also find that interesting in itself, that I know something about what happened in the past or about the mass itself, how the mass runs, what things in the church are, and so on*".

The field of teaching methods played a major role in all discussions. All the interviewees without exception said that varied teaching methods that were tailored to the respective target group were crucial for the success of Religious Education at school. Some interviewees also stressed the importance of approaches that involved games, above all for pupils aged 14 to 16: "*Well, I still remember, we had in the phase after First Communion, so 5th class, 5th, 6th, 7th, 8th, 4 years with a lot of re-*

ligious games, quiz questions, where I then, or where I found that also helps, if now there is not only every week frontal teaching, where the teacher says, so-and-so; that you also have to use your brains and – at least from my perspective – I think I really learned a lot". Where such methods were used, this led, according to the interviewees, to lasting impressions that had their effects beyond the lesson in Religious Education.

Besides discussions, the opportunity to talk about experiences, and conversations of all kinds, the interviewees also experienced approaches that used media positively. For example, some emphasised that an approach that used songs and music had been helpful to them in Religious Education at school. Others mentioned a creative approach through painting pictures, an approach used extensively at primary school, and one that many interviewees still remembered fondly. Similarly, they found approaching a topic through the medium of film useful: *"I still remember that we had a really young teacher who had quite interesting, I think, I don't remember any more if it was Star Trek or Star Wars episodes, had one interestingly enough for each topic somehow and yes, I don't know anything about the (unintelligible) area, but he could say exactly, and after we had seen clips of some of these episodes, how individual people from the stars, say, behaved among themselves, that was (unintelligible) readable from that, the world religions, how they relate to each other, and that was actually very interesting, also interesting in terms of methodology"*.

The teacher of religion undoubtedly plays an important role in the perception and sustainability of Religious Education. There were several aspects here that most interviewees considered significant. For example, a teacher of religion should be open to, and respect the views and opinions of pupils. Moreover, he or she should not judge doubters or non-believers: *"And the teachers that we have now, they give us the freedom to stop, to say and also think what we want ... if someone then says, for example, I actually think football is a religion, I think, then she accepts that. And I just think that this honesty is important"*.

In addition, the teacher should not only respect the opinion of pupils, but also take his or her own position when required. The keyword "authenticity" played an important role here. The interviewees also tended to value teachers of religion who managed to create an open and friendly atmosphere without losing any of their authority. A teacher should be respectful, friendly and communicate on eye-level with pupils. On the other hand, he or she must be able to create a sense of calm and order in the classroom.

The influence of Religious Education at school on personal beliefs and values is difficult to separate from the influence of other areas such as the family, the person's environment and catechesis. None of the interviewees expressed explicitly that Religious Education had influenced their development or formation of values. However, the interviewees often described how, especially in the interplay between Religious Education and catechesis, the Christian faith as a whole had had an influence on their personal values: *"So the commandment to love your neighbour is very much implanted in me. That was also a very, very important topic, also in Religious Education, I think also in the seventh, eighth year, so now, where it just pops up. Exactly, so that's something that still really shapes me to this day in terms of values, but also in terms of these causes, that everything will somehow turn out good".*

4.2 Context of learning: catechesis

For all the interviewees, the first contact with religious education in the parish was when they prepared for the sacrament of the Eucharist, i.e., catechesis for First Communion. At the time of the interviews, this period already lay quite some time in the past for the 16- to 18-year-olds, and even longer for the 26- to 28-year-olds; nonetheless, all the interviewees could still call up more or less concrete memories of the period. Indeed, if the interviewees had felt comfortable in the setting in which they prepared for Communion, and were also provided with hands-on, child-friendly approaches to the topics, then they were able to remember the different teaching methods as well as the various contents of teaching in great detail. *"We had grape juice there. … Red grape juice and bread. And that was always so cool, because then you always felt a bit like the disciples, because you thought we've got bread and wine".* What had a positive effect was what was dealt with in a clear and (in a literal sense) graspable way: *"During the trip, where we had Jonah and Nineveh, the first trip, I still remember, we rebuilt Nineveh a little bit for ourselves from empty cardboard boxes, so it was already then, I think, done in a way that suited us".* The vast majority of the interviewees described various child-friendly and creative activities, with frequent mention also being made in general of *"stories"*, *"Bible stories"*, *"parables"*, and *"(modern) thought-provoking stories"* to which the children were introduced. Thus, several interviewees had positive memories of topics dealt with in the preparation for Communion in connection with experiences in the church space or in church services: *"And we, I don't know the motto any more, but something with an illustrated path, and at every service together we moved a wooden figurine that we had painted ourselves one step forward. I think there were four fields and started at the first service and at the end the last field was very grand, just to show, Communion, something special, just to symbolise, we are getting closer and closer to our goal".*

All the interviewees described regular meetings with a fixed group of people of their own age, which often took place in the context of their own home or the home of another child in the group: *"Yes, so we were divided into groups, and there were five, six of us, and then each time two parents did the teaching".* It was usually the mothers who were the catechists in this setting. But, even if the groups were not led by their own mothers, but instead by other catechists, the interviewees still had positive memories: *"Yes, so our, the preparation for First Communion, both preparations, the parish assistant helped organise. And she already, she has known me all my life, and I already knew her, in a kind of group for little children".*

After the preparation for Communion, catechesis for Confirmation is another formal learning opportunity in the parish. For some young people, this period encouraged them and provided them with the opportunity to deal with their own faith more intensively. What can be seen is that, where the interviewees already had a close bond to the parish and a lively practice of faith before this period, then they experienced the voluntary character of Confirmation as something that reinforced their own faith and that strengthened their bond to the parish. The positive group dynamics during the period of preparing for Confirmation were often also experienced as a source of encouragement and affirmation. The interviewees assessed the link between puberty and the sacrament of Confirmation in contrasting ways: while some attributed their low motivation to participate in preparing for Confirmation to this period of transition, others cited their increased interest during this period in existential questions of life as a positive motivation. As a result, some of the interviewees even argued that the time of preparation for Confirmation should be postponed until later adolescence. The interviewees had vaguer memories of the actual topics that they had dealt with in the preparation for Confirmation than they had of "people" and "teaching methods/setting". What can be observed in general is that those topics that had been taught in a setting that fostered a sense of togetherness, and that had used a broad range of methods, including practical activities, were more likely to remain in the memory. Particularly popular were those topics that the young people or young adults could link to their own lives, and that were taught in an unconventional way, e.g., through the use of modern media: "*Yes, our topic at the time was 'Media: Broadcasting and Reception'. How the topic came about, I don't know, we weren't told. But it was a really fascinating topic, because it was done in a very interesting way by our parish assistant, loads through the media, SMS and stuff like that …*" The fact that preparation for Confirmation and Religious Education at school were offered parallel had a different effect on the interviewees in terms of their level of interest in the topics dealt with during the period of preparation for Confirmation: "*Yes, OK, some discussions I found a bit, well, I don't know, because the topics were already a bit worn-out*". But, looking back, other interviewees saw the deepening of topics that they had dealt with in their preparation for Communion, together with the particular group setting, as being worthwhile: "*But the lessons themselves are not bad, I must admit. The stuff itself, it's more or less dealing again with the Communion lessons, or continuing them. And sometimes it's nice to repeat something from the Communion class and then develop something from it*".

The types of catechism used in preparing young people for Confirmation vary from parish to parish, but there seem at first glance to be no regional idiosyncrasies. Most of the interviewees had gone on a trip during the phase of Confirmation, something that they still remembered largely positively. The mode of preparing for Confirmation ranged from an intensive week to a regular fortnightly meeting. Also, the strength of connection that the young people had to the church as a concrete place of worship varied, and especially so because, unlike in the preparation for

Communion, there was no obligation on them to attend Sunday services. The period of preparing for Confirmation also often included recreational activities such as playing football, going climbing and geocaching.

While the memories of the actual contents of what had been taught in the preparation for Confirmation had with a few exceptions faded just as much among the 16- to 18-year-old interviewees as among those in the group of 26- to 28-year-olds, the memories of those participants involved in catechesis were often stronger. Sometimes it was again mothers who, working on a voluntary basis, prepared the young people for Confirmation, but, more often than with the preparation for Communion, it was sometimes also full-time employees. What is worth noting is that the interviewees gave a consistently positive evaluation of the relationship that they had had with the catechists for Confirmation, although there were of course variations in the intensity of the bond.

4.3 Context of learning: Voluntary work

What emerged within voluntary work as a separate and independent context of learning was altar service. This was something that had not been previously considered, which is also due to the fact that until a few years ago altar service was not a prominent context of church youth work. Rather, young people usually belonged to a youth association and were at the same time altar boys or girls as a matter of course. It is only in recent years that the work of altar service seems to have detached itself somewhat from youth work and become a context of youth work with its own importance. It now seems to be the case that the work of altar service can be denoted as an independent and important context of religious learning that plays an important role in enabling young people to acquire knowledge and the practice of faith. This work sometimes occurs alongside traditional youth association work, and sometimes replaces it – for example, in East German dioceses, where often no traditional youth-association work was established after reunification. Children are encouraged to begin altar service as a positive experience when they prepare for Communion, and in many cases altar service also offers a bridge between Communion and Confirmation. The motives are manifold, ranging from the desire for group affiliation, the feeling of being among like-minded people, the sense of taking on a task in/for the parish, the possibility of organising something independently or guiding the younger altar boys and girls – up to feelings of personal vocation and the specialness of serving at the altar. To give just one example: "*Yes, I would now simply speak in my personal situation simply of a call to serve at the altar*". The analyses presented here have also shown clear synergies between altar service and Religious Education at school, to such an extent in fact that altar service raised religious and theological questions that then entered the Religious Education classroom at school, and vice versa. "*… now, … I know that what the teacher is saying up there gives me something*". Young people also often continued with altar service beyond

Confirmation, this however depends on their age at Confirmation. For more religiously minded young people, altar service also seems to be a way for them to live their own religiosity and to deal with religious/theological issues. "*... the church, everything you can do there. That's one thing ... that the church is somewhere you can feel comfortable, but that you don't just sit, stand, kneel and fold your hands quietly ...*" However, taking up this activity is not always a *conscious* decision; in regions that still have a relatively high level of Catholicism, taking up altar service is often simply a result of tradition. To end being an altar boy or girl happens either consciously or by "growing out" of the average age and by experiencing changed living conditions. In summary, though, it can nevertheless be said that altar service is becoming, and has become, an increasingly central place of religious youth work, but that there is also a considerable need for further research here.

The analysis here has also shown that neither the gender nor the educational background of the interviewees was significant. In terms of age, it was especially the group of 18-year-olds that attributed greater importance to the people at the different places of learning. In the analysis of regions, the Magdeburg area must be mentioned – that is, the sampling from East Germany. Here, preference was usually given to religious instruction in the parish, since such instruction at school often only took place in a mixed-denominational class or did not take place at all. In addition, the interviewees noted a close link between school and parish, with the same person teaching religion at school and working in the parish, and this person then often being influential over a longer period of time.

5. Comparing the goals

Overall, there proved to be agreement between magisterial goals and the practice of religious education in three areas. First, both the German bishops (see Die deutschen Bischöfe 2005) and teachers of religion at school are concerned with showing the importance of the Christian faith for the lives of children and young people today. Second, both wish to contribute in a targeted way to the development of a religious identity (see Die deutschen Bischöfe 1996). Finally, both are concerned with developing the capacity for dialogue, which means above all interreligious dialogue and dealing with religious plurality (see Die deutschen Bischöfe 2005).

Analysing the interviews yielded further insights on all three points. Thus, the interviewees (and particularly those in the older group) valued very highly the common goal in Religious Education at school as well as in catechesis of showing and developing the importance of the Christian faith to life – providing that this took place through discussion that left room for disagreement. Two prerequisites can be identified here. First, an atmosphere of trust, and a way of moderating and leading the discussions that values the pupils, while at the same time structuring and steering the debate towards a particular goal. Second, it becomes particularly clear in how the interviewees remembered the contents of teaching that they were especially able to recall those topics where they could find points of connection to the reality of their own lives. In short, the objects of learning referred to by Paulo Freire as "generative topics" continue to be relevant to the young people surveyed.

Developing religious identity, which is described as a central goal of religious education both in the magisterial documents as well as in the empirical studies of teachers of religion, seems to depend especially on how the teacher relates to what he or she is teaching; and in a second step, how they relate to pupils. What emerged as a further component in the investigation is the choice and application of (teaching) methods. The interviewees remembered clearly in all interviews the forms and ways of teaching in both Religious Education and catechesis.

Most of the interviewees tended to reject the goal of Religious Education set by the magisterium – namely, to enable a relationship of trust with lived forms of faith. Rather, Religious Education may and should have affective elements, because otherwise it is criticised for being too theoretical; nonetheless, practice in, for example, direct liturgical forms or prayer routines are usually not remembered positively. In catechesis, it is in particular the group focus that is welcome as a setting conducive to learning; if young people are also offered something relevant after Confirmation, then this setting can lead to their further involvement in the church. This enables them to be involved through the church in the parish in a way that is appropriate to their age – probably one of the reasons why altar service is popular. Unlike other contexts of learning, however, catechesis tends to be perceived in biographical memory as a one-time event.

Finally, the interviewees generally experienced the last goal – the capacity for interreligious dialogue – as being too weak and indistinct, and this although their Religious Education and processes of catechesis are only two to five years in the past for one group, and not more than 12–15 years in the past for the older group. Almost all the interviewees wanted to deal even more with the religions of the world, and criticised the frequent focus on Judaism in the time of the Third Reich and the Holocaust. Debates about religious traditions outside Christianity, and thus about the form that interreligious learning should take, barely take in catechesis, something that many of the interviewees criticised.

6. The attempt at a model

What is perhaps not entirely surprising at first glance is that the investigation conducted here has shown a close connection between person, method and content of teaching. The connection between person and content – that is, the teacher's enthusiasm for and commitment to a topic (or, in the language of the magisterium: the authenticity of the witness) – is well-known and pertinent. However, there have been few findings so far in the field of research on religious education on the importance and effectiveness of *methods* as tools of teaching. All the more surprising when it came to evaluating the study was that, besides the connection between content and person, method emerged as the third factor determining effectiveness and sustainability. A clear distinction between or separation of the three components is barely possible regarding effectiveness. Thus, a model has been developed at the end of the study that speaks of an "amalgamation" of the three factors of person, method, and content determining effectiveness in the context of religious education today. Future research should investigate more closely how these three factors relate to each other – whether they are, for example, equally balanced in their importance, or whether one of the factors is particularly strong in general or in a particular situation. The question of which methods receive particular attention here should also be elucidated more clearly. And, finally, it is necessary to examine more closely the question of what this means for processes of religious education.

These are all initial questions that resulted from evaluating the twelve interviews in a qualitative-reconstructive procedure. This is not a representative study. It is crucial to continue this limited pilot study on a larger scale. Besides the questions just formulated about the relationship between the factors of person, content and method, and methods as a teaching instrument, what should then also be investigated is the importance of the context of learning of voluntary work, and here especially the importance of altar service. The relationship between altar service and traditional youth-association work should then also be investigated again. An interesting hypothesis to be evaluated could be, for example, whether altar service and youth-association work relate to each other in such a way that adolescents more intensely interested in religion are more likely to find themselves in altar service, while young people who are more socially interested tend to participate in the traditional church youth associations. Regardless of these questions, which are more concerned with content, a further study should above all include other age groups.

References

Bucher, A. (2000). *Religionsunterricht zwischen Lernfach und Lebenshilfe. Eine empirische Untersuchung zum katholischen Religionsunterricht in der Bundesrepublik Deutschland.* Stuttgart: Kohlhammer.

Bucher, A., and Miklas, H. (eds.) (2005). *Zwischen Berufung und Frust. Die Befindlichkeit von katholischen und evangelischen ReligionslehrerInnen in Österreich.* Münster: LIT.

Die deutschen Bischöfe (1996). *Die bildende Kraft des Religionsunterrichts,* edited by Sekretariat der Deutschen Bischofskonferenz (= Die deutschen Bischöfe 56). Bonn: Deutsche Bischofskonferenz.

Die deutschen Bischöfe (2005). *Der Religionsunterricht vor neuen Herausforderungen,* edited by Sekretariat der Deutschen Bischofskonferenz (= Die deutschen Bischöfe 80). Bonn: Deutsche Bischofskonferenz.

Englert, R., and Güth, R. (eds.) (1999). *"Kinder zum Nachdenken bringen". Eine empirische Untersuchung zu Situation und Profil katholischen Religionsunterrichts an Grundschulen.* Stuttgart: Kohlhammer.

Feige, A., Dressler, B., Lukatis, W., and Schöll, A. (2000). *'Religion' bei ReligionslehrerInnen. Religionspädagogische Zielvorstellungen und religiöses Selbstverständnis in empirisch-soziologischen Zugängen*. Münster: LIT.

Feige, A., Dressler, B., and Tzscheetzsch, W. (2006). *Religionslehrerin oder Religionslehrer werden. Zwölf Analysen berufsbiographischer Selbstwahrnehmung*. Ostfildern: Schwaben.

Feige, A., Tzscheetzsch, W., Dressler, B., Lukatis, I., Lukatis, W., Schramm, M., Boehme, K. et al. (2005). *Christlicher Religionsunterricht im religionsneutralen Staat? Unterrichtliche Zielvorstellungen und religiöses Selbstverständnis von ev. und kath. Religionslehrerinnen und -lehrern in Baden-Württemberg. Eine empirisch-repräsentative Befragung*. Ostfildern: Schwaben.

Forschungsgruppe "Religion und Gesellschaft" (2015). *Werte – Religion – Glaubenskommunikation. Eine Evaluationsstudie zur Erstkommunionkatechese*. Wiesbaden: Springer VS.

Glaser, B., and Strauss, A. (1967). *The Discovery of Grounded Theory*. Chicago: Aldine.

Gläser, J., and Laudel, G. ([3]2009). *Experteninterviews und qualitative Inhaltsanalyse*. Wiesbaden: Springer VS.

Hopf, C. (1996). Hypothesenprüfung und qualitative Sozialforschung. In: R. Strobl and A. Böttger (ed.). *Wahre Geschichten? Zu Theorie und Praxis qualitativer Interviews*. Baden-Baden: Nomos, 9–21.

Jakobs, M., Riegel, U., Helbling, D., and Engelberg, T. (2009). *Konfessioneller Religionsunterricht in multireligiöser Gesellschaft. Eine empirische Studie für die deutschsprachige Schweiz*. Zürich: TVZ.

Kelle, U., and Kluge, S. ([2]2010). *Vom Einzelfall zum Typus. Fallvergleich und Fallkontrastierung in der qualitativen Sozialforschung*. Wiesbaden: Springer VS.

Kliemann, P., and Rupp, H. (2000). *1000 Stunden Religion. Wie junge Erwachsene den Religionsunterricht sehen*. Stuttgart: Calwer.

Kruse, J. ([2]2015). *Qualitative Interviewforschung. Ein integrativer Ansatz*. Weinheim: Beltz/Juventa.

Lück, C. (2002). *Religionsunterricht an der Grundschule. Studien zur organisatorischen und didaktischen Gestalt eines umstrittenen Schulfaches*. Leipzig: Evangelische Verlagsanstalt.

Lück, C. (2003). *Beruf Religionslehrer. Selbstverständnis – Kirchenbindung – Zielorientierung*. Leipzig: Evangelische Verlagsanstalt.

Schmidt, C. ([9]2012). Analyse von Leitfadeninterviews. In: U. Flick, E. von Kardorff and I. Steinke (ed.). *Qualitative Forschung. Ein Handbuch*. Reinbek: Rowohlt, 447–456.

Sekretariat der Deutschen Bischofskonferenz (ed.) (1989). Der Religionsunterricht in der Schule. Ein Beschluss der Gemeinsamen Synode der Bistümer in der Bundesrepublik Deutschland 1974. In: *Nachkonziliare Texte zu Katechese und Religionsunterricht*, ed. Sekretariat der Deutschen Bischofskonferenz. Bonn: Deutsche Bischofskonferenz, 263–303.

Strauss, A., and Corbin, J. (1996). *Grounded Theory: Grundlagen qualitativer Forschung*. Weinheim: Beltz/PVU.

The characteristics of non-formal religious education in a folk church
The Norwegian education reform

Heid Leganger-Krogstad

1. Separation of formal and non-formal religious education

The separation of formal and non-formal religious education in Norway is the result of two acts of the parliament, Stortinget: first in the school reform of 1997 and later in the Faith Education Reform in religious and life-stance communities (Trosopplæringsreformen) of 2003. The current Norwegian situation provides an excellent case, suited for investigating the characteristics of non-formal education in relation to formal education – legally and empirically. Material for this present investigation was taken from three main sources: the relevant legal regulations, formal changes in the school system, and publications and reports from the broad evaluation research that has been conducted to guide the shaping and implementation of the Faith Education Reform in the majority church, Church of Norway (CofN), in English named the Christian Education Reform. The research was conducted by teams from different academic institutions at three different time periods: ETOR 2003–2008, KIFO 2009–2012 and MF 2012–2018 (cf. list of web pages at the end of this chapter). This research will be reviewed in this chapter with a goal of extracting the main debates that are most relevant for the study of non-formal education.

This reform was implemented during a time in which the bonds between state and church were loosened, and a folk church gradually substituted a state church. When confessional Christian education was transferred from schools to churches in Norway (Krupka and Leganger-Krogstad 2013), the National Council of the Church of Norway found that the reform was an opportunity to encourage the development of local congregations. The reform underwent a broad political and ecclesiastical hearing and has become regarded as the church's key strategic mission for the coming years.

Models of religious education depend on the history of the country, the constitution, the religious context and demography, and the legal framework for schools and religious communities (Jackson et al. 2007). In Norway, since the school reform of 1997, the chosen model has been multireligious education (Skeie 2007) in the public school system (only 3.7 % of all pupils attend private schools), in combination with support from the state to uphold non-formal religious education in the folk church and all registered life-stance and religious communities. This is different from Denmark where there is a combination of folk church and mainly

Christian education, as well from Finland where there is a combination of two national Churches and Religious Education according to the confession of the pupils
in schools. In England, for example, churches are deeply involved in formal education through ownership of schools (Church of England Education Office 2016). The
Norwegian solution presents certain challenges for shaping non-formal education
in CofN in a specific way, which is worth a closer look. The questions are: How can
the Norwegian case contribute to the understanding of the characteristics of non-
formal education? And: To what degree can non-formal education be understood as
a tool to uphold a folk church?

1.1 A general national reform of non-formal education

In 2003, the Norwegian Parliament implemented the Faith Education Reform
(Trosopplæringsreformen), affecting all religious and life stance communities by
making them, together with the families, responsible for the upbringing and nurturing *into* a worldview or religion. This came as a consequence of changes in the
school system. In 1997, optional confessional – mainly Lutheran – Religious Education was substituted by compulsory multireligious Religious Education (Christianity, Religion and Worldviews under the abbreviation KRL, and later KRLE as
ethics was added to the name). Schools are responsible for knowledge and impartial teaching in a multireligious society, with the goal of enhancing tolerance and
interreligious dialogue. All of this is linked closely to increasing plurality in the
Norwegian society from individualization, secularization, immigration and global
influences.

   The Church of Norway, a Lutheran church, was formally freed from its status
as a *state church* in 2012 and is today a *folk church* according to the Constitution
§ 16 and has the responsibility to provide its services in Norwegian and/or the
Sami language in all places where Norwegians live, at home and abroad. 72 % of all
inhabitants of Norway are members of the Church of Norway, which is 3.7 million of the total population of 5.3 million. 620000 inhabitants are members of
other religious and life-stance communities and have official support from the state
and municipality per member (capita), equalling the support given to members of
the Church of Norway. Other Christian Churches have 340000 members, Muslim
communities 150000 members, the Secular Humanist Organization 100000 members, Buddhist communities 17000 members, and other religious communities have
smaller numbers (SSB official statistics from December 2017). In this way, the Norwegian state practises religious freedom in a positive way as opposed, for example,
to current practice in France.

   The 2003 education reform has a general character of separating *nurturing* into a
conviction, which takes place in families and religious and life-stance communities
and *religious education* which means teaching about beliefs and convictions for all
citizens. Formal and non-formal education are in this way divided between insti-

tutions that each have their own legal status, regime and objectives. There is still a cooperative zone between them due to the history of collaboration and influence in local communities, and the fact that families relate to both schools and religious institutions and children frequently move between the two.

1.2 Church of Norway. The Christian education reform

The reform affects CofN in a most profound way, since baptismal education for all citizens was the background for the founding of a common school system in 1739. Christian education had a central place in this state school until 1969, when its legal status changed. Formal religious education no longer served the needs of the church, but was reformulated to serve the child and the society. The Christian education reform from 2003 intends to be a compensation for the loss of Christian education in schools. Throughout the 250 years in which formal education functioned as baptismal education, research focused almost exclusively on formal education, and practical theology in Norway developed without a strand focusing on non-formal religious education. The evaluations mark the starting point for research on church-related religious education as a separate field of research. The reform has made stakeholders in the Church of Norway realise the need to re-establish a systematic, continuous lifelong education program on its own premises. This goes together with demands from the Norwegian parliament. The politicians expect church educators to develop learning strategies different from those of schools and a 'non-schoolish' reform of education in church is a term in a parliamentary policy document (Innst.S.Nr.200, 2002/2003, part 2.2). These recommendations from the Parliament builds on both an official Norwegian report (NOU 2000:26, 2000) and a White Paper (St.Meld. Nr. 7, 2002/2003). The parliament also decided that the project period of five years should be organised by a committee independent of the regular church structure to enhance creativity and makes new ways of thinking about education in church flourish.

A general definition of non-formal learning in the youth sector, promoted by the Council of Europe, states:

> "Non-formal learning is purposive but voluntary learning that takes place in a diverse range of environments and situations for which teaching/training and learning is not necessarily their sole or main activity. These environments and situations may be intermittent or transitory, and the activities or courses that take place may be staffed by professional learning facilitators (such as youth trainers) or by volunteers (such as youth leaders). The activities and courses are planned, but are seldom structured by conventional rhythms or curriculum subjects. They usually address specific target groups, but rarely document or assess learning outcomes or achievements in conventionally visible ways" (Chisholm 2005).

Keywords here are purpose, voluntary, teaching/training and learning, activities, transitory, professionals/volunteers, planning/curriculum, assessment and learning outcomes. This definition can function as a tool to focus on relevant issues when reviewing the evaluation research on the reform in CofN in three periods:

(a) Grassroot projects 2003–2008
(b) Implementation in all congregations 2009–2014
(c) Reform in a church perspective 2015 to date.

2. Development and evaluation during the grassroot period

Continuous funding of the reform was made dependent of a positive evaluation of the project phase, the first five years of grassroot initiatives and experimentation. The implementation period was set to 10 years and full funding of the reform allocated 250 million NOK in 2003 (about 30 million EUR) adjusted in 2018 to approximately 35 million EUR. This initial period was organised by a committee set up explicitly for this purpose and which functioned rather independently of the regular church structure. The politicians in the parliament wanted new initiatives, creative set-ups, a diverse grassroot development, and had the expectations that new educational programs should have the same number of participants as the rather successful confirmation program which reached 70 % of 15-year-olds at the time. In 2017, 58 % of all 15-year-olds took part in the confirmation program (Kirke-rådet 2018, 22–23). To reach such numbers, the politicians thought non-schoolish education would be a prerequisite.

The evaluation of the grassroots projects, ETOR, resulted in periodic reports as formative input and feedback to the committee (*Underveisrapporter*), as well as subreports (*Delrapporter*) on specific parts of the reform such as the application process, the organization of the project, comparison of education in parishes included in the project and those not involved, and Sami Christian education. Two books were published, one as a case study report (Hegstad et al. 2008) and a summative report (Hauglin et al. 2008). A review of the process is also available in German (Leganger-Krogstad 2009). The research is seen both as advice for the project committee and the steering group and to inform the public and politicians.

2.1 Local or national strategy?

A period of flourishing has been observed. Around 1000 of the 1282 congregations developed projects and applied for funding during the first five years of the reform, and 479 parish projects received funding. Educational staff from other sectors, including schools, kindergartens, child welfare, music and drama were employed and many creative programs took place.

Parallel with the facilitation of all the local development projects, the committee paved the way for a nationwide movement. This was done by professional branding through a common design program, with information material including a reform logo, motto, clothes, and equipment. The congregations were provided with information sheets, templates and videos. The ETOR-team affirms some of the committee's strategic steps in making the reform a common national project. From the very beginning, a yearly national conference gathered up to 1800 participants who were involved in education, both staff and volunteers, for updating, inspiration and networking. Every parish in the project was allocated a professional tutor who at first guided the process of the grassroot project, and later with the formation of a local curriculum. A national competency network was appointed by the committee to review the development of the project and give feedback. Regular academic conferences were held as a forum to discuss completed or ongoing research and to have consultations on specific issues at request from the committee. To support the process more closely, the committee had both a reference group for advice and a steering group to make decisions. Nationwide educational programs have been developed, materials provided for all congregations and specific week-ends during the year allocated for these events: Stay awake (*Lys våken*), Agents in the tower (*Tårnagenter*) and Code B (*Kode B*). Gradually, local congregations not yet included in the reform were influenced by the nationwide new way of thinking and increased their effort in non-formal education. Information on successful and non-successful projects were made available to guide other parishes. Development of non-formal education took place through parallel local and national strategies.

2.2 The target group?

The difference between pre-existing programs for children and youths, which mainly recruit children and young people of religiously practicing parents and the regular churchgoers, and the new programs established by the reform to reach all baptised children has been a continuous discussion. Baptism does not discriminate infants, so education is to be given irrespective of children's ability. Investigations into information and recruitment strategies which sought to find the intended target group and investigations of the participants which attempted to identify who actually participated were also part of the evaluation.

All congregations were instructed to develop invitations with a rubric where parents could indicate that their child has special needs, so that the educator could provide for this. All reports to the committee were to also report how many participants were given special care. Through this, some of the organizational reform instruments created new habits in the local congregations, and gradually also the ability to have a state of preparedness to respond to different types of special needs. During the project period a learning process was started to provide congregations with an inclusive mind-set and resources to take care of vulnerable children and children with special needs (Kaufman and Sandsmark 2015, Engedal et al. 2015).

In CofN membership is established by baptism and infant baptism dominates. The baptism rate of new-borns has been falling by approximately one percent per year over the last fifteen years and in 2017 53% of all one-year-olds were baptised (Kirkerådet 2018, 17–18). With this, the question which children are defined as *belonging* to the church becomes important. Children who have only one parent who is a member of CofN have a belonging status until the age of 15, which is the age of religious majority. Changing the established tradition that baptism should take place either with infants or with confirmands takes time. Non-baptised children in educational programs are gradually encouraged to consider baptism and become members. The church's non-formal education aims at reaching all members and associated children but has no instruments to make it obligatory.

2.3 What activities are considered part of the reform?

Only activities or events where individual invitations were sent to all baptised children in the age group enrolled for the activity, could be reported as reform activities. After each activity, reports were given to the committee including the number of participants and in percentage of the age group, boys and girls, and information on how many children with special needs took part. Youth ministry organizations within CofN, especially those responsible for continuous programs such as Sunday Schools, choirs and scouts were offended by these new regulations as they considered their work as being important and valuable part of Christian education in the parish. Mediation was needed and more co-operation eventually took place. These organizations developed their own ways of recruiting participants to be fully inclusive in line with CofN. They also had to relate more consciously to the total program in the parish. This way their activities could be enrolled in the reform program and in the reports, often with mainly volunteers as responsible educators.

In order to be recognised as non-schoolish programs, many creative concepts appeared in the applications and many of them were funded. There were several ideas for different sorts of cafés and after school activities, places for doing school homework and for dialogue, LEGO-clubs, and workshops for motor, woodwork, cooking, etc. Others had more obvious intentions of being educative such as: Christian education in nature or in relation to different sports, and teaching about *the meal* as a theological concept. Empirical studies from the first period had to question the broad variety of programs where the aims or practices showed little educational interest and where the goals for the activity were nearly invisible, and this is still the case (Frøyen 2017). Many of the activities could be held in a cultural club or elsewhere outside the church. In the meal project, for instance, most of the time was allocated to preparing the food or going shopping. In the evaluation, clearer objectives and a more conscious value base was asked for, and clearer statements on the theological content. It showed a need to verbalise the cultures in church that are taken for granted (Hauglin et al. 2008).

At the same time, the evaluation showed that use of the church buildings in education had increased rapidly and that children and young people preferred church to classrooms and basements (Leganger-Krogstad 2008b). An overall impression was that the participants wanted to be introduced to and exercise the practice of religion in a broad sense and do "the real and serious stuff" (as they expressed it) rather than take part in activities that could happen anywhere. The advice from ETOR was: church should do what church is good at. It means also non-formal education should be intentionally educational and not mainly entertaining activities.

2.4 Education as lifelong learning

The parliament decided that the general non-formal education reform should include programs for those up to 18 years. This means that confirmation, which has been considered the final goal of baptismal education by the CofN, no longer marks a finishing point. This change in duration might be the reason for the church's use of the general name *trosopplæring* (faith education) instead of *dåpsopplæringsreform* (baptismal education reform) used in the preparatory papers. The age of majority in Norway is 18 and the political demand for an educational program up to this age can be considered a way to indicate that lifelong learning affects Christian education as well as learning in all other fields of life. In Norway, it is common for young people to leave their home and local congregation at the age of 18, moving elsewhere to start their student lives. Thus, offering programs until the age of 18 is logical, but in practice, it is very difficult to create programs of interest for large numbers of young people in this age group. Leadership training programs, as a follow up to confirmation, however, are in rather general use.

Lifelong learning is part of the reform through interaction with parents that takes place in conjunction with educational programs for the infants, children and youth in the form of gatherings such as baby-singing, parent meetings or meetings with confirmands and parents. In some parishes, the instruction that is part of the Christian education for confirmands, is likewise offered for parents, in an adjusted adult version. A majority of the programs combine education in the church with the distribution of educational material for continuous use at home. Information on Christian nurture for the age group and ideas for religious practices for use at home is part of these meetings with parents. Involving the whole family is a crucial part of the reform and has been evaluated in a specific study. Whether parents are interested in having support, what sort of information and support, and what reasons parents have for relating differently to information and participation in educational programs was investigated (Høeg and Trysnes 2012). To gain this type of knowledge is important, since non-formal religious education is meant to primarily take place in the families, and the church supports the parents by providing material, advice and intergenerational activities.

2.5 Education – a practice of sharing

Prior to the reform, education in the church was widely considered the individual congregation's task and responsibility. As the project management, however, demanded written reports in digital versions, the sharing of programs, information, knowledge, ideas, teaching materials, and methods of working increased rapidly. Today thousands of reports and ideas are available in one common database, *Ressursbanken*. It is possible to conclude that a digital reform in the education sector took place simultaneously with the reform, aided by new equipment, digitally competent employees from other sectors, and the demand for digital reports from the committee (Leganger-Krogstad 2007).

The planning process of the grassroot projects in the first period was developed cooperatively in the local congregations, and many educators established cooperation with partners outside of church, such as cultural and local historical institutions, art-, drama- and dancing groups and other religious communities in the neighborhood. Many new partners were brought into contact with the church (Fuglseth and Haakedal 2012). The reform brought fresh money, so new staff was employed and many of them started a second career in the church bringing with them experience from outside the church. This called for sharing knowledge and experience within the congregation between those with long theological and pedagogical experience and those with other types of work practice. This has, of course, been experienced as both fruitful and problematic among the established professions – pastors, deacons, cantors, and catechists – in the church. The reform demands a more interprofessional working manner.

2.6 From voluntarism and tacit knowledge to professionalism and formal texts?

Inclusion of all children irrespective of their ability and belonging demands considerable changes in the established programs in churches. The application process to have a grassroot project funded led to a higher level of formalization of church programs. Programs that formerly involved primarily tacit knowledge and that were not structured according written plans and schedules, now had to be presented in written versions with explanations of contextual, pedagogical and theological grounds. This changed the way of working. The level of professionalism in the local educational work increased. An information- and knowledge-based society demands a similar development. Parents, often highly competent, expect a certain level of information on the programs being offered. The demands for reports to the funding authorities had the same effect as volunteers had no access to the digital report system. This, however, also caused a certain degrading of valuable tacit knowledge and voluntary effort in the educational field. The non-formal sector was gradually professionalised and volunteers more seldom took responsibility for educational programs, but were given more and more practical and organizational tasks which in the long run seems to have led to less interested and motivated volunteers (Fretheim 2014 and 2016). The demand for local curricula made all parishes develop formal texts (Fuglseth et al. 2012) and continuous development of these texts can be considered a working method (Botvar et al. 2015). Non-formal education became professionalised.

2.7 Open-ended activity

Non-formal education stands in opposition to formal education where children always are to meet certain standards, their outcomes are assessed and graded. Non-formal education can have aims on the program or curriculum level, but at the individual level it is much more disputed. Individual evaluation of knowledge or performance is out of the question. Non-formal education in the church is mainly understood as an environment where assessment, grading and giving certifications is unnecessary and not in accordance with the aims of the institution. Typical formulations of aims in programs are: "The church should offer the children and young people an arena of freedom and space, a place for personal development" or "a place to feel at home, and a place where they can hang around."

What kind of aims can be formulated in educational programs for *all* baptised children? This discussion has only just started in Norway. What is the difference between stating aims in the program and stating aims on behalf of every child? Is the focus then back to teaching rather than learning? What type of goals can all children fulfil? Aims stating competences seem difficult in an all-inclusive program. Individual goals stating: "have experience from" and "have taken part in" certain tasks or events, could be considered non-discriminating. How open-ended need non-formal education in the church be?

3. Development and evaluation in the implementation period

During the first 10 years of the reform, all parishes were to be able to participate by having some fresh funding for educational staff. Small congregations were supported with small sums, and cooperative positions in the rural deanery or in the diocese, were often the solution. Envy and competition in relation to the successful parishes enrolled early in the project was a topic in this period.

3.1 Curriculum for non-formal religious education

The most crucial step in the further development of the Christian education reform was to establish a national curriculum. The experiences from the evaluation were subsumed into an extensive curriculum from 2010 named: "Plan for Christian Education. God gives – we share" (Church of Norway National Council 2010). The education is meant to be learning for life:

"The aim of the *Plan for Christian Education* in the Church of Norway is to contribute to a systematic and continuous Christian education that

– awakens and strengthens Christian faith
– imparts knowledge of the Triune God
– helps in interpreting life and mastering the art of living
– encourages interest and involvement in the life of the church and the community
– for all baptised persons aged 0–18 years, irrespective of their degree of functionality." (p. 6)

This is explained further:

> "Christian education should equip children and young people to live in their baptism. Through helping them to become familiar with the local church, daily rituals, the celebration of Christian festivals and important phases of life, the home and the church can co-operate in this process. The disciples who accompanied Jesus are good role models for those travelling on the path of faith. They got to know Jesus by being with him, being taught by him, experiencing things for themselves and taking part in a working community. In this way they developed a sense of belonging and an identity of their own as disciples. To be a disciple of Jesus is to live and learn in a lifelong relationship to God. Christian education is therefore lifelong learning" (p. 5).

The reform has as a main focus taking the children's faith seriously (Krupka and Leganger-Krogstad 2007). The reform has a motto: *Greatest of all* with a double reference, both to the place of children in the Kingdom of God and to *faith, hope and love* as the heart of Christian education (Church of Norway National Council 2010) and in the parallel Plan for Sami Christian Education.

The general curriculum is mainly a framework and a resource for developing a local curriculum. In the hearing process, demand for a minimum of given common content came up, and it was solved by providing one list of *Key Bible passages* and one of *Examples on Key activities* in an appendix to the curriculum (pp. 45–47) as a resource text for local planning. The reason for this hesitancy for giving a minimum curriculum is the wish to respect the local freedom and the diversity in parishes in our vast and sparsely populated country. The curriculum is mainly stating the aims, the pedagogical and theological grounds on which the Christian teaching reform is built.

Size requirements for the program is an ongoing debate. Is there an acceptable minimum for the program to function as compensation for the loss of education in Christianity in schools, as was the intention of the reform? The loss of Christian education that serves as the basis for the reform was calculated with 315 hours per child (NOU 2000:26, 12). This number has been repeated as the aim for the reform since then. Especially parishes in the bigger cities and those in the most rural areas have severe problems meeting this goal. It means that each and every child should participate in 315 hours of activities, and confirmation, the most used program, accounts for 60 of these hours. CofN's annual report from 2017 contains statistics of the educational offerings in all eleven dioceses and after several years of rising rates of participation, rates have fallen over the past year. Simultaneously, the average of-fer of educational hours per parish in 2017 is 291 hours, down from 328 hours in 2016 (Kirkerådet 2018, 20). The local plans are under constant revision, which is in accord with the guidelines for the reform. Every local plan goes to the bishop's office for approval every fifth year. Most of the offices demand at least one activity/event for every age-group between the ages 0 and 18.

The influence of the national curriculum which is the basis for the use of Bible texts in local curricula was studied in the project "The Bible in Christian educa-tion", and the influence of the list of key Bible passages is rather significant. Signs of influence from traditional catechesis are also visible in the way that some texts not included in the list are in use in many parishes, such as the stories of Zaccha-eus, Bartimaeus, and Jesus calming the storm. Narratives are most often in use, but longer narratives especially from the Old Testament seem to be left out in order to gain space for more texts on Jesus (Midttun et al. 2018, 79).

The case of Norway is an example of a national curriculum for non-formal edu-cation and that the type of curriculum in use is then understood more as a framework and guideline than statutory, and local freedom is encouraged by the church author-ities, who are in charge of the reform after the project period.

3.2 Education based on socio-cultural understanding of learning

The politicians expect church educators to develop learning strategies different from those of schools in the 'non-schoolish' reform. This term seems to presuppose that learning in school is dominated by individual acquisition of given knowledge as a property that can be acquired. This view of learning is necessary for testing and individual measuring of knowledge in formal education (cf. educational policies of the European Union, the Council of Europe and the Organisation for Economic Co-operation and Development). Norwegian school education uses competence-based curricula. Acquisition of knowledge is according to Anna Sfard one of two domi-nant metaphors for learning in educational theory; the other being the participation metaphor (Sfard 1998). The acquisition metaphor dominates where the learner is looked upon as a receiver and knowledge is a cognitive property the consumer pos-sesses (in the brain). The teaching mainly operates with closed questions. Possessed knowledge can be demonstrated individually and assessed.

In the process of developing a curriculum for non-formal education, the in-tention of facilitating learning according to a socio-cultural view was articulated (Holmqvist 2012, Holmqvist and Afdal 2015). Thus, the reform seeks to develop learning strategies according to the participation metaphor, meaning that the child should, on the basis of Evangelical Lutheran baptismal theology, be offered op-portunities to equally partake in tasks and activities according to the individual's capacity, ability and style. Belonging and partaking are keywords in the learning strategy. The child is invited to participate in activities and situations, according to her/his own interest and pace on equal bases in the church community as a specific setting for non-formal learning. This is in line with terminology used by Jean Lave and Etienne Wenger in "Situated learning. Legitimate peripheral participation" (Lave and Wenger 1991). Learning is described as situated and as highly dependent upon support structures of human, technical and contextual type. Learning is here a trajectory from the periphery towards the center where the novice advances from 'peripheral legitimate participation' to 'full participation'. The move can also stagnate or turn away from the learning community. Church as a learning community is dependent on sharing. Contributions from one participant can change the community. The name of the reform *God gives – we share* is a sign of the aim to develop church as a learning community where children and young people have a given place in their present state, not because they are needed later or represent the future.

The learning process in churches has been in the focus of an extensive study in LETRA (LEarning TRAjectories) 2009–2014 with a double aim, both to construct knowledge on practiced church education and to develop the field of non-formal education (Afdal 2013, and 2014, Holmqvist 2014, Holtedahl 2017, Mogstad 2013, Leganger-Krogstad, 2014, Johnsen 2014). In a socio-cultural understanding of learning, *situated learning* is a key term used to try to get hold of the high degree of complexity in particular learning settings. Learning is a generally social activity in a given cultural setting and not an individual phenomenon. In real life, learning is a cooperative activity, and experience from a range of such activities decides how the individual can cope and act or perform in different situations. Information in modern societies is distributed in quite new ways, holding information, however, should not be confused with learning. Learning in socio-cultural theory is seen as a much more complex phenomenon than being able to repeat certain informational facts. After the digital revolution, learning takes place in so-called information loaded societies, and learning takes place when these intelligent instruments are used in fruitful ways in real life situations.

A socio-cultural view on learning gives specific meaning when intelligent instruments are involved in the activity like computers, projectors, mixing board, cameras, loud speakers, music notes, music instruments, or digital Sunday service agendas. All these instruments can be seen as extensions of the human brain in the way that they help humans to function or perform beyond their individual ability. Knowledge is therefore seen as *distributed* to a much higher degree in digitalised societies. Neither knowledge nor learning can be seen or measured directly, but are always mediated through language, signs, activities and practices.

A third understanding of learning in addition to acquisition and participation is therefore knowledge creation. This means that every new task or activity has to be solved in new ways as it is seldom a skill that just can be repeated. This creation happens when an activity takes place in a social setting.

Research shows that learning is not an automatic response to participation (Fredriksen 2017). Are confirmands learning Sunday services by taking part in them several times? They may behave and act adequately, but do they understand the relationship between the different parts, the rhythm of the worship service as a drama or the weekly rhythm: six days of work to maintain the planet and one day for worship and rest? Does experience lead to learning without reflection upon gained experience? Informed action (Leganger-Krogstad 2008a) seems to be necessary to gain learning from a shared activity. The point in Sfard's outlining of the two metaphors of learning is that both are needed and learning as knowledge creation provides a third. It seems that all types of learning are necessary, and the need for acquisition of knowledge should not be downplayed even in an inclusive reform. "Christian education must both show that faith has contents that we can become familiar with and at the same time make it clear that no-one can understand God fully" (p. 9).

Non-formal education in the church takes place in a real life situation allowing for different learning strategies. It is situated, because many of the activities are church specific, and, at the same time, it offers meaning for life, cultural understanding, values for mastering the art of living and training in societal action. Simultaneously, the evaluation shows how difficult it is to transfer learning from one setting to another (Fredriksen 2017). The church has a lot of tacit knowledge which is not verbalised or reflected in relation to other lifeworlds children take part in as for instance school and social media, and what the children experience in church, is difficult for them to transfer to other settings. Educators in church could build more consciously on children's competences from school, on their literacy, digital and multicultural competencies (Leganger-Krogstad 2018).

3.3 Voluntary participation and systematic learning

The stated aim of the national curriculum is a systematic and continuous learning in a non-formal educational setting, which is tremendously demanding. The national curriculum should be both systematic and open for local adaptation. The demand for formulations of local curricula in every parish has functioned as a good tool. Intense efforts have been made locally and have raised attention to non-formal education. The systematic learning should, however, be an experience of the learner and a well-prepared curriculum is a prerequisite. In a folk church, like CofN, the children come and go, and so far no regulations for continuation have been established, other than those which families uphold. This is a problem for the choice of the content of education. All too often, the educator needs to start from scratch with their lessons, which may be perceived as boring repetition for those children who attend regularly. Differentiation in teaching has not been investigated, and more mandatory programs have not yet been developed.

Evaluations show that the group of children participating in Christian education after the reform is broader than earlier. More children than before the reform experience teaching in a church setting and with Christian representatives. The average participation in 2017 for all program activities was 31 % of all members (Kirkerådet 2018, 21). This is far from the goal to reach every baptised child. Certain organizations within CofN have continuous program offerings for Christian activities and present educational opportunities with a systematic progression for children who meet more regularly over several years. A report on professionalization and voluntarism in this cooperation between organizations and the reform is given by KIFO (Aagedal et al. 2014).

There is a continuous discussion in Norway about where the boundary between formal and non-formal education is, especially connected to what is considered religious practices in school, which are not allowed within the school subject Religious Education. Exemption is offered from all activities which parents consider religious practices or practices offensive to their convictions (Education act § 2–3a). The right to exemption is important when schools offer, for example, Christmas worship during school hours. The new regulations meant a decrease in school and church cooperation. Many pedagogically good and informative lessons, reaching *all* members of CofN and others, were no longer offered. And when they still were offered, the line between pedagogical practices and religious practices in school projects involving excursions to churches was blurred, and new discussions took place. An empirical study (Opsal 2013) led to debate (Winje 2016, Opsal 2016). The decrease of school and church cooperation is an effect also of more attention to non-formal education among educators in church.

The question remains: Can non-formal education and learning be continuous and systematic as long as it is voluntary?

4. The reform in the folk church

4.1 The reform as a positive driver

A research project asked in what ways the reform has influenced the way pastors and parish council leaders think about congregational development. There are many signs that the educational reform is seen as the main driver, and even more influential than the parallel liturgical reform (MUV-project) (Birkedal and Austnaberg 2017, Austnaberg and Birkedal 2017).

Most programs combine education with worship and Sunday service or services for the target group on weekdays. The evaluation shows that Sunday services have changed character towards a more family-oriented profile including more involvement of all age groups during this education reform. Children and young people are given liturgical tasks, and several new practices in Sunday services take place. Sunday service is an arena for cooperation among all staff members; volunteers are involved together with children and youths. Sermons can be held by others than the pastors and a greater variety of sermon genres is seen.

A homiletic project will study how preaching is done, received and inter-preted when children and adults attend the same Sunday service (FoSS at MF) (Kaufman 2019). The habit of announcing Sunday services under the name of a certain target group from the Christian education activities has been discussed (Leganger-Krogstad 2017). The use of children in liturgical functions has not been without opposition (Johnsen 2008).

The cooperation among staff members in congregations has been explored in re-lation to the educational reform as part of innovative action research (Sandsmark and Holmqvist 2018). The staff members have different professional training, lan-guage, rhythm, habits of planning and goals, and they still need to cooperate around the reform. Engeström's activity theory is the basis for this innovation project (Engeström 2001). Pastoral leadership has also been focused on in relation to pro-fessional learning and parish leadership (Saxegaard 2017).

The reform has led to an increase of educational staff in churches from around 200 positions to 800 nationwide. A mapping of educational personal as a whole, who is employed, their motivation, and competence is investigated in a mainly quantitative study. Since many of the positions are part-time and often rather small, expectations were that many had rather weak formal competence. This showed to be only partly true, since 87 % of them hold a bachelor or a master's degree. Only 13 % had neither theological nor pedagogical education. Many of the smallest posi-tions are held by lay persons with solid non-formal competences (Horsfjord et al., 2015).

The church is losing its function as a folk church unless it recruits new members through baptism and education (and for unbaptised learners and converts education comes before baptism). A folk church is meant to be national with a certain status of service. In Norway as a state church it was considered a welfare service in line with health and social services. It is all too early to say whether a folk church can be upheld in Norway. Secularization sweeps all western societies and concerns all life sectors. Most citizens seem to be more concerned with individual freedom than being part of a nationwide collective. Can a folk church (or national church) have less than half of the population and maintain its function?

The educational reform as a nationally organised project has contributed to some optimism in times when church is losing influence and authority. Children and young people approach religion in an experienced and oriented way and want to be taken seriously as members and participants. They want to gain competence. Without the fresh blood from the reform, the picture would have been more pes-simistic.

4.2 Critical view on the evaluations

The evaluations have been dominated by the use of qualitative research methods focusing on gaining understanding of the reform strategies, dynamics in staffs and congregations and the implementation phase. There is a certain lack of quantitative research which could give more exact figures on participation, outreach and outcome. Who are the participants and which responses do they give? What do they gain from the teaching and participation in church activities?

There has been a lack of focus on what defines non-formal religious education. Organizational issues, recruitment, cooperation with partners inside and outside church, pedagogical development and cooperation between church professions have been priorities, but the theology of the reform has mostly gone uncommented. This means that there has been marginal focus on the educational content and purpose of the reform. How comprehensive and systematic is the reform in practice? Exceptions from this are two projects from the recent years: Theologies practiced in selected teaching activities have been studied in several congregations, and the project shows that theological diversity within CofN is visible also in the educational programs of the church. The four different types of theology found were kerygmatic theology, spiritual community theology, traditions and folk church theology, and contextual theology (Fagermoen and Lauritzen 2018). This variety is seen even when the study focuses on events following a certain national teaching kit. The national curriculum is meant to be adapted to local contexts, but it is still an open question whether it is the context or the educators who decide on the theological profile of the teaching. The second project "The Bible in the Christian education reform" (BIT) uses a variety of methods to study the Bible in the teaching practice and the responses of children and youths to those teachings (Leganger-Krogstad 2018, 2019).

5. Summary

The Norwegian case raises a lot of common issues concerning formal and non-formal religious education. The line between them is not clear, as there are historic and existing relations between them; moreover, the children are moving between them. The cooperative field is considered complicated and is treated cautiously. The most influential difference is that of individual assessment and grading. To reach a target group of all baptised children in Christian education puts the utmost demands on educators both in description and performance. The grade of inclusion and outreach is extraordinary in non-formal education. A most diverse group of children takes part and individual adaptation takes place continuously. The fact that non-formal education has voluntary participation makes systematic, comprehensive teaching with the aim of progression nearly impossible. Differentiation strategies need to be investigated. Non-formal education demands pedagogical creativity and a non-schoolish approach with an emphasis on participation in activities and knowledge creation during common tasks to solve or perform in real life settings in the congregation. Non-formal education is life-long, continuous and open-ended. Non-formal education demands voluntary work. The professionalization of the field, however, means that volunteers are less involved in curricular educational activities and more in practical tasks. Volunteers are more trusted and responsible for education in the organizations within the church working with the formative and continuous programs that are offered. Due to this, a lot of tacit knowledge and continuity gets lost. Non-formal education as a field without assessment and grading of children and young people does not mean that response, knowledge, and learning results should be ignored, but need to be looked upon as needed in a learning community. Focus on content and learning, satisfaction and motivation among participants is needed. A more solid theoretical basis for evaluation of non-formal education is needed, and the theology of the reform deserves more attention in the future.

The Christian education reform has, to a certain degree, slowed the speed of the secularization process and given hope for the possibility of upholding a folk church. The reform has been organised and performed as a national project with important tools: new employees, a national curriculum and database. The cooperation among staff members in the development of local curricula led to an exchange of competence, to the benefit of the reform. Gradually the obligation to confirm and support *all* families that come to church, not only the regulars, is sinking in. The relation between baptism and Christian education is part of pastors' consciousness. Parents take part in church activities along with their children and are provided with material for Christian practices and storytelling at home. Pedagogical thinking is changing in a socio-cultural direction, and influencing Sunday services to a high degree. The Christian education reform is in the center of development of the local congregations, with a whole church effect that has made non-formal education a common field of interest between practical theology and religious education.

References

Evaluation web pages with open access reports:

http://etor.no
http://www.kifo.no/publikasjoner/rapporter/ especially 2012-publications
https://www.mf.no/forskningphd/pagaende-prosjekter/forskning-pa-trosopplaeringsreformen

Church of Norway:

National curriculum in English version: http://www.kirken.no/?event=doLink&famID=38865
Educational resources: https://ressursbanken.kirken.no/

Aagedal, O., Haakedal, E., and Kinserdal, F. (2014). Profesjonalisering og frivillighet: trosopplæringsreformen og samarbeid mellom Den norske kirke og de kristne organisasjonene. In: *KIFO rapport.* Oslo: KIFO.no.

Afdal, G. (2013). *Religion som bevegelse: læring, kunnskap og mediering*. Oslo: Universitetsforlaget.

Afdal, G. (2014). Modes of learning in religious education. In: *British Journal of Religious Education* 37(3), 1–17.

Austnaberg, H., and Birkedal, E. (2017). Trusopplæringa sitt potensial i utvikling av menigheten. In: *Prismet* 68(3), 169–188.

Birkedal, E., and Austnaberg, H. (2017), Planarbeid i trosopplæring som ressurs for menigheten? In: *Prismet* 68(3), 189–209.

Botvar, P.K., Brottveit, Å., Hoel, N., Elisabet, H., and Schmidt, U. (2015). Avsluttet reform eller fortsatt læring og utvikling? Trosopplæring som arbeidsform i menighetene. In: *KIFO-rapport* (ed.). Oslo: Institutt for kirke-, religions- og livssynsforskning.

Chisholm, L. (2005). *Bridges for Recognition. Recognising Non-formal and Informal learning in the Youth Sector*. https://pjp-eu.coe.int/en/web/youth-partnership/home: Council of Europe.

Church of England Education Office (2016). *The Church of England Vision for Education: Deeply Christian, Serving the Common Good*. www.churchofEngland.org/: Church of England.

Church of Norway National Council (2010). *Plan for Christian Education: God gives – we share*. Church of Norway National Council, Kirkerådet.

Engedal, L.G., Fagermoen, T., and Sandsmark, A. (eds.) (2015). *Trosopplæring for alle? Læring, tro og sårbare unge,* Oslo: IKO-forlaget.

Engeström, Y. (2001). Expansive learning at work: toward an activity-theoretical reconceptualisation. In: *Journal of Education and Work* 14(1), 133–156.

Fagermoen, T., and Lauritzen, S.M. (2018). Teologier i trosopplæringen. *MF-rapport* 2/2018. Oslo: mf.no.

Fredriksen, I. (2017). *Bønnen som synes – bruk av bønnetreet som forbønnsform i gudstjenesten for store og små*. Oslo: Det teologiske menighetsfakultet.

Fretheim, K. (ed.) (2014). *Ansatte og frivillige: Endringer i Den norske kirke,* Oslo: IKO-forlaget.

Fretheim, K. (ed.) (2016). *Fellesskap og frivillige. Om trosopplæringen i Den norske kirke.* Oslo: IKO Prismet Bok.

Frøyen, E. (2017). *Klatring som trusopplæring? Ein empirisk studie av aktivitetar i ein ferieklubb i trusopplæringa*. Oslo: Det teologiske menighetsfakultet.

Fuglseth, K., and Haakedal, E. (2012). Samarbeid på tvers: Samarbeid mellom Den norske kyrkja og offentlege institusjonar innan utdanning og kultur. In: *KIFO-rapport*. Oslo. Stiftelsen Kirkeforskning.

Fuglseth, K., Haakedal, E., and Schmidt, U. (2012). Lokale trusopplæringsplanar: innhald og prosess. In: *KIFO-rapport*. Oslo: Stiftelsen kirkeforskning.

Hauglin, O., Lorentzen, H., and Mogstad, S.D. (eds.) (2008). *Kunnskap, opplevelse og tilhørighet: Evaluering av forsøksfasen i Den norske kirkes trosopplæring*. Bergen: Fagbokforlaget.

Hegstad, H., Selbekk, A.S., and Aagedal, O. (2008). *Når tro skal læres: Sju fortellinger om lokal trosopplæring*. Trondheim: Tapir Akademisk Forlag,.

Holmqvist, M. (2012). Trosopplæring som livsstil? En analyse av læringssyn i Trosopplæringsplanen. In: *Prismet* 63(1), 17–33.

Holmqvist, M. (2014). *Learning religion in confirmation: mediating the material logics of religion. An ethnographic case study of religious learning in confirmation within the Church of Norway*. Oslo: MF Nowegian School of Theology.

Holmqvist, M., and Afdal, G. (2015). Modes of learning and the making of religion: the Norwegian and Finnish curricula for confirmation. In: *Nordic Journal of Religion and Society* 28(1), 1–20.

Holtedahl, Ø.K. (2017). *"Community", "God from above" and "God from below": an ethnographic study of religious knowledge practices in two youth ministries in the Church of Norway.* Stavanger: VID Specialized University.

Horsfjord, H., Sørensen, T., Heiene, G., Leganger-Krogstad, H., and Holmqvist, M. (2015). Kompetanse, utdanning og motivasjon: en kartlegging av undervisningstjenesten i Den norske kirke. *MF-rapport 1:2015.* Oslo: mf.no.

Høeg, I.M., and Trysnes, I. (2012). Menighetenes samvirke med hjemmet: evalueringsforskning på trosopplæringsreformen. *KIFO-rapport 1:2012.* Oslo: Stiftelsen Kirkeforskning.

Innst.S.Nr. 200 (2002/2003). *Innstilling fra kirke-, utdannings- og forskningskomiteen om trosopplæring i en ny tid. Om reform av dåpsopplæringen i Den norske kirke.* Stortinget.

Jackson, R., Miedema, S., Weisse, W., and Willaime, J.-P. (2007). *Religion and education in Europe: developments, contexts and debates.* Münster: Waxmann.

Johnsen, E.T. (2008). Barn og unges deltakelse i gudstjenesten som ekklesiologisk utfordring: En diskursanalytisk refleksjon med utgangspunkt i to praksisfortellinger. In: *Prismet* 59(4), 247–256.

Johnsen, E.T. (2014). *Religiøs læring i sosiale praksiser: en etnografisk studie av mediering, identifisering og forhandlingsprosesser i Den norske kirkes trosopplæring.* Oslo: Universitetet i Oslo.

Kaufman, T.S. (ed.) (2019). *Mer enn ord,* Oslo: IKO-forlag.

Kaufman, T.S., and Sandsmark, A. (2015). Spaces of Possibilities. The Role of Artifacts in Religious Learning Processes for Vulnerable Youth. In: *Journal of Youth and Theology* 14, 138–154.

Kirkerådet (2018). *Årsrapport 2017.* Oslo: kirken.no.

Krupka, B., and Leganger-Krogstad, H. (2007). Das Größte unter ihnen. Die Glaubenserziehungsreform in Norwegen. In: M. Spenn, D. Beneke, F. Harz and F. Schweitzer (eds.). *Handbuch Arbeit mit Kindern – Evangelische Perspektiven.* Gütersloh: Gütersloher Verlagshaus, 518–527.

Krupka, B., and Leganger-Krogstad, H. (2013). Der Umzug des Religionsunterrichts von der Schule in die Kirche. In: *Zeitschrift für Pädagogik und Theologie* 65(1), 54–67.

Lave, J., and Wenger, E. (1991). *Situated learning: legitimate peripheral participation.* Cambridge: Cambridge University Press.

Leganger-Krogstad, H. (2007). Trosopplæringsreformen – som digital reform. In: *Prismet* 58(4), 221–232.

Leganger-Krogstad, H. (2008a). Learning Religion without Involving Experience? In: H. Streib, A. Dinter and K. Söderblom (eds.). *Lived Religion – Conceptual, Empirical and Practical-Theological Approaches: Essays in Honor of Hans-Günter Heimbrock.* Leiden/ Boston: BRILL, 363–376.

Leganger-Krogstad, H. (2008b). Pedagogisk innhold og utvikling. In: O. Hauglin, H. Lorentzen and S.D. Mogstad (eds.). *Kunnskap, opplevelse og tilhørighet: Evaluering av forsøksfasen i Den norske kirkes trosopplæringsreform.* Bergen: Fagbokforlaget, 123–142.

Leganger-Krogstad, H. (2009). Evaluationsforschung zur Glaubenserziehungsreform in Norwegen. In: F. Schweitzer and V. Elsenbast (eds.). *Konfirmandenarbeit erforschen: Ziele – Erfahrungen – Perspektiven.* Gütersloh: Gütersloher Verlagshaus, 140–157.

Leganger-Krogstad, H. (2014). From Dialogue to Trialogue: A Sociocultural Learning Perspective on Classroom Interaction. In: *Journal for the Study of Religion.* 27(1), 104–128.

Leganger-Krogstad, H. (2017). Trosopplæring og gudstjenester: menighetsutvikling i dybde og bredde. In: *Prismet* 68(3), 243–258.

Leganger-Krogstad, H. (2018). Hvordan foregår bibelundervisning i trosopplæringen i Den norske kirke. In: *MF-rapport* 4/2018. Oslo:mf.no.

Leganger-Krogstad, H. (2019). Barns og unges respons på bibelundervisning i Den norske kirke. In: *MF-rapport* 1/2019. Oslo:mf.no.

Midttun, A., Tveito, H.-B.S., and Joachimsen, K. (2018). Bibelen i utvalgte trosopplærings-planer i Den norske kirke. *MF-rapport 1:2018.* Oslo: mf.no.

Mogstad, S.D. (2013). Fra matavfall til NÅDE: medierende handlinger i søndagsskolen. In: *Prismet* 64(3), 79–94.

NOU 2000:26. *"– til et åpent liv i tro og tillit": dåpsopplæring i Den norske kirke.* Oslo: Kirke-, utdannings- og forskningsdepartementet.

Opsal, R.R. (2013). *Påskevandring: påskevandring som arbeidsmåte i RLE-faget og grenseobjekt i samarbeidet mellom skole og kirke.* Oslo: Det teologiske menighetsfakultet.

Opsal, R.R. (2016). Et mulig og nyttig samarbeid. In: *Prismet* 67(3), 233–236.

Sandsmark, A., and Holmqvist, M. (2018). Vår trosopplæring? Stab, samarbeid og trosopplæring. *MF-rapport 3:2018.* Oslo: mf.no.

Saxegaard, F. (2017). *Realizing church: parish pastors as contributors to leadership in congregations.* Oslo: MF Norwegian School of Theology.

Sfard, A. (1998). On Two Metaphors for learning and the Dangers of Choosing Just One. In: *Educational Researcher* 27(2), 4–13.

Skeie, G. (2007). Religion and education in Norway. In: R. Jackson, S. Miedema, W. Weisse, and J.-P. Willaime (eds.). *Religion and education in Europe: developments, contexts and debates.* Münster: Waxmann, 221–241.

St.Meld. Nr. 7 (2002/2003). *Trosopplæring i ei ny tid. Om reform av dåpsopplæringa i Den norske kyrkja.* Oslo: Kultur- og kyrkjedepartementet.

Winje, G. (2016). Et vanskelig samarbeid. In: *Prismet* 67, 229–333.

Religious education in the Swiss Reformed Churches as a promising hybrid between non-formal and formal education

Thomas Schlag, Rahel Voirol-Sturzenegger

1. On the situation of religious education in the Swiss Reformed Churches

1.1 Background

In Switzerland there is a specific relationship between church and state responsibility for religious education which can be described as an institutional "double-track"-system: The cantons are responsible for organising Religious Education as a non-denominational school subject. Denominational education is the responsibility of the churches. In other words: Apart from some cantonal exceptions, religious socialization (in its specific form of introducing the pupils to a certain tradition) is not a matter or concern of the Swiss public school system, which is considered religiously neutral (cf. Cebulj and Schlag 2014).

This did not pose a major problem as long as religious education was more or less guaranteed and a matter of course within families, supported by a fairly self--evident ecclesial surrounding. Due to the significantly decreasing effects of church commitment in Switzerland over the past decades, the churches are facing the unavoidable challenge of facilitating religious experiences and making them available to children and young people (Schlag 2013).

For this reason, the cantonal churches have developed over the last years, or are currently developing, programs for religious education for children and young people (children's work, confirmation work, youth work) intended to at least initiate a kind of basic religious socialization and also a form of identification ("Beheimatung") with the church. This form of catechetical learning has the following characteristics:

- it is based on certain institutional frameworks and regulations;
- it is often based on the idea of a comprehensive catechetical program;
- it is (in a certain sense) obligatory (e. g. as a prerequisite for confirmation);
- it has school-like elements (fixed number of hours, curricula, teaching materials; the place of learning can also be in the school buildings!);
- it is usually carried out by professionally trained staff (ministers and/or catechists).

Bearing in mind the somewhat classical differences between formal and non-formal education, it is obvious that catechetical learning in the Swiss Reformed Churches can hardly be clearly assigned to either side. Of course, some specific characteristics of formal education – like degree-orientation or employability – can be found here only on the edge. But other elements, like obligatory forms, standardization, predetermined regulation or professional responsibility, are clearly evident in the programs of catechetical learning. These programs can therefore – at least within the time between primary school and confirmation – be seen as a hybrid between non-formal and formal religious education, while the clearly non-formal, voluntary programs largely happen at pre-school level (Sunday School) or church youth work (like participation in camps, youth groups and meetings, organization of weeks for children, etc.).

1.2 Approaches to the research topic

With regard to the current state of research, extensive studies on confirmation work and the overall concept of religious education in the Canton of Zurich are available (cf. Schlag et al. 2016; Voirol-Sturzenegger 2014); a major comparative study on the youth work of the Catholic and Reformed Churches is currently in preparation (for first results cf. Schenker 2017).

However, in the field of comprehensive catechetical programs as a whole and in the cantons, a broader systematic survey beyond cantonal borders has not yet been carried out. In this respect, the following presentation aims, on the one hand, to explore the profile of the catechetical programs as a whole and, on the other hand, to identify desiderata of research.

This is performed with an exemplary view of Zurich and with some references to other programs in individual cantonal churches (Thurgau, Aargau, Graubünden/Grison, St. Gallen and Berne). The main focus is on:

– objectives, concepts and church frameworks
– target groups (ages)
– conditions of participation/terms of participation (obligatory – voluntary)
– program structure and teaching/learning materials
– responsible persons (full-time and volunteers) and training
– effects
– indications of problems and open questions.

2. The Comprehensive Catechetical Program (rpg) of the Reformed Church of Zurich

Among the concepts of denominational education in Switzerland, the Comprehensive Catechetical Program concept of the Reformed Church of Zurich (Religionspädagogisches Gesamtkonzept, rpg) has been the most thoroughly researched so far (Voirol-Sturzenegger 2014).

2.1 Research design

Since in the field of religious education there are hardly any in-depth research results available, the rpg was studied as broadly as possible. The main focus of the survey was on those responsible for religious education in the congregations (councils, ministers, catechists/teaching staff). The aim was to describe how this cantonal church concept was implemented in the individual congregations and what experiences have resulted from it. The results are based on data from the following sources:

- from 385 quantitative online questionnaires with – depending on the function of the person interviewed – 14–61 questions and around 100–300 items;
- from 16 group interviews with 4th grade children;
- from interviews with parents of these children;
- and from eight mainly qualitative short questionnaires for parents whose children did not participate in the rpg.

2.2 Brief description of the rpg concept

The overall goal of the rpg is "to experience faith in God with children, adolescents and families, to learn, to live and to shape it". These four "forms of expression of faith" each characterise a phase of the overall concept of religious education, from working with preschool children and primary school children to adolescents and young adults. While the congregations should develop voluntary "pre-school", "post-school" and "during the school years" voluntary programs of children's and youth work, a comprehensive concept of 192 hours of teaching was developed for the school years, focusing on forms of content-based learning. Participation is a prerequisite for admission to confirmation. The rpg speaks here of obligation (Verbindlichkeit). So anyone who wants to be confirmed at the end of the 9th school year must participate in religious education courses offered by the church starting in the 2nd school year. The concept envisages 30 hours each for the 2nd–4th school years and a total of 30 hours for the 5th–7th school years. In addition, there is the confirmation work, which comprises 72 hours. These programs are designed for the primary level by trained catechists according to elaborated working material. At the secondary level, ministers are usually responsible for the teaching.

2.3 Some main results

The rpg as a model for success

The rpg can be considered a success in many respects: A large number of the Reformed children of the Canton of Zurich take part and are motivated and interested.

As part of the empirical studies on implementation of the rpg, a total of 62 children were surveyed in group interviews. The interviews took place during the lessons in the 4th grade. The interviewed children had also taken part in the programs for the 2nd and 3rd grades in the previous years. The basic tenor is clear (cf. Voirol-Sturzenegger 2014, 176 f.): Most of the children are happy to participate in the church's educational programs. Even if they know about the obligatory aspect of the programs, very few of them feel compelled, but state that they like to come and feel no pressure to do so. Sometimes they may not feel like going to meetings, or they would rather go home or to the swimming pool after school, but once they arrive they like it. They are happy to experience something together with other children, and some of them are convinced that they want to continue to attend church religious education. In the words of the children, "the lessons are fun", the programs are "mega cool" or "super cool". Asked what they like best, they name games and playful learning, drawing, handicrafts, baking, or "designing a poster". It becomes clear that the children appreciate it when they can "do something" by themselves. Where a meal is offered, the children appreciate the lunch table, which makes their school life easier, and enjoy eating together. Special highlights are excursions or films and television, but also celebration of the Lord's Supper in class, or participation in and experiencing of worship.

The congregations were motivated for implementation. Several of them have since had positive experiences (Voirol-Sturzenegger 2014, 95–97). Quantitatively seen, nearly two thirds tendentially regard implementation of the rpg in their congregation as successful, whereby the pastors display significantly more sceptical attitudes. 12 % say that the introduction got off to a good start, but then came to a standstill. More than half see a high level of motivation for implementation in their congregation, while 5 % say they are not motivated at all. High motivation can also be felt from some qualitative results of the rpg survey – as one person said: "Despite the shortcomings, it is a good thing that religious education and 'Beheimatung' are offered, which is why we are all very committed to the rpg".

In some places the rpg also seems to have a positive effect on the life of the congregation (cf. Voirol-Sturzenegger 2014, 149–150). For example, a 40-year-old church administrator states: "We have had only positive experiences in our congregation. Through various new events, more people are coming together and also more are coming into the church. The lessons are more fun for everyone." Parents, too, are sometimes very positive about the church initiatives, although they also express the fear that it could be a bit too much for the children. Above all, the efforts to achieve variety and an exciting design are praised.

Where congregations care about the needs and resources of families and adopt an inviting attitude towards them, the rpg has positive consequences for parents and families (cf. Voirol-Sturzenegger 2014, 235). The interviews with parents show that parents who find it difficult to convey religious content appreciate the support provided by the church's educational programs and in any case see it as an enriching addition ("The children will thus hear more."). If children relate at home their experiences in the church programs, or if parents are occasionally invited to events, they can refresh religious topics themselves. It was mentioned that the topics are discussed and further developed at the family table. Parents can expand their local network of relationships through cooperation on certain church occasions. A mother says clearly that such engagement is positive for her. A father sees it as a benefit for the whole family when the church becomes a place where it is always possible to celebrate together. Important events in the family are celebrated in the gradually more familiar church, the family experiences an anchoring and a feeling of being at home in a larger community.

However, the research results also draw attention to challenges that should be considered more closely and included in the (further) development of comprehensive catechetical programs.

Challenges at concept level

The rpg is strongly imprinted and influenced by the general idea of a formal, reliable structure, followed by all congregations in the whole of the Reformed Church of Zurich. In its obligatory part, it focuses on learning contents and the development of religious knowledge. The especially developed elaborated materials and ready-made lessons are oriented to single or double lessons. The obligation itself is a clear characteristic of this program.

The Reformed Church of Zurich provides work aids (Arbeitshilfen) specifically geared to the programs and obliges the teachers to use them. In the 2nd grade ("minichile"), under the title "We belong together", the affiliation of the individual to the ecclesial community, the birth and childhood of Jesus, Biblical stories of wandering and the amazement at God's creation are discussed (Marugg 2008). The children of the 3rd grade (3. Klass-Unti) deal with baptism, Our Father, the Lord's Supper and Pentecost. (Bosshardt 2008). A year later, the participants embark on a journey of discovery through the Bible. This includes a "Bible research project", the prehistories and stories of David, the question "Who is Jesus" and the preoccupation with Christian symbols (Meyer-Liedholz and Voirol-Sturzenegger 2008).

The work aid "Juki" for the obligatory programs from the 5th to the 7th grade makes available elaborated lessons and church services on the following topics: "Prophet Jeremia", "Paul – Life as a Christian", "The Zurich Reformation", "Worldwide Church – Worldwide Community", "Encounters with other life worlds" and "Images of life offer orientation". The work aid for confirmation work (Evangelisch-reformierte Landeskirche des Kantons Zürich 2014) also offers ready-made modules on the topics "Finding Yourself", "Living in Relationship", "Knowing Its Roots", "Celebrating Your Faith", "Broadening Your View" and "Acting Responsibly".

Overall, the rpg benefits from the fact that at a conceptual level it strengthens the congregation as a place of religious education by emphasising intergenerational events, mutual support in the community and celebrating together. The family is also mentioned as a place of religious education: The concept involves families as a whole in the educational process.

The Church of Zurich has also developed a work aid for working with parents and families (Evangelisch-reformierte Landeskirche des Kantons Zürich 2017). It makes suggestions for programs in the areas of "church space" pedagogy, pilgrimage paths, intergenerational learning, parental education, experiential education and actions in the church community. In addition, it offers ideas regarding how, and on which occasions, contacts can be made with families in the parish.

Challenges at impact level

The results of the study show that the rpg is perceived primarily from its obligatory side and that this pressure is also highly controversial. Therefore, the answers and estimations on the possible impacts of this program vary quite significantly. The Church Council of the Reformed Church is currently dealing with a motion that was submitted in 2017 and calls for the obligatory nature of rpg programs to no longer include the threat of not being confirmed.

Professionalization – catechist as a profession

The extension to an obligatory religious educational program as a prerequisite for confirmation also results in a greater need for professional religious education. The Church of Zurich therefore trains catechists for the conducting of these programs.

This training is structured in modules and includes the basics of developmental psychology, pedagogy/didactics/methodology, social psychology, singing and making music, celebrations, theology, dealing with the church environment, and with the situation of parents and families in the rpg. In so-called "advanced modules", the topics of the curriculum and working with the work aids are taught. The practical training takes place in practice school lessons and through coaching in working with one's own classes. With the elective compulsory (Wahlpflicht) modules (youth service, theater pedagogy, song repertoire, play pedagogy, church history, Bible plus, theology plus, integrative support and symbol didactics), individual focuses can be set to a small extent. Diplomas for primary and middle school education can also be obtained separately.

Although with the introduction of the rpg, congregational conventions have been established in which those responsible for different fields of action in the congregation come together for exchange, it still seems difficult to connect these obligatory programs of the rpg with the life of the entire congregation. The interest of the cat-echists lies strongly with the individual children and their concrete teaching group. The catechists are full of energy and personal commitment, but mostly pursue indi-vidual goals, which might well be seen as a somewhat hidden agenda. For example, the quantitative survey of those responsible for education in the congregations has shown that teachers are more concerned about the effect of faith on individuals and about children's individual experiences of faith than about the world-wide aspects of the Christian faith. Goals directly related to the development of children seem more important than goals that relate to a peaceful coexistence. Home and religious socialization are more important than knowledge about religion. Being a member of the Church as a whole – perhaps also the denomination, this is not quite clear from the questions asked – is classified as more important than the developments of the local church congregation. Finding an identity is more important than dealing with plurality (cf. Voirol-Sturzenegger 2014, 114). The professionalization of work with children and young people also has the drawback that church volunteer work loses one important field and branch of activity, because the volunteers might be perceived as "not professional enough".

This might particularly be the case for volunteer work with school-age children and adolescents. The obligatory programs compete with the voluntary programs for children and young people, which are often (co-)supported by volunteers. Above all, programs during primary school have lost participants, which means that fewer leaders are needed. Where a distinction is made between obligatory and volun-tary programs, there is also a structural devaluation of voluntary programs, which also influences the motivation of employees. However, there are now municipalities that successfully employ young volunteers in the obligatory programs, especially in confirmation work, but also to some extent as helpers in programs for chil-dren.

2.4 Interim conclusion: The rpg between formal and non-formal religious education

The challenges mentioned above show that the rpg can hardly be described as a clearly non-formal educational concept. The characteristic features of non-formal religious education (voluntary, relatively low level of order and regulation, volun-teers' responsibility) are here – mainly due to the explained obligatory nature and its consequences – not very pronounced. In addition, the type of textbooks and ma-terials provided prejudge a rather close proximity to the formal school programs – not to mention terminological uses similar to those used in schools, such as "teach-ing", "class", "school year" or "school lessons/hours".

3. How do other regional church projects address these challenges? A brief orientation to other models in Switzerland

In the following, some exemplary references to various cantonal models shall indicate that – despite the basic distinction mentioned above between state and church responsibility in the field of religious education – there are not only hybrid forms of learning and teaching, but also of teaching responsibility itself.

3.1 Thurgau: Church, Child and Youth ("Kirche, Kind und Jugend") – Holding on to the place of the school

In the canton of Thurgau, denominational religious education takes place mainly in the school building and class rooms, and normally as part of the regular school timetable. Although the concept does indeed also provide for stronger congregational orientation, the church clearly welcomes the fact that it is allowed to stay at the school. However, catechists face the challenges of the school as a secular location, which also include demands on the pedagogical quality of the programs and the qualifications of the teaching staff.

3.2 Aargau: Pedagogical action ("Pädagogisches Handeln") – Partial obligation

The Aargauer Landeskirche has opted for a partial obligation in the conceptualization of its "pedagogical action" (Pädagogisches Handeln). The participants have to register for each individual phase of the pedagogical action, so that successful group processes and continuous learning processes are possible.

   The partial obligation is also accompanied by experiences with different aspects of confirmation within the educational process: admission to the Lord's Supper takes place through a celebration in primary school, the pedagogical activities in secondary school take on the character of an examination, religious maturity is celebrated in the confirmation itself and in remembering baptism celebrations for young adults.

3.3 Graubünden/Grisons: Building congregation ("Gemeinde bilden") – Religious learning on the basis of Religious Education as a school subject

In the Canton of Graubünden, Religious Education as a school subject has so far been the responsibility of the churches, with 2 weekly lessons at school from 1st to 9th grade. At the beginning of the school year 2018, the cantonal church handed over one of these lessons to the state, which introduced the subject "Ethics, Religions, Community". The saved human and financial resources are to be used by the congregations for projects within the framework of the project "Building Congregation": This is an organizational development concept that invites congregations to create educational projects for the congregation based on a careful situation analysis. This might indeed create a form of non-formal education that could serve as an example for further developments in the field.

3.4 St. Gallen: Spiritual Accompaniment ("Geistliche Begleitung") – a program of religious experiences

The "Spiritual Accompaniment" introduced in 2011 builds on the four pillars of celebration, formation, accompaniment and experience. This program includes worship services, religious and confirmation classes, parental work, experience programs, music and youth culture, child and youth work. The aim is to help shape transitions in congregational education, foster a continuous relationship and parental work and offer adventure programs for young people at secondary school age. The "Spiritual Accompaniment" program thus wants to build an overall structure from baptism to adulthood. At the same time, in addition to the likewise reduced denominational religious education at primary school, it uses a diverse congregational or supra-congregational "experience program" with an obligatory character (as a prerequisite for confirmation) for adolescents of 30–50 "program hours" (over two years). This experience program offers different routes, in the form of optional compulsory (Wahlpflicht) courses, to the destination "confirmation". The St. Gallen Regional Church has developed the "Pfefferstern" platform (https://pfefferstern. ch) to provide information about these programs and organise individual routes. It networks young people with local and regional experience programs. The young people book the programs online – whether through the website or on the go via an app – and collect the obligatory credit points in their personal account on their way to confirmation. Meanwhile, the platform "Pfefferstern" is also used by other Reformed regional churches for the organization of regional youth work and Catholic pastoral units within the framework of the "Firmweg ab 18". A first evaluation of this ("Pfefferstern") program is currently under way.

3.5 Berne: Religious Pedagogical Action ("Religionspädagogisches Handeln") – a redesign

In the Cantonal Church of Berne, the redesign of the religious education concept – formerly known as KUW (Kirchliche Unterweisung [church instruction]) is currently underway. Although KUW has over time become a label, "instruction" no longer corresponds to the didactic orientation of KUW. Thus, with the new development the name "Religionspädagogisches Handeln (RpH) Refbejuso" will probably be established. Until now participation in the programs is also a prerequisite for admission to confirmation at the KUW in Berne. However, the number of obligatory programs is lower in most congregations than in the Canton of Zurich – the concept obliges congregations to offer 140–220 hours – and the programs are more strongly related to the congregational life (cf. Bereich Katechetik der Reformierten Kirchen Bern-Jura-Solothurn 2016; Kessler 2015). It will be seen to what extent the existing concept can develop more strongly as a non-formal educational concept. At present, a working group is developing a concept which shall connect church education more closely to youth work and work with families in the sense of intergenerational religious education. The close connection between baptism and confirmation, the question of the prerequisites for confirmation and thus the obligation to participate in the programs of the church are also under discussion. A stronger orientation towards congregational education also has an impact on the distribution of tasks and responsibilities in the church congregation and leads to more intense networking of teaching staff at different levels.

4. Outlook and research desiderata

4.1 The important relation between empirical research and educational practice

The religious-educational landscape in Switzerland has been characterised for some years now by a markedly stronger dynamic, not least due to the severe changes in education policy, challenging the churches' influence on public religious education. Thus, the cantonal churches and congregations are challenged to develop contemporary and comprehensive concepts of religious education for all their members. But, generally speaking, the collaboration between researchers and practitioners in the field of religious education in Switzerland is not yet very pronounced. In many places there is still a certain theoretical deficit with regard to the churches' religious educational programs. The connection between congregational development and educational programs has not yet been examined in more detail, which seems to be problematic in view of the claim of the entire catechetical projects to provide identification and "Beheimatung". Beyond the territorial borders, historical and psychological cantonal borders make cross-border cooperation and the financing of joint empirical projects difficult. Hence, an empirical basis for the actual effects of the different catechetical programs can be extremely helpful for decision making in the future. It could help to develop new concepts by shedding light on their frameworks, intentions, outcomes and relevance in terms of individual and congregational religious life.

4.2 Hybrid forms and places of learning – Catechetical learning and congregational development

Some cantonal concepts have emerged as congregational development concepts which mainly aim at retaining members or regaining new members. This rather narrow focus is somewhat dissatisfying. The development of non-formal educational vessels in particular would require a theoretical reflection of the place of theological learning as substantial religious communication and theological productivity of the participating subjects (Müller 2018) in its broader context to the overall system of the congregations and the church in a wider ecumenical sense.

Some of the religious pedagogical concepts do not prescribe the places of religious education: "School or Church"? This indicates that the awareness of the educational significance of the congregation itself in many places is still poorly developed and the self-positioning in relation to school education is not clearly marked and explained. Reflected concept development therefore requires well-founded decisions about the adequate learning location, including a kind of "learning-location theory" which discusses specific opportunities, challenges and limits of the learning spaces school and church. Here the unclear hybrid leads to various tensions in terms of educational claims and perspectives.

4.3 Religious plurality: Does one religious "size fit all"?

Today's religious education concepts have to be aware of the plurality of very different church affiliations of their members. Currently often still quite rigid ideas of church education for children can hardly do justice to this plurality. The data of the rpg's investigation show a – not surprising, but still very often in church practice ignored – considerable difference between the meaning of religion and "classical" theological contents of those responsible for church religious education activities and that of the average Protestant church member. Thus, the importance assigned to religion for personal lifestyle and resulting needs differs significantly in terms of religious education. The aim is therefore to take more careful account of the needs and expectations of the religious education target groups. An educational partnership with the families and room for participatory education, which takes into consideration this plurality, is certainly necessary. Here, too, empirical studies with regard to religious educational needs of families could be helpful in order to ensure that church concepts are not developed "above the heads" of the target groups.

4.4 Standardization and its impacts on children, young people, families

As already indicated, a strong form of obligation – making confirmation dependent on participation in religious education programs – is quite controversial. The empirical results on the rpg have shown the problematic side of this. There is a tension between the equal treatment of all children and the effort to do justice to individuals. For reasons of educational justice, catechetical education should not be based on standardization. A "standardization of church education and socialization", such as the rpg concept, for example, is neither realistic nor theologically desirable. The different approaches to religion are hardly taken into account. One perspective could be self-obligation without standardization.

In addition, confirmation cannot be regarded as a completion of a general religious education in analogy to the completion of elementary school years. For where confirmation is understood as the final point of the congregations' educational activities, the processual character of religious education threatens to be lost. Above this the possible – and most fruitful! – connection with church youth work after confirmation is not yet fully taken into consideration. For this reason, non-formal educational programs must be strengthened programmatically before and after the confirmation period.

4.5 Professionalization: Research of competences and educational practice of catechists

Some first comparative synopses and surveys on the training of catechists in Switzerland are now available which at least reveal certain tendencies and a certain image of professionalism in this field. In addition, reference can be made to the results of the Swiss confirmation studies with regard to pastors and volunteers.

In Zurich, for example, there is a strong link between training and curricular teaching materials. However, a truly creative approach to teaching content requires adequate Biblical, systematic and practical theological knowledge. The Berne concept, on the other hand, explicitly relies on the ability to plan a wide variety of life and faith themes from the ground up and to lead worship-related celebrations. However, more experience-based and project-oriented working methods are required.

In this respect, empirical research has to ask:

- What competences do "congregational educators" need for developing religious pedagogical concepts?
- What do leaders of denominational educational practice need to know in terms of theological and pedagogical contents?
- How can they be enabled to do justice to the specific challenges of the different target groups and individuals, as well as the different places of learning?

These questions can be linked to the recent studies on confirmation work in various respects, in particular with regard to questions of religious socialization before the confirmation period, the integration of young people into the congregation during this period, and the willingness to participate within and outside the church after the confirmation period.

5. Conclusions

Too narrow and too formal structures can no longer do justice to today's religious plurality within the target groups and the diversity of the individual religious conduct of life. Related to this is the question of whether religious identity-building and church socialization should focus more strongly on the individual person or more on the church. An essential congregational-educational task is to establish forms of religious education as places of action, through which children and young people can be strengthened in their personal development and at the same time gain religious experience through their personal encounter with the church. Therefore, it would be most regrettable for both the target groups and the church as a whole if such a culture of encounters was undermined by excessive forms of formal education and inflexible formal standards.

In this respect, it is worth reflecting on church education in an empirically supported way in order to make the best use of the content sources and personal resources which the church and its congregations can provide. Therefore, it seems essential to make well-founded educational considerations for the Swiss context, to establish and promote new forms of church pedagogy as such – not least by exploring and developing consistent and promising hybrids of non-formal and formal education. Launching this on a supra-cantonal scale would be a novelty, but without doubt of great importance for all Reformed Churches in Switzerland.

There is good reason to assume that the socialising effect of religious education at school will continue to decline in the coming decades, not only in Switzerland, but also in other European countries. Despite all critical questions about these programs, the enormous financial and personnel investments in such initiatives should not be underestimated in their positive impacts and consequences. In addition, the teaching and learning materials created so far are impressive in terms of their contents, and no less in their professional style. In this respect, the intensive efforts made so far by the Swiss Reformed Churches to create attractive programs regarding faith- and church-based religious socialization undoubtedly possess an inspiring international significance.

References

Bereich Katechetik der Reformierten Kirchen Bern-Jura-Solothurn (ed.) (2016). *Dokumentation Zukunftswerkstatt Religionspädagogisches Handeln Refbejuso*, v. 5. Dezember 2016, Bern [http://www.refbejuso.ch/fileadmin/user_upload/Downloads/Katechetik/Zukunftswerkstatt/KA_PUB-Doku-Zukunftswerkstatt-161205_170421.pdf].

Bosshardt, J. (2008). *3. Klass-Unti. Wir leben Kirche: Arbeitshilfe für Katechetinnen und Katecheten. 3. Schuljahr*. Zürich: Theologischer Verlag Zürich.

Cebulj, C., and Schlag, T. (2014). Der Schweizer Lehrplan 21 – eine (nicht nur) ökumenische Herausforderung. In: *Theo-Web*. In: *Zeitschrift für Religionspädagogik* 13 (2), 198–206.

Evangelisch-reformierte Landeskirche des Kantons Zürich (ed.) (2014). *Wir leben in Beziehungen: Arbeitshilfe für die Konfirmationsarbeit mit 2 Begleit-DVDs und 103 Karten [Eure Wahl!]*. Zürich: Theologischer Verlag Zürich.

Evangelisch-reformierte Landeskirche des Kantons Zürich (ed.) (2017). *Eltern und Familien in der Kirche: Handbuch für die Eltern- und Familienarbeit mit Begleit-DVD*. Zürich: Theologischer Verlag Zürich.

Kessler, A. (2015). Konfessioneller, reformierter Religionsunterricht im Kontext kirchlich-gemeindepädagogischer Bildung. In: A. Kessler and I. Noth (eds.). *Lernen in Freiheit. Herausforderungen und Chancen des reformierten. Religionsunterrichts in der Deutschschweiz*. Zürich: Theologischer Verlag Zürich, 15–18.

Marugg, R.E. (2008). *minichile. Wir gehören zusammen: Arbeitshilfe für Katechetinnen und Katecheten. 2. Schuljahr*. Zürich: Theologischer Verlag Zürich.

Meyer-Liedholz, D., Metzenthin, C., Voirol-Sturzenegger, R., and Widmer Hodel, M. (2011). *Juki. Wir glauben in Vielfalt: Arbeitshilfe mit Begleit-DVD für das kirchliche Angebot im 5.–7. Schuljahr*, Illustrations by Nicole Lang. Zürich: Theologischer Verlag Zürich.

Meyer-Liedholz, D., and Voirol-Sturzenegger, R. (2008). *Club 4. Wir entdecken die Bibel: Arbeitshilfe für Katechetinnen und Katecheten. 4. Schuljahr*. Zürich: Theologischer Verlag Zürich.

Müller, S. (2018). *Gelebte Theologie. Impulse für eine Pastoraltheologie des Empowerments*. Zürich: Theologischer Verlag Zürich.

Schenker, D. (2017). *Organisierte Freiheit. Jugendarbeit der katholischen Kirche in der Deutschschweiz. Ein Handbuch*. Zürich: Theologischer Verlag Zürich.

Schlag, T. (2013). Schulische und kirchliche religiöse Bildung im Kanton Zürich. Entwicklungen – Spannungen – Perspektiven. In: D. Helbling, U. Kropač, M. Jakobs and S. Leimgruber (eds.). *Konfessioneller und bekenntnisunabhängiger Religionsunterricht. Eine Verhältnisbestimmung am Beispiel Schweiz*. Zürich: Theologischer Verlag Zürich, 87–104.

Schlag, T., Koch, M., and Maaß, C.H. (2016). *Konfirmationsarbeit in der Schweiz. Ergebnisse, Interpretationen, Konsequenzen*. Zürich: Theologischer Verlag Zürich.

Voirol-Sturzenegger, R. (2014). *Kirchliche Religionspädagogik in der Schweiz. Reformierte Perspektiven am Beispiel des Zürcher Religionspädagogischen Gesamtkonzepts (rpg)*. Zürich: Theologischer Verlag Zürich.

Researching non-formal religious education in Islamic contexts

Studies from Germany

Fahimah Ulfat

1. Introduction

As described in the introduction of this book, the field of non-formal education, especially in the field of religious education, is a neglected field in research. This applies in particular to non-formal religious education in the Islamic context.

Especially in Western Europe and the United States there is a relatively large amount of research on Muslims, especially Muslim youths, particularly since 9/11, dealing with a wide range of topics: migration, education, integration, identity/generational orders, violence/extremism, gender roles, democratic orientation and human rights. These topics are often examined and discussed in connection with the religion and religiosity of young Muslims, whereby both formal and informal settings are examined.

It becomes clear, as Boris Geier and Nora Gaupp formulate, that young Muslims are "often the target of research work from a problematic perspective" (Geier and Gaupp 2015, 221).

In this sense Isabel Diehm draws attention to the aspect of "Muslimization" of migrants from Islamic countries in discourses: "In European immigration societies the feature of cultural difference – mostly shortened as a national culture – has played the dominant role so far, but when it came to the description of the respective social majority and minority relationships, the category religious affiliation to Islam has gained social relevance since September 2001" (Diehm 2010, 70).

Levent Tezcan also points out in his literature report that studies on Islam/Muslims in Germany are usually about the question of the relationship between Islam and Muslims and the modern era. The question of religion is mainly discussed and narrowed in the context of the integration debate. This is particularly evident in the fact that the relevance of research results is often taken as the basis for the presentation of integration solutions (cf. Tezcan 2003).

Geier and Gaup point out three research fields on young Muslims that are not clearly distinguishable:

- "Young Muslims as a specific subgroup of young people with immigrant backgrounds (migration research)"
- "Integration and radicalization (processes) of Muslims"
- "Socialization processes and life-world aspects of young people with a Muslim background" (cf. Geier and Gaupp 2015, 222).

In order to analyse research in the field of non-formal religious education, the first step was to find out which studies are to be expected in this area. This results in a problem of definition. The distinction between the three kinds of learning and education – "formal", "non-formal" and "informal" learning, is very complex and there is no generally valid definition in the German education debate. In English literature, on the other hand, there seems to be a common denominator.

Therefore, the following definition is based on the expertise of Stephanie Baumbast, Frederike Hofmann-van de Poll and Christian Lüders.

"Non-formal learning:

– takes place outside of formal educational institutions,
– is usually not certified, but may lead to certification, but this certification does not imply any further educational entitlement,
– is less structured than formal learning" (Baumbast, Hofmann-van de Poll, and Lüders 2014, 17).

In the German education debate, a distinction is also made between "educational places" and "learning worlds". Learning worlds include, for example, family, peer groups and media.

The present article focuses on empirical research on "non-compulsory non-school-type settings which, however, still imply some kind of institution or institutional framework as their basis" (Schweitzer 2017, 1).

The focus is on the presentation of the research designs and methods of research on "mosque catechesis", as well as their results and is primarily limited to the current literature on the situation in Germany. Most of all, presuppositions and the effects of non-formal religious education are of particular interest, which are also important for formal learning at school.

2. Empirical studies on non-formal religious education in religious communities and mosques

In the following, the work on non-formal religious education in communities and mosques by Hasan Alacacıoğlu (1999) and Rauf Ceylan (2014) are presented.[1]

The focus lies on the following questions:

– Are there any differences or developmental lines between the two studies and what challenges do they pose?
– Does the research reveal whether attitudes and orientations of Muslim youths are influenced by religious socialization in mosques?

---

1 Non-formal religious education in Islamic kindergartens is addressed in another chapter of the present volume (see Rothgangel and Jäggle in this volume), with special reference to the work of Ednan Aslan (Vienna).

2.1 Hasan Alacacıoğlu 1999

Non-formal religious education in the communities in Germany began in the 1970s, triggered by the family reunion of the so-called "guest workers" (cf. Ceylan 2006, 140 ff.).

Hasan Alacacıoğlu examined the five largest Turkish-Islamic communities and their self-understanding in North Rhine-Westphalia (VIKZ, IGMG, Nurculuk movement, DITIB and the Alevite communities; cf. concerning Muslim organizations in Europe: Kreienbrink and Bodenstein 2010). Methodically, he used guideline interviews for the survey and a content analysis method for the evaluation. The interviews were conducted with representatives of the associations or umbrella organizations and their communities. DITIB plays a special role in this respect because, unlike the other associations, it is parastatal and is subject to the Turkish Ministry for Religious Affairs. His study focused on the content, aims and methods of religious instruction offered by the communities in their so-called "Qu'ran schools".

When asked about the goals of teaching, the main goals mentioned were related to social and ethical-religious fields. In the social field, the interview partners were primarily concerned with educating children and young people to become "law-abiding citizens" and accompanying their socialization processes. Alacacıoğlu notes that none of the interviewees in this area mentioned support for the integration of young people into the local society. In the field of religious goals, the focus is only on the mediation of one's own faith and one's own religion, also among the Alevis.

Alacacıoğlu also presents political goals which in his view are beyond the scope of a narrow sense of religious education:

The VIKZ, DITIB and Nurculuk Movement indicated the preservation of their own culture as a political goal of religious education. As ethical goals the VIKZ, the Nurculuk movement and the IGMG indicated the mediation of traditional values.

> "Above all, DITIB clearly promotes political propaganda within its religious education, as this political goal of religious education is clearly defined in the program published by the Turkish Ministry of Religious Affairs for Turkish children living abroad" (Alacacıoğlu 1999, 246).

The contents of the lessons included reading, reciting and memorising the Qur'an, as well as an introduction to the contents of the faith, rituals and duties. In addition, Islamic history, law and ethics are also included. Above all, DITIB has also quoted patriotism as a topic. Only the Nurculuk movement dealt with topics such as the comparison of religions, the relationship of the believers to their environment and society, as well as environmental protection. In addition, the Nurculuk movement also deals with the worldview of its founder and spiritual leader Said Nursi (cf. Alacacıoğlu 1999, 248).

Alacacıoğlu points out that the books of the IGMG and DITIB contain "attacks on dissidents and nationalist propaganda". In the newer textbooks of the IGMG, these contents are omitted, but not in the textbooks of the DITIB. The Nurcu-luk movement, on the other hand, has a "curriculum" that offers "modern ideas with child-friendly language and current, problem-oriented topics" (cf. Alacacıoğlu 1999, 248–249).

Methodologically, frontal teaching and memorization dominate in most communities. Only the teaching of the Nurculuk movement and the Alevi communities prefers methods such as group work and text work, stimulates discussions, tries to use a language suitable for children and encourages the children to become independent.

The teaching language is almost exclusively Turkish. The learning groups consist of 40–70 students. Apart from the Alevi communities, boys and girls are taught separately. The teaching staff have theological but no pedagogical competences (cf. Alacacıoğlu 1999, 250). They come almost exclusively from Turkey and have limited German language skills. Decisive for the recruitment of the teaching staff at IGMG and DITIB is also the political orientation of the applicants (cf. Alacacıoğlu 1999, 252).

2.2 Rauf Ceylan 2014

Rauf Ceylan elaborates in his empirical study the connections between secularization, migration, "mosque catechesis" and attitudes towards Islamic religious education.

He first developed theoretical search and evaluation categories and then carried out expert interviews on their basis. He evaluated these with the qualitative content analysis in order to get "a detailed outlining of the mosque catechesis of the communities in Lower Saxony (goals, contents, structures, etc.)" (Ceylan 2014, 323). The main focus of interest was the information received from the Muslim representatives, officials and the religious support staff of the DITIB and the Shura[2] about the social contexts, internal processes and structures in the communities (cf. Ceylan, 2014, 234–235).

Ceylan describes processes of individualization among Muslim youths, which is shown inter alia in their self-confidence in dealing with religious authorities and religion. The young people want to deal consciously with their religion and do not want to simply follow authorities without first reflecting. This causes uncertainties in the communities (cf. Ceylan 2014, 276).

The mosque communities are also aware of the changed living conditions and lifestyles of the young people. Ceylan explains that, although the young people want to live in an autonomous manner, they do not give up their ties/bond to

---

2 Muslims in Lower Saxony are organized in the two large regional associations Schura Niedersachsen e. V. and DITIB, which are both contact partners for politics.

the community, which he believes is related to the migration context: "The migration context is crucial, as young people tend towards self-ethnicization and self-muslimization by societal attributions, so that the – if only in their symbolic function – ethnic-religious identity and mosque communities as socio-cultural retreats do not lose their meaning, even if these young people with their lifestyles do not correspond to the image of a practicing Muslim from the point of view of the communities" (Ceylan 2014, 425).

By *ethnicization* he means that young people at school are stylised as experts on political developments in their parents' home countries. By *Muslimization* he means that young people, especially since 9/11, tend to be regarded as theological experts. Such external attributions lead to the fact that they inevitably have to deal more strongly with their religion in order to be able to explain, for example, religiously motivated terrorist attacks. Ceylan, however, notes restrictively: "Muslimization and ethnicization processes" can lead to a stronger identification with the home countries of the parents and grandparents. But they can also lead to "disengagement from their old cultural orientations as well as ethnic identity markers" or to the formation of new "syncretistic identities" with elements from the identity of origin and from the surrounding majority society (cf. Ceylan 2014, 282).

Social change and the pluralization of adolescent lifestyles are discussed controversially by experts in mosque communities. However, Ceylan describes the reaction of the experts as an "act of desperation" as they try to make the mosque attractive to young people through "material-oriented solutions", for instance through "more kicker and billiard tables". The public space is rated by them as "risky". They want to keep the youths away from the public space to protect the "Islamic identity" (Ceylan 2014, 320).

The "Mosque catechesis" takes place mainly on weekends in the communities. Children are usually registered in courses when they start school. Usually, adolescents stop attending "Mosque Catechesis" at the start of puberty. According to Ceylan, however, there are no figures on the number of participants or the scope of the lessons. The response of the parents to these courses is very positive according to Ceylan, so that there are even waiting lists for participation. One does not have to be a mosque member to register one's child for class (cf. Ceylan 2014, 345–347).

The "Mosque catechesis" is intended to "impart religious content and ethnic-cultural content", to be "identity-forming", to strengthen the "bond to the community" and thus also to attract "trainees for volunteer roles and functions", which, according to Ceylan, is a kind of "hidden curriculum" (Ceylan 2014, 350).

The profile of the teachers is as follows: Besides the active imams, many of the teachers are pensioners or graduates of religious high schools. Regarding their qualifications, they are almost always autodidactic (cf. Ceylan 2014, 351).

Ceylan concludes that "mosque catechesis" has a low efficiency because

– "there are no uniform standards or curricula,
– no well-qualified (religious) educational staff is available,

- it is still predominantly taught according to classical content and methods,
- due to the language problems of the imams and their poor knowledge about the living conditions of the children and adolescents, there is no positive teaching-learning relationship,
- no educational materials are available, but only traditional ones,
- no evaluation of the learning outcomes takes place,
- there are no adequate spaces that could guarantee a pleasant learning atmosphere,
- only sparsely furnished classrooms exist, so the pupils have to kneel on the floor,
- due to the high number of pupils a high burden for the imams is recorded,
- the children and adolescents come to the mosques with very different learning backgrounds and thus there is a great learning gap,
- there is no widespread introduction of a class system and thus larger units with different learning levels and different age groups arise,
- individual support is more or less excluded" (Ceylan 2014, 428–429).

According to Ceylan the presented problem constellations are not problematised in the communities. However, the functionaries see a special opportunity for themselves in the attempt to also influence Islamic Religious Education in schools as it is introduced on the basis of the German constitution. This influence would give them "an official status in order to be actively involved in the conception of teaching and the selection of religious teachers on the basis of the teaching permission (iǧāza ruling)" (Ceylan 2014, 430). However, such participation can lead to significant problems, as community leaders often lack professionalism in the field, and thus can not constructively support the development of Islamic Religious Education in schools.

According to the conviction of the community representatives, the "mosque catechesis" is intended to convey Muslim foundations which serve "to be socialised to become a practicing Muslim" (Ceylan 2014, 348). The identity-forming objective does not focus on an overall societal context, but is closely linked to the development of an awareness "as part of the Muslim world community", even though Ceylan rightly notes that this goal is in contrast to the more ethnically compounded and oriented communities (cf. Ceylan 2014, 349). In addition to the content-related goals, there are also "community-political goals" such as "strengthening the community-bind", "motivating young people, assuming honorary duties", "qualifying new trainees" and "winning new members" (cf. Ceylan 2014, 349–350).

3. Which challenges can be identified?

The results presented by Alacacıoğlu (1999) and Ceylan (2014) on non-formal religious education in mosque communities show that this non-formal religious education is problematic in many ways. A limiting factor in comparing the two studies is that, despite their methodological similarities, they focus on different content priorities. Nevertheless, there are considerable similarities:

– In the foreground of non-formal religious education is a static concept of religion. "Mosque catechesis" is limited to teaching children and young people texts, rituals and rules without reflection. In such a way, Islam can not be regarded as a life enriching resource, but as a collection of commandments and prohibitions that make life difficult, especially in a context in which these rules and limits are critically questioned by the majority society.

– A crucial issue is addressed in the study by Ceylan, namely the changing living conditions and lifestyles of young people. Since the static concept of religion in the communities continues to dominate, it is not surprising that the communities are trying to engage young people by becoming more attractive through better leisure time opportunities.

– "Mosque catechesis" still continues to focus on creating a kind of defensive identity preservation through Islamic knowledge, rather than creating a mobility of thought that also involves critical thinking. If this were the case, it would strengthen the individual and not isolate him or her from the supposed "risky" environment. The preservation or strengthening of an "Islamic identity" which is understood as static, is visibly in the foreground for the communities in both investigations. However, it is not quite clear what the community representatives actually understand by this. This static identity-forming objective is problematic, above all, because it is intended to be exclusive and does not pave the way for young people to become Muslims and pluralistic in a globalized world.

– In the "mosque catechesis" traditionalism, the collective and community ideology are in the foreground and not the situations of the children and adolescents, their individual thinking and life worlds and their subject autonomy. This is hardly to be expected because the teachers come almost exclusively from Turkey, they barely speak the German language and do not know the socio-political context in which the young people live.

– A detailed criticism of methodology could be formulated. However, it would overshoot the target, since "mosque catechesis" is not conceptually framed and shows no professionalism in religious education. Therefore, to be fair, it cannot be compared and measured in relation to Religious Education at public schools.

– Interreligious components are missing completely.

– A major problem is the political propaganda in the classroom, which, however, is no longer a subject of discussion in Ceylan's investigation.

4. Does the research show an influence of the religious socialization in mosques?

The question arises whether the attitudes and orientations of Muslim youths are influenced by religious socialization in the mosques.

The public and scientific interest in "mosque catechesis" regularly focuses on concerns about possible fundamentalist influences from the teaching staff on those participating in their lessons.

Regarding this area of attitudes and orientations of Muslim youths, there are relevant studies which give a differentiated picture, for instance the study of Wilhelm Heitmeyer, Joachim Müller and Helmut Schröder (cf. Heitmeyer, Müller and Schröder 1997) or of Katrin Brettfeld and Peter Wetzels (cf. Brettfeld and Wetzels 2007), furthermore of Yasemin Karakasoğlu (cf. Karakaşoğlu-Aydın 2000), Nikola Tietze (cf. Tietze 2001) or Michael Tressat (cf. Tressat 2011).

However, Wensierski makes clear that these studies "do not give any information about the origin, the development and the biographical process of social attitudes and biographical behavior patterns" (Wensierski 2013, 58). The vast majority of studies dealing with the attitudes of Muslim youths are methodically working with open interview forms in which the biography and attitudes of young people are surveyed directly in conversation with them. This procedure is not able to identify the origin of the attitudes and orientations. This means that it is *not* possible to establish a connection between the attitudes and orientations of young people and non-formal religious education, which is assumed to be the factor behind the attitudes.

Even if empirical findings show that there are Muslim, predominantly male, adolescents who are strictly religious and have anti-democratic orientations, it is by no means possible to say clearly where these orientations come from. The character of previous empirical findings does not allow such a conclusion (cf. Wensierski 2013, 59).

In order to give the reader an insight into the current attitudes and orientations of Muslim youths, a study by Stephan Weyers will be considered as an example.

In his study, he interviews religiously engaged youths from the mosque communities of Ditib and Milli Görüs. Catholic youths from the youth organization BDKJ (Federation of Catholic Youths) and KHG (Catholic University Communities) were interviewed for comparison. The survey was conducted in the Rhine-Main area in 2006 and 2007 (cf. Weyers 2011, 124).

In the interviews, the interviewees were asked to evaluate actions, norms and conflicts with justification (cf. Weyers 2011, 134). Through the analysis, a "typology of religious-normative thought" was created (Weyers 2011, 135). Weyers focused on the question of the relationship between religious commandments, moral norms and private matters.

Weyers sums up that "there are significant differences between young Christians and Muslims in the evaluation of norm conflicts. The latter have more traditional moral concepts and evaluate potential norm violations much more negatively. The biggest difference is in the area of sexual morality, which is evaluated completely in the opposite direction. Especially in the case of homosexuality, the evaluations of many Muslims are in conflict with secular legal norms and human rights. Issues of sexual morality and actions such as theft, abortion, suicide and religious change are interpreted by almost all Muslim youth as violations of religious commandments, but only by a few Catholics. Not a single Muslim, but two-thirds of Catholic youths judge secularly in the interviews without any recourse to religious norms. For Muslims, religion is a central foundation of normative orientation, but this seems to apply only to a few Catholics. These rarely judge religiously and contradict mostly the church doctrine. Although Muslims interpreted many norm violations religiously and understand the Qur'an as God's direct word, the interviews show a great diversity of interpretations" (Weyers 2011, 166).

However, this study also does not make it clear which influences are coming directly from religious teachers of the mosque and which from family members, peers or other agents of socialization.

5. Conclusion

For further research, the question arises which effects "mosque catechism" has on the attitudes and orientations of Muslim youths and also in formal Religious Education. As shown, this question can not be answered by reconstructing the attitudes and orientations of the adolescents. So far, research has been unable to establish any systematic correlations.

Alacacıoğlu and Ceylan illustrated the discourses in the mosques, analysed teaching materials and conducted interviews with the teaching staff. In addition, it would be interesting to conduct teaching research (work shadowing). However, even this does not answer the question, how much of the teaching content of the "mosque catechesis" is adopted by the young people and which of the taught contents will be relevant to their actions in what way. Even through these research settings, no complete causal chains can be depicted.

In order to examine the effects of "mosque catechesis" on young people, a three-step process has to be carried out, which firstly researches what the young people learn in the "mosque catechesis", secondly, how they assimilate what they have learned and thirdly, in what way what they have learned becomes relevant for their actions.

The study of the impact and effects of non-formal religious education thus requires not only the study of "mosque catechesis" or the study of attitudes and orientations of active youth in mosque communities. Rather, a differentiated reception research design is needed which focuses on the entire field of discourse.

References

Alacacıoğlu, H. (1999). *Außerschulischer Religionsunterricht für muslimische Kinder und Jugendliche türkischer Nationalität in NRW. Eine empirische Studie zu Koranschulen in türkisch-islamischen Gemeinden.* Münster: Lit.

Baumbast, S., Hofmann-van de Poll, F., and Lüders, C. (2014). *Non-formale und informelle Lernprozesse in der Kinder- und Jugendarbeit und ihre Nachweise (Expertise).* München: Deutsches Jugendinstitut.

Brettfeld, K., and Wetzels, P. (2007). *Muslime in Deutschland – Integration, Integrationsbarrieren, Religion sowie Einstellungen zu Demokratie, Rechtsstaat und politisch-religiös motivierter Gewalt – Ergebnisse von Befragungen im Rahmen einer multizentrischen Studie in städtischen Lebensräumen (Befragung).* Berlin: Bundesministerium des Innern.

Ceylan, R. (2006). *Ethnische Kolonien: Entstehung, Funktion und Wandel am Beispiel türkischer Moscheen und Cafés.* Wiesbaden: VS Verlag für Sozialwissenschaften.

Ceylan, R. (2014). *Cultural Time Lag: Moscheekatechese und islamischer Religionsunterricht im Kontext von Säkularisierung.* Wiesbaden: Springer VS.

Diehm, I. (2010). Religion ist im Spiel – oder virulent. Diskursive und interaktive Inszenierungen ethnischer Differenz. In C. Hunner-Kreisel and S. Andresen (eds.). *Kindheit und Jugend in muslimischen Lebenswelten. Aufwachsen und Bildung in deutscher und internationaler Perspektive.* Wiesbaden: VS Verlag für Sozialwissenschaften, 59–76. https://doi.org/10.1007/978-3-531-92237-9_4

Geier, B., and Gaupp, N. (2015). Alltagswelten junger Musliminnen und Muslime unter Bedingungen sozialer Ungleichheiten. In: *Diskurs Kindheits- und Jugendforschung* 10(2), 221–236.

Heitmeyer, W., Müller, J., and Schröder, H. (1997). *Verlockender Fundamentalismus: türkische Jugendliche in Deutschland.* Frankfurt am Main: Suhrkamp.

Karakaşoğlu-Aydın, Y. (2000). *Muslimische Religiosität und Erziehungsvorstellungen.* Frankfurt/M.: IKO, Verl. für Interkulturelle Kommunikation.

Kreienbrink, A., and Bodenstein, M. (eds.) (2010). *Muslim organisations and the state – European perspectives (Vol. 1).* Nürnberg: Bundesamt für Migration und Flüchtlinge.

Schweitzer, F. (2017). Researching non-formal religious education: The example of the European study on confirmation work. In: *HTS Teologiese Studies/Theological Studies* 73(4), 1–8. https://doi.org/10.4102/hts.v73i4.4613

Tezcan, L. (2003). Das Islamische in den Studien zu Muslimen in Deutschland. In: *Zeitschrift für Soziologie* 32(3), 237–261.

Tietze, N. (2001). *Islamische Identitäten.* Hamburg: Hamburger Ed.

Tressat, M. (2011). *Muslimische Adoleszenz?* Frankfurt am Main et al.: Lang.

von Wensierski, H.-J. (2013). Jugend, Jugendkultur und radikaler Islam – Gewaltbereite und islamistische Erscheinungsformen unter jungen Musliminnen und Muslimen in Deutschland. In: M. Herding (ed.). *Radikaler Islam im Jugendalter Erscheinungsformen, Ursachen und Kontexte.* Halle (Saale): Deutsches Jugendinstitut e. V., 57–78.

Weyers, S. (2011). Zwischen Selbstbestimmung und religiöser Autorität, säkularem und göttlichem Recht. Normative Orientierungen christlicher und muslimischer Jugendlicher. In: K.F. Bohler and M. Corsten (eds.). *Begegnungen von Kulturen.* Wiesbaden: VS Verlag für Sozialwissenschaften, 105–180.

Cooperation between Christian youth work and schools in Germany

A research project

Lena Wolking

1. Cooperation between Christian youth work and state-sponsored schools in Germany

1.1 Starting point: State-sponsored schools as places of learning and living

Within the last decade, the amount of time German youths spend at school has steadily increased. This development is due to several developments, most of them are political. One of the notable reasons is the increasing number of all-day schools. It has only been fifteen years since ministries of education in various federal states in Germany started to change more and more state-sponsored schools from half-day to all-day schools (for further information about different types of all-day schools in Germany, see KMK 2015). In addition to other reasons, this change has been motivated by the fact that German pupils showed poor results in inter-national comparative studies like the PISA study (for further details see BMFSFJ 2017, Gärtner and Kempfer 2016, KMK 2015). Consequently, as pupils now spend a significant amount of their time at school, the schools not only serve as places of study but have also taken on additional importance in other respects. From this perspective, schools have become places where learning and living are combined. Aside from the teaching during traditional lessons, extracurricular activities take place as well. These programs are supposed to assist pupils in gaining experiences which support their social and personal development (for a general overview see e.g. Wermke 2014).

These changes hold new challenges both for schools and for youth work. For one, schools are responsible for the organization of extracurricular programs, run either by their own staff or by external partners. At the same time, youth work orga-nizations fear losing participants and youth group leaders because the young people spend more time at school, including afternoons which used to be the typical time for youth work activities when half-day schools were still the norm (Lange and Wehmeyer 2014). Given the new presuppositions, collaboration between schools and youth work is a logical consequence which promises a win-win situation, meet-ing the needs of everyone involved. Schools frequently depend on partners to offer extracurricular activities and youth work organizers are interested in effectively reaching their target audience. Unsurprisingly, the empirical data show a steady increase in the number of cooperations between youth work and schools (e.g. Lange and Wehmeyer 2014, Ilg in this volume).

Today, the cooperation between schools and youth work has become a new field of work referred to as school-related youth work. Definitions found in articles or research papers, however, show that the term school-related youth work is often used as a general category which includes the new extracurricular programs at all-day schools as well as traditional forms of cooperation like religious services at school, pastoral counselling and social work in schools (e.g. Spenn and Fischer 2005 or Lehmann et al. 2014, 168; different terminology: Schröder 2006). This understanding of the term is also used in this article. However, as the considerations and results from the research project presented in the following suggest, school-related youth work, being at the interface of formal and non-formal education, provides an interesting test case for the cooperation between both spheres of learning.

1.2 How is school-related youth work carried out?

School-related youth work features characteristics of classical youth work, i.e. principles such as accepting and tolerating mistakes, implementing flat hierarchical structures and not assessing achievements (Ilg 2013, see also Spenn and Fischer 2005, 17). The main difference to classical youth work is its proximity to the domains of formal education: "children and youth [being] on or near school grounds" (Schröder 2006, 24). Usually, these extracurricular programs take place weekly but in some cases, they are offered as full-time project days. Extracurricular programs are organised by the schools, by the heads of the school or teams of teachers. In some cases, the organization and implementation can be delegated to youth work organizations.

Depending on the type of all-day school, the attendance of extracurricular programs is obligatory for pupils, e.g. in so-called "binding elementary schools" (KMK 2015). Volunteers, who frequently run the activities, are either organised by the school or external partners such as youth work institutions. However, the latter rely on part- or full-time employees if volunteers are not readily available. Depending on the background of the youth work institution (sport, music, denominational, etc.), the contents of the offered programs vary.

1.3 Presuppositions for (Christian) school-related youth work: the principle of subsidiarity

In Germany, the legal frameworks of the cooperation between state-sponsored schools and external partners, such as religious and non-denominational youth work organizations, are defined by legislation at different levels. The principle of subsidiarity is a crucial aspect of this legislation and helps to better understand the cooperation between schools and external partners such as Christian youth work organizations.

German social law encourages institutions and associations of civil society to participate in educational programs. With roots in the Weimar Republic, the principle of subsidiarity emphasises the role of non-governmental (institutional) actors and their responsibility for the development of the civil society, including the field of education (for a general overview see Spenn and Fischer 2005, esp. 16–19). Based on this concept, the Child and Youth Welfare Act (§ 3.1) defines the active role of religious and non-denominational partners in general education, including societal diversity in educational processes. Lawmakers aimed to create "a diverse landscape of institutions, which offer different value orientations and various contents, methods and approaches" (BMFSFJ 2014, 13). In this way, education is supposed to take into account societal diversity, for instance, in terms of differing religious worldviews.

In the case of school-related youth work, the principle of subsidiarity applies to religious (e.g. Christian youth work) as well as non-denominational partners such as sports or music associations. These actors of the civil society can be understood as contributors to the educational mandate of state-sponsored schools (as it is defined in the respective state constitutions). They are considered equal partners rather than service providers. By transposing non-formal education to a formalised context, these actors can enrich the profile of the schools by introducing non-formal elements such as accepting and tolerating mistakes as mentioned above (see Ilg 2013). It is no surprise that the synergy of formal and non-formal education in all-day schools nurtures the ongoing general debate on terms and concepts such as "all-day education" (*Ganztagsbildung*, see e.g. Coelen and Otto 2004).

1.4 Research about Christian school-related youth work in Germany

Christian school-related youth work is an emerging field of study in religious education and Christian churches. Researchers, however, encounter an immense structural diversity, a circumstance in many respects due to Germany's federalist structure.

On the one hand, each of Germany's sixteen federal states is responsible for its own school education policy and legal conditions for cooperation between schools and extracurricular partners. On the other hand, the Protestant Church in Germany subdivides into twenty independent Protestant Churches, each defining different conditions for cooperation. For logical reasons and to stay abreast of the varying conditions for school-related youth work, empirical research projects most often only focus on one selected federal region and a single denomination such as the Catholic Church (e.g. Gärtner and Kempfer 2016) or the Protestant Churches. This is also the case for the research project presented here.

2. Protestant school-related youth work in Württemberg

2.1 Three examples of school-related Christian youth work in Württemberg

The three following case reports taken from this study are examples of a wide variety of school-related youth work.

Example 1: Martin and Paul

Martin attends a primary school in a rural area. Once he has finished school in the morning, he attends an obligatory afternoon program until his parents pick him up. First, Martin takes part in a homework supervision program. Afterwards, he can choose from various extracurricular programs. The options differ from day to day and include physical and mental stimulations such as volleyball and chess. As his parents have given written consent, Martin is allowed to attend a weekly Christian youth group as one of the extracurricular program options. Together with other members of the group, he participates in singing, listening to Christian stories and playing games. The Christian youth group is run by local YMCA volunteers, the majority being between 40 and 50 years of age. While Martin participates in the Christian youth group, his friend Paul takes part in a music group. All extracurricular programs that take place at Martin's school are organised by a full-time coordinator who is financed by the local YMCA as well as the municipality.

Example 2: Sarah

Sarah attends a middle school (*Realschule*) in a small town (5000–20000 inhabitants). Some months ago, she and her parents received a letter of invitation to participate in a pupil-mentor-training (German: *Schülermentorenprogramm*). She signed up for the program sponsored and run by the local YMCA and the Protestant parish. This training program, supervised by a full-time employee, takes place over the course of six months and teaches skills such as communication, team-work and taking responsibility. Initially, participants complete a weekly theoretical training course. After completion, they move on to a practical training unit, for example in the local Protestant parish. Then, the participants receive a certificate which qualifies them as youth group mentors. The program is financed by the local Protestant parish, the church district and a group of donors.

Example 3: Anna

Anna attends a middle school (*Realschule*) in a medium-sized town (20000–100000 inhabitants). Whenever she has some spare time at school, she can contact Oliver, a youth worker of the church district, who is responsible for open youth work options at Anna's school. At the drop-in center, he plays table tennis with pupils and he has an open ear for their concerns. Anna is aware that he is working for a Christian organization and once in a while, Oliver invites her and other pupils to Christian youth work events. This program is financed by the Protestant church district, fundraising campaigns and private initiatives.

2.2 The regional project "Church – Youth Work – School"

There are two factors which prompted the synods of the two regional Protestant Churches in the federal state of Baden-Württemberg (i.e. the Protestant Church of Baden and the Protestant Church of Württemberg) to fund empirical studies on school-related youth work: 1) The aforementioned shifts in the educational landscape and 2) the immense increase of Christian school-related youth work as shown in a previous study funded by both Protestant Churches (Lehmann et al. 2014, for more details see Ilg in this volume).

Both Churches established specific projects for Protestant school-related youth work: in 2010 in Baden, and 2012 in Württemberg. For further information about the project in Baden, see Schweizer, Sommer and Stange 2016. The project "Church – Youth Work – School" ran in Württemberg from 2012 to 2017 and had three key components:

1) A *central full-time employed coordinator* served as advisor for all cooperation projects in Württemberg which were run by the Protestant Church and the Protestant Youth Work.
2) Innovative local projects in Württemberg could apply for additional *funding*. As mentioned before, these projects were supposed to fulfill different criteria, e.g.:
   – Establishing new cooperations between Church, youth work organizations and schools
   – Involving volunteers in extracurricular programs
   – Improving the reputation of Christian youth work as extracurricular partner among decision-makers
   – Providing access to further financial and human resources in order to ensure the continuity of the local projects.
3) *Scientific monitoring* which evaluated the projects that received extra funding. The aim was to identify factors leading to success when formal and non-formal education cooperate.

2.3 Scientific monitoring of the project "Church – Youth Work – School"

The following section offers a brief summary of the research project (for further details see the main publication, Wolking 2016).

Formative evaluation and research questions

The scientific evaluation took place between autumn 2014 and summer 2015, i.e. halfway through the ongoing main project (2012–2017, see Figure 1). Therefore, the evaluation is to be characterised as formative, being influential in that its findings might give input to the ongoing project and make changes necessary.

The following two questions were central to the research project:

a) How can cooperation between schools, youth work and church succeed?
b) What kind of basic arrangement between schools, youth work and church is necessary?

As the questions illustrate, the project's focus was to identify possibilities as well as challenges regarding structural and financial aspects in the local programs. However, contents and participants of these programs were not analysed.

Research object: Local cooperation projects

At the onset of this study (autumn 2014), twelve cooperation projects received funding (see the three examples presented in 2.1). At a later stage, fourteen additional projects received funding which, however, were not included in the analysis.

The twelve chosen projects were highly diverse in structure and content. Due to the limited personnel resources for the evaluation process, the research object needed to be confined to a manageable size. Thus, the twelve projects were grouped into three categories (Group A, B and C) based on structural differences:

– Group A: These projects were actively involved within an entire church district, sought to work with many different state-sponsored schools and were sponsored by the church district itself.
– Group B and C focused on cooperations with only one or a few schools. In group B sponsors were single local groups such as a parish or a youth work group (e.g. local YMCA), whereas in group C projects were sponsored by the church district.

Figure 1: Timeframe of the scientific evaluation

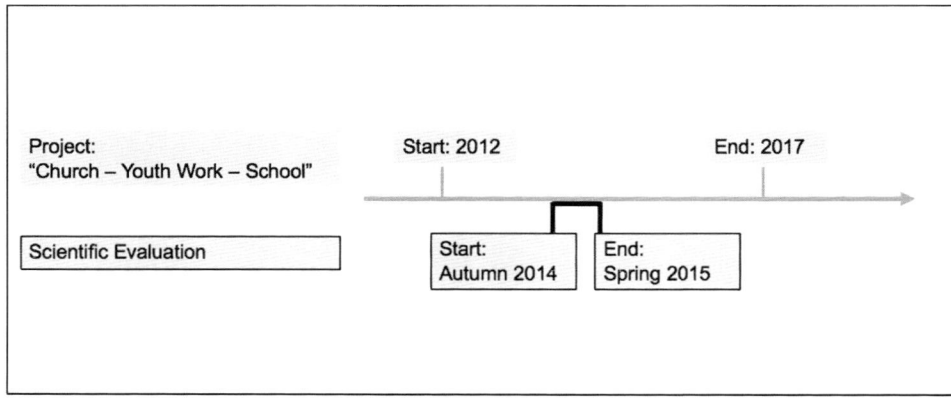

Seven out of the twelve projects were randomly selected, however, it was equally ensured that at least one project of each of the three categories was chosen (see Table 1). By reducing the number of projects analysed, the evaluation aimed to provide a detailed description and a deeper understanding of the project's specific circumstances.

Table 1: Number of analysed local projects, classified by sponsors and number of cooperating schools

Group	Sponsored by...	Cooperation with ... school(s)	Number of analysed projects
A	Church district	Many	2
B	Parish/local YMCA	One/few	3
C	Church district	One/few	2

Design

As illustrated in Figure 1, the design consists of two qualitative approaches. The greater part consisted of 27 interviews that, in three cases, were enhanced by participatory observations.

To assess the experiences from the local projects, expert interviews were conducted with thirty-seven participants. As illustrated in Table 2, five different types of guideline interviews were generated. The interview types took into account the different functions the interviewees had in the projects themselves. Most interviews were audio-taped, transcribed and studied using content analyses (Mayring 2015). Written documentation by the interviewer was used to a lesser extent.

The participatory observations took place a) in an extracurricular program, b) in a church district conference and c) in a meeting of the advisory group of the project "Church – Youth Work – School".

Figure 2: Design of the scientific evaluation

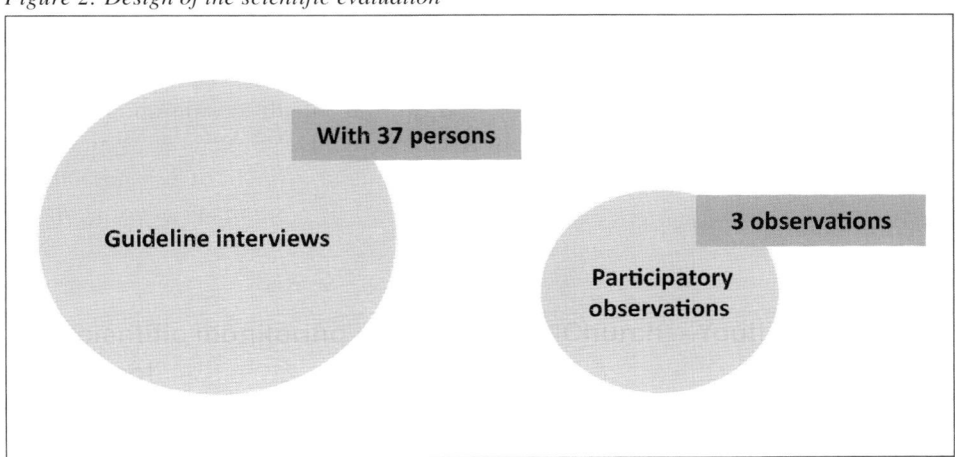

Table 2: Overview of interviewees, types of interviews and documentation

Respondents within the local projects	Type of interview/Documentation
All full-time employees who run, organise and/or work directly with children/adolescents	Interview/Audio-recording and transcription
Two advisory groups consisting of full-time employees and/or volunteers	Interview/Audio-recording and transcription
Almost all heads of schools that cooperate with the local project	Telephone interview/notes taken from memory
Volunteers within two out of seven projects	Interview/Audio-recording and transcription
Three deans of church districts dealing with matters of schools (German: *Schuldekane*)	Telephone interview/Audio-recoding and transcription

3. Results of the research project

3.1 Factors for successful collaboration between schools, youth work and church

Four factors for success were identified: (1) the existence of well-established personal contacts, (2) transparent communication between the actors, (3) professionalism and reliability of the extracurricular partners and (4) supportive programs for local projects run by youth work and/or church.

Personal contacts

All projects and all types of respondents confirmed that well-established contacts were a key factor, as illustrated by the quotation of a full-time employee: "Personal contacts are a central pillar". Moreover, full-time employees identified further aspects, e.g. sufficient time to establish contacts, being present at schools and keeping in touch with key players such as heads of schools and teachers involved in the organization of extracurricular programs.

Transparent Communication

Full-time employees from youth work and church identified three aspects for transparent communication with schools:

1) A clear understanding of the legal frameworks, including the principle of subsidiarity, for the cooperation between *Christian* youth work and schools. Thus, employees often criticised the need to justify the legitimacy of a *Christian* extracurricular partner when dealing with heads of schools, teachers and parents. Some employees went further and experienced that not every school displayed openness for *Christian* school-related youth work. This is despite the fact that the

constitution of Baden-Württemberg states that children and adolescents should be raised, e.g. in reverence for God and in the spirit of Christian "brotherly love" as rooted in the Christian faith (see Art. 12 of the Constitution). Additionally, two relevant agreements exist which regulate the cooperation between the federal state of Baden-Württemberg, municipalities and extracurricular partners. The Agreement of 2014 (Rahmenvereinbarung 2014) incorporates the cooperation with all extracurricular partners whereas the Agreement of 2015 (Rahmenvereinbarung 2015) exclusively describes the cooperation between all-day schools and the Christian Churches.

2) Transporting the principles of (Christian) youth work. In some cases, youth work employees experienced that parents and heads of schools could not grasp the benefits of these particular programs for pupils. As opposed to programs like the pupil-mentor-training, their usefulness did not always seem obvious to heads of schools as well as parents. Employees stated that unlike in the classical context of youth work, they were required to emphasise the particular advantages of their particular program, i.e. to explain the principles of Christian youth work, but also point to its distinctiveness with regard to other extracurricular programs. However, many respondents confirmed that the initial scepticism subsided with time.

3) Clarity with regards to the Christian profile of the local program. Extracurricular Christian programs do not always have a religious or spiritual character. When in contact with schools, employees report that the religious or spiritual nature of the program is often, however, a central issue. One employee recorded the headmaster's reaction that he deemed typical for the topic: At the initial meeting to discuss a possible cooperation, the headmaster's first question was: "Are you coming to do missionary work?"

The headmaster's uncertainty confirms the employees' experience in the context of formal education where Christian youth work is required to provide clarity with regards to the nature of its Christian profile, its contents and aims as further reflections show (see below). According to employees' experiences, these particular circumstances play less of a role within the ordinary context of youth work (i.e. outside the school context).

Professionalism and Reliability

Although schools welcome volunteers in the extracurricular programs, heads of schools stated that they prefer working with full-time employees. Full-time employees were attributed to be more professional, reliable, better organised and having pedagogical skills. Not surprisingly, full-time employees confirmed this view.

Supportive Programs for Local Projects

Facing the above mentioned ambivalence regarding Christian youth work at school, many respondents appreciated the fact that there was a central project coordinator who helped to advertise as well as establish school-related Christian youth work. This central project coordinator provided practical advice for establishing new programs and the possibility of networking with other local programs.

3.2 The basis for cooperation between schools, youth work and church

The second research question examined from the perspective of the study participants what basic agreement between schools, youth work and church they deemed essential. In the following, the different institutional protagonists within the field are examined and different ways of cooperation are considered: Firstly, Christian youth work, church and schools, secondly, Christian youth work and church and lastly, Christian youth work itself. The analysis includes the successes as well as obstacles of these collaborations in order to evaluate conditions for a successful basis.

Christian youth work, church and schools: Financial support

Factors such as professionalism determined successful cooperations and underlined the importance of full-time employees. Many projects had full-time employees who were largely funded by the project "Church – Youth Work – School". Nearly all participants referred to the challenge of guaranteeing long-term funding and they sought to retrieve additional funding via fundraising campaigns, private initiatives and ventured to secure other sponsors such as city councils, municipalities, etc. Some projects were able to establish creative local solutions (see examples 1 to 3), however, only with great efforts.

Although there are programs within the federal state of Baden-Württemberg which offer financial support, in order to apply to these programs additional organizational expenses are required from heads of schools and for youth work organizations and churches. In many cases these programs do not cover all costs. In Baden-Württemberg financial support is based on the model of monetarization: In the context of all-day primary schools, heads of schools are granted additional teachers' hours (*Lehrerstunden*) in order to offer extracurricular programs. Every head of school decides whether he or she gives half of the funding to external partners (for an overview, see Ilg 2014). In 2015, Baden-Württemberg had approximately 2500 primary schools (Statistisches Landesamt 2015) of which 172 were all-day schools. Only 60 % of this group of 172 all-day schools made use of monetarization (Landtag in Baden-Württemberg 2015). Currently (2018), Baden-Württemberg plans to simplify this model by abolishing the application process and allocating a general budget to all-day schools.

In the evaluation, the respondents confirmed the need for high quality programs but also acknowledged that they are difficult to finance. Thus, school-related youth work is in need of long-term funding by the three institutional protagonists, i.e. Christian youth work, church and school.

Christian youth work and church: Raising the awareness for school-related youth work

The local projects adopted different structural approaches (as previously illustrated by the categories A, B, C). According to the interviewees, Christian institutional protagonists themselves (Christian youth work and church/parish), did not always work well alongside each other. Respondents from parishes and from Christian youth work observed, for example, either a feeling of distrust coming from one group to the other, or personal conflicts. Hence, teamwork became a complex task. Some respondents belonging to the youth work and the church side confirmed problems assigning the responsibilities for running extracurricular programs and aligning their self-conceptions with the respective other side.

However, school-related youth work requires the two institutions to collaborate in an unfamiliar setting. It is, therefore, important to raise the awareness that school-related youth work is a shared *common* ground where personal and financial resources of Christian youth work, church and school can be merged. Only then is it possible for churches/parishes and Christian youth work organizers to really tackle the immanent challenge, i.e. to establish a thriving cooperation between the Christian sector and schools.

Christian youth work: Change of premises?

Christian youth work can be characterised by different standards, principles and methods (see Ilg 2013). Interviews have shown the need to redefine some of the principles with regards to the two following aspects: firstly, the principle of volunteering and secondly, the principle of Christianity in Christian youth work.

a) Young and professional volunteers

Naturally, youth work involves many, and, in particular, *young* volunteers. The respondents from youth work and church/parishes emphasised that this premise had a weakening effect on the field of school-related youth work. Many of the evaluated projects were not able to involve young volunteers because these volunteers had to attend school themselves. Different strategies were used by the projects to deal with this situation, for example, by involving older volunteers. At the same time, however, youth work employees have reservations to involve, for instance, older volunteers although for different reasons. A full-time employee regarded young volunteers as essential because their "closeness of age to the adolescents them-selves".

As the findings show, schools prefer professionals when it comes to coopera-tion with external organizations. Some projects met this need by accompanying volunteers with professionals or providing advanced training for volunteers. Some respondents, however, regarded this phenomenon critically: one full-time employee stated that volunteers did "not have to be experts". Following the principles of youth work, this particular respondent understands volunteers to be on eye-level with chil-dren and adolescents, i.e. that they are part of the group themselves (see also Ilg 2013, 6). This is, of course, in some way contrary to the idea of high professional-ism. Hence, the principles of youth work are challenged when asking what degree of professionalism is required. On the whole, these examples confirm that the ten-dency for schools to desire a degree of professionalism equally influences the field of school-related youth work (see also BMFSFJ 2017, 362).

Therefore, a more general question regarding (Christian) youth work needs to be asked: How much should non-formal Christian education adapt to formal educa-tion, and how much does it have to adapt itself?

b) Christian programs: Profile and content factors

The question of Christian content plays an important role regarding the extracurric-ular program. In the project evaluations two types of Christian programs have been identified (see also Rahmenvereinbarung 2015):

Firstly, there are programs run by Christian youth work organizations that are open to all pupils (see examples 2 and 3) – that is, the pupil-mentor-training pro-gram and open youth work at schools. These kinds of cooperative programs are entitled to funding from the state / school administration.

Respondents working in these types of programs stressed the importance of being there for young people and supporting them in their development. In their opinion, a Christian profile is defined by the Christian principle of taking care of young people and taking their concerns seriously. Naturally, the persons in charge of the program ought to be Christian themselves. Some of the respondents working in these types of programs noticed the absence of distinct Christian activities, like, for example, prayers, and sensed a feeling of loss regarding a clear Christian pro-file. They noted a huge gap between classical and school-related Christian youth work.

Secondly, there are programs that have a distinct Christian touch. However, they remain optional for pupils, since pupils must have the freedom to choose between extracurricular non-religious and religious programs (see example 1). Schools wel-come these forms of cooperation, yet these extracurricular activities do not receive financial support from state / school administration.

Respondents working in those types of programs underlined the importance of implementing Christian elements. According to them, a Christian profile was de-fined by practical religious elements like the telling of Bible stories or prayer.

In practice, it is not always possible to draw a clear distinction between the two above mentioned types of programs. On the one hand, these programs show how diverse extracurricular Christian programs are, on the other, this diversity raises questions concerning the identity and self-conception of Christian youth work itself, its employees and volunteers in that the context of formal education questions these well-established premises.

Adolescents with various backgrounds and motivations

According to the employees and volunteers, all their Christian extracurricular programs are accessible to all adolescents regardless of their cultural background, religion, etc. A full-time employee of one of the projects described the participants as follows: "Considering religious backgrounds, it was quite colorful: atheists, New Apostolics, Buddhists, adolescents with a Christian and a Muslim background, also Greek-Orthodox". But what led adolescents want to join such programs? According to the opinion of full-time employees, social aspects like community-feeling or the experience of receiving attention played a crucial role. Moreover, the chance to acquire qualifications within programs like the pupil-mentor-training program attracted many pupils.

4.   Summary, reception and methodological conclusions

4.1 Summary and reception of the research project: Tasks for Christian school-related youth work as non-formal education at school

All in all, in the context of non-formal education, the research project and its results illustrate the challenges faced when non-formal religious education takes place in the context of formal education, for example in state-sponsored schools. Firstly, schools demand reliable and cost-effective partners. Although there is an openness for collaboration, schools not only face obstacles and challenges, such as the internal structure of Christian youth work and church/parishes, but also profile-related diversity within the programs themselves. For schools, clarity with regards to Christian school-related youth work is not always easy to achieve and sometimes renders cooperation difficult. Secondly, in funding cooperative projects some parishes hope to attract more participants for their own programs taking place outside of the school context. These expectations put additional pressure on the extracurricular programs. Thirdly, cooperating with the formal sector questions characteristics and principles of Christian youth work, that is, for example not focusing on achievements, while simultaneously offering programs with a certificate such as the pupil-mentor training program. Notwithstanding the above, the advantage of school-related youth work is that it reaches children and adolescents from a multitude of backgrounds. This, however, implies that further strategies are needed which take, for example, into account the religious diversity of adolescents participating in extracurricular Christian programs.

Before discussing more general methodological issues of the research project, some pertinent examples of this project's impact will be given. First of all, decision-makers of the Protestant Church in Württemberg decided to continue the project by extending the central project coordinator for five more years after 2017. Moreover, based on the project's results the Protestant Christian youth work in Württemberg developed a guideline on school-related youth work, its profile and principles (EJW 2017). Thus, the central aim of the evaluation as a formative analysis, namely to describe and clarify the practice of Christian school-related youth work as non-formal religious education, is apparent. Likewise, procedures were initiated on evidence of empirical results in order to improve practice (Schweitzer 2008).

4.2 Methodological considerations – critical perspectives

The research project shows that school-related youth work finds itself in a grey area, vacillating between formal and non-formal education. This is a characteristic also facing research in the field itself.

Designed with a focus on structures as well as issues referring to the basic agreements needed for successful work, a useful supplement to research projects like the present study lies in incorporating young people's voices. A crucial starting point for educational processes needs to acknowledge school-related youth work and its participants as a form of religious education. Future research should include more in-depth analysis of the perspectives and desires of adolescents, as well as dealing with questions such as their views about specific extracurricular programs and the differences between the curricular and extracurricular programs they take part in. Further aims for school-related youth work might arise by gaining insight into the perspectives of children and adolescents.

The interaction between the formal and the non-formal sector points to the urgent need for a further development of research methods. In the case of school-related youth work, the non-formal sector interacts on a conceptual level with the formal sector. Thus, the leaders of these programs are faced with challenges of formalised standards, yet, there is no detailed curriculum or catalogue of competences to refer to. Non-formal activities follow another logic as they, for instance, do not have a defined nor established curriculum. Therefore, future research ought to focus even more on non-formal criteria within its designs.

Aside from this, the research project, which was designed as a formative evaluation, had to deal with complications such as diverging interests of different stakeholders (see e.g. Brandt 2007). This became evident during interviews with full-time employees who depended on a positive evaluation of their programs so that their workplaces would continue to exist. An external researcher was, therefore, hired to avoid these particular conflicts of interests. However, this researcher still needed to have a certain knowledge of the field in order to guarantee a professional familiarity and an understanding of the overall topic (in the present case, the researcher had a university degree in Protestant theology).

Considering these specific crucial aspects, the question arises whether research which follows formalised designs, standards and principles is not in need of some direct form of interaction with the research object of non-formal education itself. A direct form of interaction would allow to assess the research object from within its own way of thinking and perception of its context. Action research, for instance, offers the opportunity for developing an interactive "research togetherness" which allows the research object to participate in a more active role in the research itself. Naturally, certain research particulars, such as the actual data collection (e.g. guideline interview), are exempt from this specific methodology. This approach could give further impetus (for this particular example, see Nicolaisen 2007) and could be applied to either collecting data or to the process of interpreting and analysing collected data. Following the logic of interactive "research togetherness" and developing concrete methods that implement such kinds of research partnerships, the gap between (formal) research/researcher and the (non-formal) object of research could be minimised and a more profound understanding of non-formal educational practices and processes might be gained.

References

Brandt, T. (2007). Sozialer Kontext der Evaluation. In: R. Stockmann (ed.). *Handbuch zur Evaluation. Eine praktische Handlungsanleitung*. Münster: Waxmann, 164–194.

Bundesministerium für Familie, Senioren, Frauen und Jugend [BMFSFJ] (ed.) (2014). *Kinder- und Jugendhilfe. Achtes Buch Sozialgesetzbuch*. Berlin.

Bundesministerium für Familie, Senioren, Frauen und Jugend [BMFSFJ] (ed.) (2017). *15. Kinder- und Jugendbericht: Bericht über die Lebenssituation junger Menschen und die Leistungen der Kinder- und Jugendhilfe in Deutschland*. Berlin.

Coelen, Th., and Otto, H.U. (2004). Auf dem Weg zu einem neuen Bildungsverständnis: Ganztagsschule oder Ganztagsbildung? In: T. Coelen and H.U. Otto (eds.). *Grundbegriffe der Ganztagsbildung. Beiträge zu einem neuen Bildungsverständnis in der Wissensgesellschaft*. Wiesbaden: Verlag für Sozialwissenschaften, 7–16.

Evangelisches Jugendwerk in Württemberg [EJW] (2017). *Den Aufbruch wagen – Im Lebensraum Schule präsent sein!* Stuttgart. www.schuelerarbeit.de/fileadmin/schuelerarbeit/upload/2017-05-20-Grundlagenpapier_Einzelseiten.pdf [01.06.2018].

Gärtner, C., and Kempfer, K. (2016). Jugendverbände in die Schule? Empirische Erkundungen in einem Kooperationsprojekt von Ganztagsschule und katholischer Jugendverbandsarbeit. In: *International Journal for Practical Theology* 20(1), 26–50.

Ilg, W. (2013). Jugendarbeit – Grundlagen, Prinzipien und Arbeitsformen. In: T. Rauschenbach and S. Borrmann (eds.). *Enzyklopädie Erziehungswissenschaft Online*. Weinheim and Basel: Beltz Juventa, 1–21.

Ilg, W. (2014). Die Kinder- und Jugendarbeit als Partnerin der Ganztags-Grundschule. In: *Die Gemeinde (BWGZ)* 18, 1018–1022.

Kultusministerkonferenz [KMK] (ed.) (2015). *Ganztagsschulen in Deutschland. Bericht der Kultusministerkonferenz vom 3.12.2015*. Berlin.

Landtag von Baden-Württemberg, *Drucksache 15/6726* (2015). Antrag von Abg. Wacker u. a. CDU, Stellungnahme des Ministeriums für Kultus, Jugend und Sport. Ausbau der Ganztagsgrundschulen in Baden-Württemberg, Stuttgart. www.landtag-bw.de/files/live/sites/LTBW/files/dokumente/WP15/Drucksachen/6000/15_6726_D.pdf [01.06.2018].

Lange, M., and Wehmeyer, K. (2014). *Jugendarbeit im Takt einer beschleunigten Gesellschaft*. Weinheim and Basel: Beltz Juventa.

Lehmann, P., Ilg, W., Heinzmann, G., and Cares, M. (2014). Schulbezogene Kinder- und Jugendarbeit. In: W. Ilg, G. Heinzmann and M. Cares (eds.). *Jugend zählt! Ergebnisse, Herausforderungen und Perspektiven aus der Statistik 2013 zur Arbeit mit Kindern und Jugendlichen in den Evangelischen Landeskirchen Baden und Württemberg*. Stuttgart: buch+musik, 164–175.

Mayring, P. (2015). *Qualitative Inhaltsanalyse. Grundlagen und Techniken*. Weinheim und Basel: Beltz Verlag.

Nicolaisen, T. (2007). Pluralitet, planer og praksis. Mangfold i klasserommet når KRL står på timeplanen. Perspektiver på aksjonsforkning i en grunnskole i Oslo. In: *Prismet* 58(1), 3–16.

Rahmenvereinbarung zwischen dem Land Baden-Württemberg – vertreten durch den Minister für Kultus, Jugend und Sport –, den nachfolgend unterzeichnenden außerschulischen Partnern und den Kommunalen Landesverbänden: Kooperationsoffensive Ganztagsschule (2014). www.ganztagsschule-bw.de [01.06.2018].

Rahmenvereinbarung zwischen dem Ministerium für Kultus, Jugend und Sport Baden-Württemberg und der Diözese Rottenburg-Stuttgart, Erzdiözese Freiburg, Evangelische Landeskirche in Baden, Evangelische Landeskirche in Württemberg über die Zusammenarbeit im Rahmen der Ganztagsschule gem. §4a Schulgesetz (2015). www.ganztag.de/rahmenvereinbarung [01.06.2018].

Schröder, B. (2006). Warum 'Religion im Schulleben'? In: B. Schröder (ed.). *Religion im Schulleben. Christliche Präsenz nicht allein im Religionsunterricht*. Neukirchen-Vluyn: Neukirchener Verlagshaus, 11–26.

Schweitzer, F. (2008). Wissenschaftliche Begleitforschung als Aufgabe der Religionspädagogik. In: C. Gramzow, H. Liebold and M. Sander-Gaiser (eds.). *Lernen wäre eine schöne Alternative. Religionsunterricht in theologischer und erziehungswissenschaftlicher Verantwortung*. Leipzig: Evangelische Verlagsanstalt, 125–136.

Schweizer, M., Sommer, L., and Stange, K. (2016). Nachgefragt – Jugendarbeit und Schule in Baden. In: W. Ilg and F. Schweitzer (eds.). *Jugend gefragt! Empirische Studien zur Realität evangelischer Arbeit mit Kindern und Jugendlichen in Baden-Württemberg*. Stuttgart: buch+musik, 307–340.

Spenn, M., and Fischer, D. (2005). *Ganztagsschulen gemeinsam entwickeln. Ein Beitrag zur evangelischen Bildungsverantwortung,* ed. Comenius Institute, Münster.

Statistisches Landesamt Baden-Württemberg (2015). *Statistische Berichte Baden-Württemberg: Unterricht und Bildung. Allgemeinbildende Schulen in Baden-Württemberg im Schuljahr 2015/2016*. Artikel-Nr. 3231 15001, Stuttgart.

Wermke, M. (2014). Religion in school outside Religious Education. In: M. Rothgangel, T. Schlag and F. Schweitzer (eds.). *Basics of Religious Education*. Göttingen: Vandenhoeck & Ruprecht, 95–111.

Wolking, L. (2016). Kirche, Jugendarbeit und Schule machen sich auf: Wissenschaftliche Begleitung des Projekts "Kirche – Jugendarbeit – Schule". In: W. Ilg and F. Schweitzer (eds.). *Jugend gefragt! Empirische Studien zur Realität evangelischer Arbeit mit Kindern und Jugendlichen in Baden-Württemberg*. Stuttgart: buch+musik, 233–306.

II
Kindergarten

Researching interreligious and intercultural education in German kindergartens

Three empirical projects – their approaches and methodologies

Alexandra Wörn, Golde Wissner, Lena Wolking, Rebecca Nowack

This chapter offers an overview of three empirical research projects in the area of non-formal religious education in German kindergartens with a particular focus on interreligious education. For the past ten years a succession of ensuing research projects in the area of interreligious and intercultural education have been carried out by an interdisciplinary research team at the University of Tübingen (Protestant and Catholic Faculties of Theology). Various quantitative and qualitative research methods have been employed, tested and adapted to the groups examined, i.e. children, parents, kindergarten staff and those in training. All three research projects identify interreligious education as an integral part of intercultural education. An important dialogue partner in interreligious and intercultural matters is the Center for Islamic Theology at the University of Tübingen.

1. Terminological questions: Kindergartens as places of non-formal education?

When discussing non-formal education, kindergartens are not the educational institutions which initially come to mind. At first glance, kindergartens do not seem to have much in common with typical non-formal educational contexts such as youth work. Rather, kindergartens are seen to be more analogous to schools, i.e. educational places representing formal education. However, as the following discussion shows, the elementary sector (in this article this term refers to education for children before school) can indeed be considered as a place of non-formal education, despite the fact that a certain degree of formal education takes place within them. Thus, kindergartens can be understood as educational loci which are "in between", bridging formal and non-formal education. The following overview of three empirical projects on religious education in German kindergartens looks at two types of institutional affiliation, municipal as well as church-sponsored kindergartens. The age range of the children attending the discussed kindergartens is up to six years.

In the context of official general education policy in Germany, kindergartens are generally characterised as places of non-formal education: although kindergartens offer an organised form of education, elementary education is optional and conducted in a way, which inspires rather than demands participation (Rauschenbach et al. 2004, 29). Likewise, kindergartens are seen in sociological terms as part of a range of educational institutions, yet unlike schools or universities kindergartens are not required to be impartial and degree oriented (Rauschenbach et al. 2004, 30–33; see also European Commission and Council of Europe 2004). Thus, kindergartens can be located outside the formal educational system comprising schools, vocational training and universities. In sum, kindergartens offer a type of non-formal education that is intentional in character and planned, they are staffed by teachers who are employed full or part-time, have programmatic goals, and a specific interest or ethos (European Commission and Council of Europe 2004).

Notwithstanding this, some of these non-formal characteristics exhibit formal qualities, which is why kindergartens inhabit a place in between formal and non-formal education. The following presents an overview of some of the characteristics:

a. The German state suggests an educational curriculum for kindergartens entitled "Orientierungsplan" offering pedagogical guidance for kindergarten teachers. In the case of Baden-Württemberg, this curriculum provides guidance to both kindergarten teachers and parents and is concerned with the individual development of each child (Ministerium für Kultus, Jugend und Sport Baden-Württemberg 2011, 6). Hence, the curriculum's starting point is the child's own intrinsic motivation (p. 25). Even though this "Orientierungsplan" is only seen as a guideline, it is nevertheless reminiscent of formal curricula in the sense that it reflects on the role and the competences of kindergarten teachers and focuses on important pedagogical notions, i.e. so called "educational fields" which include topics such as the body, the five senses, language, thoughts, feelings and empathy, as well as the meaning of life, values and religions (pp. 27–47).
b. In the final year of kindergarten, children take part in a school entrance test. Only by passing this test are they then allowed to attend primary school. This particular test is similar to a formal certificate in that it offers official confirmation that a child is now ready and able to attend school.
c. When parents enroll their child in kindergarten, it is customary that the child will continuously and conscientiously attend kindergarten. This kind of constancy is redolent of formal attendance at primary and secondary school level, even though non-formal education at elementary level is neither compulsory nor legally binding.

Furthermore, it is important to draw attention once more to the difference between municipal and church-sponsored kindergartens, in particular the ones with denominational affiliations. Non-formal characteristics are particularly prevalent for church-sponsored kindergartens. In the following sections, denominational kindergartens will serve by and large as an example for non-formal religious education. Denominational kindergartens are structurally as well as educationally linked to local parishes. These parishes offer a variety of groups, which all belong into the area of non-formal religious education. The denominational kindergartens are supposed to be an integral part of the life of the parish and its non-formal programs: it is hoped that children attending such kindergartens will experience Christian fellowship, education in Christian faith and the chance to learn from each other (for Protestant kindergartens, see Evangelische Kirche in Deutschland 2005, for Catholic kindergartens, see Deutsche Bischofskonferenz 2008). This explains why denominational kindergartens naturally have a closer link to non-formal education than, for example, municipal kindergartens.

There is a general consensus today concerning the importance of early childhood education. For the past 15 years, the previously mentioned "Orientierungspläne", i.e. a voluntary curriculum offering educational guidance for the education of pre-school children, have been available. One of its components is also religious education. Research in the area of interreligious and intercultural education, especially within the elementary sector, is still the exception rather than the rule. However, there is an increasing interest in religious and interreligious elementary education as the need for interreligious exchange and competences in a pluralistic society such as Germany is growing fast (Edelbrock 2014). Likewise, results show that the cornerstone for a fruitful and respectful intercultural and interreligious dialogue is set in pre-school education. However, the question still remains whether and in what manner the individual kindergartens actually offer interreligious and intercultural education. Thus, the results of the three research projects conducted at the University of Tübingen and presented in this article give crucial answers to pressing questions that until now have not been given full scientific attention. As recent political developments confirm there is an urgency for further research in this particular field of inquiry.

The following sections will offer an overview of the three empirical studies undertaken within the last decade. All three projects have in common that they scientifically investigate interreligious and intercultural education in German kindergartens; interreligious education is understood as an integral part of intercultural education. The first project, the foundation of all ensuing projects, set out to discover the status quo regarding interreligious and intercultural education within German kindergartens. One of its aims was to analyse interreligiously and interculturally sensitive teaching modules for kindergarten teachers in training on the basis of its scientific findings. Following on from Project I, the second (still ongoing) project has a stronger focus on the kindergarten teachers themselves and on the training courses through which they gained their interreligious and intercultural competences. A particular emphasis of Project II are also kindergarten teachers and kindergarten teachers in training with Muslim backgrounds. Finally, the third project deals solely with kindergarten teachers in training. This study, likewise still in progress, examines the content and significance of religious education within the professional training itself and asks whether the vocational schools sufficiently prepare these future kindergarten teachers for work in a multi-religious context.

2. Project I: Researching intercultural and interreligious education in German kindergartens

This empirical research project based at Tübingen (Edelbrock, Schweitzer and Biesinger 2010; Biesinger, Edelbrock and Schweitzer 2011; Schweitzer, Edelbrock and Biesinger 2011) was sponsored by the Stiftung Ravensburger Verlag. It represents a pioneering study investigating intercultural and interreligious education in kindergartens. As mentioned above, these results laid the foundation for further research in the field. The research carried out in this first project comprised several different elements: questionnaire-based surveys and interviews with kindergarten teachers, parents and children on the one hand, and on the other, description of best-practice-models as well as the collection of evidence to further develop teaching modules for kindergarten teachers in training.

2.1 The pilot project

Before describing the research project and its methodologies in more detail, a brief overview of the pilot project (Schweitzer, Biesinger and Edelbrock 2009) which preceded this present study is necessary. This pilot project examined religious and interreligious education in kindergartens and included both qualitative and quantitative parts: 37 interviews with kindergarten teachers were conducted in seven different cities throughout Germany. The analysis of these interviews assisted in developing the questionnaire used in this survey, which in turn was filled out by 364 kindergarten teachers in different parts of Germany. One interesting result gained from this questionnaire was the distribution of the religious affiliations of the children who attended the respective kindergartens: only half of the children were Christians, 19% Muslims, 3% had other religious affiliations and 27% were without any religious affiliation. This was similar both in church-sponsored as well as in municipal kindergartens and confirmed that religious pluralism is an undeniable reality in German kindergartens, especially in urban areas. Simultaneously, the results showed that the diversity of religious and cultural backgrounds is frequently overlooked in the work with pre-school children, and therefore, it does not come as a surprise that interreligious education was not adequately supported by the kindergarten teachers in most kindergartens.

Central issues

Three central questions emerged from the pilot study which led in turn to the research project in question:

1. Would the results of the pilot study be replicated in a larger and more representative sample?

2. What further insights regarding religious, interreligious and intercultural education can be gained through parent and children surveys?
3. What can be learned from kindergartens that "successfully" implement an interreligiously sensitive education?

Different components of the more representative research project suggest answers to these questions which are summarised in the following sections.

2.2 Children survey

Background

As previously mentioned, there is very little research on how pre-school children perceive religious diversity and difference. Interviewing this particular group is obviously challenging: it was necessary to interview parents and teachers, but more importantly also the children themselves. Hence, a children's survey was developed.

Design and sample

140 pre-school children were interviewed; their average age was 4.9 years. The sample consisted of 65 Christian, 48 Muslim and 20 religiously non-affiliated children. The interviews took place within municipal, church-sponsored as well as Muslim kindergartens[1]. These kindergartens were located in the vicinity of four larger cities within different parts of Germany. The conversations were recorded and transcribed for later analysis. The children were interviewed in groups of three or four, and the interviews lasted between 20 to 45 minutes. Each group was interviewed three times by the same interviewer, in order for the children to build up trust with their interviewer. Due to the intimate interview situation, in-depth conversations were possible in the final round of interviews. The interviewer used pictures, objects (i.e. a Muslim prayer chain or a simple wooden cross) as well as role play in order to initiate a conversation with the children. However, the goal was not to evaluate or dictate the contents of the conversation itself but rather to facilitate and inspire conversation with and amongst the children themselves. The following questions guided the research: What do the children *know* about different religions? How do the children *experience* religious rituals and festivals in other religions? Which *attitudes* do they hold with regard to members of a different religion? Which *language skills* do they possess with respect to interreligious themes?

---

1 Muslim kindergartens are still extremely rare in Germany. They exist in some of the larger cities. The project visited some of them, so that it was possible to perceive attitudes of Muslim children towards other religions not only from a situation of minorities like in the other kindergartens.

Results

The analysis confirmed that children are indeed capable of distinguishing and discerning differences between the various religions; some of them even possess interreligious knowledge. More generally speaking, most children seemed tolerant as well as demonstrated an interest in other religions; some of them had developed friendships with children from other religious and cultural backgrounds. Some children were unsure about specific contents concerning their own religion and as a result began to develop their own explanations, for example, for the differences in the customs of other religions when they did not have the opportunity to engage in interreligious learning. Some of the children's explanations were regarded as objectively disturbing and again served as a proof of the importance and necessity for interreligious education in kindergartens. Positively speaking, only a few of the interviewed children expressed negative attitudes towards other religions. Another result proved that problems regarding the ability of a child to express religious views seemed to coincide with a more general deficiency regarding language skills. Furthermore, children who did not possess much knowledge on religious matters, were predictably not experienced in talking about religion, and could not understand children who had experience in talking about their religion in another language, such as Arabic or Hebrew. (For further information on the research findings, see Dubiski et al. 2010.)

2.3 Parent survey

Background

A child's own family is obviously his/her first and central living environment. The family is crucial for the child's own development. Whether and how religious education is part of this familial environment varies greatly in contemporary Germany. The kindergarten then becomes the child's second living environment and educational context and hence, it is crucial that parents have knowledge of the kind of education their child's kindergarten offers. Likewise, it is essential for the teachers to be aware of the parents' own beliefs and values. The aim of the parent survey was therefore, to discover what kinds of attitudes, experiences, concerns and hopes parents hold with regards to religious and interreligious education in kindergartens.

Design and sample

In the qualitative part of this survey, interviews based on an interview guideline were conducted with 41 mothers and 4 fathers with different religious backgrounds. All of them had one or several children in kindergarten. For the ensuing quantitative part of the study, a questionnaire was developed on the basis of the insights gained from these interviews. In the end, 590 parents from 54 kindergartens located in

14 different German states participated in these interviews. The questionnaire was also translated into Turkish and every kindergarten received German and Turkish questionnaires, which the teachers distributed to the parents.

Results

The kindergarten's pedagogical concept including religious and interreligious education only played a minor role for most of the parents. However, interestingly only eight of the interviewed 590 parents stated that religious education in the home is not an issue for them. Although many parents expect support from the kindergarten teachers in the education of their children, it seems that only the parents who are not religious or those who are highly religious hold reservations towards religious education in kindergartens. Most of the parents believe that interreligious education is important, although some fear that this topic might go beyond their children's mental capacities. The quantitative results confirm that the parents' attitudes towards religious and especially interreligious education varies greatly; and again, only a small group of the respondents were opposed to religion. The results confirm the challenges kindergarten teachers face and furthermore, highlight the importance of regular exchange between teachers and parents on this topic.

2.4 Teachers' survey

Background

The teachers' survey set out to determine whether and in what form interreligious education is part of religious education in German kindergartens. A particular focus was on the challenges as well as opportunities as perceived by teachers themselves.

Design and sample

The representative sample was secured with the help of GESIS (Leibniz Institut für Sozialwissenschaften), a randomly computerised process: 2838 teachers from 487 different kindergartens participated in the study and filled out the questionnaire which was a revised version from the pilot study.

Results

A first question to the teachers referred to the religious composition of the groups they are working with. This question was necessary because there are no official statistics concerning the religious affiliation of the children in kindergartens. According to the teachers' responses, most of the children were of Christian background (around 70%), about 15% were of Muslim background and about 16%

had no religious affiliation. With this data it was possible for the first time to provide information about the religion-related composition of the children in German kindergartens. This heterogeneous mix of children from different religious backgrounds confirms yet again the importance of and need for religious and interreligious education. Most of the teachers were open to being asked (inter)religious questions by the children themselves. One important finding was that not many of the teachers seem to deliberately incorporate religious and interreligious topics into their educational program. In spite of that, differences were noticeable between church-sponsored and municipal kindergartens: one common example is the fact that the children in municipal kindergartens are rarely encouraged to say grace before eating while most kindergartens with a Christian foundation encourage this religious practice. Muslim education is rarely practiced in either type of kindergarten. Intercultural education seems more commonly practiced than interreligious education. In sum, the study confirms the teachers' need for support regarding interreligious education within German kindergartens. This particular result led on to a further research project with kindergarten teachers in training which will be discussed in a later part of this chapter.

2.5 Best-practice models

Background

Some kindergartens can indeed serve as an inspiration for further developing interreligious education. A central goal of this research project was to find such best-practice models. The first step was to identify German kindergartens, which were engaging successfully in interreligious education, the second to visit these kindergartens and document their pedagogical innovations.

Design and sample

180 addresses of kindergartens which seemed successful in further advancing interreligious education were compiled. These kindergartens were identified with the help of elementary education experts, kindergarten associations as well as online searches indicating that kindergartens had a particular emphasis on interreligious education. The following criteria were crucial in the decision-making and selection of 26 kindergartens: firstly, the quality of their work, secondly, a wide range of different educational profiles and models for documentary purposes. The chosen facilities were then visited on several occasions in order to interview their teachers and to conduct observational studies.

Results

The following pedagogical insights and concepts for interreligious education were observed and documented, such as visiting churches, mosques and synagogues within the neighborhood, encouraging parents to mix with parents of other religious backgrounds and affiliations or celebrating different religious festivals together (for further information: Schweitzer, Edelbrock and Biesinger 2011).

2.6 Conclusion

The project confirms the need for different methodological approaches when analysing non-formal (religious / interreligious) education in kindergartens. Qualitative and quantitative surveys specifically tailored to the target group offered a comprehensive picture; qualitative surveys were not only effective when questioning parents and children, but also with the teachers themselves. The analysis of pedagogical concepts of kindergartens and observational studies in the kindergartens themselves on the basis of the above-mentioned surveys further provided a more comprehensive picture of the state of religious and interreligious education. At the same time, it should be stressed that the quantitative approach with questionnaires and a large representative sample is indispensable for valid assessments.

3. Project II: Researching interculturally and interreligiously sensitive education in kindergartens. A scientific evaluation of 16 intercultural and interreligious kindergarten projects in Baden-Württemberg

Background

Between 2015 and 2018, the Baden-Württemberg Foundation/Kinderland Foundation funded 16 intercultural and interreligious projects in almost 80 municipal and church-sponsored kindergartens in Baden-Württemberg. Individual kindergartens as well as representative bodies in charge of several kindergartens were able to apply for this funding. The Departments for Religious Education of both the Catholic and Protestant Theology Faculties at the University of Tübingen were jointly responsible for the evaluation of these projects in cooperation with the Centre for Islamic Theology as well as the Institute of Education, also based at the University of Tübingen.

Aims

The following six points highlight central issues investigated in Project II:

1. In continuation of the first project, the aim of this study was to compile knowledge of already existing intercultural and interreligious competences of kindergarten teachers who work in institutions, which engage in intercultural and interreligious projects. A particular focus was to assess the teacher's own pedagogical experience in order to improve future design of intercultural and interreligious training courses for kindergarten teachers themselves.
2. From this followed a comparison of the efficacy of the various types of interreligious and intercultural training courses through which the chosen kindergartens had gained their respective competences. This second aim was inspired and further developed by the results of Project I; Project III also continues this line of research, which will be discussed in more detail in a later part of this chapter.
3. The results of the first two steps resulted in establishing a range of different criteria that training courses for intercultural and interreligious competences should meet if they are to further such competencies effectively.
4. One of the central aims of collecting knowledge of intercultural and interreligious skills from the above mentioned 16 projects was to share this practical knowledge with and return it to the source from where it originally came from, i.e. the kindergartens themselves. The study therefore aimed to capture and describe the experiences of the kindergarten teachers it surveyed, in order to make it available, for instance, for conducting parents' meetings.
5. An aim unique to this study is the strong focus on the increasing religious diversity amongst the kindergarten teachers themselves. Kindergarten teachers and kindergarten teachers in training with Muslim background were chosen as a good example to reflect upon on how these (prospective) teachers might contribute to future intercultural and interreligious education.
6. Finally, another pioneering aspect of this study is to analyse elementary educational material, e.g. children's books, which further intercultural and interreligious education. The reason for this was to sensitise kindergarten teachers to different pedagogical approaches and encourage a reflected use of material for interreligious education. Here it was crucial to include the advice of Jewish, Christian and Muslim experts.

Design

The six points described above are the basis of the scientific evaluation. The study consisted of project-specific tasks, especially the training courses which took place during the course of the project itself. To begin with, the kindergarten teachers were asked to fill out questionnaires: all staff participating in the study had to complete the same questionnaire twice with an interval of at least one year between the first and second completion (points 1, 2 and 3). Secondly, qualitatively guided interviews took place at the beginning and end of the scientific evaluation. Considering the different structural conditions each project faced, it was necessary also to interview different stakeholders (i.e. kindergarten teachers, kindergarten management or institutional representatives) regarding the extent to which they were responsible for and involved in the execution of the respective projects (points 3 and 4). Qualitatively guided interviews were also used in the case of Muslim kindergarten teachers (in training) (point 5). Finally, children's books were evaluated from a Christian, Jewish and Muslim religious pedagogical perspective and compared with the findings from the 16 projects and the additional independent research work undertaken by members of the reach group (point 6).

Results and discussion

The evaluation of the results from this project is still ongoing. Nonetheless, preliminary findings within the quantitative analysis confirm the above mentioned results and highlight the fact that intercultural and interreligious education, a supplementary part of the education for kindergarten teachers, has not essentially improved within the last ten years. Nevertheless, as the quantitative and qualitative analysis show, positive approaches and developments can be found within interculturally and interreligiously active kindergartens. However, these educational implementations often demand huge efforts on the part of the kindergartens themselves, i.e. applications for funding to cover the cost of extra staff, staff training and extra educational material. Likewise, a lack of awareness concerning the potential for interreligious competences in the case of teachers with, for example, a Muslim background is a common phenomenon in many kindergartens.

Finally, and on a positive and more hopeful note, there are a variety of possible methodologies which enable the examination of intercultural and interreligious education from various different angles. Despite that, there is a definite need for a further improvement and refining of standard methodological approaches in the area of non-formal religious education.

4. Project III: Enhancing interreligious competences for kindergarten teachers in training

Analogously to Project II, this study investigates the significance of interreligious and intercultural competences within the education of kindergarten teachers, however, the focus in Project III is exclusively on kindergarten teachers in training. As became evident in Project I, there is an urgent demand for further training courses within the area of interreligious and intercultural competences, thus, Project III tries to establish what is theologically and pedagogically required in order to gain such expertise.

Aims

As mentioned above, this study investigates the content and significance of religious education for kindergarten teachers in training and asks whether the vocational schools sufficiently prepare them for work in a multi-religious context;
hence, teaching units, which further the acquisition of interreligious competences
are a natural part of this study. Similarly to the first two projects, the approach chosen for Project III is that of an intervention study in order to measure and evaluate
the enhancement of interreligious competences for future kindergarten teachers.

Design

The intervention consists of two different treatments, i.e. teaching units on the topics of "tolerance" and "prayer" which contain six lessons each comprising 45 minutes. Before the start of the teaching units as well as after their completion, students
are asked to fill out the same questionnaire; the questionnaire filled out before the
teaching units is identified as t_1 and after the intervention t_2.

The first implementation of this study was in 2015/2016 with over 300 students
from 17 different classes in the federal state of Baden-Württemberg. Eight classes
received the teaching unit on "prayer" and nine classes the teaching unit on "tolerance". 358 questionnaires were returned at the t_1 stage and 302 questionnaires
at the t_2 stage. A total of 251 students filled in the questionnaires at both stages:
hence, it was possible to directly compare the data of 251 students before and after
the intervention. In addition, this study also includes a qualitative part consisting of
written feedback by the students themselves as well as interviews with students and
teachers on the teaching units.

In order to extract measurable indices for interreligious competences, Project
III concentrates on four core components which are considered essential for developing interreligious competences, and which consequently enable a person to act
competently within interreligious contexts. The four core components are stated
below.

A hypothesis regarding these four core components has been developed which have
all been integral to the questionnaire used in this study and which is analogous to
Project II. It is also partly based on Project I as well as on another past project in the
area of the efficacy of interreligious learning within religious education in the training
of future caregivers. To have interreligious competences includes the following:

– knowledge about other cultures and / or religions
– a positive attitude towards other cultures and / or religions
– ability to adopt the perspective of someone from another culture and / or religion
– ability to self-reflect on one's own attitude and / or behaviour (with regards to
  religion and / or culture).

Results and discussion

The results that have been presented so far are preliminary as this project is still ongoing. The qualitative analysis confirmed that teachers as well as students appreciated the teaching units.

However, the quantitative analysis of the questionnaires shows that not all of the (sub-)scales which were developed could actually be confirmed empirically. The exploratory factor analysis (EFA) produced reliable factors for the dimensions of "self-reflection" and "attitudes", yet the analysis did not produce reliable results for the dimensions "knowledge" and "perspective taking". Nevertheless, one or several reliable (sub-)scales were discovered for all of four core components.

In terms of evaluating the effects of the treatments, reliable scales are a vital presupposition for comparing results at t_1 level with those from t_2. At this point, the scales are still being revised in order to improve measurements of the individual dimensions, especially with regards to the dimension of perspective taking.

5. Conclusion: Analysing the results the three studies

5.1 Interreligious education in German kindergartens

When looking at the overall results of the three research projects conducted between 2009 and 2018, a growing societal awareness is noticeable with regards to the necessity of interreligious education, also within early childhood education. This topic has an ever-increasing presence in the kindergartens themselves as well as in the education and further education of pedagogical staff, although it has to be said that differences are evident with respect to how and when interreligious education is being implemented in the individual kindergartens themselves. What is equally apparent is the strong need of the pedagogical staff themselves to learn how to meet the requirements of children and their families from different religious and non-religious backgrounds.

5.2 Methodological challenges and suggestions for researching non-formal early childhood education

The Tübingen research projects are exceptional in the field in that all three studies are ground-breaking with regards to empirical standards, such as in their choice of methodology and design. Thus, these projects can indeed be seen as inspiring and influencing further research in the area of non-formal early childhood education. Of particular interest are the questionnaires that were developed, the manner in which the samples were acquired, the way in which the various reference groups were interviewed as well as the employment of different methods of inquiry.

A well-planned and well-accompanied questionnaire survey

The acquisition of data through questionnaires is necessary and until now there is no alternative methodology available which might offer representative results for general use. However, during the various different projects it became increasingly obvious, what should be observed when conducting research into early childhood education in kindergartens. The findings are helping to develop ideas which might alleviate or even overcome certain common problems and could further assist future research in this area. Here are a few of the challenges encountered in the studies as well as some possible solutions:

– Concerning the construction of the questionnaire: The questionnaires in all three projects passed a test run and the feedback given by the pedagogical staff was always taken into account. However, in some individual cases a number of kindergarten teachers were dissatisfied with regards to the questionnaire's intelligibility and scale. It therefore seems advisable to take into account the input of the pedagogical staff itself from a very early stage, i.e. when developing the questionnaire. It might even be considered viable to include a kindergarten professional as part of the research team.
– Regarding personal support during the survey: The significance of quantitative studies depends especially on high participation rates. In order to enhance the response rate among kindergarten teachers as well as parents with regards to the questionnaire, it might be feasible for the research team to provide extra personal support. For example, as it is equally relevant to emphasise the importance of the teachers' as well as the parents' contribution, a possible solution might be to have a member of the research team introduce the study, i.e. during a training course, team meeting at the kindergarten or vocational school, or at a parents' meeting. The advantage of such an approach, even though it is labour intense, would be the possibility to deal instantly with questions and thus increase motivation among participants.

A representative sample

In order to offer reliable conclusions in the area of non-formal education, the first and essential step is to establish a valid, i.e. representative sample of different kindergartens. This starting point already proves challenging: How to find kindergartens which are willing to participate in the study in the first place; but likewise, a representative sample is not only determined by its quantity but also by the allocation of the kindergarten according to specific criteria (namely, a balance between regions, an equal distribution between urban and rural areas, etc.).

Different approaches

For a more comprehensive understanding of non-formal education in kindergartens, it is essential to interview various reference groups, that is, not only the teachers themselves but also the responsible bodies, kindergarten supervisors, parents and children. From a pedagogical perspective, the children's survey (i.e. interviews) is of particular importance, as the children themselves are, in this instance, the educational focal point. For a more conclusive picture it therefore seems necessary that both qualitative as well as quantitative approaches should be used.

References

Biesinger, A., Edelbrock, A., and Schweitzer, F. (2011). *Auf die Eltern kommt es an! Interreligiöse und Interkulturelle Bildung in der Kita.* Münster: Waxmann.

Deutsche Bischofskonferenz (eds.) (2008). *Welt entdecken, Glauben leben. Zum Bildungs- und Erziehungsauftrag katholischer Kindertageseinrichtungen* (Die deutschen Bischöfe; 89). Bonn: Deutsche Bischofskonferenz.

Dubiski, K., Essich, I., Schweitzer, F., Edelbrock, A., and Biesinger, A. (2010). Religiöse Differenzwahrnehmung im Kindesalter, Befunde aus der empirischen Untersuchung im Überblick. In: Edelbrock, A., Schweitzer, F., and Biesinger, A. (eds.). *Wie viele Götter sind im Himmel? Religiöse Differenzwahrnehmung im Kindesalter.* Münster: Waxmann, 121–191.

Edelbrock, A. (2014). Empirische Forschung zur interreligiösen Bildung im Kindergarten. In: Schreiner, P., and Schweitzer, F. (eds.). *Religiöse Bildung erforschen. Empirische Befunde und Perspektiven,* Münster: Waxmann, 79–90.

Edelbrock, A., Schweitzer, F., and Biesinger, A (eds.) (2010). *Wie viele Götter sind im Himmel? Religiöse Differenzwahrnehmung im Kindesalter.* Münster: Waxmann.

European Commission and Council of Europa (2004). *Pathways towards validation and recognition of education, training & learning in the youth field.* .]www.pjp-eu.coe.int/documents/1017981/1668227/Pathways_towards_validati.pdf/caf83fd5-b4db-4b56-a1ab-3b1178e182db) [28.11.2018].

Evangelische Kirche in Deutschland (EKD) (ed.) (2005). *Wo Glaube wächst und Leben sich entfaltet. Der Auftrag evangelischer Kindertageseinrichtungen. Eine Erklärung des Rates der Evangelischen Kirche in Deutschland.* Gütersloh: Gütersloher Verlagshaus.

Ministerium für Kultus, Jugend und Sport Baden-Württemberg (2011). *Orientierungsplan für Bildung und Erziehung in baden-württembergischen Kindergärten und weiterer Kindertageseinrichtungen.* www.kindergaerten-bw.de/,Lde/Startseite/Fruehe+Bildung/Material_Orientierungsplan [28.11.2018].

Rauschenbach, T., Leu, H.R., Lingenauber, S. et al. (2004). *Konzeptionelle Grundlagen für einen Nationalen Bildungsbericht – Non-formale und informelle Bildung im Kindes- und Jugendalter,* ed. Bundesministerium für Bildung und Forschung. Berlin: BMBF.

Schweitzer, F., Biesinger, A., and Edelbrock, A. (eds.) (2009). *Mein Gott – Dein Gott. Interkulturelle und interreligiöse Bildung in Kindertagesstätten.* Weinheim/Basel: Beltz Verlag.

Schweitzer, F., Edelbrock, A. and Biesinger, A. (eds.) (2011). *Interreligiöse und Interkulturelle Bildung in der Kita. Eine Repräsentativbefragung von Erzieherinnen in Deutschland – interdisziplinäre, interreligiöse und internationale Perspektiven.* Münster: Waxmann.

Strohm, F., and Nowack, R. (2017). Interreligious Competence for Kindergarten Teachers in Education. In: Schweitzer, F., and Boschki, R. (eds.). *Researching Religious Education. Classroom Processes and Outcomes.* Münster: Waxmann, 245–256.

Islamic kindergarten

A controversial debate on non-formal religious education in Austria

Martin Rothgangel, Martin Jäggle

There is a wide range of non-formal offers of religious education in Austria. Apart from kindergartens, which are described in more detail in this article, one of the non-formal religious education offers for children and adolescents in Austria in the domain of the Catholic Church is the First Communion preparation for children around the age of 8 years as well as confirmation preparation courses for children of at least 12 years of age. At this point we should also mention Protestant confirmation work. The "Katholische Jungschar", the children's organization of the Catholic Church for Children until the end of the 9 years of compulsory education, is considered "a central place of non-formal education in Catholic parishes in Austria" (Kromer and Hajszan 2015). So-called Sunday Schools are rare in Austria, but the widespread practice of children's services (and also family worship services) can be considered non-formal religious education. In Islamic terms, these include the Koran schools connected to mosques. The small Jewish domain has its own offers, whereas those of Orthodox Christians are only being developed. Overall, it can be assumed that well over half of all children in Austria are reached by these non-formal education programs.

A special role is played by the kindergartens in Austria for quite different reasons: Over the past ten years, kindergartens have received heightened public scrutiny due to, among other things, their role in educational achievements of children. As a result, since 2009 one kindergarten year with a focus on language skills is mandatory. One of the impulses for this reform was the OECD Austrian Country Report titled "Starting strong: Early childhood education and care policy" (2006). In Austria, this led to the development of All Austrian Educational Guidelines (= bundesländerübergreifender BildungsRahmenPlan) for Preschool Educational Institutions (Ämter der Landesregierungen der österreichischen Bundesländer, Magistrat der Stadt Wien and Bundesministerium für Unterricht, Kunst und Kultur 2009).

Another issue that has recently sparked a heated debate is that of the so-called "Islamic" kindergartens in Vienna. For a long time, Viennese city officials claimed that there were no Islamic kindergartens in Vienna. This stance was contradicted by a preliminary study commissioned by the Ministry of Integration and conducted by Ednan Aslan (2016), Professor of Islamic Religious Education at the University of Vienna. This study found that there were in fact about 150 Muslim childcare facilities (Aslan 2016, 8) and that some could be described as having "Salafist orientation and isolationist tendencies". The dispute over this study even became a central issue in the 2017 Austrian parliamentary elections and probably contributed to the Ministry of Education, Science and Research adopting the coordination of preschool education as its explicit remit.

In order to properly understand these discussions, it is important to first look at the specific Austrian framework for kindergartens, especially legal aspects and educational plans for preschool education. Following this, the much-debated commissioned studies (Aslan 2016; Aslan 2017; Hover-Reisner et al. 2017) on so-called "Islamic" kindergartens will be presented and discussed. Finally, there are the two doctoral theses (Stockinger 2017; Brandstetter 2017) on this topic that give interesting insights beyond the troubled waters of the commissioned studies.

1. The guidelines as background

1.1 Legal aspects and background

According to the Federal Constitutional Law, preschool education is not regulated by the federal government but by the individual federal states (B-VG, Art. 14, Item 4[b]). This leads to a diverse regulatory environment in which Vienna plays a special role. The following is a rough overview of the legal situation in the states of Lower Austria, Carinthia and Vienna.

In the state of Lower Austria, one of the stated purposes of kindergarten is to make a "fundamental contribution to religious and ethical education" (Lower Austrian Kindergarten Act 2006, Sec. 3[1]). Also a "crucifix shall be displayed in all classrooms of such kindergartens in which the majority of pupils belong to a Christian denomination" (Sec. 12[2]).

A separate paragraph is devoted to religious education: "The kindergarten operator and administration shall grant legally-recognised churches and religious communities the opportunity to hold religious education classes for the children of their denomination in the public kindergarten for a maximum of one hour a week. The parents or guardians may withdraw their children from participating in such classes at any time, doing so in written form" (Sec. 29).

The state of Carinthia provides for a similar regulation concerning religious education in preschool: "Family education must be supported and supplemented according to social, ethical and religious values" (Carinthian Childcare Act 2011, Sec. 2).

By contrast, the Vienna Kindergarten Act (2003) does not contain any reference to religious education. The reasons for this are various: On the one hand, Vienna has a history of conflict between a politicised Catholic Church and Social Democrats, in particular during the Austrian "Ständestaat" of 1934 to 1938. To this day, the ubiquity of the phrase "Red Vienna" signals the influence of social democracy in the Austrian capital. On the other hand, the Viennese slogan that "Vienna is different" ("Wien ist anders") can be freely interpreted to mean that Vienna is also different in religious respects from other Austrian states, namely it is viewed as being more pluralist and secular. Unfortunately, there has been no reliable survey of Austrian religious affiliation since 2001. And yet, even the data from the 2001 census emphasises the more pluralist and secular character of Vienna.

Table 2: Religious denominations in Vienna and in Austria

Religious denominations	in Vienna		in Austria
	1991	2001	2001
Roman Catholic	57.8 %	49.2 %	73.6 %
No affiliation	19.8 %	25.6 %	12.0 %
Islamic	4.0 %	7.8 %	4.2 %
Orthodox		5.8 %	2.2 %
Protestant	5.4 %	4.7 %	4.7 %
Unspecified		4.2 %	2.0 %
Jewish	0.4 %	0.5 %	0.1 %
Old Catholic		0.5 %	0.2 %
Jehovah's Witnesses		0.3 %	0.3 %
Buddhist		0.3 %	0.1 %
Hindu		0.2 %	< 0.1 %
Other		0.8 %	1.3 %

According to the 2001 census, Roman Catholics represented about 49.2 % of the population in Vienna – in contrast to about 73.6 % throughout Austria. At the same time, the number of people reporting no religious affiliation was twice as high in Vienna than in Austria in general. This trend has continued in recent years. For example, in 2011, 11175 people in Vienna left the Roman Catholic Church (= 1.5 % of self-professed Catholics in 2001) and in 2017, 9839 members (= 1.6 %). Accordingly, 41.3 % of the Viennese population was Catholic in 2011, but only 32.9 % were Catholic at the turn of the year 2017/2018 (620434). So while the population of Vienna has grown significantly since 2001 (from 1.55 million in 2001 to 1.89 million in 2017), the number of Catholics is declining in absolute and relative terms.

Despite this, the city of Vienna remains on good speaking terms with its churches and religious communities and seeks cooperation with them. For several years now, the city has arranged and supported interreligious neighborhood fora. Naturally, another important basis for kindergartens are the education plans for preschool education, which are examined below.

1.2 Educational guidelines for preschool education

The *Austrian Educational Guidelines for Preschool Educational Institutions (Ämter der Landesregierungen der österreichischen Bundesländer et al. 2009)* were already mentioned in the introductory remarks. The guidelines' religious provisions are rather marginal because they must be in account with Vienna, which has no legal provisions for religious education in kindergarten. The relevant provision may be found in the education section, item 3.2 "Ethics and Society" and reads as follows:

> "The interest of children in the philosophy of life and the values of others can be engaged through conversation. In the process, questions of meaning and moral issues can be raised or addressed. The basis for this is furnished by children's intuitive approach to philosophical questions and their ability to transcend and transgress the subject matter boundaries. Various group traditions, worldviews and religions can serve to foster engaged discussion and become the basis for a respectful togetherness." (Ämter der Landesregierungen der österreichischen Bundesländer et al. 2009, 12)

The different ways in which the federal states refer to the religious dimension can also be demonstrated by comparing Vienna with Lower Austria: The *Educational Guidelines for Viennese Kindergartens (Magistratsabteilung 10 2006)* tend to avoid explicit mention of religion. Namely, there is an "area of emotional, social and ethical (ESE) competence" as well as an "ethics and values" category with three learning sub-areas. However, the word "religion" only appears incidentally. The *Educational Guidelines for Lower Austria (Amt der NÖ Landesregierung 2010)* are completely different. Here one finds, for example, a section in Article 2 titled "Ethics, religion and society", in which among other things, there is the following passage:

> "Kindergartens are reflections of society at large. Children from different nations, cultures and religions are therefore not uncommonly found in most kindergartens. Human rights form the basis for intercultural and interreligious coexistence, which demands respect for human dignity, respect for the diversity of cultures and religions, and the protection of minorities. Religious and interfaith education means stimulating learning processes that introduce children to the world of religions, allowing them to discover differences and similarities, and empowering them to engage each other with openness and interest" (Amt der NÖ Landesregierung 2010, 12).

The section titled "Key questions for reflecting on educational processes" states the following:

> – "To what extent is cultural and religious diversity taken into account in the children's group?"
> – "How important is the cultivation of values, traditions and interreligious education in my work, and what experience do I have with them?" (Amt der NÖ Landesregierung 2010, 16)

In all of this, it should be remembered that irrespective of the Austrian government, the church exerts a relatively large influence on preschool education. On the one hand, this may be observed in the large proportion of church-operated kindergartens. There are 700 Catholic, 37 Protestant, a few Jewish and a rapidly growing number of Islamic kindergartens. On the other hand, this is also made clear by the fact that 12 out of 30 of the educational institutions for training kindergarten teachers (Bildungsanstalten für Elementarpädagogik) in Austria are sponsored by the Catholic Church. Furthermore, Austria's only journal specialising in education and care in early childhood, "Unsere Kinder", is published by Caritas Austria.

With this in mind, it is not surprising that in 2010, under the scientific guidance of Silvia Habringer-Hagleitner (2006), the St. Nikolaus Children's Day Care Foundation (Archdiocese of Vienna) and Caritas (Austria) worked out guidelines explicitly for religious education. This document sought to supplement the Austrian guidelines by "formulating and elaborating religious educational work in preschool education" (Frick et al. 2010, 11). Philipp Klutz rightly points out in his analysis that these guidelines situate the child as a subject of religious learning and that also the elementary sphere now deals with philosophy for children and theology for children (2011, 68).

Last but not least: The Viennese municipal government has recently published explicit declarations in respect to religion in Kindergarten. Not only because of the highly controversial discussion about the Islamic kindergarten studies, a guideline was published in 2017, which is titled "Ethics in kindergarten" (Magistratsabteilung 10 2017). At first glance it appears wholly in line with earlier publications, as the title does not mention 'religion'. However, its subtitle is "Dealing with religions, worldviews and values", and also the two-page text calls for, among other things, a "culturally and religion-sensitive education" (Magistratsabteilung 10 2017, 1) for Viennese preschool educational and care institutions. Two points from these guidelines can be understood against the background of Ednan Aslan's preliminary study:

(1) "Preschool educational and care institutions in Vienna shall recognise and respect the following principles":

1. "The democratic constitutional state […] must be recognised. State laws have precedence over religious prescriptions.
2. The equality of non-religious and religious people and people of different religious affiliations shall be recognised.
3. Gender equality shall be recognised.
4. Openness and willingness to dialogue about social pluralism shall be maintained."

(2) "Viennese preschool educational and care institutions shall disclose whether and how they teach religious education". This section includes the following passage: "Religion as educational content is fundamentally not bound to a specific faith. If the day-to-day education of a preschool educational institution is based on a specific religious belief, parents or guardians must be clearly told how religious education takes place. Here, too, children shall not only be taught a single religion as an exclusive single worldview. Ethics, values, beliefs and religion figure in the lives of children attending non-denominational preschool educational institutions and are therefore also educational topics therein."

It should be critically noted, however, that this guideline does not proceed from a positive religious freedom and focuses on religion as knowledge primarily (Magistratsabteilung 10 2017, 17–18, 21–22). In our view, such statements would have been unthinkable without the commissioned study on Islamic kindergartens in Vienna by Ednan Aslan. Accordingly, the following section will examine this research in closer detail.

2. The commissioned studies on "Islamic kindergartens in Vienna"

Before looking at the commissioned studies themselves, it is important to pay attention to the context of these studies: in autumn 2009, a compulsory kindergarten year was introduced throughout Austria for 5-year-olds. At the same time, the City of Vienna established the "free kindergarten" (without fee) for everyone and fundamentally changed their kindergarten policy. Instead of expanding the public kindergarten, Vienna promoted private sponsors, who receive start-up funding for the creation of new kindergarten facilities. In addition, private providers receive support for the operation of the kindergarten in order to provide all parents with a "free kindergarten". While there were 74858 children in Vienna's kindergartens in 2008/09, this number increased to 96037 in 2016/17, of which only one third were in municipal kindergartens. In this expansion phase, there were numerous initiatives with special offers for Muslim children, including special food ("halal"). While Catholic and Protestant kindergartens are labelled as such, the label "Islamic" is not yet permissible. The Islamic Religious Community in Austria does not run kindergartens and so far has no regulations for the recognition of kindergartens as Islamic. Thus, a civic platform was created which was influenced by religion, but as such did not represent a legal entity. Since they made a specific contribution to the rapid expansion of kindergarten places (almost 30% in seven years), they were politically desirable as long as the formal quality standards were met. In fact, they have enabled traditionally Muslim families access to kindergarten who typically have difficulties accessing this public service. In municipal kindergartens, children whose parents can prove that they are both gainfully employed are preferred. This often is not the case for families with a so-called migration background, many of whom are engaged in precarious forms of employment. In addition, halal food is not offered in municipal kindergartens. Thus, the paradoxical situation arises that in municipal kindergartens Muslim elementary educators wear headscarves, while relatively few of the children are Muslim.

2.1 The preliminary study (Aslan 2016)

The vehemence of the quarrel that erupted in the media over Ednan Aslan's preliminary study entitled "Evaluation of selected kindergartens and groups: Trends and recommendations" (Aslan 2016) may be understood if one considers party political backgrounds: Initially, the City of Vienna, headed by the Social Democratic

Party of Austria (SPÖ) and the Green Party, commissioned Ednan Aslan to investigate the alleged existence of Islamic kindergartens and their Islamic character
in a scientific study. After this commission failed due to insufficient funding and
probably also political considerations, the Federal Ministry of Europe, Integration
and Foreign Affairs headed by Sebastian Kurz (ÖVP) took over this assignment
and made the preliminary study of Aslan possible. During the 2017 election cam-
paign, the weekly magazine *Falter* reported that ministry employees had revised
the study, sharpening certain statements within it. This led the University of Vienna
to commission the Austrian Agency for Scientific Integrity (OeAWI) as an external authority to conduct an audit. The audit detected no scientific misconduct, but
noted methodological shortcomings.

In terms of methodology, this 177-page project report on the one hand conducted
a document analysis of several Islamic organizations sponsoring kindergartens. On
the other hand, guided interviews were conducted with kindergarten administra-
tors, teachers and parents. The author points out that only eight of the requested
fifteen kindergartens were available for the interviews. The data analysis was carried out "in the manner of" Uwe Flick's thematic coding (Aslan 2016, 13). In fact,
the inter-subjective traceability of the coding is limited. Regarding the results of
this preliminary study, the focus here is on the document analysis of the sponsoring organizations. Four tendencies were identified: "Programmatic, mono-religious
orientation with Salafist traits and a tendency towards isolationism (A); political
and cultural Islamism with isolationist features (B); pragmatic religious orientation with strong economic interests (C); and expression in which an unconditional
openness to other cultures and religions prevails (D). Representatives of political
and cultural Islamism (B) as well as representatives with strong economic interests
(C) make up the majority of Islamic childcare facilities in Vienna. These tendencies were identified in the investigated kindergartens" (Aslan 2016, 111). This said,
the author makes sure to point out the following: "However, the amount of data is
not sufficient to support claims about the characteristics of these four tendencies
among the kindergartens. Doing so would require more comprehensive research"
(Aslan 2016, 111).

2.2 The main study (Aslan 2017; Hover-Reisner et al. 2017)

This highly anticipated main study, which was commissioned jointly by the City of
Vienna (Municipal Department 11 – Vienna Youth and Family Offices; hereunder,
abbreviated as MA 11) and the Federal Ministry for Europe, Integration and Foreign Affairs, was published in the form of two sub-studies: On the one hand, Ednan
Aslan published a 75-page study titled "Islamic kindergartens and groups: Motives
and strategies of the operators in the context of the City of Vienna (MA 11) and
expectations of the Muslim parents", in which 30 providers and 15 parents (only

women!) were interviewed and an analysis of the City of Vienna's handbooks was performed.

On the other hand, a project team from the FH Vienna Campus and the University of Vienna published a 212-page study titled "Plurality in Viennese kindergartens and children's groups with special consideration of so-called 'Islamic' institutions: Final report of the project part for the study of orientation and process quality". The design of the project team's sub-study can be described as follows (Hover-Reisner et al. 2017, 35–39): Initially, a quantitative questionnaire survey was conducted, aimed at all Viennese kindergartens and groups. Following this, the authors conducted a qualitative investigation by means of four group interviews, participatory observations in eleven kindergartens and an analysis of the City of Vienna's handbooks on "19 institutions with special emphasis on Islam" (Hover-Reisner et al. 2017, 120).

The differences between the two sub-studies lie not only in the study of different aspects of "Islamic" kindergartens, but also in a different understanding of the subject of the study. Aslan's sub-study defines certain characteristics that identify a kindergarten as "Islamic": Halal provisions, sponsoring organizations, kindergarten policies, classes on Islam and the Qur'an, kindergarten homepages, Islamic symbols and respective telephone information. If more than one of these characteristics applies, it can be called an Islamic kindergarten (Aslan 2017, 11–16). By contrast, the project team did not want to provide such a definition and preferred a discursive understanding of terms (Hover-Reisner et al. 2017, 11–13) such as the phrase "so-called 'Islamic' kindergartens and children's groups" or "preschool educational institutions with special emphasis on Islam" (Hover-Reisner et al. 2017, 13). However, it should be noted critically that in the course of the study, the authors did not attempt to discursively clarify these terms with, for instance, Muslim sponsoring organizations, leaders, teachers or parents. Instead, the authors used items in the questionnaire study to approximately identify and select kindergartens and children's groups with special emphasis on Islam for further group discussions (Hover-Reisner et al. 2017, 60). These questions referred to regular visits by religious scholars, Halal foods, or changing the way religion has been treated in the institution in the last two years.

One strength of the project team's study is that its analysis of the Ethics Guidelines of the City of Vienna (Hover-Reisner et al. 2017, 21) as well as other documents clearly shows that positive religious freedom in Vienna has not been sufficiently maintained and tendencies toward segregation and homogenization can emerge from the social majority (Hover-Reisner et al. 2017, 156–157). Another strength is the processing of the relevant research literature as well as the specific background of Viennese kindergartens (Hover-Reisner et al. 2017, 5–31). Fundamentally, the authors' decision to introduce "non-denominational" as well as "Christian" kindergartens for the purposes of contrasting is also informative (Hover-Reisner et al. 2017, 58–59). However, the disadvantage of this methodical approach is that only a limited number of cases can be analysed within the framework of a qualitative study, and thus the potential diversity among "Islamic" kindergartens as well as the potential issues associated with their categorization (e.g. as in Aslan's preliminary 2016 study with its four categories presented above) is not sufficiently represented.

Beyond the questionnaire survey, which was directed at all Viennese kindergartens and children's groups, only two group discussions (with three and six participants) were conducted with "Islamic" kindergartens. In retrospect, it emerged that of the nine participants from "Islamic" kindergartens who volunteered for the group interviews, most were non-denominational or Christian. Furthermore, the use of "Christian" kindergartens as contrasting foils is by no means successful within the scope of the group discussion, since only two persons were available, which fundamentally calls into question comparative and further inferences derived from doing so.

From a methodological point of view the participatory observation is questionable insofar as the observation was limited to one half a day. Helena Stockinger's dissertation (2017) has recently shown the limitations of such relatively brief field access. Also the questionnaire proves indirectly that some of the self-reporting by "Islamic kindergartens" should be treated with caution, due to the media and socio-political climate in which the responses were given. Indeed, according to the questionnaire study, only one institution indicated that it was guided by Islam (Hover-Reisner et al. 2017, 60), which would equal 0.2 % of the total sample of N=452 (Hover-Reisner et al. 2017, 47–49). And yet, the project team assumes that 35 institutions from the overall sample are Muslim (34.3 % of religiously oriented kindergartens and children's groups; Hover-Reisner et al. 2017, 49) basing this on its aforementioned definition.

Furthermore, with regard to the observation part, it is not unproblematic that in addition to the six kindergartens used for piloting the survey instruments, only five other kindergartens were observed for half a school day. In the process, also a kindergarten in Germany was interviewed without explaining the reasons for it, and the six kindergartens visited to pilot the survey instruments were also included in the evaluation without distinction. Finally, it is not easy to see how many "Islamic" kindergartens were observed for half a day. For all these reasons, it becomes clear that the scope of "Islamic" kindergartens in the project team's sub-study is not fully represented in terms of the potential diversity, as suggested by Aslan's preliminary study from 2016.

Speaking bluntly, it remains unclear to what extent the project team's study is able to elucidate the category of "Islamic" kindergartens in any differentiated way, which is certainly due to the uncertain situation in this research area after the preliminary study (Aslan 2016) was appropriated by the media and wider socio-political discourse.

Ultimately, this problematic research situation is also reflected in the main study of Aslan, which states as one of the main findings of his study: "Responses to the question of the importance of religious education in Islamic institutions vary

according to the source of information – interviews, websites and parental statements – or contradict each other." (Aslan 2017, 1)

3. The doctoral theses of Stockinger (2017) and Brandstetter (2017)

Against the background of the heated discussion about the commissioned studies, the
two doctoral theses of Stockinger and Brandstetter deserve attention, particularly as
their data collection was completed before the Aslan 2016 preliminary study.

3.1 Dealing with religious difference in kindergarten (Stockinger 2017)

The religious educational study by Helena Stockinger "Dealing with Religious
Difference in Kindergarten" investigates kindergartens of various religious institutions. For a year, the trained kindergarten teacher regularly visited both a kindergarten in Catholic and a kindergarten in Islamic sponsorship. Both are located in the
same district of the City of Vienna with a comparable catchment area. The children
in both kindergartens come from different religious traditions, with the majority of
children belonging to the religion of the responsible institution. Stockinger does
not present a comparative study because her subject was not a comparison between
a Christian and an Islamic kindergarten. Neither did she want to identify any specific characteristics of Islamic kindergartens. Her research question was a double
perspective: "How is religious difference treated in elementary educational institutions in Catholic and Islamic sponsorship in Vienna, and how do children address
them?" (Stockinger 2017, 60) Thus, the study looks at the children as actors and at
the same time the institutional parameters.

Based on the UN Charter on the Rights of the Child, the researcher attributes a
"right to difference" (Stockinger 2017, 16–17) to children, whereby difference is
understood as plurality and not exclusivity. Also the concept of religion has "the so-
cial-scientific dimension, with the concept of religiosity the anthropological dimension is in the foreground" (Stockinger 2017, 29). "Religious difference" includes
both dimensions that are considered inseparable. At the same time, "'religious difference' is seen as a dimension of difference that is intimately interwoven with
other dimensions such as cultural and linguistic difference" (Stockinger 2017, 40).
The methods of data collection were participatory observation, spontaneous and
initiated group discussions with children, but also with pedagogically responsible
persons as well as guided expert interviews. The author combines the ethnographic
approach with Grounded Theory (Corbin and Strauss 2008) and Thematic Coding
(Flick 2012) in the evaluation and offers a fitting example of triangulation. In accordance with the qualitative research approach and practical-theological claims,

she makes the subjectivity of the researcher recognisable in a separate chapter entitled "Reflection on Examination" (Stockinger 2017, 121–123). The "reflection of one's own ideas and one's own feelings" contributes to "achieving results that are as reliable and as valid as possible" (Stockinger 2017, 77). In conclusion, the author reflects on the results of her study in the context of the organizational discourse according to E. Schein and others, which constitutes the particularly original and innovative characteristic of this study.

While in kindergartens in Catholic sponsorship religion is an integral part of the kindergarten's daily routine (Stockinger 2017, 152–153), in kindergartens in Islamic sponsorship religion is treated exclusively in specific lessons on religion, commonly known as "Quran-lessons" and constitutes a voluntary supplementary offer. This is offered daily "in a reserved space, at a fixed time and with a colleague trained for it". So "religion should be clearly distinguishable from the rest of kindergarten everyday life and play no role in it" The degree of participation is determined by the parents (Stockinger 2017, 153). In both cases the principle of voluntariness is emphasised, but the conceptual considerations are incomplete "as religion and religious difference should occur in kindergarten" (Stockinger 2017, 154). Communication about religious difference may not take place for several reasons (Stockinger 2017, 162–167), e.g. because one wants to treat all children equally and avoid conflicts, because of the lack of knowledge or because religion is assigned to the realm of the "private". There is a link between the lack of communication about religious difference and the empirical fact that children of religious minorities avoid bringing up differences in religious background and generally refuse to talk about their religion and their religious expressions. "Instead of mentioning that they have not been present at certain festivals, the children maintain the appearance of having been there. The Muslim children, who were not present at St. Martin's festival, do not admit this in retrospect, do not comment on this or mention it only quietly and reservedly towards the end of the conversation" (Stockinger 2017, 175). Thus, Rw, a Muslim girl, does not respond to criticism about her absence at the St. Martin's festival in the group discussion, she barely speaks and does not respond to a question addressed to her about her attendance. "Only toward the end of the group discussion does she mention her absence at the celebration barely audibly by stating 'wasn't there'" (Stockinger 2017, 140). Children of minority religions see their affiliation to the group endangered if they are considered religiously different. "The children who recognise religious difference, often have no explanation for it and prioritise participation in the group over discussion of their religious identity." (Stockinger 2017, 244) A key challenge for kindergartens should be to enable group participation regardless of religious differences. There are clear differences between the children in the two kindergartens: In the "Catholic" kindergarten "it is apparent that children tend not to discuss religion and religious differences", in the "Islamic" kindergarten, however, Muslim children often talk about "religion and religious difference" and are "curious what other religions are like" (Stockinger 2017, 168).

The dominating religion of the majority proves to be determining of normality in both kindergartens. At the same time, religious differences are not addressed and the smaller religions receive little recognition. "Children of the minority religions can either adapt or remain absent from certain offers, the potential of their own religion is not visible in the everyday life of the kindergarten." (Stockinger 2017, 245) The study shows how much the children's willingness and ability to address their own religion and its expressions is dependent on how religious practice is lived and reflected in the organization. The reflection of the study in the horizon of the organizational discourse of E. Schein (1992) makes these connections comprehensible. In conclusion, Stockinger calls for the development of a non-discriminatory "culture of recognition". According to the results of their study, children need a "safe space" of recognition to be able to address differences, especially religious differences. "In kindergarten it is possible to recognise religious differences and to practice respect for different religions with children." (Stockinger 2017, 245)

The importance of organization and organizational culture, as identified in Stockinger's study, should be considered in the future, especially in projects on childhood research. One should not focus solely on the child's opinion, but include the organizational context. It is highly relevant for further research to focus on kindergartens in secular sponsorship as well as in rural areas and to pay particular attention to differences in the worldviews (Stockinger 2017, 245–246).

3.2 Between homogenization and pluralization (Brandstetter 2017)

The intercultural-theological study by Bettina Brandstetter, a trained kindergarten teacher, sees kindergarten as a "place where public discourses on culture, religions and identities take place". Brandstetter "pursues those confrontations and complexities within kindergarten that are primarily related to cultural diversity and religious plurality" (Brandstetter 2017, 12). Elementary educators employ forms of action for securing a serene experience of childhood in the kindergarten, the discursive strategy of which the researcher calls "homogenization" ("We are all one family") and "pluralization" ("diversity is enriching"). They focus primarily not on (religious) pedagogical issues, but their "interest lies in the intercultural cross-sectional task that the kindergarten shares with intercultural theologies" (Brandstetter 2017, 12). She sees the "kindergarten as locus theologicus alienus" and locates it "in the mirror of intercultural theologies".

The study explores the question: what role do discourses play in cultural diversity and religious plurality in everyday working life of elementary educators? In the opening theoretical discussion, the author argues for the "necessity of a critical discourse analysis" (S. Jäger 2015) and a "postcolonial perspective in kindergartens". Thus, "power and power relations at the kindergarten […] are to be disclosed" to what extent "orders and action strategies work with precarious constructions of identity that bring children, families but also the educators into situations in which they struggle for recognition of their dignity" (Brandstetter 2017, 83). The author sees the possibility of transgressing into spaces "as a space of negotiation of cultural and religious identities" (Brandstetter 2017, 79). This happens "when problems cannot be solved using current strategies" (Brandstetter 2017, 85). Brandstetter uses the research attitude (not method) of Grounded Theory. Twenty-two observation protocols obtained by participatory observation at a kindergarten in the City of Salzburg serve as an exploratory preliminary survey. The transcripts of eight interviews with elementary educators (23 to 52 years old) of various professions in Austria were subjected to a content analysis (Mayring 2010) and a "post-colonial informed discourse analysis" (Brandstetter 2018, 8). "The paraphrased and category-based interview sections" were "analysed along the previously created discursive network" to highlight "the characteristics of homogenization and pluralization, highlighting underlying dominant discourses and their disciplinary effect". Especially elaborated "were identity constructions, representations and discourse positions". With the help of "different readings, hidden and repressed positions could also be revealed" (Brandstetter 2017, 101). In the public debate on so-called "Islamic kindergartens", the religious coding "Islamic" also connotes topics such as educational quality, language development, training of pedagogical personnel and social connectivity (Brandstetter 2017, 8). This is clearly shown in the "Interview with Helena" (Brandstetter 2017, 190–212). The interviewee graduated with a focus on migration studies, is in her first year of service and changed after one semester from a "Muslim kindergarten" in private sponsorship into a "municipal kindergarten". She describes these two kindergartens differently, associating one with religion ("Muslim") and not the other. She assigns a homogenising orientation to the former, while emphasising pluralization to the latter.

The interviewee refers to the "Muslim kindergarten" in an interview "as pre-modern and educationally remote" with a poorly trained staff, an "untimely pedagogy" in which "the children did not learn German". This private kindergarten would be "a 'parallel society' that lags far behind local claims" (Brandstetter 2017, 8). With the help of "a post-colonially informed, discourse-analytically guided reading" (Brandstetter 2017, 8), a completely different approach opens up for the same kindergarten. The 'Turkish Muslim' head of the kindergarten completed her training in Turkey and Austria, something the interviewee does not believe. She focuses on education and the acquisition of the German language, but fails, according to her surveyed colleague. The director deliberately presents the kindergarten as secular, open and social. Nevertheless, he is marked by the interviewee as 'Muslim' and stigmatised as pre-modern (Brandstetter 2017, 8). The interviewee experiences "little recognition in this kindergarten", feels like a "stranger" despite belonging to the majority society. She cannot live up to the educational requirements "and cannot assume her – otherwise socially self-evident – hegemonic position" (Brandstetter 2017, 9). As the interviewee feels "lost" here, after one semester she moves to a "municipal kindergarten", which she describes as the complete opposite of the "Muslim kindergarten". The narratives are based on a black and white construction, according to which the "municipal kindergarten" was completely successful and the "Muslim kindergarten" had completely failed. However, she is not deterred by the contradictions and breaks in her story. Brandstetter shows how much the discourse about "Islamic" kindergartens takes place in the dichotomy "German-speaking" versus "Muslim". Religion functions as a social difference category and binary identity politics dominate. The argument, according to Brandstetter, makes use of "the construction of a 'we' confronted with the construction of the 'others'." The strategy of homogenization (the unification associated with "we") and the strategy of pluralization (the 'others' constructed in their 'otherness') support this state of affairs and are linked to the generated dichotomy of intensifying discourses.

According to Brandstetter, there is an "in-between space" between homogenization and pluralization (Brandstetter 2017, 77–85), because neither of the two strategies (homogenization, pluralization) can be enforced in the long run, they "reach their limits and demand the failure of their binary coding for something else, they call for creative solutions and alternatives" (Brandstetter 2017, 11). Thus, between the two there arise – often surprising – creative spaces. In these spaces "identity discourses and power relations can be processed", the "binary coding" can be overcome. There are several examples of such gaps in the Brandstetter study interviews. For example, if an elementary educator "recognises the underlying question of identity in the child's orientation search" and does not resolve it. "In doing so, he or she opens up a space for a negotiation process, which the child will finally resolve for him or herself." (Brandstetter 2017, 11) Or if a teacher succeeds in "opening a space for parents of different religions to meet and discuss their own tradition or religion in dialogue" (Brandstetter 2017, 11–12). In all the cases, "educators take the limitations of homogenization and pluralization seriously", perceive related discourses of identity and open possible alternatives. In this way identity issues, religious plurality and cultural imprints can be related to each other (Brandstetter 2017, 12). The author argues for a specific "competence of the in-between space" (Brandstetter 2017, 289–293). On the one hand, this refers to the space between homogenization and pluralization and, on the other hand, to those competences resulting from Salzburg's intercultural theologies (responsive competence, polyloge competence, alterity competence, localization competence for hybridity, comparative competence) (Brandstetter 2017, 290). This "competence on a meta-level" enables elementary educators to "deal with the surprises that arise through cultural diversity and religious plurality in pedagogical everyday life", also because they resist "the gravitational pull of either pure homogenization or pluralization" (Brandstetter 2017, 290). Brandstetter comes to the following conclusion after completing her study: "A religious pedagogy that allows for in-between spaces, that transcends dichotomous logics and resolves ambiguities not by immediate homogenization or pluralization, can contribute to the discussion of precarious social identity politics, discourses and power relations in a space dedicated to that purpose." Associated conflicts and ambiguities should be kept in suspension and attended to in a sensitive manner. In these in-between spaces, "it would be possible to reverse power relations and empower disadvantaged individuals". This requires "discourse-sensitive religious education" (Brandstetter 2017, 12–13).

4. Summary and outlook

With regard to fundamental questions of research, the commissioned studies draw attention to the problem of contractual research. If party political interest decides on the approval or rejection of such socially relevant research assignments, then the research results are subject to party interest and exploitation. There are currently no legally and ethically clear rules for the design of the relationship between client and contractor in place which are designed to protect the researchers and the research project. Overall, it would have been desirable for both sub-studies to have been brought closer together: Ednan Aslan's sub-study examined issues of certain types of "Islamic" kindergartens as well as religion-displacing activities of the City of Vienna, which started as a result of his preliminary study (Aslan 2017, 16–33, 65–66). On the other hand, the project team's study reveals rather critical points, how the Viennese social majority contributes to the segregation of Muslims – while "Islamic" kindergartens are inadequately considered in their potential diversity and issues.

In summary, it can be stated that the overall study of "Islamic" kindergartens demonstrates how scientific research in the field of "Islamic" kindergartens in Austria is currently reaching its limits. Simply put, reliable data is difficult to collect amid the current media and socio-political climate. This was further impaired by the main study being subjected to a great deal of time pressure on the part of the client, which can explain methodological problems such as the insufficient dataset in the group interviews as well as the brief field observations.

Nevertheless, a positive effect of the two sub-studies can be identified. Their results became "motivation boost" for the Islamic Religious Community in Austria (IGGÖ) to create a set of approval standards for "Islamic kindergartens": "The focus would be on child-friendly mediation of spiritual aspects, 'with special attention to diversity and mutual acceptance.' The highest value would be placed on inter-Islamic pluralism as well. Images of a punitive God, as criticised by Aslan, are just as taboo as black-and-white thinking."

The studies of Stockinger and Brandstetter show how theology can be relevant as a reflection and reference horizon for empirical religious pedagogical research: in Stockinger's case, this is the reference to practical theology (Norbert Mette), in Brandstetter's the anchoring in intercultural theology. Both show how fruitful the integration of discourses foreign to the field is for empirical research in religious education: in Stockinger's case this is the organizational discourse, in Brandstetter's it is postcolonial discourse. It would be desirable to set the conceptions of kindergarten as a "safe space", for which Stockinger argues, and of the kindergarten as an "in-between space", which Brandstetter unfolded, in relation to each other. It is still unclear how these designs can be understood as complementary rather than exclusive.

All of the studies presented here provide a wealth of clues as to how much of pre-primary education lacks mature concepts for culturally and religiously heterogeneous contexts, so efforts are made in state/city institutions and so-called "Islamic" kindergartens to stage religion-free everyday life. Conversely, in church kindergartens the church year and everyday life are associated with the Christian faith, yet other religious traditions that are important to children do not receive suitable attention.

Finally, looking back at the Austrian discussion on Islamic kindergartens with regard to the question of formal and non-formal education, there are also fluid transitions and changing transitional areas: on the one hand, education in pre-schools is becoming more formal as there are several new regulations, on the other hand, due to the regulations of Vienna, the religious education in Islamic Kindergarten is becoming less formal, as it is more often more hidden than before.

References

Amt der NÖ Landesregierung (2010). *Bildungsplan für Kindergärten in Niederösterreich.* http://www.noe.gv.at/noe/Kindergaerten-Schulen/Bildungsplan_Niederoesterreich_.pdf [08.03.2019].

Ämter der Landesregierungen der österreichischen Bundesländer, Magistrat der Stadt Wien and Bundesministerium für Unterricht, Kunst und Kultur (2009). *Bundesländerübergreifender BildungsRahmenPlan für elementare Bildungseinrichtungen in Österreich.* https://bildung.bmbwf.gv.at/ministerium/vp/2009/bildungsrahmenplan_18698.pdf [08.03.2019].

Aslan, E. (2016). Projektbericht. *Evaluierung ausgewählter Islamischer Kindergärten und -gruppen in Wien. Tendenzen und Empfehlungen.* https://www.bmeia.gv.at/fileadmin/ user_upload/Zentrale/Integration/Studien/Abschlussbericht__Vorstudie_Islamische_ Kindergarten_Wien_final.pdf [08.03.2019].

Aslan, E. (2017). *Islamische Kindergärten und -gruppen. Motive und Strategien der BetreiberInnen im Kontext der Stadt Wien (MA11) und Erwartungen muslimischer Eltern.* http://medienportal.univie.ac.at/uploads/media/KIGA_STUDIE_FINAL_ASLAN_14. 12.2017-2.pdf [08.03.2019].

Brandstetter, B. (2017). *Zwischen Homogenisierung und Pluralisierung. Der Ort der Kindergartenpädagogin in der Heterogenität von Kulturen und Religionen* (unpublished dissertation). Universität Salzburg, Austria.

Brandstetter, B. (2018). Die umstrittene Religionspluralität im Kindergarten. Elementarpädagogik im Zwischenraum. In: *ÖRF* 26, 7–14. http://unipub.uni-graz.at/download/pdf/ 2568674?name=Brandstetter%20Bettina%20Die%20umstrittene%20Religionspluralit% C3%A4t%20im%20Kindergarten [08.03.2019].

Corbin, J., and Strauss, A. (2008). *Basics of Qualitative Research.* Los Angeles et al.: Sage Publications [1990 and 1998 eds. present Strauss as the first author and Corbin as second].

Flick, U. (2012). *Qualitative Sozialforschung. Eine Einführung.* Reinbek bei Hamburg: Rowohlt.

Frick, E., Haas, S., Peterseil, J., Stadlbauer, U., and Walter, E. (2010). *Religionspädagogischer BildungsRahmenPlan für elementare Bildungseinrichtungen in Österreich*. Wien, Linz: Fachverlag UNSERE KINDER.

Habringer-Hagleitner, S. (2006). *Zusammenleben im Kindergarten. Modelle religionspädagogischer Praxis*. Stuttgart: Kohlhammer.

Hover-Reisner, N., Steiner, E., Fürstaller, M., Habringer, M., Eckstein-Madry, T., Schluß, H., Andersen, C., and Medeni, E. (2017). *Pluralität in Wiener Kindergärten und Kindergruppen unter besonderer Berücksichtigung sogenannter "islamischer" Einrichtungen. Abschlussbericht des Projektteils zur Untersuchung von Orientierungs- und Prozessqualität*. https://www.fh-campuswien.ac.at/fileadmin/redakteure/News/Dokumente/Abschlussbericht-PLUKI-Wien-Islam-Qualitaet-Final2.pdf [08.03.2019].

Jäger, S. (2015). *Kritische Diskursanalyse. Eine Einführung*. Münster: Unrast.

Klutz, P. (2011). Religiöse Elementarbildung in Österreich. Vorstellung und Analyse des Religionspädagogischen BildungsRahmenPlans. In: *Österreichisches Religionspädagogisches Forum* 19, 68–70.

Kromer, I., and Hajszan, M. (2015). Jungschar als zentraler Ort non-formaler Bildung in katholischen Pfarren Österreichs. Ausgewählte Ergebnisse einer umfassenden empirischen Studie. In: *Österreichisches Religionspädagogisches Forum* 23, 121–129.

Magistratsabteilung 10 (2006). *Bildungsplan für Wiener Kindergärten*. https://www.wien.gv.at/bildung/kindergarten/pdf/bildungsplan.pdf [08.03.2019].

Magistratsabteilung 10 (2017). *Ethik im Kindergarten. Vom Umgang mit Religionen, Weltanschauungen und Werten*. https://www.wien.gv.at/bildung/kindergarten/pdf/ethik-kiga.pdf [08.03.2019].

Mayring, Ph. (2010). *Qualitative Inhaltsanalyse. Grundlagen und Techniken*. Weinheim/Basel: Beltz.

OECD (2006). *Starting Strong: Early Childhood Education and Care Policy. Country Note for Austria*. http://www.oecd.org/education/school/36472878.pdf [08.03.2019].

Schein, E. H. (1992). *Organizational Culture and Leadership*. San Francisco: Jossey-Bass.

Stockinger, H. (2017). *Umgang mit religiöser Differenz im Kindergarten. Eine ethnographische Studie an Einrichtungen in katholischer und islamischer Trägerschaft in Wien* (Religious Diversity and Education 35). Münster, New York: Waxmann.

III
Sunday School

Researching non-formal religious education in the Orthodox Church

The first empirical study on Sunday Schools in Belarus

Yauheniya Danilovich

Non-formal religious education has an important place in the Orthodox Church. Through religious education, the Orthodox Church assumes its responsibility for the processes of the tradition and supports the church's socialization of church members. The field of non-formal education in the Orthodox Church includes many formats for people of different ages. One of them is the well-established format of the Sunday School. With the existing theoretical foundation and reflection of religious education, the practice of non-formal religious education in the Orthodox Church has so far been covered by empirical research only marginally. Conducting research on the practices of religious education of the Orthodox Church not only provides critical insights and new impulses for further developments, but also can stimulate a kind of reflection on the theory of Orthodox religious education.

1. Non-formal Orthodox religious education in the Orthodox Church

This article will focus on Sunday Schools in Belarus (Belarussian Orthodox Church, Patriarchate of Moscow). At the same time, the aim is to present an Orthodox perspective on non-formal religious education, which is more or less common for all Orthodox churches. References are made to several Orthodox churches and contexts of Orthodox religious education.

The Orthodox Church sees itself as the one church in uninterrupted continuity with the Old Church, preserving and proclaiming (unadulterated) the doctrine of Christ and the entire Apostolic tradition. Despite the existence of several Orthodox Churches, it sees itself as the one Orthodox Church. There are no dogmatic, canonical or substantial liturgical differences between the individual Orthodox Churches. There is a full ecclesial-sacramental community between the different Orthodox Churches. The one Orthodoxy consists of a community of (autocephalic) Churches (Leb and Ursa 2016, 11).

The main aim of Orthodox religious education is the integration of the person into the church life. In this context, "church" is understood as "the mystical Body of Christ". Constance Tarasar explains the aims of (non-formal) Orthodox religious education with the following citation: "The aim of all religious teaching in the Orthodox Church is to introduce the child (or the adult) into the Church, to integrate him into her life – the life of grace, communion with God, love, unity, and spiritual progress towards eternal salvation, for such are the essential aims of the Church." (Tarasar 1966, 459) In brief, the main aim is the integration into the Church life, which in Russian is called "Воцерковление" (Wotserkowlenie). In English it can be translated with "Churching". The emphasis lies on catechetical contents, like knowledge about the Orthodox faith, tradition, Orthodox worship and festivities but also on the study of the Bible and ethical issues.

2. Sunday School as a concept of non-formal religious education

First some general information on the concept of Sunday School and its role in the Orthodox Church should be given. Sunday School is in contrast to "normal" schools non-compulsory. However, Sunday School has an institutional framework as its basis. This institutional reference allows Sunday School to be categorised as non-formal education and not as informal education (Schweitzer 2017, 1). This contribution is based on Sunday School in the Russian Orthodox Church.

The beginnings of Sunday School in the Russian Orthodox Church can be found in 1840. Before 1917 (the October Revolution), the original aim of the Sunday School was alphabetization. Priests invited adult people to come together on Sunday in order to learn to read (and to write). After the October Revolution and during the next 70 years of Communism, practically all forms of religious education were forbidden. It was only in the 1990s when Sunday Schools were reopened. The main aim of the present concept of Sunday School is the catechesis of children and youths.

2.1 Institutional presuppositions, didactics, participants

As mentioned before, participation in Sunday School is not mandatory. Usually, there is no age limit for the participants. From pre-school age on, children can attend Sunday School. Some Sunday Schools also have adult participants. At the end of Sunday School attendance, there is no kind of initiation rite like First Communion or confirmation.[1] Contents and organization, like group size, number of teachers and schedule of the Sunday School are decided upon by the individual parishes. In a small village parish, for example, there may only be one group in which children of different ages come together. In the large parishes, if there is enough space and teachers, there is often the opportunity to teach in age-differentiated groups. The duration of Sunday School attendance also varies from parish to parish. In terms of didactics, Sunday School falls between general youth work and traditional school

---

1 In this respect Sunday School is not a kind of equivalent of confirmation work.

teaching. Sunday School usually includes formal teaching with the lessons usually taking place on Sundays. Sunday School includes also many other activities like playing games, doing creative projects, internships, camps, outings, pilgrimage, theatrical performance, choir, etc. The teachers can be priests or other persons.

There is no exact data concerning the participation rates. This is partly because participation is usually not tightly controlled. Furthermore, there is no statistical data on the size of individual parishes. But it still can be said that Sunday School is the biggest and best developed offer of religious education in the Russian Orthodox Church. This can partly be explained by the fact that religious education is not a regular subject at school.

3. Research on non-formal Orthodox religious education

The current discourse about Orthodox religious education merely comprises historical accounts and systematic analysis. So far, empirical studies on Orthodox religious education have not gained much interest. But there are some studies, that more or less indirectly, have to do with religious education and are thus beneficial for the research work in this field.

Until now, studies on Orthodox youth mainly emphasised religious attitudes, religious self-assessment (Kulakov 1997), discrepancy between church integration and religious attitudes (Kozyrev 2003; Bakrač 2011; Mora, Stavrinides and McDermut 2014), attitudes towards Religious Education at school (Карасёва and Шкурова 2015) and values.

In 1993, for example, James A. Athanasou did research on Greek Orthodox youth in Australia, who attended Sunday School. He collected data from 254 youth (113 female and 141 male) with an average age of 14.3 years (Athanasou 1993). The emphasis of the study was on religious practices like attendance at Sacraments (Lord Supper, confession), fasting, reading the Bible and praying. This study did not emphasise Sunday School as non-formal religious education.

The lack of empirical research on Orthodox religious education concerns not only the field of non-formal religious education; empirical work has not yet enriched the Orthodox religious education. But why has Orthodox religious education been, so far, so much neglected by empirical research? In the following, some first considerations to this point will be made.

First of all, in many countries Orthodox religious education as an independent theological discipline of theological education is not very developed. Here the example of Belarus can be made: Although theological education is developed to a certain extent, there is no institutional research facility for Orthodox religious education, as for example a professorship (see http://minda.by). There is the same situation in Germany. The emphasis is on theological contents (studies on church history, New and Old Testament, liturgical theology) but not on religious education. Religious education as a discipline of practical theology has definitely not the same prominence as other theological disciplines in the Orthodox theological education. So if there is no significant awareness for the field of religious education, research in the field is also not very significant. From this point of view, there is no structural opportunity for the field of Orthodox practical theology to take initiative for research in the field of non-formal religious education.

The Orthodox Church itself does not take the initiative to research non-formal religious education. For this kind of research, though, a form of cooperation between the Church and the researchers is needed. So, very often the initiative is not taken by church leaders like bishops, but by representatives of the sciences, for example, the social sciences. It has to be stated, though, that their research is only rarely supported by the Orthodox Church.

Also the legacy of the Communist era plays an important role in this context: During Communism, every development of religious education was prohibited, which is why there was no research on religious education.

Further, in the Orthodoxy tradition plays a very important role in comparison to other Christian denominations. Tradition is understood in two ways within Orthodoxy. On the one hand, it is more or less of a fix content: The tradition includes, for example, liturgical heritage, decisions of ecumenical councils, legacy of the church fathers. The processes of change in terms of tradition within Orthodoxy are difficult to imagine. On the other hand, tradition is understood as the living faith and God-experience of the church as the body of Christ (Florovsky 1951; Ivliev 2000).

As it has been pointed out above, one of the goals of formal as well as non-formal Orthodox religious education is the integration of children or youth into church life. At the same time, religious education processes are predominantly conceived as traditional processes whereas the focus is not always on youth as subjects. This can be clearly seen, for example, in the statements of the Orthodox Bishops' Conference in Germany on Orthodox Religious Education at school. According to the pastoral messages from the year 2011 and 2017, the main task of Orthodox religious education is the transmission of tradition (Orthodoxe Bischofskonferenz in Deutschland 2011, 2017). Tradition in this sense prevails over pupils as active subjects of religious learning. The learners should be integrated into tradition. It should be considered to what extent this objectification and authority of tradition leads to religious didactics that is less subject-oriented. A presumption could be made here: authority of tradition is so dominant that it could almost replace religious didactics and make subject orientation superfluous. Such a normative attitude can inhibit empirical research on religious education.

In sum then, it has become clear that both formal and non-formal Orthodox religious education have not been a main concern of empirical research so far. Also the topic of Sunday School has not yet been the object of major empirical studies.

Recently, awareness for the need of empirical research on Orthodox religious education has developed. One of the reasons for this awareness is, from the author's point of view, the gap between a systematical approach which means for example the theory of Orthodox religious education, and practice, as for example, the disillusioning real situation. One of the examples for this gap is the already mentioned concept of integration into the church life ("Churching"). This aim is contrary to the real process of continuous dis-integration of the youth from the church. This process is seen as problematic, because also young people who were integrated in the church are leaving the church (Orechanov 2015, 400). It becomes clear that the dis-integration of young people from the church life is a real problem (Orechanov 2015). At the same time, there is no empirical research or empirical data about this phenomenon. In the discourse there are some attempts to identify the reasons and to find solutions for this problem, but these attempts are based on theory. In this context, a negative image of youth is constructed. It is said that they did not really understand the meaning of Orthodox religious education. At the same time, the situation and attitudes of youth are sometimes ignored in Orthodox religious education.

These problems can be identified because of this gap between the aims of religious education and the disillusioning reality. So it could be beneficial to evaluate these assumptions with empirical research.

4. The first study on Sunday Schools in Belarus

4.1 The aims of the study and the research questions

The main aim of the present study was to gain first insights in the field of religious education in the Orthodox Church as well as to get to know the perspective of the Orthodox youth who attend Sunday School. The aim of the study was to achieve an empirical description of religious education from the perspective of the youth. The main questions refer to the experiences of the youth who attend the Sunday School. What do they want to know? What are their motives for participation? What religious and social attitudes do they have? Do the youth see the effect of religious education of Sunday School?

Religious education is not only limited to Sunday School lessons, but also extends to the Orthodox worship. Many Orthodox theologians make reference to the parish and especially worship as a central place of religious education and learning processes. In this respect the present study emphasised the following questions: How do the youth encounter the Orthodox worship services? How can we describe worship as a place to learn and as a place of religious education? What kind of problems do the youth face during worship? Do they really learn something new during worship and how can we describe the effects of the learning process?

4.2 Research design and procedures

In the following, first a brief description of the project's design and procedures will be given and then some of its main results will be summarised.

Sample

The present study is concerned with the Sunday Schools of the Belarussian Orthodox Church, which is a canonical part of the Russian Orthodox Church (Patriarchate
of Moscow). When the study was conducted (2012), the Belarussian Orthodox
Church consisted of 11 dioceses[2] with 1555 parishes and 654 Sunday Schools. Not
every parish, though, had a Sunday School (Danilovich 2016b, 234).

All dioceses of the Belarussian Orthodox Church were asked to participate in
the study. Finally, the study was conducted in six (of eleven) dioceses collecting
data from 38 Sunday Schools of the 654 Sunday Schools in Belarus (5.8% of the
Sunday Schools and 11.3% of the 336 Sunday Schools in the involved dioceses).
479 youths (295 females and 184 males) with an average age of 12.9 years were
interviewed. It is hard, though, to judge the representativeness of the sample because no data is available on how many children and youth attend Sunday school in
Belarus.

Questionnaire

This study was the first of its kind in terms of research about non-formal Orthodox
religious education. For this reason it was considered useful to use experiences from
other studies in this field. So, the present study is partially based upon research on
confirmation work in Germany (Schweitzer et al. 2010); for example, some items
were taken from the questionnaire used in this study in order to make it possible
to compare the results of both studies. At the same time, the present study had to
be sensitive to the different presuppositions in Belarus. Many of these differences
were based on denominational differences. This means that the questionnaires had
to be adapted to the country-specific and denomination-specific settings. Although
the questionnaire also included qualitative items, the study is mainly based on a
quantitative approach.

The questionnaires were filled out by the youth during their Sunday School lesson at only one point of time. All of them were assured that the results would be
anonymous. All questionnaires were recorded manually into the software SPSS and
analysed statistically, which was the task of sociologist Yuri Chernyak from Belarussian State University. The analyses affirm that most youth were indeed very
open to the questions and felt that they were taken seriously by the questions about
their experiences and opinions. The results of the study are accessible in two publications (Danilovich 2016b; Danilovich et al. 2014).

---

2 For comparison: today it consists of 15 dioceses. The territory did not become larger, only
  some larger dioceses were divided into some smaller ones.

4.3 Selected results

In the following, some of the results will be presented concerning the situation of Sunday School, the effects of religious education at Sunday School and the issue of worship services as a place of Orthodox religious education.

Participants

The age limits were set to only include youth aged 12 to 15 years. The aim of the study was a comparison with confirmation work in Germany. Therefore, respondents at this age were selected. The age range is approximately the same as the age of the German confirmands. However, Sunday School participants in general also include children and adults. Table 1 displays the sample in terms of ages. The mode (the most frequent value) is 12 years. In terms of the age of the participants, there is a clear tendency, the older the youth were, the less often they attended Sunday School. This can be explained in two ways. First, some Sunday Schools set an age limit for the participants. A second explanation could be that with increasing age the interest of youth to attend Sunday School decreases and Sunday School is no longer competitive anymore with other free time opportunities.

Table 1: Proportion of age groups

12 years	43.2%
13 years	27.6%
14 years	17.1%
15 years	10.0%

Most of the participants come from a religious family or perceive their family as religious. Table 2 displays how often youth attend a church service. The answers indicate that the participants have quite a close relationship to church attendance. Overall, 82.1% of the respondents attend a church service at least one time per month. Almost half of the respondents (46.7%) attend a church service every Sunday and the major holidays. In Sunday School, attending church services is usually not mandatory.

Table 2: Participation in worship services

How often do you attend services?	
Every Sunday and the major holidays	46.8%
A few times a month	35.3%
Only on special occasions	18.0%

The questionnaire included a question about which persons children and youth go to church with (Table 3). There was more than one answer possible. 69.3% mentioned their parents, followed by friends (32.4%), grandparents (27.3%), and other relatives (15.9%).

Table 3: "With whom do you attend services?" (more than one box could be ticked)

With my parents	69.3%
With my friends	32.4%
With my grandmother and (or) grandfather	27.3%
With other relatives	15.9%
Someone else	7.5%

In terms of the church attendance of the parents, the situation is different. Some of them attend church services very often, at the same time some parents rarely do so. Fasting[3] is practiced by most of the families. Overall, 83.4% of the families fast in one way or another. Only 8.6% of the respondents declared that their families do not fast in any way. The items in terms of central contents of Christian belief like "God created the world", "There is life after death" and so on received high approval from the youth.

In summary, it became clear that the youth who attend Sunday School have a close relationship to the church and worship services as well as Christianity and church practice play an important role for them.

Sunday School lessons

The three most important factors of motivation to attend Sunday School (Table 4) named by the respondents are the own decision (75.2%), the will of the parents (22.3%) and the friends (18.0%). In terms of the answers to the open questions, participants appreciated Sunday School as a place to meet youth with similar interests. Respondents expressed the wish that their peers would join Sunday School and the church life. At the same time, every fourth (26.3%) agreed with the item "Sometimes I am ashamed to tell my friends that I participate in Sunday School". This could indicate that Sunday School attendance is not to be taken for granted in Belarus.

---

3 Fasting at certain periods of the liturgical church year (for example, before Christmas or Easter) and on single days (for example on Wednesdays and Fridays) forms an essential element of Orthodox spirituality and piety and includes food regulations such as abstinence from all meat, dairy and egg products as well as oil and wine.

Table 4: Reasons to attend Sunday School (more than one box could be ticked)

Because I wanted that myself	75.2%
Because my parents wanted me to do so	22.3%
Because my friends do so as well	18.0%
Others, i.e.	9.6%
Because my grandparents wanted me to do so	9.4%
Because I have been told that Sunday School is fun	8.4%
Because I was invited personally (by a priest, by somebody from the parish)	6.7%

The youth's preferences of topics to be brought up during the Sunday School lessons are shown in Table 5, ranked by importance. The issues "Miracles" (70.6%), "The Stories about the Saints" (68.9%), "Jesus Christ" (60.5%) and "God" (57.8%) interest most of the Sunday School participants, whereas they are not very interested in issues such as "Sects" and "Other Religions".

Table 5: Topics in Sunday School

What about your interest in these topics?	
Miracles	70.6%
Stories about the saints	68.9%
Jesus Christ	60.5%
God	57.8%
Bible stories	55.9%
Pray	43.4%
Sacraments	42.8%
Mother of God	40.9%
The Bible	38.8%
Faith and not-faith	31.9%
Course and meaning of the worship service	25.1%
Problems in school and family	24.8%
Other religions	19.2%
Sects	16.3%

Some items of the questionnaire aimed at an evaluation of the Sunday School lessons. The respective results are presented in Table 6. In this regard, most participants show high approval of the effects of religious education at Sunday School. No matter which question was asked, less than 10% would disagree with the idea that Sunday School has positive effects in one way or another. It is noteworthy, that especially competences in terms of individual religious attitudes were approved of most, that is competences that are difficult to evaluate and cannot be grasped as only cognitive ones, like: "to know more about God and faith", "to have been strengthened in my faith". All other items considered more the cognitive competences. Respondents appreciated also the activities beyond the regular lessons, like excursions or different projects.

Table 6: "How does Sunday School help you?"

How do Sunday School lessons help you ...?	help a lot/rather help	rather don't help/don't help at all	difficult to answer
to understand Orthodox tradition	96.5 %	1.2 %	2.3 %
to understand the meaning of procedure during the worship	95.2 %	1.5 %	3.3 %
to know more about God and faith	97.5 %	0.2 %	2.3 %
to have been strengthened in my faith	97.1 %	0.4 %	2.5 %
to understand the meaning of religious texts (Bible, prayers, preaching, icons, etc.)	94.2 %	1.7 %	4.2 %
to discuss competently about religious topics	90.6 %	2.7 %	6.7 %

The general satisfaction with Sunday School is high. Across the participating dioceses, Sunday School receives very high approval from the youth. The average for the participating dioceses is 95.4 % approval from the youth – a result that should be counted as a real success, even if the present study is only a snapshot.

Worship services as a place of religious education?

Worship and especially liturgy are often seen as a core characteristic of the Orthodox Church and the place of realization of Church in the sacrament of the Lord's Supper (Kallis 1986; Schmemann 1993). In the discourse of Orthodox religious education, worship services are an integral part of the religious education (Tarasar 1974). At the same time, it is a given in most CIS (Commonwealth of Independent States) countries as well as in European countries that young people rarely attend worship services.

So it was interesting to find out if those participating in Sunday School encounter church services as a place of religious education. As mentioned above, the youth attend church services quite often. But not all of them participate actively in the preparation of church services (Table 7). 66.6 % do not participate in any way in the preparation of church services. Most of the youth participating sing in a choir or help in the sanctuary. There are some gender differences concerning the kind of participation. 20.6 % of the male respondents help in the sanctuary in contrast to none of females. This can be explained by the fact that according to the Canon rules of the Orthodox Church, women may not enter the sanctuary.[4] 30 % of the female respondents sing in a choir, compared to only 6.5 % of the male respondents.

---

4 The Council of Laodicea (around 364), rule nr. 44.

Table 7: Participation in the preparation of church services

Do you participate in the preparation of the church services?			
	all	male	female
No	66.6 %	70.1 %	64.4 %
I sing in the choir	21.3 %	6.5 %	30.5 %
I help in the sanctuary	7.9 %	20.6 %	0 %
I read the liturgical texts	6.3 %	5.9 %	6.4 %
Something else	2.7 %	2.7 %	2.7 %

In most parishes of the Russian-Orthodox Church, worship services are held in the Church-Slavonic language. This language is used only in the church context (for example, in the worship). So it was relevant to know if the youth understand Church-Slavonic; through the language one can encounter the contents of the worship, so that possible educational processes can take place during the service. To the item "Do you understand the worship language?", only 22.1 % answered "I understand everything". Most respondents (59.7 %) answered: "I understand only the common meaning/content." It is difficult, though, to identify or describe what is meant by "common meaning/content". 16.3 % of the respondents claimed to understand only some words, 1.9 % understand nothing at all. To emphasise the importance of this question: The respondents are youth who regularly attend Sunday School and worship services as well. There was one similar item in the questionnaire concerning the worship language: "Sometimes it is hard for me to understand what is sung and read during the worship". Almost half of the respondents agreed with this statement (47.1 %). Another item referred to understanding of the Scripture readings during the service: "If something in the church is read out of the Holy Scripture (Bible), I do not understand what it is about (can not understand acoustically, do not understand the language in which it is read)". Here, 11.9 % stated not to understand the readings. 55.7 % of the respondents did not agree with this statement. Another item asked about knowledge of the meaning of the procedure during the worship. Almost half of the respondents (46.2 %) considered themselves not competent enough in this respect while almost as many considered themselves competent. Another item referred indirectly to the effects of worship as a place of informal religious education, asking "What does attending worship give you?" 45.1 % answered that they experience or encounter or learn something new from the worship. 37.6 % answered that they get to know themselves better. 36.1 % answered they get answers to the questions that they think about. Another item asked in a more concrete way about the learning processes during worship: "During the worship services I get something new for me (about God, about Jesus Christ, about Mother of God)". This item was highly approved by the youth. 65.6 % agreed totally and 25.3 % agreed partially with this statement.

There was also a special "Orthodox" item about experiences with icons. Icons have a relevant position in the Orthodox theology, liturgy practice and also for religious education (Vrame 1999). Consequently, it was interesting to know how youth encounter icons. The item "In the Church I often look at the icons" got 93.9% approval from the respondents. The item "I try to understand what is drawn on the icons" was answered positively by 91.9%. So, it seems that most youth are interested in icons. Another item was about how icons help to understand Bible contents. Most respondents (66%) stated that they totally agreed with it and every fourth (25.1%) agreed partially with this statement. Unfortunately, there are only these quantitative results, which do not show anything about the relationship of the youth to the icons and their role in religious education.

4.4 Scope and limits of the study on Sunday Schools in Belarus

While its pioneering character makes the study innovative and especially valuable, it also implies several limitations. Interpretation of empirical data always requires points of reference in order to make comparisons. For the present study, there does not exist a t_1 and t_2-data collection, what makes it, from this point of view, a kind of snapshot.

The results can be interpreted in two ways. First, the results give insights in the concrete situation, opinions and attitudes of the Orthodox youth in the year 2012 in Belarus. They show a homogeneous group of young people who attend Sunday School und show high approval rates. But at the same time, the present study raises new issues: What are the reasons why other youth do not attend Sunday School? Why is the group of the respondents so homogeneous? With the results of this study, no statements about the long-term effects of non-formal religious education can be made – a questionnaire at a later stage would be very interesting.

It is clear that some results give just first insights in the processes of formal and non-formal religious education. Yet another way to interpret the data could be to check if there are some results that confirm some more far-reaching assumptions. This would be possible although only to some degree. Some results indicate und confirm empirically long-term problems in the Orthodox Church. One of those is the Church-Slavonic language used merely during the worship in the Orthodox Church, which is a very old problem.

All in all, the present study gives a first overview that should be supplemented by special qualitative studies on specific aspects, like language in the worship services, relationship to icons, relationship between active participation in the worship service and other aspects.

5. Implications for further research on non-formal religious education

The lack of empirical studies on (formal, non-formal and informal) religious education is a serious weakness of the field of Orthodox religious education.

In the following, several observations and considerations concerning this issue will be made.

A critical mirror for the practice of Sunday School and worship services

"Research always implies some kind of evaluation, at least to some degree." (Schweitzer 2017, 7) Through such empirical research, the Church leadership and the workers could reflect more intensively about the role of the Church and their role as a relevant sponsor of religious education. It is also a challenge for the believers to reflect on their role in the church as not just only visitors of the worship services and receivers of the Sacraments, but also as co-shapers of a church, as co-shapers of the Body of Christ (Schmemann 1966).

The Orthodox Church is one of the relevant sponsors of non-formal religious education, especially in countries where there is practically no religious instruction in schools like Belarus and Russia. But how does the church see itself in this role as a sponsor of religious education? And does the Orthodox Church see this role also as an important duty and task? Is the Orthodox Church interested in educational work and respective contributions to the society?

Reasons for further empirical research. Further perspectives

What kind of needs and reasons for empirical research in Orthodox religious education can be discerned?

Breakdown of the process of tradition?

As mentioned above, Orthodox religious education places an emphasis on the processes of tradition; "tradition" also means transfer of religious experiences and integration into the church life. But there is also a gap between contents and forms of tradition.

Georgij Orechanov writes: "We need to rethink the church tradition in the current life and a new search for such forms, through which the Good News will be accessible for today's youth, in the language that can be understood by the youth." (Orechanov 2015, 408) The reason to stick to tradition should not be tradition itself. When tradition is preserved in such a way, but there is no one who would like to participate in this tradition, what can be achieved except for conservation work?

The language ensures here an important access to the forms as well as to the contents of tradition. In a language that is not understandable for most of the church-integrated youth, the contents of tradition are not accessible to them. In this way, the gap between the forms of tradition and the content grows. The forms become themselves autonomous. How has this gap influenced the relevance of the Gospel for the youth? This question is impossible to answer without further empirical research. Empirical research could disclose and indicate the problems and gaps between forms and contents of tradition and ratio to religious education.

Subject orientation in Orthodox religious education

The first change which is needed concerns what can be called a new appreciation of the needs and personal interests of individual church members in general and of young people in particular. Currently, there is no growing openness in church and theology for the questions and views of the individual believers, especially youth. But, from a theological and ecclesiological point of view, there are also no arguments against subject orientation in Orthodox religious education.

A characteristic of Orthodoxy is that the Church has a certain authority, not only as an institution, but rather as the Body of Christ. This implies that the person should be incorporated in the Church, not in the institution, but in the Body of Christ. At the same time the child, youth or adult is incorporated not only in the relationship to the others, but remains a person in his individuality and freedom. This diversity and emphasis on the personhood can be seen as an argument for subject orientation.

Ecumene

In some discourses, international comparative research in religious education is seen as "an outgrowth of the idea of *ecumene* and as one of its contemporary forms of realisation." (Schweitzer et al. 2010, 23) So far the Orthodox perspective has not been sufficiently included in this kind of research work. This study is one of the first to use the experiences of the research work from another church. In this respect, the empirical research can be not only international, like the study on confirmation work in Europe, but also the perspectives of inter-denominational studies can be discussed.

Interplay of formal, non-formal and informal religious education

With any kind of religious education (non-formal, formal and informal), there are still spaces where there is interplay of different forms. The question is how these intersections can be taken into account by empirical research on effects of non-formal religious education: If non-formal religious education has an influence on the informal und formal religious education. As in the case of the present study, a specific question is investigated: Does the attendance of Sunday Schools influence the processes of informal religious education during the worship services and how can this influence be described? Through the sample that is linked with non-formal religious education we gain first insights into informal religious education. A similar question was asked also in the framework of the confirmation study, for example, the ratio between participation in confirmation work and experiences with the worship services. So, it can be considered if it is always possible to strictly divide these two forms in relation to the effects of religious education by empirical research. It can also be tested in more detail which opportunities and perspectives can come from intersectional research of non-formal and formal religious education. The reciprocal relationship of effects of non-formal and formal religious education can also be further explored.

References

Athanasou, J.A. (1993). Analysis of religiosity and practice: A study of Greek-Australian Orthodox youth. In: *British Journal of Religious Education* 16(1), 51–57.

Bakrač, V. (2011). Religiosity of the Orthodox Youth Montenegro. In: M. Blagojevic and D. Todorovic (eds.). *Orthodoxy from an Empirical Perspective*. Belgrade-Niš, 101–114.

Danilovich, Y. (2016a). Orthodoxer Religionsunterricht in Deutschland. In: S. Altmeyer, R. Englert, H. Kohler-Spiegel and F. Schweitzer (eds.). *Ökumene im Religionsunterricht (Jahrbuch der Religionspädagogik 32)*. Göttingen: Vandenhoeck & Ruprecht, 123–132.

Danilovich, Y. (2016b). *Religiöses Lernen im Jugendalter. Eine internationale vergleichende Studie in der orthodoxen und evangelischen Kirche*. Göttingen: V&R unipress.

Danilovich, Y., Chernyak, Y., and Schweitzer, F. (2014). Sonntagsschulen in Weißrussland. Eine empirische Untersuchung. In: *Zeitschrift für Pädagogik und Theologie* 66, 55–68.

Florovsky, G. (1951). Offenbarung und Deutung. In: A. Richardson and W. Schweitzer (eds.). *Die Autorität der Bibel heute. Ein vom Weltkirchenrat zusammengestelltes Symposium über "Die biblische Autorität für die soziale und politische Botschaft der Kirche heute"*. Zürich: Gotthelf-Verlag, 184–205.

Ivliev, I. (2000). Die Macht der Kirche und die Auslegung der Bibel. Eine orthodoxe Perspektive. In: J. D. G. Dunn (ed.). *Auslegung der Bibel in orthodoxer und westlicher Perspektive*. Tübingen: Mohr Siebeck, 73–79.

Kallis, A. (1986). Theologie als Doxologie. Der Stellenwert der Liturgie in der orthodoxen Kirche und Theologie. In: K. Richter (ed.), *Liturgie – ein vergessenes Thema der Theologie?* Freiburg: Herder, 42–53.

Kozyrev, F. (2003). The Religious and Moral Beliefs of Adolescents in St. Petersburg. In: *Journal of Education and Christian Belief* 7(1), 69–91.

Kulakov, P.A. (1997). Religion and Young People in School. In: *Russian Social Science Review* 38, 28–46.

Leb, I.V., and Ursa, I. (2016). Einführung in die Geschichte der Orthodoxen Kirche. In: I.V. Leb, K. Nikolakopoulos and I. Ursa (eds.). *Die Orthodoxe Kirche in der Selbstdarstellung. Ein Kompendium*. Berlin: LIT, 11–59.

Mora, L.E., Stavrinides, P., and McDermut, W. (2014). Religious Fundamentalism and Religious Orientation Among the Greek Orthodox. In: *Journal of Religion and Health* 53, 1498–1513.

Orechanov, G. (2015). Jugend, Kirche und Säkularisierungsprozesse im heutigen Russland. In: R. Flogaus and J. Wasmuth (eds.). *Orthodoxie im Dialog: Historische und aktuelle Perspektiven*. Berlin: De Gruyter, 395–409.

Orthodoxe Bischofskonferenz in Deutschland (ed.) (2011). *Hirtenwort der Orthodoxen Bischofskonferenz in Deutschland zum Religionsunterricht*.

Orthodoxe Bischofskonferenz in Deutschland (ed.) (2017). *Hirtenwort der Orthodoxen Bischofskonferenz in Deutschland zum Religionsunterricht.*

Schmemann, A. (1966). *Introduction to Liturgical Theology*, London: Faith Press.

Schmemann, A. (1993). *Liturgy and Life: Christian Development through Liturgical Experience,* Syosset, New York: Department of Religious Education Orthodox Church in America.

Schweitzer, F. (2017). Researching non-formal religious education: The example of the European study on confirmation work. In: *HTS Teologiese Studies/Theological Studies* 73(4), 1–8.

Schweitzer, F., Ilg, W., and Simojoki, H. (eds.) (2010). *Confirmation Work in Europe. Empirical Results, Experiences and Challenges. A Comparative Study in Seven Countries.* Gütersloh: Gütersloher Verlagshaus.

Tarasar, C.J. (1966). An Orthodox Curriculum in Development. In: *Religious Education* 61(6): Nov. 1, 459–462.

Tarasar, C. J. (1974). Liturgical Education for Community Life. In: *Religious Education* 69(2), Mar 1, 243–246.

Vrame, A. C. (1999). *The Educating Icon: Teaching Wisdom and Holiness in the Orthodox Way,* Brookline, Mass.: Holy Cross Orthodox Press.

О религиозно-образовательном и катехизическом служении в Русской Православной Церкви, документ утвержден определением Священного Синода Русской Православной Церкви от 27 декабря 2011 года (журнал № 152). http://www.patriarchia.ru/db/text/1663546.html [08.03.2019]. = On religious, educational and catechetical ministry in the Russian Orthodox Church, document approved by the definition of the Holy Synod of the Russian Orthodox Church dated December 27, 2011 (register nr. 152). http://www.patriarchia.ru/db/text/1663546.html [08.03.2019].

Карасёва, С., and Шкурова, Е. (2015). *Знания о религии в школах Беларуси. Состояние и перспективы* (= Wissen über Religion in den Schulen Weißrusslands. Stand und Perspektiven). Минск: Изд. центр БГУ.

http://minda.by/ [08.03.2019].

Sunday School and worship activities with children

Empirical findings and perspectives from the Protestant church in Germany

Peter Schreiner

Sunday School and worship activities with children have come into the focus of empirical research on non-formal religious education only recently. This chapter presents findings of a first quantitative study concerning the professional staff and volunteers responsible for these programs on the level of the Evangelical Church in Germany (EKD). The wider context for this study includes the observation that in Germany data-based reports on the educational programs and institutions in general have come to play an increasingly important role for politics as well as public opinion, including the media. Such reports are provided by the social sciences, often in connection with the government. A major example that encouraged other initiatives is the National Report on Education (Autorengruppe Bildungsberichterstattung 2018). It periodically presents a major empirical review, with the intention of covering the entire German education system. The focus is mainly on formal fields of education. Published every two years, each report provides indicator-based information about the general conditions, features, results and output of education processes.[1] As a data-based, problem-centred analysis the reports do not include assessments and recommendations.

Encouraged and guided by this development, empirical research on church-based programs in education started some years ago. The synod of the EKD recommended in 2008 that the Comenius Institute, a Protestant Centre for Research and Development of Education, should organize a report on church-based education programs. A first step was to identify and look closer at those areas where churches actively contribute to formal and non-formal education. First pilot studies were organised. These first reports underlined the potential of a data-based reporting for those working in these educational institutions for scientists and church staff. But it also became clear how complex each of these fields really are.

So far, such reports have been compiled for a number of fields which are important for the German Protestant Churches – church-sponsored pre-school education, Sunday School, Religious Education at school. Other studies on adult education and counselling programs at school are in preparation.

---

1 See https://www.bildungsbericht.de/en/the-national-report-on-education/education-in-germany?set_language=en

1. Research design, basic data and preliminary remarks

The focus of this article is on the design and selected outcomes of a study on Sunday School and worship activities with children (Comenius Institute 2018). The study is based on a representative online-survey among coordinators and staff for Sunday School and other worship activities with children in all member Churches of the EKD. The survey took place between June and October 2015. The report was initiated because very few data existed on this field. In a first step 4510 randomly selected congregations were contacted and asked to provide email addresses of those staff who were responsible for Sunday School and other worship activities with children. Depending on the size of the congregation more than one person could be mentioned. Each person was asked to fill in the questionnaire for the most offered activity (per year). Altogether 2297 staff received a link to the survey and 1252 filled in the questionnaire. The return flow was 54.5% of the contacted persons. For making the sample more representative, the data were weighted and adjusted. In the end 1198 participants took part in the survey.

The field of Sunday School work has changed over the years (cf. Ruddat 2001). Being traditionally the worship service for young children, often taking place parallel to the main service for adults, alternative and innovative forms and projects have produced a rich and manifold collection of activities. This is why the study was based on a broad understanding of the field covered by the key term "Sunday School and worship activities with children". The different models of Sunday School and other specific worship activities with children that exist on a local level cannot be identified from outside. So the participants of the study were encouraged to choose an activity related to Sunday School and worship with children from a given list or to name their main program themselves. The range of mentioned activities in the field of Sunday School led to the understanding that *the one model* of Sunday School no longer exists.

Other general considerations were as follows.

1.1 The theological definition of Sunday School

The standard theological definition of Sunday School that is also the basis of the "Conception for Sunday School" (cf. Gesamtverband 2017, 12–13) understands Sunday School as a double relational act: God comes near to worshippers in God's words and sacraments, the parish addresses God through singing and prayer. The service follows a recurring process that consists of four parts: arrival and opening; listening and replying, celebrating and sharing; ministry and blessing. Programs with children that follow this process can be identified as worship activities with children and as the focus of the report.

1.2 Worship in day care centers and schools

Due to pragmatic reasons, church services in day care centers and schools were not included in the study. Those who are responsible for these programs are not the same persons as those who are responsible for institutionalised Sunday School and worship activities with children. Furthermore, basic conditions differ such as spatial arrangements and the general setting (voluntary activity during leisure time/weekend versus the integration in everyday routine).

1.3 Sunday School and worship activities with children and education

One can ask if Sunday School and worship activities with children can be linked to education or provide an educational context,[2] especially when one values church worship as a holistic act including the experience of awe and wonder and a possible touch by the finger of God as well as spiritual experience. However, the different parts and elements of worship also include 'educational offers' e.g. singing, praying, storytelling and being together in a community. Sunday School and worship activities with children represent elements of non-formal education as described in other contributions in this book. It is a voluntary activity outside the formal education system. It is person-oriented and has flexible forms. Sunday School is intentional and planned but also marked by a strong influence of the participants. And finally, the activities are staffed by volunteers and/or professional staff. When people reflect on their religious upbringing and education, many refer to their participation in Sunday School.

1.4 Christian teaching and children's groups – why are they included in the study?

The programs with primary school aged children of the Protestant Churches in the east of Germany are dominated by a specific type of Christian teaching (Christenlehre[3]) developed during the period of the German Democratic Republic (cf. Comenius Institute 1998; Aldebert 1990; Steinhäuser 2016). It was established at a time when Religious Education in school was not allowed. The parishes and local churches initiated this type of program for catechetical and educational reasons and have kept it going until today. The program itself is heterogeneous but existing surveys show that worship activities are included in this program of Christian teaching.

---

2 Sunday Schools were first set up in the 1780s in England to provide education to working children. This was a period when education was not compulsory.

3 The term exists nearly exclusively in the east German Protestant churches (cf. Steinhäuser 2016).

The inclusion of children's groups in the survey under the rubric of Sunday school and worship activities with children takes into consideration that in some regional churches more and more mixed programs of children's groups exist which include worship activities (cf. Lehmann, Widmann and Wolf 2014, 203).

2. Selected results

2.1 Overview of the different formats

Each participant of the survey was asked to identify the main program they are responsible for. It is therefore not surprising that a range of formats appeared. The list includes the following formats:

- Sunday School (65.8%)
- Bible days for children (27.8%)
- Family church (26.2%)
- Devotions (16.3%)
- Toddler services (15.2%)
- Christian teaching (Christenlehre) (11.6%)
- Children's groups (Jungschar) (10.3%)
- Messy church (Überraschungskirche) (0.3%)
- Other programs (18 categories) (16.4%).

The main offer is Sunday School followed by a range of other programs. While multiple answers were possible the majority of staff (54.2%) describe themselves as responsible for one program, 21% for two programs and still 14.4% for four and more programs.

The item "Other programs" was marked relatively often (16.4%). It includes 18 different categories such as family services, services at specific dates, World Day of Prayer, etc. This can indicate a rich and differentiated range of activities in the field or a lack of understanding of what has been asked for.

The participants were asked to complete the questionnaire for the most relevant format of their work. Sunday School (54%) was mentioned as the main offer, followed by Christian teaching (9.7%) and "Other programs" (8.2%), a format that includes 18 different categories. Bible days for children (6.8%) and family church (5.5%) were also chosen.

2.2 Structure, aims and methods

The presentation of the programs refers to structural elements such as the regular cycle, the duration of the offer and the day of the week.

Christian teaching (Christenlehre) and children's groups are offered on a weekly basis, Sunday School which traditionally was organised once a week (on Sunday)

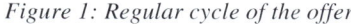

Figure 1: Regular cycle of the offer

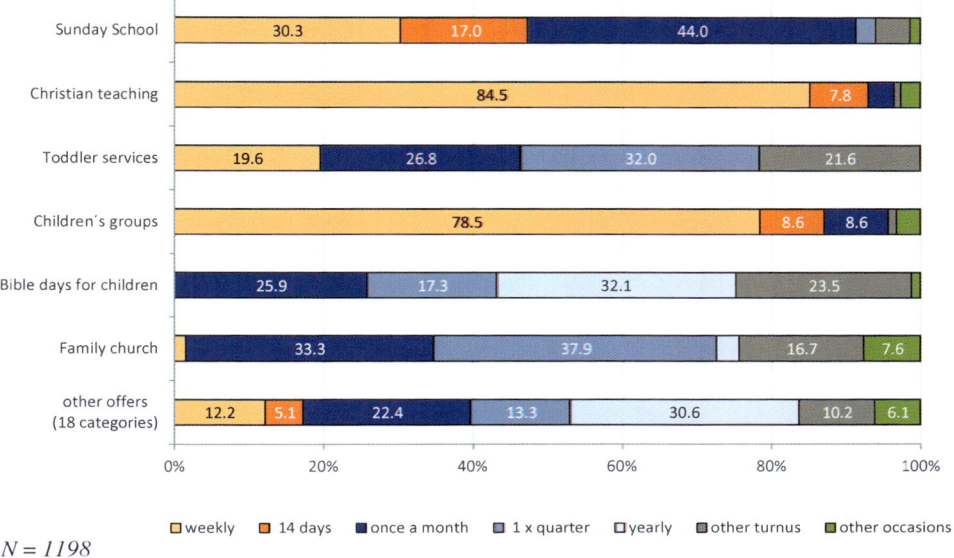

N = 1198

Figure 2: Day of the week of the offer

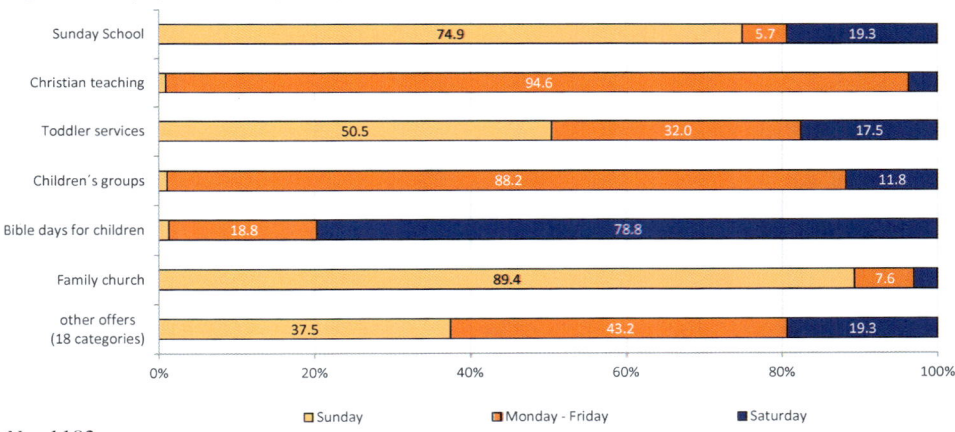

N = 1182

changed to once a month in more than 40% of the responses. Also family church takes place mainly every 3 months. The duration of the program differs very much due to specific characters.

Figure 2 shows that Sunday is the main day for Sunday School and family church, Bible days are offered on Saturdays and children's groups and Christian teaching during the week.

Figure 3: Main aims

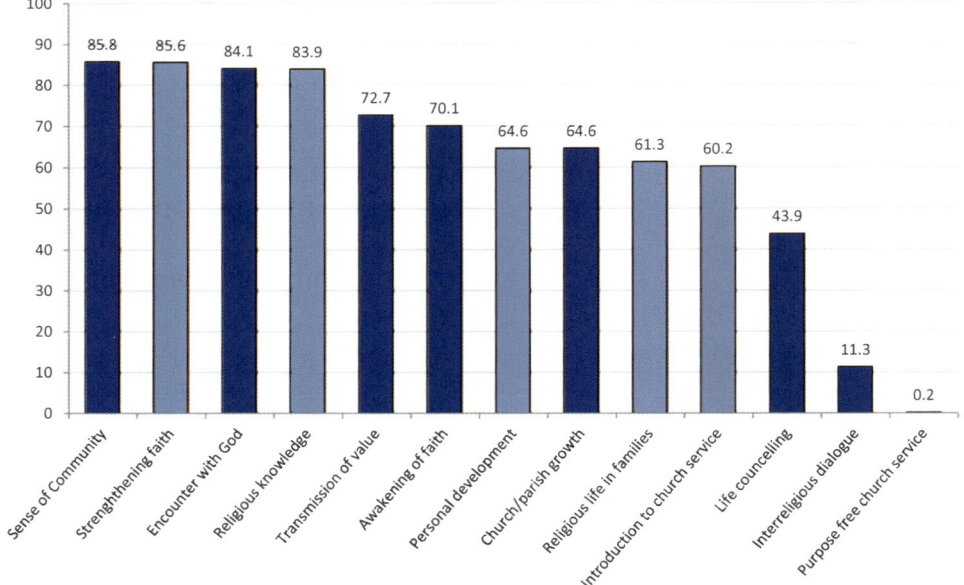

N = 1198; multiple answers possible

Figure 4: Used methods

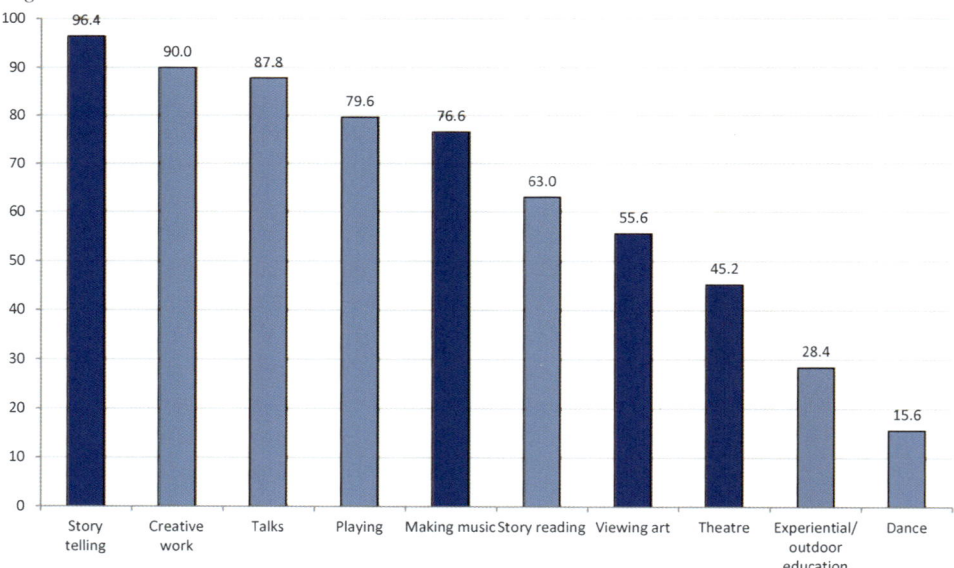

N = 1198; multiple answers possible

The participants named the main aims of their offer, which are summarised in Figure 3. The dark blue columns represent aims that are named for all formats, the light blue columns represent aims that differ between the formats. For example, the toddler services do not aim at religious knowledge or strengthening faith due to the age of the children.

Four aims reached more than 80 %: sense of community, strengthening faith and encounter with God, however the last one may be difficult to measure.

Most of the mentioned aims scored high, just three out of 13 received less than 44 % (multiple answers possible). The top three were sense of community (85.8 %); strengthening faith (85.6 %) and encounter with God (84.1 %).

Figure 4 summarizes the methods used in all formats. The dark blue columns show methods that were used in all formats whereas the light blue columns indicate significant differences between the formats.

2.3 Participating children

Time and fluctuation

Concerning the duration of participation, in most programs, except toddler service and family church, the majority of children participate three years or longer (according to the estimation of the responsible persons) (cf. Figure 5). For Sunday School and Bible days for children the proportion of long-term participants is more than 50 % and for Christian teaching even more than 80 %.

Only Christian teaching and Children's Bible days have stable numbers of participants, all other formats show a high percentage of fluctuating numbers of participation (cf. Figure 6).

Figure 5: Duration of participation of children

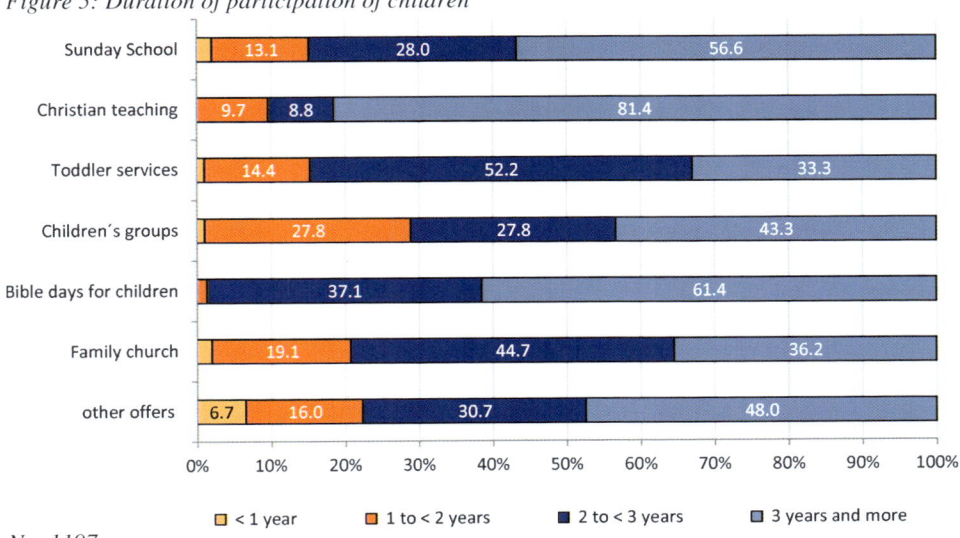

N = 1197

Figure 6: Variations in numbers of participation (Question: Were there variations in the number of children that participated normally in the activity?)

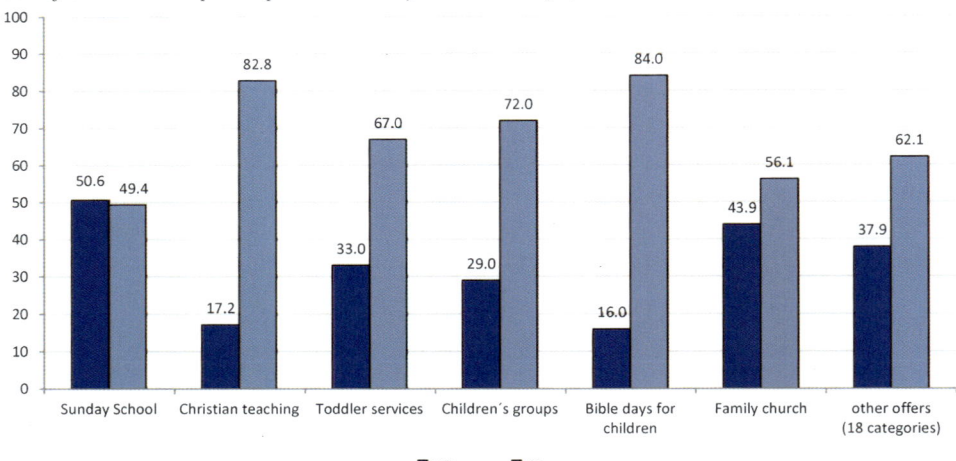

N = 1194

Sociodemographic attributes of children

Children who participate in Sunday School and worship activities are similar in a number of respects. While both boys and girls participate, more girls than boys attend (59% and 36%). The majority of the participants is baptised (73.8%) and has a Protestant background (74.2%). The fact that one-fourth of the participants are not baptised marks the welcoming character of Sunday School and worship activities with children in general.

A large majority of participating children have German as mother tongue (95.6%) and come from families with strong or mainly strong income (92.5%). Also they are mainly or exclusively without disabilities (96.2%). The overview of the sociodemographic characteristics can lead to the conclusion that the activities attract mainly church-oriented well situated families. However, "mainly" indicates that there are also children from church-distant families that participate in the programs.

A question on age distribution was included, to document how often the four different age groups participate in the program. The division was: up to 2-years; 3–6 years; 7–10 years, more than 10 years. For children in each of the groups, the question was if the respective age group is attending, and if so with less than 50%, about 50%, more than 50%.

The groups are mainly heterogeneous in terms of the age of the participants. In all formats, except children's groups, there are significant numbers of activities where all age groups come together (cf. Figure 7).

Figure 7: The age distribution in the programs

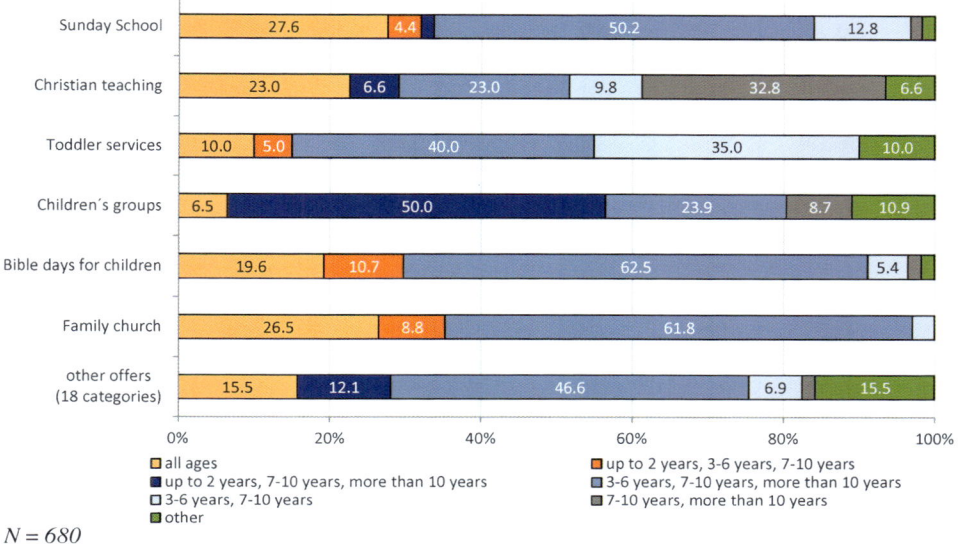

N = 680

2.4 Responsible staff

Concerning the responsible staff (the persons leading a program) professionals form the majority for most of the activities. However, Sunday School, the most chosen program, is mainly organised by volunteers. The highest percentage of professionals is found for Christian teaching (92%) and for family church (86.4%) (cf. Figure 8).

Figure 8: Volunteers and professionals responsible for the offers

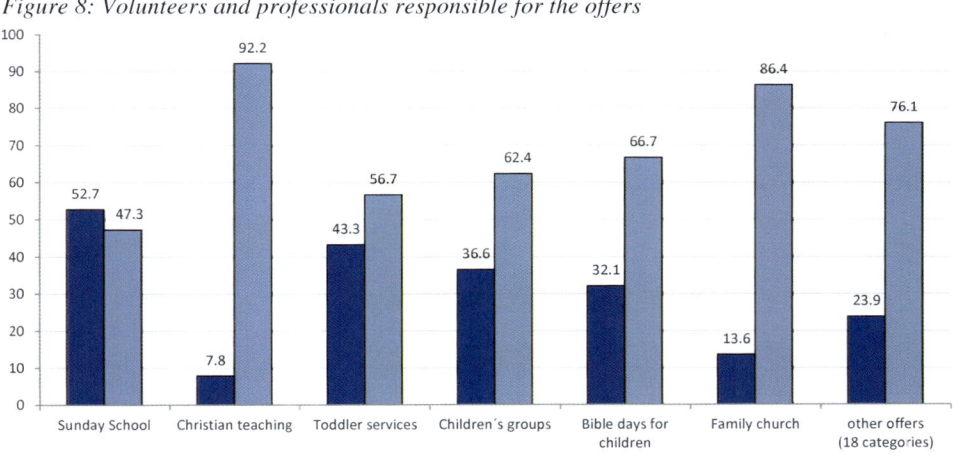

N = 1190

Figure 9: Work alone or in a team

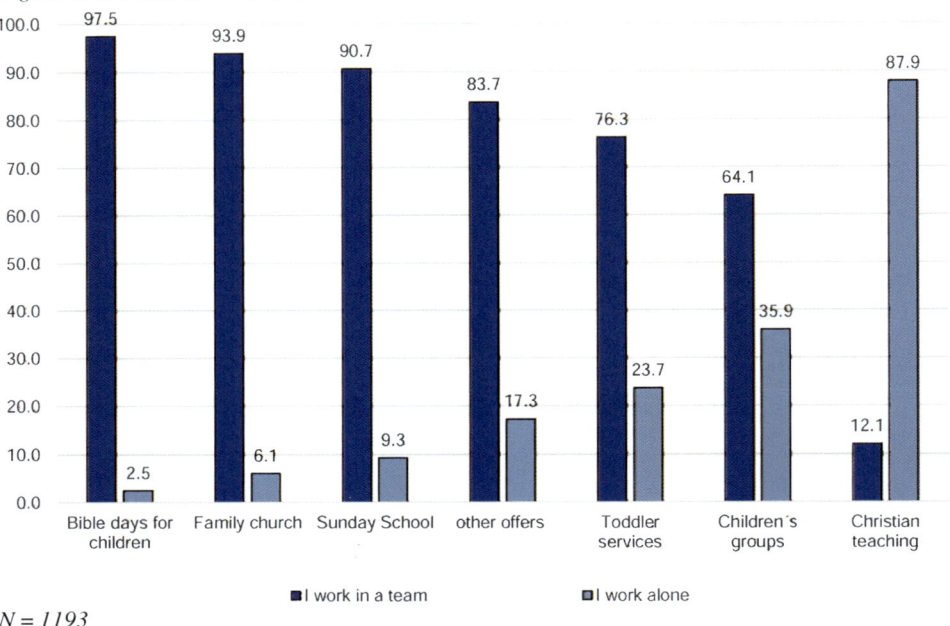

N = 1193

Other indicators are that the staff is mainly female (73.8%), mainly between 36 and 45 or between 46 and 55 years old (23.4% or 46.1%) and mainly with a highschool diploma or an academic degree (71%).

How do they work? Alone or in a team?

In most Sunday School and worship activities with children a team is responsible for planning and running of the program (cf. Figure 9).

Working in a team is very common in most of the programs. An exception is the Christian teaching where 87.9% of all activities are organised by one person. These persons are mainly parish educators and as already mentioned – this type of program is mainly offered in eastern Germany due to the specific background and history.

Networking

In addition to the conditions and the content of the work also the question of cooperation with other institutions or groups was asked. In the fields of Sunday School, toddler services and Bible days for children more than 2/3 of the programs do not cooperate with others. This is different for Christian teaching, children's groups and family church where a majority do cooperate with others. Concerning the type of cooperation partner, day care institutions and primary schools play a crucial role.

Figure 10: Type of cooperation with other institutions

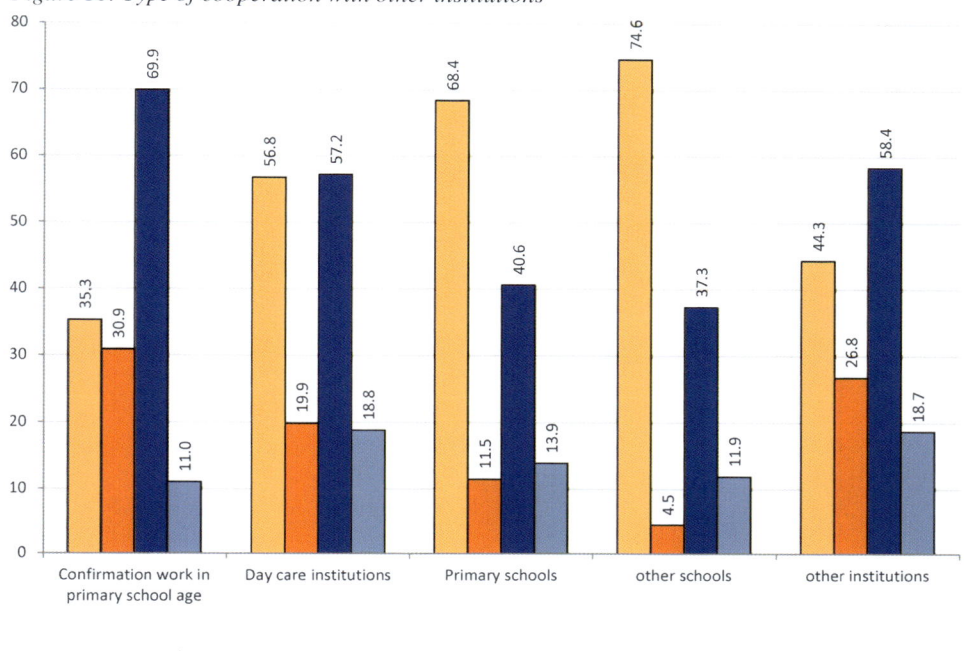

Confirmation work in primary school age: N = 136; day care institutions: N = 271; primary schools: N = 244; other schools: N = 67; other institutions: n=332; multiple answers possible.

Figure 10 shows the type of cooperation with the different partners. The figure identifies the main types of cooperation which is: exchange of information, meeting of staff, common events, other forms.

With confirmation work for primary school age, day care institutions and often other institutions organize common events whereas programs of children's groups related to schools mainly exchange only information.

3. Summary and perspectives

In the following, the main outcomes of the study are summarised in six points.

Sunday School and worship activities with children are characterised by innovation and by tradition

Innovation happens mainly in terms of organization and structure. The rhythm of church service programs includes weekly as well as fortnightly or monthly formats. Also yearly and quarterly events take place. The days for the offers vary; there is a clear preference for Sunday for Sunday School, toddler services and family church.

About one out of three Sunday School services start with a common opening together with the main service for adults. Other offers take place on Saturdays and some formats, for example children's Bible days, are mainly organised in cooperation of more than one parish. This readiness for innovation goes along with an awareness of existing tradition. The tradition of telling Bible stories is kept nearly everywhere, a rich set of methods is used for that. The basic orientation is on the liturgical year and about half of the offers take up the themes that children bring along. How can classical contents be presented in modern structures? Concepts of Sunday school and worship activities with children have to be positioned within this tension.

The staff responsible for coordination is mainly female, well educated, happy and work mostly as volunteers in a team

The majority of the mainly female staff in Sunday School and worship activities with children belong to the age group of 46 to 55 years old. In some forms also younger staff (eg. toddler services) or older staff (eg. children's Bible days) participate.

Teams of three to six members coordinate most of the offers. They often belong to different age groups. In Sunday School and worship activities with children, many volunteers are active, however, different formats exist.

The findings underline that getting new staff happens mainly through personal contacts. Also there is a high level of satisfaction among the staff. The appreciation given by the children as well as by other parish members to the workers plays a role as well as the opportunity to grow personally, eg. through workshops and training. The environment of the work is seen as good.

The participating children stay for a long period, they show a great age span as well as an inner ecclesial background, attendance fluctuates greatly

Most of the children participate in the Sunday School and worship activities for three years or longer. However, about 40 % of the Sunday School and worship activities have fluctuating numbers of participation. Sunday School activities can range between 5 and 40 children. That means that on one day 5 children participate and on another day 40 children participate

There is also a high level of mixture of the age of the participating children. In nearly half of the groups children between three and ten years participate, in nearly a quarter of the offers under two-year-olds also participate.

Concerning other characteristics, great similarities exist. In the Sunday School and worship activities with children mainly or exclusively baptised, Protestant children with German as mother tongue and without disabilities come together.

"Mainly" means that also a certain number of children from more church-distanced families, or with a migrant background or with disabilities attend the programs.

Many programs are attended equally by girls and boys. In about 1/3 of the programs mainly girls participate.

Sunday School and worship activities appear as places of education with their own profile

Church services are characterised by an explicit orientation towards God. This makes a difference to other places of education. If and how God's presence is experienced is beyond planning and acting.

Beyond that special characteristic, the staff is guided by specific aims in their programs and uses different methods to make them real. These aims include catechetical as well as liturgical contents.

Sunday School and worship activities with children have their own profile: church services include varied ways of Christian-based communication where children of different age participate. They listen and experience stories of the Bible, and can grapple with them in a holistic, creative way. Music plays an important role too. Sunday School and worship activities with children include cognitive learning processes and emotional elements. Part of the special conditions of this place of learning is also the common celebrations of different age groups together and a special relationship which develops between the different age groups.

Sunday School and worship activities create relations with families

Encounters with adults as companions are part of most Sunday School and worship activities with children. In about half of the programs, adults can also participate in the services, partly with special elements for adults. Offers such as family church or toddler services are popular, in which the common celebration of adults and children are part of the concept. Obviously many adults want to celebrate services with their children.

More than a fifth of the staff became active because of their participating children. Sunday School and worship activities with children can obviously encourage an ongoing church involvement of adults.

Cross-linking of Sunday School and worship activities with other programs happens in different ways

Cooperation with other institutions or organizations happens with the Christian teaching or children's groups but this is rare in other formats.

Important partners of cooperation are day care centres and primary schools; confirmation work for primary school aged children or cooperation with other schools play a minor role. Possibly one reason for the intense cooperation is due to the fact that Christian teaching and Christian youth groups attract more "church-distanced" children than it is the case in other formats. Joint events may have similar effects.

4. Conclusion

The outcomes of the first survey of the staff of Sunday School and worship activities with children provide a rich picture about the current situation of Sunday School and worship activities with children concerning the profile of the programs, the participating children and the responsible staff. It proves that this field of church activities includes important educational elements. It is a point of discussion if all mentioned programs are close to Sunday School activities. This is especially the case concerning Christian teaching and children's groups. In a traditional perspective, these programs do not belong to Sunday school activities. In a more open view and due to changes in church activities with children it indicates that the existing programs are more differentiated and flexible than their traditional profile. The main reason to include them in the survey is that they are named as part of Sunday School and worship activities with children according to the self-reporting of the responsible staff for this type of program. One can argue that the inclusion of these programs makes it more difficult to determine a clear profile for Sunday School activities. So, it is no surprise that more questions came up that definitely point to the need for ongoing research in this field. Children are not the future of the church but decisive contributors and beneficiaries for and of today's church activities.

The responsible staff for Sunday School and worship activities with children was addressed with an online questionnaire to investigate their views and perspectives which have been discussed in this chapter. They had to identify the main program they are responsible for and filled in the questionnaire on the background of that program. The questionnaire with 41 items allowed a differentiated insight into structure, activities, participating children and methods. A number of topics came up that could be used for further research. For further research in this field, the focus should be also on the perspectives of the participating children and the parents who take part in many activities in a remarkable number.

References

Aldebert, H. (1990). *Christenlehre in der DDR. Evangelische Arbeit mit Kindern in einer säkularen Gesellschaft; eine Standortbestimmung nach zwanzig Jahren "Kirche im Sozialismus" und vierzig Jahren DDR.* Rissen: E.B.-Verlag (Pädagogische Beiträge zur Kulturbewegung, 8).

Autorengruppe Bildungsberichterstattung (2018). *Bildung in Deutschland 2018.* https://www.bildungsbericht.de/de/bildungsberichte-seit-2006/bildungsbericht-2018/pdf-bildungsbericht-2018/bildungsbericht-2018.pdf, English summary of the 2016 report: Education in Germany, https://www.bildungsbericht.de/en/the-national-report-on-education/education-in-germany?set_language=en [23 08 2018].

Comenius Institute (ed.) (1998). *Christenlehre und Religionsunterricht. Interpretationen zu ihrer Entwicklung 1945–1990*, with G. Kluchert, A. Leschinsky, D. Reiher, G. Doyé, F.G. Friemel, R. Degen, J. Henkys et al. Weinheim: Dt. Studien-Verlag.

Comenius Institute (ed.) (2018). *Gottesdienstliche Angebote mit Kindern. Empirische Befunde und Perspektiven.* Authors: N. Bücker, K. Greier and P. Schreiner. Münster/New York: Waxmann (Evangelische Bildungsberichterstattung, Band 1).

Gesamtverband für Kindergottesdienst in der Evangelischen Kirche in Deutschland (EKD) e. V. (2017). *Plan für den Kindergottesdienst 2018 2019 2020. Leitfaden für Verantwortliche.* Münster: Gesamtverband.

Lehmann, P., Widmann, F., and Wolf, C. (2014). Kindergottesdienst. In: W. Ilg, G. Heinzmann and M. Cares (eds.). *Jugend zählt! Ergebnisse, Herausforderungen und Perspektiven aus der Statistik 2013 zur Arbeit mit Kindern und Jugendlichen in den Evangelischen Landeskirchen Baden und Württemberg.* Stuttgart: buch+musik, 196–205.

Ruddat, G. (2001). Art. Kindergottesdienst, Sonntagsschule. In: *Lexikon der Religionspädagogik Bd. 1*, Neukirchen-Vluyn: Neukirchener, 1023–1032.

Steinhäuser, M. (2016): Christenlehre, http://www.bibelwissenschaft.de/stichwort/100214/ [08.10.2018].

IV
First Communion Preparation and Confirmation Work

Researching the effects of First Communion preparation

Empirical results of a national survey on religious education in German Catholic parishes in the perspective of religious identity formation

Stefan Altmeyer, Reinhold Boschki

In times of increasing religious diversity, multiculturalism and pluralism the question of religious identity and belonging becomes more and more important. Learning tolerance and respect for others is closely linked with a search for one's own standpoint and identity in terms of religion. Finding a spiritual home in a specific religious tradition by developing a feeling of belonging seems to be a key to gaining the ability to encounter other traditions. While formal religious education, especially Religious Education at school, widely excludes aspects of affiliation for good conceptual reasons, non-formal religious education in Christian communities provides a specific place for this. However, most empirical research has so far focused on school-based Religious Education yielding a vast number of studies and research projects (cf. Schweitzer and Boschki 2018). In comparison, the field of non-formal education in parishes is a neglected topic in religious education, although to this day offerings like preparation for confirmation – in the Protestant tradition – of adolescents aged 13 or 14 (cf. Simojoki in this volume) and – in the Catholic Church – the preparation for the so-called "First Communion" of children aged 8 or 9 are not only significant in numbers but also very important for religious socialization and religious development in childhood and adolescence.

In this chapter, results from the first national survey on First Communion preparation in Catholic parishes in Germany, conducted in cooperation with an interdisciplinary research team, are presented.[1] In this quantitative as well as qualitative empirical study over a period of more than two years, children and parents were repeatedly interviewed with the aim of determining the effects of this specific form of religious education on the development of religiosity. The results help to explain and to understand the processes and impacts of non-formal religious education in the childhood phase. The chapter discusses some selected results with a spe-

---

1 Persons and institutions participating at this research project were: Stefan Altmeyer, Mainz University; Albert Biesinger, Tübingen University; Reinhold Boschki, Tübingen University; Klaus Kießling, Philosophisch-Theologische Hochschule St. Georgen, Frankfurt; Dieter Hermann, Heidelberg University (especially responsible for quantitative data-analysis); Norbert Mette, Dortmund University. Research assistants: Monika Duda, Perke Fiedler, Simone Hiller, Michael Mähr, Nicole Toms, Angelika Treibel, Melanie Wegel.

cial focus on the question of the formation of religious identity (for all details on goals, methodology, results, and consequences see: Forschungsgruppe Religion und Gesellschaft 2015).

Before that, however, some terms and basic assumptions should be clarified. Preparation for the First Communion in Germany is not standardised, although there are parallels and common elements in preparation courses. These courses are mandatory and called First Communion Catechesis (FCC). FCC is – formally – the preparation of children for the participation in the Roman Catholic mass, the Eucharist, as part of the initiation process. In Germany, this preparation as well as the celebration of First Communion are organised by the parishes, and children of the age of 8 or 9 participate. Every year, almost 200000 children participate. FCC is often organised in small groups of 5 to 10 children, mostly lead by volunteers (catechists). But also larger groups up to 50 children exist. In most cases, catechists are laypersons (not clerics but men or women), sometimes mothers and fathers of First Communion children who participated in a special training beforehand. Catechists sing with the children of their groups, read the Bible, tell stories about Jesus, introduce children to special prayers and practices. In general, the catechetical process starts in autumn and continues over 9 months culminating with the First Communion celebration.

Concerning the term "Catechesis", it is important to note that Catechesis is the traditional term for religious education, for the learning and teaching process of people on their way to become baptised or of people who are already baptised (for example as a child) and get further instruction. The term refers back to biblical scriptures. It was first used by Paul (e.g. Gal 6,6), extensively practiced in the early church, and elaborated by the so-called Church fathers (e.g. Augustine). The term is defined in official church documents e.g. by Pope John Paul II: "Catechesis is an education in the faith of children, young people and adults which includes especially the teaching of Christian doctrine imparted, generally speaking, in an organic and systematic way, with a view to initiating the hearers into the fullness of Christian life." (John Paul II. 1979, paragraph 18) This traditional concept follows more or less a "top-down" logic and is perceived as a process to transmit the tradition and the doctrine of the Church to the next generation.

Nowadays catechesis in Germany is in most cases far away from such a narrow top-down understanding. Catechesis is no longer understood as merely teaching in a one-way manner, in which the doctrine is given from 'above' and people 'below' only have to adopt the teachings of the so-called catechism. Catechesis today is conducted in a dialogical manner in which the people who participate are respected in their own life-world, in which their own life experiences are focused on and where their questions can be discussed as well as their doubts and critical thoughts (cf. Altmeyer, Bitter and Boschki 2016; Kaupp, Leimgruber and Scheidler 2011; Jakobs 2010). Nevertheless, the term "Catechesis" is very much debated. In Protestant churches in Germany, the term is no longer common and no longer used, it has been replaced with Gemeindepädagogik ("religious education in the context of the parish"; Meyer-Blanck 2016), whereas in the Catholic tradition the term catechesis still plays a central role in Christian education of children, young people and adults in the setting of Catholic parishes.

The authors of this chapter organised a conference at Bonn University where the term and the concept of catechesis in "liquid modernity" (Bauman 2000) was discussed and a search of a dialogical and encounter-based concept of catechesis for today was initiated. The approach follows the multidimensional model of education ("Bildung") formulated and conceptualised by Karl Ernst Nipkow. The authors try to adopt this model to religious education in parishes (catechesis). According to Nipkow's educational theory (Nipkow 1992, 32–36), education can be conceptualised in at least five dimensions: (1) social and public dimension; (2) utopian and future dimension; (3) subject-oriented and identity-related dimension; (4) dimension of religious tradition; (5) dimension of dialogue and encounter. All five aspects have to be seen in close relation in order to realise a broad and holistic approach of education that will not be reduced to the mere transfer of knowledge or moral lessons.

As a consequence, religious education as well as Catechesis today is understood as a multifaceted concept. The main goal of catechesis is maturity and autonomy in religious affairs. At the end of the learning process, learners should have acquired the competence to make the decision whether they would like to continue a life within the church and with God or to follow another path – a decision to be made on their own, free from any pressure. Catechesis neither acts from a neutral standpoint nor from outside of religion but it is realised *within* a distinguished community. It is the attempt to invite (young) people to a special religious way of live, to identify with it and to get to know it from inside.

This is what Hanan Alexander (2009) calls "educating identity". It focuses on dimensions (3) and (4) of the above mentioned education theory. Religious education in parishes (catechesis) is part of the formation of religious identity as it aims to foster the development of children's identity through a deep contact with Christian tradition, communion and life. Religious education – and in this case "catechesis" – is always an act of balancing different aims and purposes within the frame of the educational poles of autonomy and identity, community and society, belonging and dialogue (cf. Cush 2014).

1. An evaluation study of FCC in Germany

In light of this theoretical background, FCC in Germany was investigated as an important process of non-formal religious education by asking: What is done by professional and voluntary workers involved? Which goals do they have? In which ways do they act? With which results? Formally speaking, an evaluation study was conducted to examine in which way FCC in Germany is practiced and evaluated (process evaluation) and to which extent the predefined goals were achieved (impact evaluation). In order to answer these questions, a nationwide quantitative and qualitative panel study was conducted. This means: the participants were repeatedly interviewed. The aim of the quantitative part was an examination of different hypotheses concerning the impacts of FCC; the qualitative part was supposed to help understand the communicative processes and to find complementary hypotheses which were supposed to be checked by using the quantitative data.

Methodology

The concept and the arrangement of the study were based on a quasi-experimental pre-post-control group design (Meyer 2007; see Figure 1). The general group of participants for the panel consisted of children living in Germany who were 8 to 9 years old in 2010. The treatment group within this panel were Roman Catholic children who attended FCC in 2010/11. In addition, one parent was included in the study for each child so that a consideration of children and parents became possible. The recruitment of participants was determined by a two-stage random sample. In a first preliminary survey, conducted by an opinion research institute (INFAS, Bonn), 81 municipalities in Germany were randomly selected (weighting by population). In each municipality, a predetermined proportion of children aged 8 to 9 years was randomly selected from the population register. From this random selection, a total number of 1877 child-parent-pairs agreed to participate in this panel study. With regard to regional distribution as well as to religious affiliation, this sample is almost representative of the population in Germany.

Starting from this random selection, three consecutive survey waves were conducted: the first inquiry was held before Catechesis began (in September 2010), the second was carried out immediately after First Communion (in May 2011) and the third inquiry took place one year later. 1383 pairs of children and parents partici-

Figure 1: Survey design

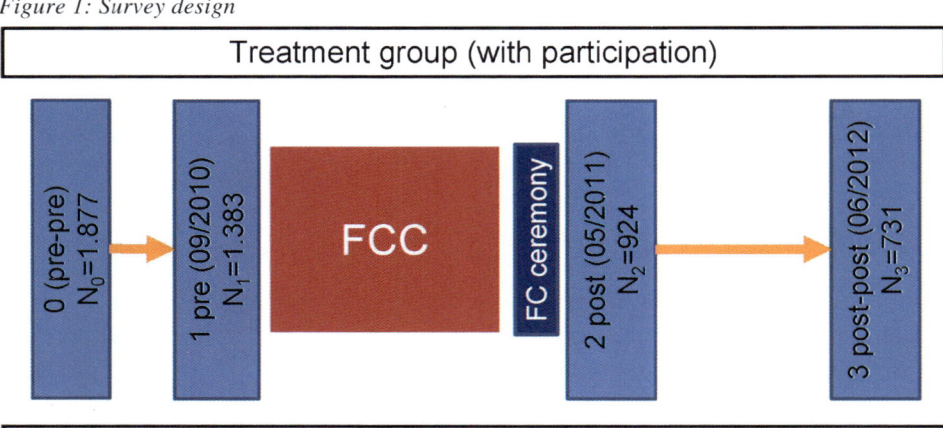

pated in the first quantitative inquiry. The number of participants decreased over the course of time to a total of 924 and then 731 children and parents pairs who participated in the second and the third inquiry. This means that 731 participants could be considered throughout the entire time period of the study. For the qualitative part of the study, three ideal-typical groups of parent-child-pairs were formed by means of a cluster analysis out of which 30 pairs were chosen and interviewed repeatedly. In addition, 165 catechists and 93 priests or lay persons as responsible professionals were included in the survey.

In order to receive valid information about the impacts, the research group drew upon elaborate evaluation research methods (Stockmann 2006). For the quantitative as well as for the qualitative part of the research, it was crucial that not only participants of FCC in 2010/11 were taken into consideration, but also a control group consisting of children of the same age who did not attend any church educational program. Otherwise, it could have been possible that all observations had been due to developments that are typical for this age cohort, rather than being an effect of Catechesis. Parallel to the treatment group, one parent was also included in the study for each child in the control group.

Concerning quantitative methodology, the question of the impact of Catechesis on religious orientation of children and adolescents cannot be answered by consulting isolated items in a questionnaire, e.g.: so-and-so many percent of the participants stated that they attend church services on a regular basis. Incidentally, the 'perceived statistics' of many professionals and volunteers in practice operates in this manner and concludes, for example, that children no longer attend regular church services after First Communion (which is certainly not uncommon) is due to weaknesses of FCC. However, one must consider correlations which are far more complex to reliably decide on absent or existing impacts. In the present study so-called structural equation models were used to meet that complexity (Byrne 2010; Kline 2011). This is a statistical approach which tests and estimates correlations between dependent and independent variables. In general, several theoretical models of how certain variables relate with and influence others are constructed. It is then tested which model matches the data best and leads to a meaningful interpretation. In evaluation research in educational contexts, the focus on a so-called effect variable is central. This addresses the question of which features are supposed to be influenced positively by an educational offer. Using structural equation models, it can be examined whether certain hypotheses concerning what the achievement of such goals depends on are in accordance with the collected data. Furthermore, additional control variables, which also produce effects, can be taken into consideration. As a result, a measure can be indicated (the so-called effect size), which shows to what degree the tested educational offer (or any single factors) influences the effect variable. Amount and +/- sign of the effect sizes can be interpreted. A neutral value of zero means no influence was exerted. A positive value stands for a progression and a negative value for a regression of the effect variable. To give a simple example, regular smoking has been proven to increase the risk of lung cancer (effect variable), as well as passive smoking. In both cases, the effect size is greater than zero, but higher for active smoking than passive. Similarly, the impact of an educational activity can be measured and compared.

In order to evaluate the impacts of FCC, the question of the effect variable to be considered had to be identified. Which skills, abilities or attitudes should be developed positively through Catechesis? Concerning this question, the focus was put on religiosity by assuming that the label "fostering of religiosity" can cover most of the goals that are typical for this process of non-formal learning in church. However, religiosity must be understood as a complex reality that includes different dimensions. There are a variety of scales for measuring religiosity (Maiello 2007, 27–36). The scale used here is based on theoretical considerations and was developed for use with children of FCC age. On the one hand, Christian-religious values are separated from Christian-religious attitudes, on the other hand different components of attitudes are distinguished considering affective, cognitive and conative dimensions (Figure 2). The construct generally assumes that religiosity can be described by these factors without postulating certain dependencies. Construct validity testing has yielded good results (for details see: Forschungsgruppe Religion und Gesellschaft 2015, 136–144).

Figure 2: Operationalization of religiosity (effect variable)

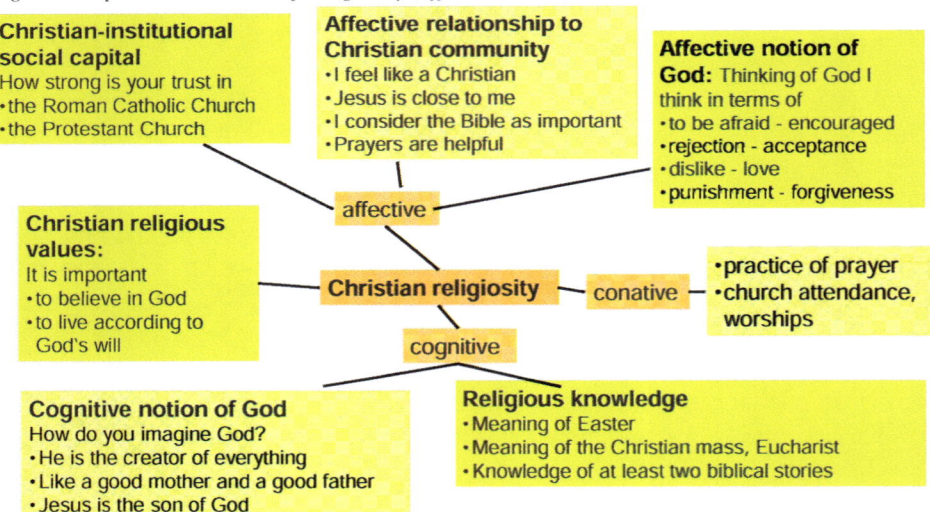

Items in the questionnaires were largely taken from already proven scales. However, to be manageable for the children, these scales were only partially used and simplified in terms of language. At the same time, parents and children were asked questions with comparable content. As the research focus was on the children, all the dimensions of religiosity mentioned were taken into consideration for them, while in the parents' questionnaire questions about knowledge and affective attachment to Christianity were left out. This is because the questions were very much tailored to the children and might seem strange to adults. With a few exceptions, the comprehensive set of questions remained unchanged over the entire research period. To illustrate this approach to religiosity, here are some exemplary insights into the items used in the questionnaire.

- Questions about *Christian religious values* cover the subjective importance of Christian religiosity for life. The children were asked: "Every person has something that is especially important to her/him. How important is it to you ...? (1) to believe in God, and (2) to live as God wants." The given answers could be rated from "very unimportant" to "very important" by means of a five-level rating scale.
- The operationalization of *affective religiosity* takes into account the following components: the affective image of God, the affective attachment to Christianity and the Christian-institutional social capital. For example, the *affective image of God* was elicited by means of typical pairs of opposites: "When I think about God, I rather think that ... (1) He scares me / He gives me courage, (2) He rejects me / He accepts me, (3) He does not like me / He loves me, (4) He punishes me / He forgives me". The participants had to specify their own positioning between these poles. The so-called *Christian-institutional social capital* was raised by a question about the trust in the Church. The *affective attachment to Christianity* was measured through the personal evaluation of seven content statements (e.g.: "I feel like a Christian" or "I know that Jesus is very close to me").
- The assessment of the cognitive dimension in religious attitudes takes into account questions about the *cognitive image of God* and *religious knowledge*. The religious knowledge was captured through the knowledge of two biblical parables and the meaning of Easter or the Eucharist. The cognitive image of God was inquired by rating eight pre-formulated statements about God and Jesus.
- The conative, action-oriented attitude dimension is measured by items on the *practice of faith*. Here the participants were asked about church service attendance and prayer practice, as well as certain prayer occasions.

Selected quantitative results

How does participation in the FCC affect the development of religiosity among children and parents? Using the presented methodological design, it was possible to answer this question and to distinguish between short-term and long-term effects. The short-term effects relate to changes between the first and the second survey wave (Figure 1). In this time, the preparation and the celebration of First Communion took place. One can therefore expect that the impressions of the special event were still present. The long-term effects relate to changes between the first and third wave of surveys. The impact analyses thus refer to the period from the time before the beginning of Catechesis to one year after First Communion. Table 1 shows the results in detail based on complex structural equation models. The underlying models cannot be comprehensively presented here (for details see:

Forschungsgruppe Religion und Gesellschaft 2015, 165–184); instead, how participation in FCC affects each aspect of the effect variable for children and parents is
reported. These influences become visible and comparable through the values given
as effect sizes. Values greater than zero indicate a positive effect; a larger value indicates a higher influence, with the theoretical maximum being 1. In an educational
context, the measured effect sizes may all count as high. The model quality (indicated by the value CFI) can also be rated as good meaning that the theoretically
assumed dependencies between variables highly agree with the data.

Table 1: Effects of FCC on effect variables. Results of structural equation models

Effect variable	Short-term effects of FCC (n_2=924)		Model quality (CFI)	Long-term effects of FCC (n_3=731)		Model quality (CFI)
	Children*	Parents*		Children*	Parents*	
Affective notion of God	.13	.08	.98	.11	.05 **	.98
Affective commitment to Christianity	.10	–	.97	.12	–	.96
Christian-institutional social capital	.11	.14	.81	.25	.09	.77
Cognitive notion of God	.07	.04	.96	.06	.06	.94
Religious Knowledge	.36	–	.94	.23	–	.96
Religious Practice	.17	.08	.96	.06	.08	.95
Christian-religious values	.07	.05	.98	.05	.05	.98

* Standardised path-coefficient, all effect sizes significant ($p \leq .05$), except for **.
– Effect variable not included

Interpreting the figures, the results mean that participation in FCC influences all dimensions of the children's religiosity positively. This means that the children who
attended FCC differ from other children (the control group) with regard to the development of religiosity during the observed period. The effects of FCC on the
religious socialization of children are, except for one dimension of religiosity, still
measurable even one year after First Communion. In addition, the participation of
the children in FCC and the involvement of the parents in Catechesis influence the
religiosity of the latter. Significant effects can be found in all considered dimensions of religiosity. However, the effects of FCC on the parents are most of the time
weaker than the effects on the children. Still, these effects are – with the exception
of one dimension – lasting.

These consistently positive results are highly surprising and encouraging, especially considering that in practice the actors are often highly pessimistic. Many
persons involved in FCC are constantly wondering whether the great commitment
is worthwhile and whether the high workload can be justified. In another recent
study, it was shown that many professional and voluntary catechists see Catech-

Figure 3: Changes in Christian-religious values. Comparison between children of treatment and control group

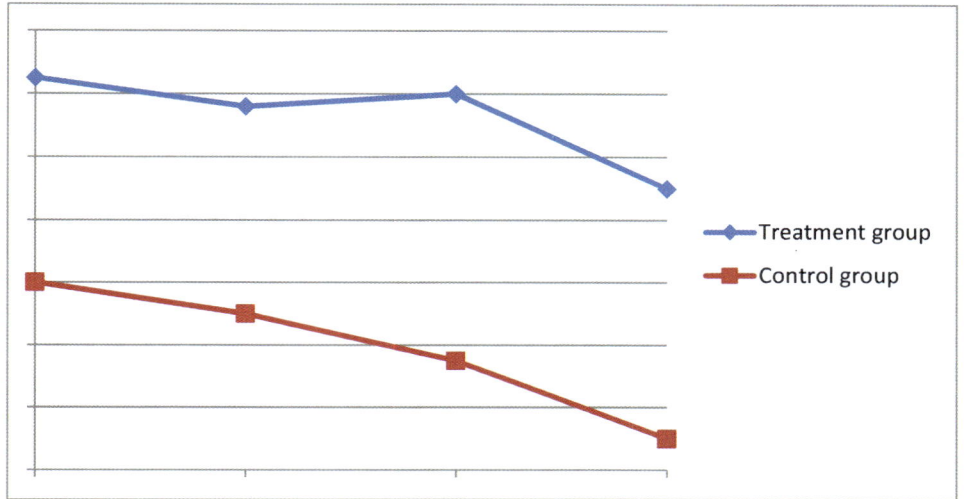

t_0–t_3 *in accordance with the survey waves in Figure 1*

esis as a major challenge burdened by many conflicts (Altmeyer 2018). In light of this, the results show that the empirical assumptions based on subjective percep-tions empiricism does not agree with the actual effects of Catechesis and that they are considered too negative. Nevertheless, the positive effect sizes just reported do not necessarily mean an absolute increase of importance of religiosity in any di-mension – the opposite is also possible in some way: the importance of religiosity decreases, but the treatment and control group differ significantly in how strong the loss of importance is. This becomes particularly clear considering in which ways the importance of religious values is changing. As illustrated in Figure 3, the *im-portance of Christian-religious values* for children decreases in the treatment and control group. This trend is only interrupted but not stopped by participation in FCC. While the importance of Christian-religious values increases among the par-ticipating children, a downward trend is measured among the other children during this period. In addition, the analysis shows that both groups differ in Christian reli-gious values even before the Catechesis starts. Thus, FCC increases this difference and slows down the process of distancing from religiously motivated values.

In *religious knowledge*, however, a real increase is recognisable. In the period of Catechesis, there is an above-average increase in knowledge among children partic-ipating in Catechesis. After the preparation time, the knowledge continues to grow but much more slowly. A reason for this may be because the scale has a maximum value and with increasing proximity to the maximum, increases are more and more unlikely.

Relevant factors with positive effects on development of religiosity

In all dimensions of religiosity – emotion, knowledge and practice as well as, to a certain extent, value orientation – positive and even lasting effects of FCC could be proven. Now, however, the question is whether this applies equally to all children and families, or whether this depends on certain positive or negative conditions. The complex structure of the quantitative study and the abundance of data make it possible to sort out relevant factors which make Catechesis successful. Table 2 shows a selection of only a few factors (for details see: Forschungsgruppe Religion und Gesellschaft 2015, 149–165). First of all, it is noticeable that a number of factors have no influence at all. Anyhow, these factors are continuously and fiercely under discussion, especially in practical fields, e.g. the duration of the catechetical process, group size or the question in which intervals the meetings take place (weekly, fortnightly, monthly, etc.). Additionally, the fact whether the children of one learning group are already acquainted with each other has no effect. However, positive environments are supportive factors (child feels comfortable, materials are appealing) and above all positive relationships: between the children and the catechists, but also between the parents and the catechists. Particularly, the family appears to be a crucial factor for the effectiveness of religious education in parishes in general. The more the parents' interests and questions are included, the more positive and lasting the whole educational project will be.

Table 2: Selected factors of FCC and effects on target variable

Without any effects	With positive effects
– duration of FCC – group size – frequency of meetings – children acquainted with each other	– positive learning environment (child feels comfortable, appealing materials) – positive relations (children-catechists, parents-catechists) – central factor: the family

Besides these rather organizational and process-related factors, individual conditions also influence the success of Catechesis. For example, a *gender-specific aspect* was found. Girls evaluate Catechesis and catechists more positively than boys. 87.6% of the female and 78.6% of the male children agree with the statement "The catechist was friendly". Asked "Did you like going to Catechesis?", 56.5% of the girls but only 43.5% of the boys answered "always". Both differences are significant. But is FCC also more successful, depending on whether one looks at girls or boys? To answer this question, the effects of Catechesis on the effect variable were calculated separately for boys and girls which showed gender-specific differences. The analysis is based on the same structural equation models as Table 1. For girls, for example, the influence of FCC on Christian religious values is significant, not for boys. Affective attachment to Christianity is significantly more effective for girls. Thus, the results point out a girl bonus or boy malus, meaning that the aspects of FCC relating to value education and affective aspects are more effectively taught to girls than to boys (for details see: Forschungsgruppe Religion und Gesellschaft 2015, 317–319).

Family was identified as a crucial influencing factor, in particular the preferred values and familial religious communication. By means of further structural equation models, it was possible to prove relevant correlations: A strong religious development is particularly evident for those children who can rely on a religious basis in their families even before the beginning of FCC. A religious basis in family can occur in form of a Christian-religious value basis or in form of a family communication culture, in which speaking about religious issues, reading from the children's Bible, celebrating church festivals, etc. is broadly integrated. When religiosity forms an integral dimension in family life, children become acquainted with it and develop their own religiosity in a quite natural way. A family life that is religiously grounded even before the FCC, strengthens religious development. This means that family values and communication culture increase or decrease the chances of FCC in a self-reinforcing process. Children who successfully participate in FCC are before they even begin more religious than others, and this difference is intensified through the catechetical process (for details see: Forschungsgruppe Religion und Gesellschaft 2015, 319–323).

Further development

The positive quantitative results lead to exciting follow-up questions. In particular, it can be assumed that the observed effects fade out over time. And moreover the effects disappear during the transition from childhood to adolescence in accordance with the typical course of religious development (Altmeyer and Hermann 2016a, b). This question was explored beyond the study design outlined above in two small follow-up surveys in the same panel at intervals of one each year. As expected, participation in these additional surveys decreased, but there are still data from $N_4=518$ child-parent-pairs from the last questionnaire administered (November 2014). The guiding question was: what will happen three to four years after the First Communion celebration, when the children are already 12 to 13 years old? So are there still effects on the religiosity of children or adolescents and parents at this later stage? The question can not be easily answered.

At first glance, it seems that the differences between the groups have almost levelled off. Religiosity is still more pronounced among children of the treatment group than in the control group. However, this is no longer measurable as a direct effect of Catechesis. The preparation for First Communion on its own – independently of the short-term effectiveness – is no longer enough to explain the course of religious development. However, such a finding of a direct long-term effectiveness would have been more than astonishing. Because compared to other central areas of life of children such as school or leisure time, religion occupies a miniscule amount of time.

Figure 4: Model of the relationship between religiosity, participation in FCC and participation in religious offerings at school or church

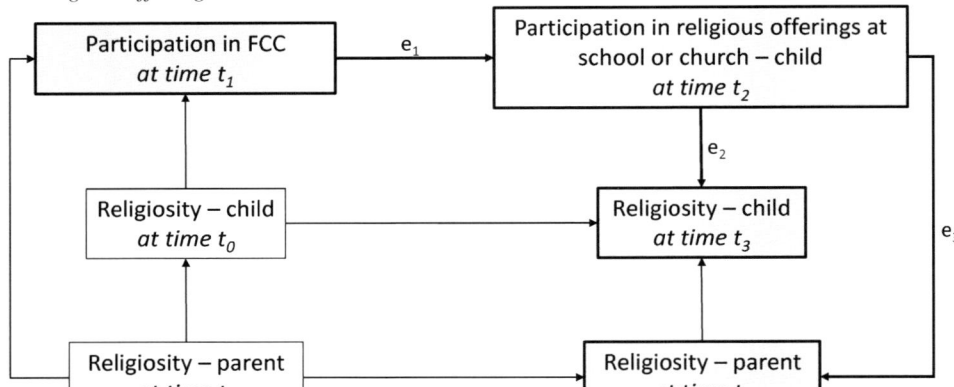

However, taking a closer look, one still gets a revealing picture. A long-term effect of Catechesis can indeed be recognised, but only an indirect one. To see this relationship, a theoretical model must be constructed that examines participation in FCC for its indirect effects. Figure 4 gives a schematic picture of this model. To answer the question of the effects of FCC on religiosity, only the marked variables and arrows are important. However, the others are interesting and necessary because they show the complexity of the causal relationships. They must be considered in the statistical analysis to achieve reliable results.

Table 3 lists all the results obtained when this model is assumed for all factors of religiosity. The values can be interpreted accordingly: FCC sets an impulse for further religious development. Religiosity fostered in FCC manifests itself in an increased participation in religious offerings at school or church – and this leads to an increase in religiosity of children and partly even of parents. If one took FCC as an isolated learning offer, there would not be a long-term effect after 4 years. Still, it can have a long-term effect, but only in its interaction with other religious offerings at school or church.

Table 3: *Effects of FCC on effect variables (4 years after the beginning of preparation, N_4=518). Results of structural equation models*

Effect variable	Effects of FCC on the participation in religious offerings at school or church* [= e_1 in Figure 4]	Effects of participation in religious offerings at school or church (child) on effect variable (child)* [= e_2 in Figure 4]	Effects of participation in religious offerings at school or church (child) on effect variable (parents)* [= e_3 in Figure 4]
Affective notion of God	.33	.20	.15
Affective commitment to Christianity	.31	.38	–
Christian-institutional social capital	.33	.26	.25
Cognitive notion of God	.36	.14	.21
Religious Knowledge	–**	–**	–
Religious Practice	.26	.96	–
Christian-religious values	.29	.15	.22

* Standardised path-coefficient, all effect sizes significant (p≤ .04)
** Religious knowledge no longer considered because original questions were oriented towards 8- to 9-year-old children and might not be appropriate for young adolescents
– Effect variable not included

2. Some selected results of the qualitative study

Complementing these statistical analyses, the qualitative interviews aimed to gain insight into the personality of the participants. In letting the persons speak for themselves, one gets a meaningful understanding of the catechetical process. Through a detailed look into individual families and their catechetical constellations, it is possible to interpret the quantitatively measured effects, and moreover to gain new insights into the course of religious socialization in the context of First Communion. In conducting the interviews, the study relied on the personal interview procedure according to Inghard Langer (2000). In contrast to other methods of qualitative social research, this method is characterised by an empathic-accepting interview style and by the congruence of the interviewer. The researcher is more than the neutral expert. His or her behavior is decisive for the coherence of inner experience and external signals. Such an approach promotes authentic presentations and evaluations as well as more in-depth self-exploration of the persons surveyed – as comparable studies show. The evaluation of conversations with parents and children from the treatment and control group led to nuanced family portraits, which traced the religious developments in the context of family relationships and communications (for details see: Forschungsgruppe Religion und Gesellschaft 2015, 280–311).

Selected findings

For the overall study, interviews with a total of six families were intensively evaluated, five of which came from the treatment and one from the control group. A total of 34 half-hour interviews with children and parents following the waves of the quantitative surveys were analysed. Summarising the findings from this enormous qualitative data, it is possible to say that if families support the development of religiosity, the effects of FCC are stronger than in families with weak religious affiliation. The effects concern the following topics:

– *Relationship (closeness) with Jesus and God:* All of these findings suggest that the children's relationship with Jesus and God is changing and deepening during the First Communion preparation and celebration. Just to quote some examples: *"It was a moving experience. I had the feeling that Jesus was very close to me."* (p. 204)[2] – *"God was close to us in our community."* (p. 207) – *"I learnt more about the Bible and Jesus, I know that Jesus restored sight to the blind."* (p. 204, 205) – *"God is merciful and nice."* (p. 205)
– *Development of the image of God:* Many children show a clear development of their image of God from a childishly naive concept to a more reflected open notion of God. For example: *(Child) "I do not believe in God because my mom says God could be anything and I cannot imagine ... that God could be anything. Then God could also be a pencil and I cannot imagine that, or a flower or bed linen or ... I cannot imagine." – (Mother) "I think I'll tell her (my daughter), everyone has to make his or her own image of God, and if you believe it, it will change again in your life, God is not the same for everybody ..."* (She also tells that her husband opposes Christian education). (pp. 270–271)
– *Meaning of prayer:* Prayers express a special relationship. God is obviously more than an "idea" to the children. They feel that one can turn to God, address Him personally, and develop a relationship with Him. Some children practice prayer on their own initiative, they know it from the family and develop it further on their own.
– *Importance of First Communion celebration:* The celebration of First Communion is an outstanding event in the children's biography. In most cases it is celebrated as a family event in which the child is the focus and gets special attention by the presence of guests, letters of congratulation, gifts, etc. Such cultural factors together with the experience of the First Communion liturgy seem to be very important for children's religious identity. This could be seen in children's narratives as well as parents' very vivid recollections of their own First Communion.
– *Development of ritual competence:* In the course of the preparation, the children experience and learn a multitude of rituals: to light the group candle, to sing a song at the beginning of the group lessons, concluding rituals, crossing oneself

2 Page numbers from: Forschungsgruppe Religion und Gesellschaft 2015.

upon entering the church, liturgical rites in devotions and services, prayers of thanksgiving before meals, evening rites in families, etc. Examples: *"I learnt how to go to church, how to sit in church and keep quiet, how to receive the Holy Bread …"* (p. 224) – *"The catechist did a great job … I always liked to join the group … I enjoyed it very much."* (p. 201)

– *Participation in parish life:* Almost all children interpret the First Communion as a full acceptance into the Christian parish. Some chose to participate in children's groups or youth groups after First Communion (e.g. altar boys or girls).

– *Religious identity:* It is important to note that the First Communion preparation makes children aware of their own confessional affiliation as one element of their religious identity and of the fact that there is a religious or denominational plurality (difference). On a personal level identity is strongly affected, e.g.: *"It was very nice to see how happy the child is, how the child develops and (…) above all, you also gain an insight into what's going on in FCC."* (p. 228)

– *Value orientation:* As noted above, the preparation and implementation of FCC contribute to raising awareness of values and moral behavior.

– *Effects on parents:* As mentioned above, parents who are actively involved in FCC get new impulses for their own religious life and faith. Example: *"The Holy Communion is a place where God and Jesus are very close by taking the (Holy) Bread, and that is the moment in which you can be closest to God. There is no other moment for me in which I can be as close to God as in Communion."* (p. 276)

– *Effects on religious family life:* Families which have already practiced a religious life before the beginning of FCC adopt new elements for their family life, e.g. rituals, prayers, or songs, e.g.: *"Jesus helps to manage conflicts and offer solutions for our life."* (p. 209) Families which have *not* been religious before did *not* change their family life.

– *Lack of exchange:* In most cases, FCC lacks inter-denominational and inter-religious aspects.

3. Conclusion and discussion

According to these results, FCC can be considered as a central part of a broad concept of religious education that comprises different stages and fields: family, parish, school, religious education for adults, etc. In all of these fields, religious education is closely connected with the questions 'who we are?' and 'to whom do we belong?' meaning: 'What is our personal and social identity in religious terms?' "For all of us in religious education, the questions of identity are central, otherwise the depth and truth of our traditions would not be effectively taught." (Seymour 2014, 109)

   FCC can be understood as an attempt to foster personal religiosity of children as well as the sense of belonging to a specific community. In this sense, the contribution of this non-formal education offer to the religious education of children could be that believing and belonging are explored in their deep mutual dependency. As seen above, this attempt is quite successful in terms of most dimensions of Christian-religious attitudes and values. However, in times of growing religious diversity and multicultural societies, these certainly most valuable effects must be put into the frame of inter-religious and inter-cultural exchange. "Educating identity" must come together with a "pedagogy of difference" (Alexander 2009).

A first step is personal encounter *within* a specific tradition. This means: "one stands inside a way of life and receives it into oneself" (ibid., 49). "To make life choices intelligently, then, I need to stand firmly within a way of life that offers me guidance in doing so." (ibid.) This educational process which Alexander describes for the Jewish tradition, can also be applied to the classical process of "Catechesis". One of the most important goals of FCC is a "deep immersion in the stories and practices of the tradition into which one is being initiated" (ibid., 50).

However, this concept would remain one-sided and exclusive if it would not be related to a "pedagogy of difference" that requires "opportunities to learn of other traditions": "To understand myself I must encounter the other; but to genuinely encounter the other I must also understand myself." (ibid., 50)

Julia Ipgrave (2016) views identity learning and learning dialogue as two sides of the same coin. Religious education varies between *auto*-referential and *allo*-referential perspectives (ibid., 54). In the context of Jewish learning she writes: "With *auto*-reference, the Jewish self determines the purposes and character of engagement, and with *allo*-reference, 'the other', from a different faith community, shapes the encounter." (ibid.)

In structural analogy, the following is suggested: Christian Catechesis is *auto*-referential by nature ("educating identity"); but in our time it should be broadened to *allo*-reference as well. Catechesis has to sensitively and seriously initiate encounters with other denominations and religions. This should be a present and future task of Catechesis in general. Summarising the findings on FCC, it is quite successful in preparing children for religious maturity (*auto*-referential perspective). However, during and after the catechetical process, it should sensitise learners for a more and more *allo*-referential perspective.

References

Alexander, H.A. (2009). Educating identity: Toward a pedagogy of difference. In: *Religious education as encounter: A tribute to John M. Hull*, ed. S. Miedema. Münster: Waxmann, 45–52.

Altmeyer, S. (2018). Blickpunkt. Zukunftsfähige Katechese. In: *Katechetische Blätter* 143, 219–231.

Altmeyer, S., Bitter, G., and Boschki, R. (eds.) (2016). *Christliche Katechese unter den Bedingungen der 'flüchtigen Moderne'*. Stuttgart: Kohlhammer.

Altmeyer, S., and Hermann, D. (2016a): Langzeiteffekte der Erstkommunionkatechese. In: *Katechetische Blätter* 141, 292–298.

Altmeyer, S., and Hermann, D. (2016b). Mit Freunden über Gott reden … Religiöse Kommunikation vor dem Übergang von der Kindheit zum Jugendalter. In: S. Altmeyer, G. Bitter and R. Boschki (eds). *Christliche Katechese unter den Bedingungen der 'flüchtigen Moderne'*. Stuttgart: Kohlhammer, 125–142.

Bauman, Z. (2000). *Liquid Modernity*. Cambridge: Polity Press.

Byrne, B.M. (2010). *Structural equation modeling with AMOS*. New York/London et al.: Psychology Press, Taylor & Francis.

Cush, D. (2014). Autonomy, identity, community and society: Balancing the aims and purposes of religious education. In: *British Journal of Religious Education* 36(2), 119–122.

Forschungsgruppe Religion und Gesellschaft (ed.) (2015). *Werte – Religion – Glaubenskommunikation. Eine Evaluationsstudie zur Erstkommunionkatechese*. Heidelberg: Springer.

Ipgrave, J. (2016). Identity and inter-religious understanding in Jewish schools in England. In: *British Journal of Religious Education* 38(1), 47–63.

Jakobs, M. (2010). *Neue Wege der Katechese*. München: dkv.

John Paul II (1979). *Apostolic Exhortation Catechesi tradendae*. Rome: Vatican. www.vatican.va [08.03.2019].

Kaupp, A., Leimgruber, S., and Scheidler, M. (eds.) (2011). *Handbuch der Katechese. Für Studium und Praxis*. Freiburg: Herder.

Kline, R.B. (2011). *Principles and practice of structural equation modeling*. New York et al.: Guilford.

Langer, I. (2000). *Das persönliche Gespräch als Weg in der psychologischen Forschung*. Köln: GwG-Verlag.

Maiello, C. (2007). *Messung und Korrelate von Religiosität. Beziehungen zwischen Glaubensintensität und psychologisch, pädagogisch, soziologisch sowie medizinisch relevanten Variablen*. Münster: Waxmann.

Meyer, W. (2007). Evaluationsdesigns. In: R. Stockmann (ed.). *Handbuch zur Evaluation. Eine praktische Handlungsanleitung*. Münster: Waxmann, 143–163.

Meyer-Blanck, M. (2016). Die Untauglichkeit des Katechesebegriffs und die Chancen des Katechismus aus evangelisch-theologischer Sicht. In: S. Altmeyer, G. Bitter and R. Boschki (eds.). *Christliche Katechese unter den Bedingungen der 'flüchtigen Moderne'*. Stuttgart: Kohlhammer, 143–151.

Nipkow, K.E. (1992). *Bildung als Lebensbegleitung und Erneuerung. Kirchliche Bildungsverantwortung in Gemeinde, Schule und Gesellschaft*. 2nd. ed. Gütersloh: Gütersloher Verlag.

Schweitzer, F., and Boschki, R. (eds.) (2018). *Researching Religious Education. Classroom Processes and Outcomes*. Münster: Waxmann.

Seymour, J.L. (2014): Knowing Who We Are: Identity and Religious Education. In: *Religious Education* 109(2), 109–110.

Stockmann, R. (ed.) (2006). *Evaluationsforschung. Grundlagen und ausgewählte Forschungsfelder*. Münster: Waxmann.

Non-formal religious education:
The notion of mini-confirmands in Denmark

Leise Christensen

1. Church, school and the idea of mini-confirmands: Historical Background

Historically there have been rather close ties between school (folke-skolen) and church (folke-kirken) in Denmark. Apart from confirmation preparation which was initiated in 1736 in Denmark much of the Christian education of children has been left to the school to administer. However, during the 20th century these ties were gradually loosened and in 1975 the ties between school and church were finally and completely cut through. The church did not take much notice of this new state of affairs and when voices began to suggest that the church itself should initiate initiatives to make sure that the children who were baptised in the Church of Denmark also would have access to a Christian education earlier than the confirmation preparation at the age of 13–14, these voices were largely ignored. The prime consideration and argument behind not wanting the church to offer any non-formal Christian education for the younger children was that it was seen as a task that is securely based within the realm of the home, i.e. it was seen solely as the responsibility of the parents. However, the waves of 1968 had not gone unnoticed by in Denmark and a lot of young parents had themselves not had any Christian education to speak of. Often it is called a time of a tremendous loss of tradition. The parents may (or may not!) have been taught about Christianity in a Lutheran understanding in school, and school and church may not officially have been separated before 1975 but in reality the world had already undergone big changes for quite a long time at this point – 1975 – and the school had also for quite some years experienced a certain weakening in the area of Christian education. The church may not have noticed but the surrounding world had long felt the wind of change.

In the mid-eighties two or three bishops – out of the ten bishops of the Church of Denmark – together with a small group of pastors decided to try out a concept which they called "The Preparatory Confirmation Preparation for Children in Third or Fourth Grade". The idea was to compensate for the loss of Christian tradition and teachings after school and church had been separated and introduce a certain opportunity for children to gain insight in these matters again in a (sort of) faith based manner. As one would image this name did not quite catch on and soon the idea was labelled mini-confirmands or Junior-confirmands.

The first groups of mini-confirmands saw the day of light in 1987 as a sort of temporary arrangement where the whole concept was tried out. In 1994 the arrangement was made permanent by the bishops. Now the parishes could – if they so wished – offer children the opportunity to participate in mini-confirmand groups. It was, however, voluntary if the parish offered this sort of education and it was voluntary, obviously, for the children to take part. The aim of the mini-confirmand groups was 'to contribute to children's familiarity with the Christian teachings for children and to contribute to the familiarity with the Sunday service of Church of Denmark in order to strengthen the fundaments for the ordinary confirmation preparation later on' (The Decree 1994). Participation in a mini-confirmation group has never been a prerequisite for participating in the ordinary confirmation preparation in 7th or 8th grade. The Decree furthermore stated that 'the children in the framework of the Sunday service meet around the telling of Bible stories, (children's) hymns, prayer and the Creed' (The Decree 1994). This rather ambitious plan was meant to be carried out by the pastors who were always responsible for the mini-confirmands – both pedagogically and theologically – with the twist that the curriculum of the actual group sessions should be planned together with the parents – "the pastor is the responsible person for the Prepatory Confirmation Preparation which is to be organised together with the parents" (The Decree 1994 §6). This last passage was partly added not to upset the groups in Church of Denmark who were very much against the notion of mini-confirmands due to the above mentioned argument of the family as the place of religious upbringing. In reality, §6 was only carried out in very few instances which will also be discussed later on in this article. It was furthermore stated in the Decree that the mini-confirmand groups should have a maximum of 40 lessons of 45 minutes each.

2. Numbers of mini-confirmands in Denmark 1995–2010

The notion of mini-confirmand groups became a rather instant success in the church. In 1995 a total of 9236 children of the age 9–11 years took part in a mini-confirmand group and one year after the arrangement was made permanent by the Decree in 1996 a total of 11645 took part (http://www.helsingørstift.dk/til-praesterne/ideer/minikonfirmand/vejledning). In 2007 a total of 25922 took part which is the equivalent of 37 % of the children in that particular year group. Three years later the percentage was around 40 % (The report 2010, 6). The following three years the number of participants seemed to make further progress and the bishops – this time all ten of them – began to consider making all parishes in Denmark offer mini-confirmand groups. At this time approximately 75 % of the parishes offered this particular type of Christian education for children. Before this decision was made, however, it was decided to undertake a study of this area of Christian education and to write a report in order to gain insight in what the contents of the mini-confirmand groups actually were: What was being taught there; how was it taught; for how long time did the mini-confirmands attend their group; were there any geographical differences in the country; what about the parents; and several other relevant matters. In the following, some of the results from the report will be presented. Further studies into this matter have not been done since this Report even though there are plans at the moment of repeating it (2018). There are no results from the new survey as yet. They will probably be published in 2019. The name of the Report is Minikonfirmand- og Konfirmandundervisning i folkekirken 2008–9, hereafter "the Report". The Report was conducted by sociologist Steen Marqvard Rasmussen as the prime writer in cooperation with Leise Christensen, then assistant professor, Povl Götke and Gert Nicolajsen.

3. The findings of the report

The questionnaire was sent out to 824 pastors, 594 pastors filled it out and returned the questionnaire which means that 72 % answered. The pastors were active in all of the ten Danish dioceses and they were working either in the countryside, small town, larger town, big city or the capital area. The children in question were not asked due to their young age and lesser ability to read and write and nor were their parents.

Table 1: Do you offer mini-confirmand groups in your parish? – results at diocese level

Name of diocese	proportion of parishes with mini-confirmands
Viborg	95 %
Aarhus	86 %
Aalborg	86 %
Copenhagen	51 %
Lolland-Falster	49 %

Viborg, Aarhus and Aalborg are the three dioceses that have had mini-confirmand groups for the longest period of time. They were the three dioceses initiating the mini-confirmand groups in 1987. The diocese of Copenhagen is the one with the second lowest number of parishes offering this type of Christian education. Lolland-Falster is a very small diocese and they started offering mini-confirmand groups much later than all the other dioceses. The rest of the dioceses responded between 66 % and 86 %.

Table 2: Reasons against the mini-confirmand concept
Why aren't you offering mini-confirmand groups in your parish?

Reasons	% of parishes without mini-confirmand groups
The parish has chosen to work with the local school in a school-church-cooperation	33 %
Lack of children in the appropriate age-group	18 %
Lack of funding	9 %
The pastor(s) does not want it	5 %
The lay council of the parish does not want it	4 %
Other non-specified reasons	56 %

Especially in Copenhagen "Lack of children" is a dominant reason for not offering mini-confirmand groups with 40%. The same is the case for dioceses like Viborg and Aalborg where there are many country parishes with only few children and no schools (65% and 38%). One must keep in mind that most parishes in Viborg and Aalborg do offer mini-confirmand groups so the 65% and 38% are percentages of a very small percentage.

Table 3: Participation rates
What percentage of the children in the appropriate age group in your parish took part in a mini-confirmation group?

Diocese	0–40%	41–80%	81–100%	Membership of Church of Denmark for the age group
Copenhagen	83%	17%	0%	56%
Helsingor	80%	15%	5%	73%
Roskilde	46%	31%	23%	83%
Lolland-Falster	36%	64%	0%	86%
Fyn	32%	20%	48%	84%
Aalborg	8%	49%	43%	89%
Viborg	10%	35%	55%	90%
Aarhus	18%	37%	45%	83%
Ribe	11%	38%	51%	90%
Haderslev	17%	48%	35%	not available

In 2018 the church membership rate is slightly lower all over. What is still relevant is that the degree of urbanization is important for the number of children who take part in a mini-confirmation group: The more urbanised an area, the fewer children take part. In the smallest towns it is only in 10% of the parishes where 40% at the most take part in a group while this percentage is steadily increasing with the degree of urbanization. In the capital area of Denmark this percentage rises to 83%. This means that in Copenhagen, 83% of the parishes have up till 40% of the children at the most in the appropriate age group. This can have at least three important explanations:

1. In Copenhagen, fewer children are baptised as infants, fewer are baptised between the age of one and nine and thus fewer are members of Church of Denmark at the age span in question.
2. Living in the capital area to which part of Helsingor also belongs, there are many leisure activities to take part in and those are often given priority over the activities of the church.
3. Children may go to school in other parishes than where they live and it can be difficult for them to reach the mini-confirmand groups in the afternoons.

Figure 1: What subject matters are being taught in the mini-confirmation group?

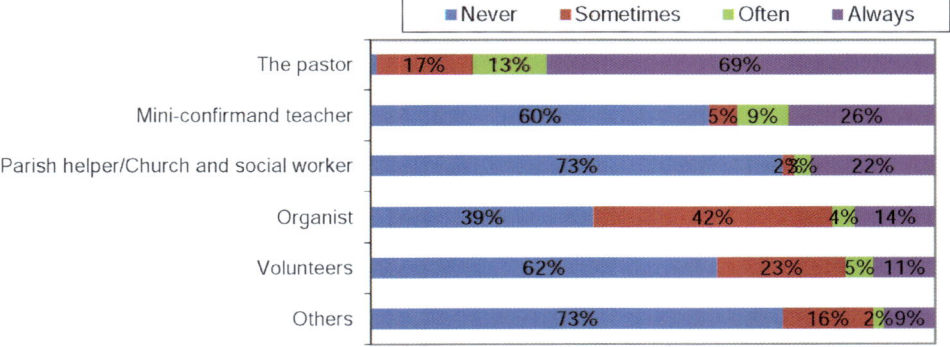

Figure 2: Who teaches and leads the mini-confirmation groups?

It appears that the content of the mini-confirmand groups is fairly traditional when it comes to the subject matters. It resembles those taught in the ordinary confirmation preparation classes. The telling of Bible stories is a rather important subject matter in mini-confirmation groups all over the country. In Denmark there is a strong tradition of rewritten Bible stories for children and re-telling the Bible stories. It is surprising to note that 31% sometimes use the Catechism in the mini-confirmation groups.

Nationwide 82% of the pastors often or always take part in the work connected to having mini-confirmand groups. Parish helpers are employed mostly in larger parishes in bigger towns. In country parishes and smaller towns mini-confirmand teachers, who have no other paid task in the church during the week, can be found in a fourth of the cases. Volunteers are not present very frequently in mini-confirmand groups. The pastors are at all times responsible for the mini-confirmation group –

Table 4: Which qualifications do the parish helpers or mini-confirmand teachers have?

Level of formal education	Share of all helpers
Medium long pedagogical education (i.e. pedagogue, teacher, diacon)	60%
Long, academic education/degree (i.e. university degrees in languages, political science, religion)	20%
Skilled worker (i.e. cook, carpenter, hairdresser)	8%
No formal education after compulsory school	6%
Other medium long education (i.e. nurse, engineer, social worker)	6%

Table 5: Number of lessons in mini-confirmation groups
How many lessons of 45 min were offered during one mini-confirmand group period?

Number of lessons	Share of groups
Less than 8	1%
8–10	21%
11–15	28%
16–22	37%
More than 22	13%

Table 6: Number of leaders
Is there more than one leader present in the mini-confirmation group at the same time?

Frequency of meetings	
Never	15%
Sometimes	17%
Often	22%
Always	45%

even in the cases where they are not present at all times in the actual work of the group, typically in groups with a parish helper or a mini-confirmand teacher.

It would appear that the parish helpers or mini-confirmand teachers are fairly well-educated with 86% having a medium long or long academic education. 60% of those have a pedagogical education or training. In addition to that, of course, come the pastors who all have a theological degree from a university. It can be added that out of the 6% who have no formal education, 83% have non-formal competences acquired through work in Christian children's clubs, missionary work, scout work and such.

At the time of the study – in 2008/09 – quite a lot of lessons were held, on an average two lessons per week. They usually took place in the afternoon after school. The hope that parents or other responsible adults in the proximity to the children would take part in the work of the mini-confirmand group was not fulfilled in spite of the wording in the Decree. This is not surprising as most Danish parents are working full-time during the day and have busy evenings as well. It can be added

Table 7: Involvement of parents, etc.

How often do the parents, grandparents, stepparents, etc. of the children get involved in the actual mini-confirmation work?

Not at all	28%
Sometimes	69%
Often	3%

Figure 3: Which pedagogical tools are used in the mini-confirmation groups?

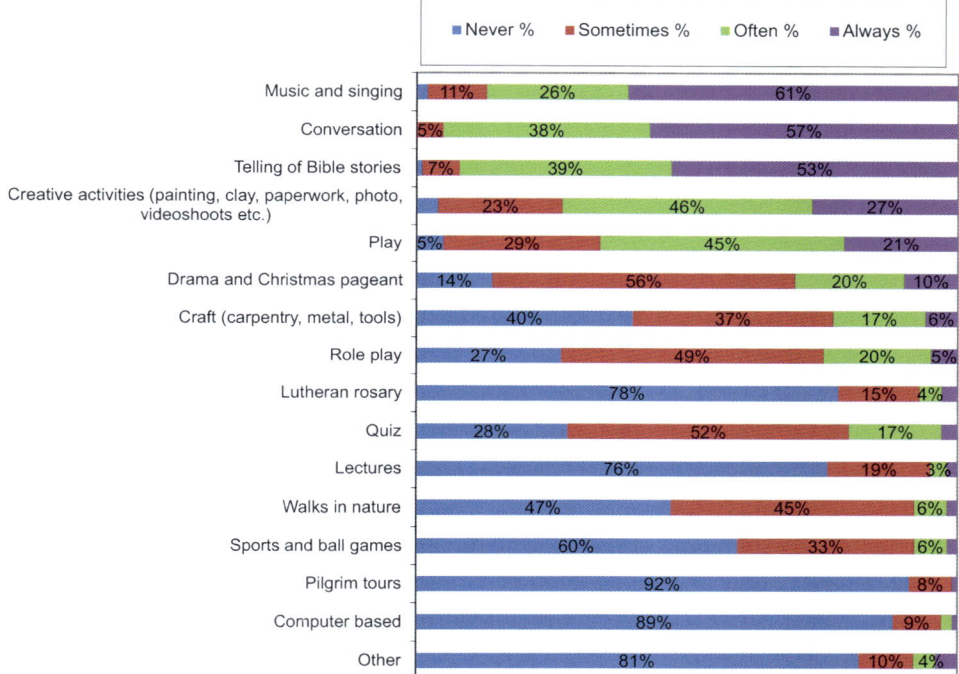

that the longer a parish has offered mini-confirmand groups the more lessons they seem to offer. If the parish has had this offer for only a short period of time they tend to offer fewer lessons. If parishes have offered mini-confirmand groups for less than 5 years, it seems that only 40% offer 16 lessons or more. If the parishes have offered it for 16 years or more, 62% offer more than 16 lessons. Apparently it all comes with the experience. Another interpretation of this matter could be that the parishes which have offered mini-confirmation groups only a short time are only moderately interested in this type of work and therefore try to 'get off' lightly. The average size of a mini-confirmand group consists of 16 mini-confirmands.

It can be seen that most of the mini-confirmation groups take place indoor and that the main tools are telling of Bible stories, music and singing, creative and play-

Table 8: What are the aims of the mini-confirmation groups?

Aims	Not at all	Somewhat	Absolutely
Knowledge about Christianity	1%	36%	63%
The practice of faith	2%	42%	56%
To pass on Christianity as a bearer of culture	18%	59%	23%
To point to Christ as the saviour of the world	3%	34%	62%
Other	50%	10%	40%

(Report 30)

Table 9: How do the pastors initiate their work with the mini-confirmand groups?

No other announcement or happening than the actual first meeting in the mini-confirmand group	53%
By an announcement or happening in a service	14%
At a meeting with the parents	14%
Other	8%

ful activities. It should be mentioned that Copenhagen has a low score on both the traditional Christian content of the mini-confirmand groups and on creative and playful activities, whereas Aarhus scores high when it comes both to the traditional Christian content and the creative and playful approach to the group. Aarhus diocese contains the second biggest city in Denmark, namely Aarhus, but also a large rural area with small or smaller towns or villages. Therefore, parts of Aarhus diocese are influenced more strongly by traditional values but it does not reflect on the pedagogical tools in use. Aarhus is as mentioned before, one of the "old" dioceses when it comes to mini-confirmand groups and therefore has a long experience concerning the groups. This reflects on the use of pedagogical tools. Copenhagen, on the contrary, is completely urbanised and the context of the inhabitants there is less likely to be a traditional one with traditional values. This probably means that the leaders are less likely to display a very traditional Christian content in their mini-confirmand groups. Why they also use rather traditional pedagogical tools which are not so creative or playful is less easy to grasp (Report 17–30). Perhaps it has to do with the rather small groups in Copenhagen compared to other places in Denmark? In Copenhagen, the average size of a group is 13 children and in Aarhus 19. It could also be noted that those pastors who put most weight on the aim "Knowledge about Christianity" also put a lot of weight on the aim "To pass on Christianity as a bearer of culture". Those pastors who were more into the aim "To point to Christ as the saviour of the world" were also into the aim "The practice of faith". That most pastors stress the "knowledge about Christianity" is hardly surprising as Denmark has had a tradition of a knowledge-based way of teaching Christianity both in school and church.

Table 10: How do the pastors finish off their work with the mini-confirmand groups?

By an announcement or happening in a service	62%
By the mini-confirmands making an appearance in a children's service (song, drama, Christmas pageant, etc.)	45%
By handing out a children's Bible, candle or such	28%
By handing out a diploma or equivalent	26%
Other	13%

Do the mini-confirmands drop out of their mini-confirmation group?

The short answer to this is "no". They do not drop out but continue to take part in the group until the end of the course. 98% of the parishes state that there are no drop-outs or only very few. The 2% who do experience drop-outs, state that boys are more likely to drop out than girls. An interesting detail could be noted even if it is based on very small numbers: In those instances where the organist takes part in the mini-confirmation group there is a tendency for the boys *not* to drop out. In those instances where there is a lot of weight on the practice of prayer, the boys have a small tendency to drop out (Report 32).

There is definitely more content and celebration at the end of the mini-confirmand group compared to the initiating phase. Mini-confirmand groups which meet for 16 lessons or more have a larger tendency to celebrate the ending of the mini-confirmand time by staging more of the above mentioned than just one of the possibilities, i.e. having both a nativity play, a handing out of diploma and handing over a candle as a memento of the day.

Confirmands and mini-confirmands

As it has been mentioned earlier it never was or is a requirement for the ordinary confirmands in 7th or 8th grade that they took part in a mini-confirmand group when they attended 3rd or 4th grade. But it appears that the pastors who head the ordinary confirmation work in the parishes can tell the difference between those confirmands who attended mini-confirmand groups and those who did not. It must here be born in mind that the confirmands were not asked in this survey, only the pastors. It is their impression that we meet in the survey.

The overall impression from Figure 4 is that the pastors find that attending mini-confirmand groups has been beneficial for the confirmands when they reach the ordinary confirmation classes later on. Especially when it comes to a more familiar relationship to the church, a more personal relationship to the workers in the church and the fact that the confirmands appear to have a more open attitude to the confirmation work, the mini-confirmand groups seem to have been fruitful. In many ways, Christianity can be described as "a religion of relationship" – relationship between people and between individuals and church – therefore the mini-confirmand groups seem to accomplish something important for the church, i.e. the groups have helped

Figure 4: Does it make a difference that the later confirmands took part in a mini-confirmand group earlier on? (Report 34)

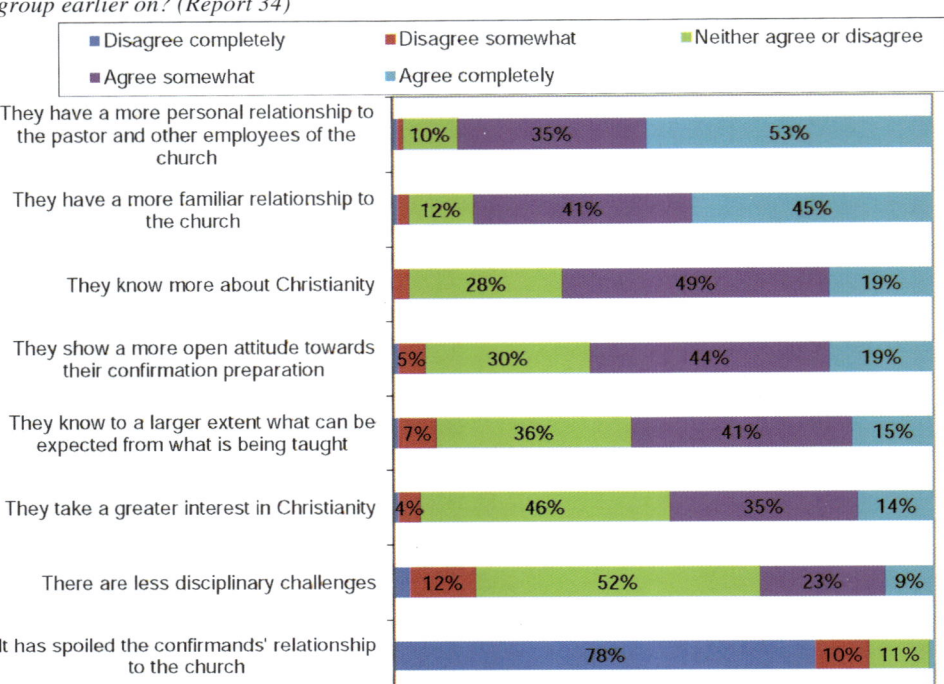

to establish a relationship between the children and the church. This experience also stresses the influence and importance of religious nurture at a more tender age than the ordinary confirmand classes.

4. From 2010 and onwards

As was mentioned at the beginning of this chapter, the Report which contained the most important results as shown above was meant to create the basis for making a new Decree with regard to the mini-confirmand work. The basis for many of the considerations with regard to the ordinary confirmands can be found in the international study on confirmation work in Europe which took place from 2007–2008 (Schweitzer et al. 2010; for the later study see Schweitzer et al. 2015) and in which Denmark participated (Christensen 2010). For the first time ever, a new Royal Decree for both confirmation work and mini-confirmand work was in sight.

The bishops appointed a committee consisting of nine members – two bishops, four pastors, one from the association of Sunday Schools, one lawyer and one university lecturer of pedagogy of religion (the author of this chapter) – and the task at hand was to make a suggestion for a new Royal Decree and also to make guidelines for both confirmation work and mini-confirmand work.

The new Royal Decree was signed in 2014 with very few changes from the suggestion submitted by the committee – the changes were mostly of a formal character – and it was put in force on October 1, 2014. When it comes to the part that has to do with mini-confirmand groups, there were various differences from the decree of 1994.

1. The first major difference to the prior decree of 1994 was that it became compulsory for all Danish parishes to establish mini-confirmand groups. If there was a lack of children in the parish or other practical matters which hindered the formation of a group, the parishes in question could work together in order to establish a group. All children living in Denmark would from now on have the possibility of joining a mini-confirmand group. This obviously also was the case for children with special needs in one way or another.
   After the initial debates over this new requirement, it seems that all parishes in different ways actually do offer the appropriate mini-confirmand groups.
2. The aim of the confirmation work and the aim for mini-confirmand work were stated to be identical: "Both the confirmation work and the children's confirmand work are based on the baptism and as such a part of the catechism instruction of the Church of Denmark. The aim is to contribute to making the children and the adolescents familiar with the basic contents of the Christian faith and the service of the Church of Denmark and to teach them what it means to live in a Christian faith and as a part of the Christian community". (Decree 2014 §1)
3. "When it comes to the children confirmands, this aim should be met by facilitating knowledge of church and Christianity by connecting them to the children's own experiences and questions. The duration of the mini-confirmand group must be at least 16 lessons of 45 minutes over at least two months or it can take place during one week in an intensive course". (Decree 2014 §3) Now there is a minimum duration where there used to be a maximum and the thoughts, questions and life world of the children are now taken seriously as a way of facilitating the subject matter at hand.
4. The parents are no longer responsible for planning the mini-confirmand work which happened only rarely anyway as stated above but the parents are still mentioned: "The aim is that the teaching takes place in cooperation with the parents". The future will show if there is any more success with this wording. (Decree 2014 §4 part 4)
5. The endearment 'mini-confirmands' was changed to the more official sounding 'children confirmands' but it must be said that this term does not seem to be used outside the committee! Mini-confirmands (or sometimes Junior-confirmands) will probably stay as the term most often used by children, pastors and people in general.

5. School reform 2014 and consequences

At the same time as the committee was working on the new Decree and having it approved by both the bishops and the Ministry of Church Affairs, the Ministry of Teaching was working on a new school reform. A lot could be said on this matter which will be left unsaid here but the bottom-line of the school reform was that the children were to have longer days in school, i.e. a whole-day-school, which was something completely new in Denmark. The concept of a whole-day-school meant that the children in the 3rd and 4th grade were at school for several more hours each day which in turn meant that time to take part in mini-confirmand groups became very limited. No numbers or percentages are yet available on this development. It has been heard from around the country that fewer children are taking part in a mini-confirmand group than before the school reform but this point of view has not as yet been validated. It has also meant that the requirement of having the minimum 16 lessons spread out over two months is not always followed. Alternative ways have been established in different parishes but no research has as yet been done on this development. How the school reform has influenced the mini-confirmand work in various ways will hopefully be established with the new report mentioned at the beginning of the article.

In many ways and despite the school reform, the mini-confirmand work is still a healthy child of the Church of Denmark. It works out well and is carried out professionally in the vast majority of parishes but still, the church must be alert. The membership rate is dropping both among infants who are not being baptised and among young people – mostly men between the age of 22 and 40 – who choose to drop out of church. Quite a few confirmands are being baptised every spring before their confirmation and there is also a growing number of grown-ups who are being baptised but there is a long way to go before the score is evened. So in time the numbers of children attending mini-confirmand groups will also probably drop – even though there are always some children attending who are not members of Church of Denmark. Membership or no membership, they are obviously all welcome. Under all circumstances the mini-confirmand work is opening a whole new world to the children which gives food to their thoughts.

6. Formal or non-formal religious education?

Normally one would differentiate between formal and non-formal education by stating that formal education is what a person meets in the established school and educational system in the society at hand whereas non-formal education is education that is not validated by exams or any qualifications. The non-formal education is not as such "controlled" by society's rules and regulations – as long as they do not do anything illegal – or "controlled" by persons who see to the academic level, the content, the duration and so forth of the non-formal education. It is not a government matter and the state as such cannot break in and promote or close down a non-formal educational offering. The non-formal education is not within the realm of the state other than by the normal laws that must be adhered to.

In this way mini-confirmand work in Denmark could be seen as non-formal religious education. The content, the duration, the leaders and such are all decided by the church itself. *But* as mentioned above, the new Royal Decree had to be signed in a rather official manner in order to be applicable. It was signed by Queen Margrethe II as she signs all laws passed in Denmark and she is the Head of State as well as the Head of the Church of Denmark. There is obviously freedom of religion in Denmark (apart from the Queen/King of Denmark who has to be a member of the Lutheran Church of Denmark) and has been so since 1849. But in the Constitution of Denmark (Grundloven) only one religious group is mentioned and that is the Church of Denmark which is, as it says, supported as such by the state. This means among other things that the Church of Denmark does not have a synod or any other regulating organ that can speak on behalf of the church. This is a much debated issue in the Danish church-life with pro- and con groups! The synod of Church of Denmark (folkekirken) is so to speak the parliament (Folketinget) which decides on all the external matters of the church whereas the church itself in form of the clergy and lay councils decide internal matters. Every now and again this balance collapses because it has never really been put into formal writing what internal and external matters are in reality. It is a matter of discretion and judgement from the minister of Church Affairs who may have the flair for it or not. So the Royal Decree on confirmation work and mini-confirmand work had to pass through the hands of bishops, lay councils, interested church members and the Ministry of Church Affairs and the Ministry's civil servants in order to finally be signed by the Queen. Other and more controversial matters are also discussed by the Folketing and voted on as for instance the law legalising same sex marriages in church (in the Registry Office it had been legal for 25 years) or women's access to ordination which the Folketing approved in 1948. In both cases the church stood divided and the decision of the Folketing became decisive.

So in some ways it could be stated that mini-confirmand groups in Denmark are an expression of both formal and non-formal Christian education. Formal after all because formally it is sanctioned by the Ministry of Church Affairs, and their lawyers and civil servants have been responsible for writing the actual Decree and thus looking into it from a legal point of view, and non-formal because it is the decision of the church and bishops that such a thing should come into existence at all with none of the above mentioned signs of it being formal. Maybe it should be called a formal non-formal religious education or a non-formal formal religious education?

7. Research in Denmark on non-formal religious education and church matters in general

In Denmark, research in practical theology has for quite a number of years been centered around research into, for example, the history of the Danish high mass, the ritual for baptism through history, hymns and their history, theories on, for example, pastoral care ('Seelsorge') and all matters relating to a very classic theological understanding of practical theology. During more recent years, the focus has also been placed on research with sociological connotations and surveys concerning, for instance, confirmation work, baby hymn singing, funeral practices in Denmark, the relation between church and society. There are several institutions active in this particular field. Both quantitative surveys and qualitative investigations containing questionnaires and focus group interviews have found their way into Danish research when it comes to church matters. In fact, in recent years three centers for research in practical theology concerning the church have either been established or long existing departments have added empirical and sociological methods to a higher degree in their work:

1. Practical Theology, University of Aarhus: At the University of Aarhus, research concerning church related matters is incorporated within the Department of Practical Theology along with the more classic issues of this area of study: a) Social and practical means of expression in the Christian, ecclesiastical and religious field are worked with and this work is both interpretive, critical and constructive; b) Interest is taken not only within the traditional boundaries of Church of Denmark but also within the area of religious practices which are not bound to a church context but are more individualised; c) Social and practical means of expression in the ecclesiastical and Christian field are interpreted as theologically productive. These social and practical means of expressions are thus seen as ways in which one can engage in theology, i.e. as reflections concerning faith; d) all research in the field is seen with a perspective to Danish society in general.

2. Center for Church Research, University of Copenhagen (see https://teol.ku.dk/cfk/): This research center was established in order to a) research the practicing forms of churches and forms of communication; b) research the institutional and social terms of the churches; c) research the contributions of the churches in relation to the identity and context of Danish society; d) research the general development of religion in Denmark.

3. The Research and Development Center of Church of Denmark (see https://www.fkuv.dk/videnscenter/om-videnscentret) was established in January 2014 and this Center aims to: a) collect and develop knowledge and research which is relevant for church and society; b) develop projects and initiate surveys in order to create new knowledge with regard to Church of Denmark; c) facilitate research and knowledge for the benefit of Church of Denmark and Danish society.

Quite an extensive amount of research has been published during the last four years from these various research institutions. When it comes to non-formal Christian education, research done on baby hymn singing can be mentioned as one example. One tentative step in Denmark has been taken in order to familiarise new parents with the church by introducing baby hymn singing where infants with one of their parents come to church once a week to sing hymns – traditional hymns of Church of Denmark or new(er) hymns – with their little ones. There is no formal teaching or explanations or 'preaching' during the course, only singing for and playing with the babies aged two months to about nine months. This type of relationship between church, parents and children has been developed over the last 15 years and now around 25–27% of all Danish babies take part in such a course in Church of Denmark centered around baby hymn singing. Between 55% and 60% of Danish parishes offer this type of early non-formal Christian education (Vejrup Nielsen and Janderup 2015). Maybe this will have a supportive role for the mini-confirmand classes in the future because the parents have already been in a 'church program' and found it meaningful? The extensive and international studies on confirmation work which have had a great impact on confirmation preparation in Danish parishes must also be mentioned in this context (Schweitzer et al. 2010; Schweitzer et al. 2015; Schweitzer et al. 2017).

Many other surveys with a wide range of methodological backgrounds could also be mentioned. One thing is for sure: the empirical research has hit the Church of Denmark!

8. Closing remarks

All in all, it would seem, at least at the moment, that the mini-confirmand work is doing quite well in Denmark. However, it is also important to be aware of the changing paradigms when it comes to infant baptism and the consequences of the school reform. Also the growing scepticism towards religion on a whole which we now experience in the Western world must be taken into consideration when looking at the future for the non-formal Christian education in Denmark. All in all, people are looking forward to the research results from the upcoming new survey on mini-confirmands in Denmark.

References

Reports and Decrees

The Report: Rasmussen, S.M., Christensen, L., Götke, P., and Nicolajsen, G. (2009): http://www.konfirmandcenter.dk/fileadmin/filer/PDF_filer/Rapport_om_kirkelig_under-visning_v_2_0.pdf [08.03.2019].

The Royal Decree 2014: https://www.retsinformation.dk/Forms/R0710.aspx?id=164454 [08.03.2019].

The Report 2010 by the Committee established by the Danish Bishops: http://www.kon-firmandcenter.dk/fileadmin/filer/PDF_filer/Daabsoplaeringsudvalgets_rapport_2010.pdf [08.03.2019].

Other literature

Christensen, L (2010). Confirmation Work in Denmark. in: Schweitzer, F., Ilg, W., and Simojoki, H. (eds.) (2010). *Confirmation Work in Europe. Empirical Results, Experiences and Challenges. A Comparative Study in Seven Countries.* Gütersloh: Gütersloher Verlagshaus, 116–138.

Demant, J., Thyssen, B., and Iversen, H.R. (eds.) (2008). *Dåbsmanual. Opskrifter til arbejdet med dåb og dåbsoplæring i folkekirken.* Løgumkloster.

Krarup, J.K. et al. (eds.) (1996). *Ud fra en gudstjenstlig sammenhæng. Håndbog om indledende konfirmationsforberedelse.* Frederiksberg: Religionspædagogisk Forlag (RPF).

Schweitzer, F., Ilg, W., and Simojoki, H. (eds.) (2010). *Confirmation Work in Europe. Empirical Results, Experiences and Challenges. A Comparative Study in Seven Countries.* Gütersloh: Gütersloher Verlagshaus.

Schweitzer, F., Niemelä, K., Schlag, T., and Simojoki, H. (eds.) (2015). *Youth, Religion and Confirmation Work in Europe. The Second Study.* Gütersloh: Gütersloher Verlagshaus.

Schweitzer, F., Schlag, T, Simojoki, H., and Tervo-Niemelä, K. (eds.) (2017). *Confirmation, Faith and Volunteerism. A Longitudinal Study on Protestant Adolescents in the Transition towards Adulthood. European Perspectives.* Gütersloh: Gütersloher Verlagshaus.

Vejrup Nielsen, M., and Janderup, H. (2015). *"Tager du barnet ved hånden, tager du moderen ved hjertet".* Aarhus, University of Aarhus

On baby hymn singing. Report published by Center for Contemporary Religion, University of Aarhus. http://samtidsreligion.au.dk/fileadmin/Samtidsreligion/Oevrige_projekter/Babysalmesang/BabysalmesangRapport.pdf [08.03.2019].

Profiling confirmation work as a marketing strategy

A case study from Sweden

Per Pettersson

In 1970, 81 % of Swedish young people attended confirmation work offered by the Church of Sweden. 46 years later, in 2017, the attendance had dropped to 24 %. Along the continuous decline, the church has taken a number of initiatives in order to reform and renew the pedagogic form and content of confirmation work. As part of new pedagogic views the label "confirmation teaching" has been changed to "confirmation work". This article gives a short background to the decline of attendance, a brief overview of Church of Sweden's response, and demonstrates by a case study one local example to meet young people's individual preferences by providing different new forms of confirmation work. The last part of the article discusses possible factors behind the fast decline of participation in Swedish confirmation work.

1. Changing social and religious conditions for confirmation work

As other European countries, Sweden has passed through a process of secularization by which the state as well as the individual has liberated themselves from the previous power of the Church (Bäckström, Beckman and Pettersson 2004). The historical strong relationship between the state and the Church of Sweden has changed from a situation of total unity towards an almost complete separation between church and state that was accomplished January 1, 2000. However, the most radical change of religious relationships has taken place on the individual level, between the Church and individual Swedish people. Relationships to the Church have changed by an increased privatization of religion, a continuous decline in people's regular participation in worship and a decreasing acceptance of the traditional dogmas and values of the Church (Gustafsson and Pettersson 2000, Sjödin 2001, Pettersson 2006).

Nevertheless, there is a prevailing formal relationship between a majority of Swedish people and the Church of Sweden (Pettersson 2000). Further, the Church of Sweden still has a dominant role in the Swedish religious scene by its size and its integration in Swedish history as well as in some official public contexts and institutions (Pettersson 2011, 2015). So the Swedish religious situation is characterised by complexity (Furseth 2018).

Presently (2017) 59 % are members of the Church of Sweden and pay around 1 % of their income as membership fee. 42 % of all children born were baptised in the

Church of Sweden, 24% of all 15-year-olds participated in its confirmation work, 32% of all marriages took place in the Church of Sweden and 73% of all dead were buried within the church setting (Church of Sweden statistics 2017). However, the percentage of members as well as participation in religious life rites in Church of Sweden is continuously declining.

When analysing and interpreting the religious change in Sweden, it is important to take into account the continuous increase of the part of the Swedish population that has a non-Swedish background. The high degree of immigration to Sweden during 2014–2016 has speeded up the religious change and increased the religious pluralism. In some respects, the secularised character of Sweden has thereby been reduced, especially through the public visibility of Muslims and Muslim religious practice. In 2017, around 23% of the population were born abroad or were children with both parents having been born abroad.

2. Confirmation is the major form of non-formal religious education

The dominant form of Swedish religious education takes place in the public school system and is named "Knowledge about religion". It is non-confessional, compulsory and according to the national curriculum, to teach about different religions and help the students develop life-skills (cf. Läroplan för grundskolan, förskoleklassen och fritidshemmet 2011). These skills are supposed to be developed by encountering different people's thoughts of what life is all about, their religions, traditions and life-views. The teaching deals with essential life-questions of the pupils and the religious traditions are used to find different possible answers to these questions (Osbeck and Pettersson 2009).

The place for non-formal and confessional religious teaching is within churches and other religious organizations. As being the major religious agent, the Church of Sweden is the major organizer of non-formal religious education, and the major educational activity consists of confirmation work. In the year 2017, 26887 young people of the age of 15 years participated and were confirmed after attending a 60-hour confirmation course. This is by far the largest educational activity focusing on religion in the Swedish society next to the compulsory school. In addition to confirmation work the Church of Sweden also runs many other pedagogic activities for children, young people and adults. Some of them have explicit educational aims, others have a more implicit educational function. Minority religious organizations provide different forms of educational activities for different age groups, sometimes linked to "rites de passage" according to their respective traditions, e.g. the Catholic Church, the Jewish community, Islamic organizations, etc.

Since the separation between state and church, there has been increasing attention within the Church of Sweden's organization to the significance and importance of confirmation work. This attention is largely caused by worries concerning the continuous decrease in participation. As Table 1 shows, figures on membership in the Church of Sweden as well as participation in all life rites (baptism, confirmation, marriages, funerals) have decreased since this type of national data collection started in 1970.[1]

Table 1: Church of Sweden statistics 1970–2017

Year	Baptism % of all born	Confirmation % of all 15-year-olds	Confirmation % of all 15-year-old church members[2]	Church marriage % of all marriages	Church funeral % of all deaths	Church membership % of whole population	Foreign background % of whole population (born abroad or both parents born abroad)
1970	81 %	81 %		79 %	96 %	97 %	
1975	83 %	74 %		65 %	95 %	95 %	
1980	76 %	65 %		58 %	94 %	92 %	
1985	74 %	69 %		61 %	93 %	92 %	
1990	72 %	63 %		64 %	93 %	89 %	
1995	79 %	51 %	59 %	63 %	89 %	86 %	13 %
2000	73 %	43 %	51 %	61 %	88 %	83 %	15 %
2005	68 %	37 %	43 %	50 %	85 %	77 %	17 %
2010	54 %	33 %	41 %	37 %	81 %	70 %	19 %
2015	46 %	28 %	43 %	34 %	77 %	63 %	22 %
2017	42 %	24 %	39 %	32 %	73 %	59 %	23 %

The most dramatic decrease during this period has taken place in confirmation work, which has declined from 81 % to 24 % in relation to the population, or down to 39 % when related only to 15-year-olds that are church members. This has activated many voices in the church arguing for increased financial resources directed to confirmation work. A number of improvement projects at the national level and different kinds of development work at the local and diocese level have been initiated, although critics argue that far too little has been done (Grahn, Eek and Pettersson 2007, Pettersson 2009).

---

1 The detailed data collection of the church has a long tradition since the national population registration was handled by the church at local level since it was initiated in 1608 until it was handed over to the state tax authority in 1991. Church statistics in the present form was introduced in 1970, building on compulsory local records and yearly reports from all parishes.
2 Statistics on confirmation in % of all 15-year old church members is available only from 1995.

3. Changed pedagogic ideology and theological understanding

Parallel with the decline in participation, there has been a continuous reformation of the confirmation work (Pettersson 2010). The Church has continuously revised its view on religious didactics along the general changing pedagogic discourse, following the same path as the public school system towards a more pupil-oriented pedagogic model. The development has moved towards an increasing focus at the pedagogic forms, methods and process in confirmation work and a decreasing regulation of the content in the teaching. This was part of the radical wave of pedagogic reforms sweeping across all European educational systems, universities as well as the ordinary school world in the 1970s. The Church of Sweden's educational board took a major step in this pedagogic direction in 1978 by adopting a principal document on a new pedagogic view on all kinds of church education. The old authoritarian educational model was abandoned and replaced by new pedagogic principles (Kyrkans utbildning, förutsättningar och principer 1978, Wadensjö 1979). This new view was further elaborated and applied in the "Guiding principles for the Church of Sweden's confirmation work" of 1978 (Riktlinjer för Svenska kyrkans konfirmandarbete 1978). The new guiding principles were to a large degree built on the results of a survey among confirmation teachers about their views on the previous more detailed curriculum of 1968 (Läroplan för Svenska kyrkans konfirmandundervisning 1968, Wallinder 1990).

The basic idea of the new guiding principles was that teaching in Christian belief should relate to the existential needs of the pupils. The questions of the participating young people should be the starting point of teaching. Theologically, this new pedagogic approach was underpinned by contextual theological reflection inspired by liberation theology and the pedagogical work of the Brazilian liberation pedagogue Paulo Freire (Freire 1975, Wallinder 1990). As part of this change in the pedagogical view, the label "confirmation teaching" was replaced by the label "confirmation work". The new guiding principles meant a radical change of the Church of Sweden's pedagogic principles for confirmation work from a traditional top-down model towards a pupil-oriented pedagogical model. This was part of a general development from religion being more or less *enforced* on people in the former relatively homogeneous Swedish society with a state church, towards the present pluralistic situation in which church membership is voluntary and religion is a *possible resource* for individual or collective needs.

As part of the pedagogical change, the concept "service" has been used in order to stress the focus on the participating young people. Confirmation work is described as a service to young people (Geyer 1989). This view of confirmation was significantly stressed in the new revised Guiding Principles of 1994 (Riktlinjer för Svenska kyrkans konfirmandarbete 1994, 6); "Confirmation work is a SERVICE to teenagers in a CRUCIAL stage of their lives. The Church has a mission to WALK TOGETHER with them and ON THE FOUNDATION OF BAPTISM present the

INTERPRETATION OF LIFE which is provided by the Christian Faith"[3]. Parallel with the pedagogical change, there was a simultaneous change of the theological view on confirmation. In the most recent version of the Guiding Principles for Church of Sweden's Confirmation Work (2008), the objectives of confirmation work are formulated in the following way (Riktlinjer för Svenska kyrkans konfirmandarbete 2008, 6):

"The confirmation work shall demonstrate the faith and life of the Church of Sweden by offering the confirmands:

- knowledge that the Christian faith and the life of the Church is dealing with the questions of life that we as human beings carry.
- a possibility to explore and test the Christian faith from the perspective of their own questions of life.
- to become familiarised with liturgical services and prayer.
- tools to form a confident identity and to develop themselves spiritually and emotionally.
- joy of living and hope for the future.
- experience of community in the group of confirmands and in the congregation.
- a possibility to express the gospel of the Church and its presence in society and the world.
- tools to relate Christian faith to other views of life, and to show respect in relation to people with other convictions."

These objectives are very short and generally formulated and do not contain any more detailed description of the expected content. The main aim is to give the confirmands insight and opportunity to explore and try out the Christian faith starting with their own questions and issues of life. Confirmation work should also support the adolescents in the process of identity formation, emotional and personal growth and their building of good relationships. A variety of expressive and creative methods are used to reach these objectives such as common experiences in the group as starting point for dialogue and reflection. These methods can be value exercises[4], drama, dance, play, singing, music, painting, etc.

According to the guidelines a confirmation course ought to include at least 60 hours of group meetings and at least four nights of confirmation camp. Camps with overnight stay are regarded as an important form of activity in order to build good relationships, to build a supportive culture for open discussions and to practice regular prayer life in the group.

There is, however, no elaborated national standardised curriculum regulating the content of a "confirmation course", and no officially accredited or recommended

---

3 Capital letters are used in the same way as in the original Swedish text.
4 Value exercises are pedagogical methods used in groups of people to express and discuss values.

textbooks. Thereby it is in practice up to the individual teachers and local teams to decide their own more specified objectives, to plan the content of the course and to construct their own curriculum. Quite often they compile their own "textbook" from different texts, articles and other material. Consequently, the form and content of Church of Sweden's confirmation work is in practice outlined and shaped at the local level. This means that the questions and subjects that are brought up, what is taught, and the actual content in a "confirmation course" can be totally different in one confirmation group compared to another group, even within the same local parish.

The development of Swedish confirmation work during the last twenty years has been characterised by increasing numbers of camp days, increasing confirmation work managed by a team of church personnel instead of just one minister, and increasing numbers of young recently confirmed volunteers who have the function of assisting leaders. In 2017 the number of young confirmed volunteers was up to 8165.

4. Differentiation and profiling of confirmation offers

Building on the quite general national guidelines there is a broad variety of how confirmation courses are practically arranged, which pedagogic forms are used, what issues are brought up and consequently how the actual "curriculum by practice" is formed.

Some confirmation groups meet weekly during the school year. Others start just before Christmas during Advent, meet a few times during the spring and conclude with a confirmation camp in the summer. There are also longer summer camps for a period of three to four weeks. Such long summer camps have existed since the 1950s, organised by the Church at diocese level or by "secular" organizations in some form of cooperation with the Church. Some dioceses offer special summer confirmation camps in which young people with and without special needs are integrated in the same camp.

Since so many activities compete with the adolescents' time and attention, there is a growing trend to combine confirmation work with other interests of young people, for example sports like ice hockey, golf, sailing, hiking, horseback riding or cultural activities like music, drama, etc. This way of profiling confirmation offers has been practiced in the longer summer camps since the 1960s. One popular form has been confirmation camp abroad in combination with an English language course, mostly taking place in England and arranged by private companies specialising in language courses for young people.

During the last ten years there has been an increasing differentiation of form and contextual packaging also for confirmation work organised by local parishes, for example, in cooperation between a number of parishes in order to offer different alternative forms of confirmation work. One such local cooperation will be described in the following section in a case study of the differentiated confirmation offer in the city of Karlstad.

5. Differentiated confirmation offer in Karlstad

Karlstad is a Swedish city of around 100000 inhabitants including suburban areas. It consists of six geographical parishes: Karlstads domkyrko parish, Norrstrands parish, Västerstrands parish, Alster-Nyedsbygdens parish, Väse-Fågelviks parish, Grava parish. The first five parishes mentioned are organised in a common pastoral unit, "Karlstads pastorat", led by a main pastor (kyrkoherde). Participation in confirmation is higher than on the average in Sweden, but the trend of declining participation is the same as elsewhere. The ongoing decline during the years 2000–2008 worried the church workers responsible for confirmation work in the six parishes of Karlstad. After a period of analysis and discussion, a decision was made to reorganise the confirmation work and to form a common organization for the confirmation work in Karlstad with a joint differentiated confirmation offer, aiming to reduce and stop further decline.

The new organization was introduced in 2009. This case study describes the different available offers of confirmation courses in Karlstad during the school year of August 2017 – July 2018, as it was published in a printed brochure and presented at the website of the Church of Sweden in Karlstad's pastorat (www.svenskakyrkan.se/karlstadspastorat/konfa accessed June 15 2017).

On the first page of the website confirmation is presented as "The journey of your life" and the following text reads: *"All of life is a journey … Certain people you meet only during a short period of time. Others follow a bit further. Confirmation time can also be a journey, geographically but most of all a journey within yourself. Choose a confirmation journey that seems exiting"*.

On the following web pages, 13 alternative forms of confirmation work are presented. They differ concerning contextual profile as well as the time of the confirmation group meetings. Four alternatives are weekly meetings spread out over the school year. Three of the offered forms of confirmation work take place during a number of weekends spread out over the school year. Two confirmation groups include a longer period of travel and a number of meetings during the school year, and four alternatives are concentrated to the summer holiday period.

The following are the 13 alternative forms of confirmation work offered to young people in Karlstad during the school year 2017–18 (the responsible parish is noted in brackets):

Weekly meetings

1. Weekly meetings (Västerstrands parish)
2. Weekly meetings combined with support of school homework (Grava parish)
3. Weekly meetings with film profile (Norrstrands parish)
4. Weekly meetings adapted for people with mental handicaps (Norrstrands parish)

Weekend meetings

5. Weekend meetings, one weekend per month (Väse-Fågelviks parish)
6. Weekend meetings, one weekend per month (Alster-Nyedsbygdens parish)
7. Weekend meetings with hunter profile (Alster-Nyedsbygdens parish)

Travel included during school year

8. Confirmation work with human rights profile (Karlstads domkyrko parish)
9. Confirmation work with skiing profile (Grava parish)

Summer confirmation

10. Summer confirmation work with one-week camp on the island of Gotland (Västerstrands parish)
11. Summer confirmation work in Karlstad with a few days camp nearby (Norrstrands parish)
12. Summer confirmation work with football profile (Norrstrands parish)
13. Summer confirmation work with music profile (Norrstrands parish).

All 13 alternatives follow the general confirmation guidelines of the Church of Sweden, but as described previously the actual curriculum in practice and the Christian educational content depends on decisions of each team of leaders. A general idea with different profiles is to contextualise the Christian content by linking the profile of the respective confirmation group to different interests of the young people. All groups follow the general advice to include a minimum of two weekend camps, and several of them include a larger number of camp days.

In the group with film profile, movies are used as a primary pedagogic tool, which is of special attraction to many young people. The skiing and football profiles combine confirmation work with social time and teambuilding around a certain sport activity. It works in a similar way in the music profile, which is a choice for young people who like singing in public or acting on a stage. Their confirmation time consists of producing a musical which is totally integrated into the confirmation teaching, and the confirmation period ends with a public performance of a musical composed and performed by the confirmands themselves.

The human rights profile integrates in a similar way confirmation teaching with a special focus on social ethics. This alternative includes a one week trip to Poland to visit a former concentration camp from the Second World War, a visit which is carefully prepared a long time before and followed up afterwards. Human rights are used as a pedagogic framing of the confirmation teaching and the visit to the concentration camp gives a special serious and personal reflective character to the atmosphere in this confirmation group.

Karlstad is located in a rural region with large forests, known for several kinds of wild animals: elk, moose, bear, wolf, etc. Two of the six parishes, Molkom-Alster and Väse-Fågelvik include large parts of the countryside. Young people in these parishes are brought up with hunting as part of their families' life, and many long for the time when they will be able to take part fully, especially in the yearly moose hunting. This is the background of forming a confirmation alternative in combination with a hunter course. The group meets one Sunday per month from 10–16:00 during the school year, and attends a hunting course every second Thursday from 18–21:00. Three weekend camps are included, one of them with moose hunting. Additionally, participants are offered to take part in practical hunting on seven occasions, arranged in cooperation with The Hunter Association. The hunter course follows parallel with the confirmation course. At the end of the school year, participants are confirmed and can receive their hunting license.

One of the confirmation groups that meet every week includes the possibility to get support for school homework. This can be especially valuable for young people with weak support options from parents. Another group that meets every week is specially adapted in form and content for young people with some kind of mental handicap. It is presented like this: *"Perhaps you have a functional variation of some kind. Perhaps you are in need of special support. Perhaps you feel better with not too many people around. Then this might be the confirmation group for you!"* The confirmation time in this group is planned in close conversation with the participants and adapted to their specific needs and possibilities.

6. Has the differentiation by profiling succeeded?

The new organization of confirmation work in Karlstad was implemented in fall 2009. Table 2 illustrates the outcome concerning participation in the five parishes of Karlstad's pastorat[5].

---

5 Grava parish is not included in the analysis since it forms a separate pastorat and the data available are based on the pastorat organizational structure.

Table 2: Confirmation statistics, Church of Sweden in Karlstad's pastorat 2007–2017 (%)

	% confirmed of 15-year-old church members	% confirmed of all 15-year-olds	All confirmed in numbers
2007	47.4 %	40.3 %	335
2008	46.1 %	38.5 %	318
2009	38.5 %	32.7 %	242
2010	47.2 %	38.7 %	279
2011	53.9 %	41.7 %	279
2012	52.2 %	40.2 %	272
2013	54.1 %	41.1 %	271
2014	49.8 %	37.5 %	239
2015	50.3 %	36.5 %	248
2016	48.6 %	35.4 %	246
2017	42.6 %	29.3 %	194

Has the new differentiated offer of alternative forms of confirmation work suc-
ceeded? Table 2 show statistics from 2007–2017 on confirmed 15-year-old church
members as well as confirmed related to all 15-year-olds in the population. The relevant and most secure figure to compare over time is the proportion of confirmed
among 15-year-old church members (first row), since the rate of 15-year-olds with
non-Swedish background in the population at large has continuously increased over
the years. So the following analysis will focus on confirmed among 15-year-old
church members.

When looking at the statistics regarding confirmed church members, the figures
show that the trend of decline seems to have been temporarily stopped after the new
organization of confirmation work was introduced in 2009. Figures show that 47 %
of the church members were confirmed in 2010. This was followed by a noticeable increase in the years 2011–13 when an average of 53.4 % of church members
were confirmed. However, the next three years from 2014–16 show an almost corre-
sponding decline down to 49.6 % on the average. The very last data from 2017 show
a dramatic drop down to 42.6 %. When looking just at the statistics, the conclusion
is that the reorganization by differentiation of confirmation work in Karlstad seems
to have been a success initially, although not sustainable. The initial successful
years would need a more careful analysis in order to identify in more detail the factors behind the increase by 6 percent points, and possible explanations for the high
figures during these three years 2011–13. In a similar way, a deeper analysis would
be needed to understand the following decline and especially the drop in 2017.

7. Differentiation of confirmation courses as part of societal differentiation

What is then the background to the development of different forms of confirmation courses? We will discuss four background factors that are linked to one another: general societal differentiation, individualization, culture of consumption and competition for young people's time.

Ever since the breaking up of unitary agricultural society in the 19th century, the process of societal differentiation has implied a continuous and still increasing pluralization in all areas of society, and thereby also individualization which is the other side of differentiation and pluralism. Pluralization means the development of individual life worlds and consequently that individuals become increasingly unique in their background, experiences, knowledge and presumably their way of thinking. Thereby societal differentiation drives individualization. Differentiation, pluralization and individualization develop in different ways in different cultural contexts. Sweden is one of the countries in which these mechanisms are most developed, as indicated in an obvious way by results from the World Values Survey program (WVS). According to WVS, Sweden is among the most individually-oriented countries in the world, in combination with being one of the countries in which traditional religious values are of least importance for the people (WVS 1981–2015).

As part of developing into one of the most individually-oriented countries, Sweden has supported individual choice and strived to provide adaptation to individual needs in a number of social areas in which just one option previously was offered. This concerns public schools, health and medical care, social care, telecommunication, post, electricity, etc. From being known as a country with a strong state and a large public sector of state monopolies, Sweden is today probably the country having gone furthest in outsourcing state activities by implementing a "Neoliberal Market Paradigm".

The outsourcing of public services has implied differentiation of offers and thereby expanded the general consumption culture to be implemented also in previously standardised public services, e.g. schools. Young people are brought up in an environment in which they are used to having the option to make individual choices from a number of alternatives. Confirmation work is today one of many possible alternatives competing for young people's time with a vast number of other possible sports, leisure and educational activities. This competition for young people's time is probably the most important background factor behind the development of differentiated forms of confirmation work. Thus, the differentiation of confirmation courses can be regarded as part of the range of consequences of the general societal differentiation process.

The marketing of confirmation profiles makes confirmation work more similar to other leisure activities and can therefore become more identified as part of the general leisure activity market. One can thus wonder if the differentiation of confirmation work makes it more invisible as something special and different from other leisure activities, and thereby less attractive as an alternative to other activities. This could be a possible contradiction to the aim of making confirmation work more attractive by combining it with some kind of leisure activity. There might, however, be no alternative than to enter the leisure activity market, although this competitive market demands continuous evaluation and renewal of confirmation work in order to keep being an attractive choice.

8. Why is confirmation loosing attraction?

As described above, the confirmation rate in the Church of Sweden has declined from 81 % in 1970 to 24 % in 2017 of all 15-year-olds, and to 39 % when related only to 15-year-olds that are church members. But why is confirmation loosing attraction? The general social and religious change by differentiation and individualization has already been mentioned as a background factor as well as the crucial change by increasing competition for young people's time with a number of other activities. There are, however, also other factors to take into account, other societal factors as well as internal factors within the Church of Sweden.

In the first part of this article, the separation of state and church was mentioned. As part of the previous close link between church and state, confirmation had an official character as a "rite de passage" that manifested young people becoming adults. This civil status merit of confirmation has long been gone, but some kind of compulsory character of confirmation stayed in the collective memory for decades, all through the 20th century.

A radical change in the traditional social position of confirmation took place when high school (Swedish: gymnasium) was made almost compulsory for all young people by a political decision in the 1980s. This means that today almost all 16- to 18-year olds attend gymnasium. After three years, they end this period of education with a big celebration that has developed into an additional common "rite de passage". This new rite has taken over the previous role of confirmation as manifesting adulthood, especially since the end of gymnasium takes place at the age of 18 when adulthood is legally acknowledged by the right to vote, drive a car, buying alcohol, etc.

The loss of confirmation's social value is one essential factor behind the changed position and attraction of confirmation. Another important factor is that historically confirmation implied access to the Holy Communion. But in 1988 child communion was introduced in the Church of Sweden and confirmation is no longer a compulsory condition or "merit" in order to take part. Thus the historical function of confirmation as providing certain specified merits of both societal and religious value has been abolished. Today the value of confirmation is purely "religious" and possible to evaluate only on a personal, individual level.

Explanations of the decline in confirmation rates are also to be found internally in the Church of Sweden and concern mainly the unclear theology of confirmation. The national guidelines as well as the confirmation ritual and practice in the parishes are vague concerning the theological motive and objective of confirmation. Is confirmation work primarily a preparation of the individual's confirmation of his/her baptism in the confirmation rite? Is confirmation work primarily a period for personal growth with a Christian profile? Is confirmation work primarily education in Christian faith? Is the confirmation rite primarily *God's* confirmation of love to the individual confirmand? All these, and other, interpretations of the theology and objective of confirmation exist in parallel, with the consequence that descriptions of confirmation and confirmation work are often very unclear and ambivalent.

A second unclear aspect is the ambiguity between an orientation towards the individual on the one hand and an orientation towards the congregation on the other hand. Should confirmation work be focused at integrating the individual in the congregation, preparing for regular Sunday service participation, etc.? Or should confirmation work first of all assist the individual in handling his/her personal life and private faith? There is often an ambiguity and tension between these two objectives and directions: the individual or the congregation.

As previously described, there is presently no national curriculum or authorised textbook that regulate or describe the content of a confirmation course. Additionally, the only existing national regulating texts are the Guiding Principles for Church of Sweden's Confirmation Work (Riktlinjer för Svenska kyrkans konfirmandarbete 2008) and the confirmation ritual in the Church's Liturgical Handbook (Kyrkohandbok för Svenska kyrkan 2018) and these texts do not give any clear declaration of the objective of confirmation work or the confirmation rite.

These unclear conditions make it difficult and in practice impossible to have a common and coordinated national strategy for development and improvement of confirmation work. Before the reformation of confirmation work through the 1970s introduction of a new pedagogic ideology, there was a common curriculum and description of the theological motivation along with common national strategies for the development of confirmation work. The introduction of a youth-oriented pedagogic profile implied many positive aspects, but the theological reflection on confirmation as well as common practical theological strategies got lost in this process of change. This is at least the author's analysis.

The unclear theological position and essence of Church of Sweden's confirmation work and the lack of a national common strategy for the development of the confirmation practice is a major negative internal factor within the church behind the ongoing decline in participation. However, even if the confirmation rate at a national level presently is down to 39% of the church members (2017), this still means that 26887 girls and boys were confirmed in 2017. If the Church of Sweden take the young church members seriously, the Church should invest national resources in order to raise the quality in confirmation work in all aspects discussed in this article, theologically as well as developmentally and strategically.

References

Bäckström, A., Beckman, E.N., and Pettersson, P. (2004), *Religious Change in Northern Europe – The Case of Sweden,* Stockholm: Verbum.

Church of Sweden statistics (2017). http://www.svenskakyrkan.se [10.08.2017].

Freire, P. (1975), *Utbildning för befrielse,* Stockholm: Gummessons Bokförlag.

Furseth, I. (ed.) (2018). *Religious Complexity in the Public Sphere. Palgrave Studies in Religion, Politics, and Policy.* Palgrave Macmillan: Cham.

Geyer, K. (1989). *Att dana människor. Om kvalitet i livsfrågeorienterad verksamhet – en diskussion i Georg Herbert Meads anda,* diss. Uppsala: Teologiska institutionen, Uppsala Universitet.

Grahn, N., Eek, J., and Pettersson, P. (2007). *Vägar framåt i Svenska kyrkans konfirmandarbete,* Karlstad: Karlstads stift.

Gustafsson, G., and Pettersson, T. (eds.) (2000). *Folkkyrkor och religiös pluralism – den nordiska religiösa modellen (Folk Churches and Religious Pluralism. The Nordic Religious Model).* Stockholm: Verbum.

Kyrkans utbildning, förutsättningar och principer (1978). Ett arbetsmaterial utgivet av Svenska Kyrkans Utbildningsnämnd, Stockholm: Skeab.

Kyrkohandbok för Svenska kyrkan (2018). Church handbook for the Church of Sweden) Stockholm: Verbum.

Läroplan för grundskolan, förskoleklassen och fritidshemmet (2011). Stockholm: Skolverket.

Läroplan för Svenska kyrkans konfirmandundervisning (1968). Stockholm: Verbum.

Osbeck, C., and Pettersson, P. (2009). Sweden: Non-confessional and Confessional Education. Religious Education in Public Schools and in the Church of Sweden. In: H.-G. Ziebertz and U. Riegel (eds.). *How Teachers in Europe Teach Religion. An International Empirical Study in 16 Countries, International Practical Theology Vol. 12.* Berlin: Lit Verlag, 211–226.

Pettersson, P. (2000). *Kvalitet i livslånga tjänsterelationer. Svenska kyrkan ur tjänsteteoretiskt och religionssociologiskt perspektiv.* diss. Stockholm: Verbum.

Pettersson, P. (2006). Swedish Young People: Religious belonging and Life Rites without Confession and Regular Practice. In: H. G. Ziebertz and W.K. Kay (eds.). *Youth in Europe II.* Berlin: LiT Verlag.

Pettersson, P. (2009). Qualität der Konfirmandenarbeit – ein Forschungs- und Entwicklungsprojekt in Schweden. In: F. Schweitzer and V. Elsenbast (eds.). *Konfirmandenarbeit erforschen, Ziele – Erfahrungen – Perspektiven.* Gütersloh: Gütersloher Verlagshaus, 125–139.

Pettersson, P. (2010). Confirmation work in Sweden. In: F. Schweitzer, W. Ilg and H. Simojoki (eds.). *Confirmation work in Europe. Empirical Results, Experiences and Challenges. A Comparative Study in Seven Countries.* Gütersloh: Gütersloher Verlagshaus, 184–204.

Pettersson, P. (2011). State and Religion in Sweden: Ambiguity Between Disestablishment and Religious Control. In: *Nordic Journal of Religion and Society* 24(2), 119–135.

Pettersson, P. (2015). Is the Swedish State Secular When Religious Service Functions are Integrated in State Institutions? In: *Studia Z Prawa Wyznaniowego* 18/(2015), 23–42.

Riktlinjer för Svenska kyrkans konfirmandarbete (1978). Stockholm: Verbum.

Riktlinjer för Svenska kyrkans konfirmandarbete (1994). Stockholm: Svenska kyrkans församlingsnämnd (revised editions 2000 and 2004).

Riktlinjer för Svenska kyrkans konfirmandarbete (2008). Stockholm: Verbum.

Sjödin, U. (2001). *Mer mellan himmel och jord. En studie av den beprövade erfarenhetens ställning bland svenska ungdomar.* Stockholm: Verbum.

Wadensjö, B. (1979). *Konfirmationen i kyrkans liv.* Stockholm: Skeab/Verbum.

Wallinder, B. (1990). *Tradition och förnyelse i Svenska kyrkans konfirmandundervisning.* Stockholm: Verbum.

WVS 1981–2015 World Values Survey, Live Cultural map – WVS (1981–2015). http://www.worldvaluessurvey.org [08.03.2019].

Researching confirmation work in Europe

An example of research on non-formal education

Henrik Simojoki

1. Introduction

This article begins with a question that really does not make much sense in the context of youth research: "Why do you go to school?" The reason why one would not even think about asking young people this question is rather simple: It would inevitably cause eye-rolling or some other kind of reaction signalling bewilderment. Because the answer is so obvious – they go to school because they have to.

In a recent study on confirmation work in Europe, adolescents from nine European countries were asked about their reasons for taking part in confirmation time (cf. Hardecker and Bromander 2015). To the more than 28000 respondents this question made perfect sense. Because they had a choice, because they had their reasons and because they grew up in a cultural context in which such a decision cannot be taken for granted anymore.

This example illustrates one central difference between formal education, non-formal education and informal learning: In contrast to formal education in schools, non-formal education is not mandatory. Young Protestants are not obliged to take part in confirmation work. However, if they decide to take part, they do have to sign up. Unlike informal education that occurs spontaneously in the everyday interaction of individuals, non-formal education is characterised by a certain degree of organization. This article argues that such specific features of non-formal education are relevant for educational research. Since non-formal education is non-compulsory, the participants' motivation for attending is more important as a research focus than in formal education.

With that in mind, the article proceeds in three steps. First, the concept of non-formal education is discussed. The aim is to identify a set of features that are characteristic for this type of education and to show how they apply to confirmation work. The second part draws upon two comparative studies on confirmation work in Europe that were conducted by an international research team between 2007 and 2017. The article ends with proposals for further research.

2. Confirmation work as a field of non-formal education

Since the concept of non-formal education is discussed more broadly in other contributions to this volume, the following considerations will not delve too deeply into the parameters and underlying theories on this specific type of education. They are limited to a very basic question: What constitutes non-formal education? The defining characteristics of non-formal education become particularly clear in comparison to formal education on the one side and informal learning on the other side. According to the widely adopted classification by Philipp Coombs and Manzour Ahmed,

– *formal education* is described as "the highly institutionalized, chronologically graded and hierarchically structured 'education system' spanning lower primary school and the upper reaches of the university",
– *non-formal education* refers to "any organized, systematic, educational activity carried on outside the framework of the formal system to provide selected types of learning to particular subgroups in the population, adults as well as children",
– *informal learning* is defined as "the lifelong process by which every person acquires and accumulates knowledge, skills, attitudes and insights from daily experiences and exposure to the environment – at home, at work, at play" (Coombs and Ahmed 1974, 8).

After the turn of the millennium, the differentiation between these three forms of education has been particularly influential for educational policies at the European level, mainly promoted by the European Commission and the Council of Europe. In their joint working paper "Pathways towards the validation and recognition of education, training and learning in the youth field", the "complementary character of formal, non-formal and informal learning" is stressed with particular emphasis on the need "to increase recognition of the value of non-formal education among young people" (European Commission and Council of Europe 2004, 7). Based on these and other publications (cf. Lafraya 2011, 7–17) the following characteristics of non-formal education can be discerned:
    In difference to formal education, non-formal education

– is *non-compulsory*,
– takes place *outside the formal educational system in schools, training institutions and universities*, with a wide range of learning fields, from sports activities to education in churches,
– is situated in *experience-oriented, often outdoor learning environments* that are less restricted in time and space, thus enabling *participative learning* and *activating teaching methods*,
– is *less professionalised* in a formal sense and *open for voluntary activity*.
– is *particular* and *partial*. Whereas in pluralistic democracies formal education in state run schools has to be impartial, non-formal education is often guided by programmatic aims (e.g. in the case of environmental associations), specific in-

terest (e.g. in the case of sport activities) or a particular ethos (e.g. in the case of Christian youth work).

As distinguished from informal learning, non-formal education is

- to some extent *socially structured* at the level of *institutions* (like the churches), of *organizations* (like NGOs), of *social movements* (like the Transition Town Movement).
- *intentional:* The activities "are planned, but are seldom structured by conventional rhythms or curriculum subjects" (Lafraya 2011, 9).
- *staffed* (by professionals or volunteers).

All these criteria apply to confirmation work as a pedagogical activity of Protestant churches. It has to be noted, though, that confirmation work is in many senses closer to formal education than many other activities in the wide range of non-formal education. It is an activity of established and complex institutions, with formalised aims and curricula that are not decided on the grassroots level. Furthermore, confirmation work is run by fully paid professionals, who are obliged to engage in this field. In most contexts, the learning is based on specific teaching material.

3. Researching non-formal education: The studies on confirmation work in Europe (2007–2017)

3.1 An overview of the studies

This contribution is based on two related comparative empirical studies on confirmation work in Europe that were conducted 2007–2010 and 2012–2017. In both studies, a large data set was collected, to insure that the results are representative for all participating countries. They included responses from the confirmands as well as from the workers (full-time and volunteers) in the beginning and in the end of confirmation time.

With the first international study which was carried out in seven European countries from Scandinavia (Denmark, Finland, Norway and Sweden) and German-speaking Central Europe (Austria, Germany and the canton of Zurich in Switzerland) systematic international comparisons on an empirical basis became possible for the first time (Schweitzer, Ilg and Simojoki 2010a).

The second study builds on the first and expands it further, not only in theoretical and empirical scope but also geographically, by adding Hungary, Poland and Switzerland as a whole, and ecumenically, by including the Methodist Church in Germany (Schweitzer et al. 2015). Based on data involving more than 28000 confirmands, this study is one of the most comprehensive studies on youth, religion and non-formal education to date. The focus was on long-term developments that can be described in two respects:

– The second study was conducted five years after the first study. Since about two thirds of the items in the questionnaire remained the same, it became possible to capture long-term developments in confirmation work. The comparisons over time show both, much stability of the overall picture but also some remarkable discontinuities.
– In the second study additional responses were gathered two years after confirmation. Consequently, the results provide clearer information concerning what comes after confirmation and, moreover, entail new insights in religious change over several years, not only at a group level but for every individual adolescent taking part in the study (Schweitzer et al. 2017).

Table 1 gives an overview on the series of studies, research designs and publications.

Table 1: The studies on confirmation work in Europe in overview

	First Study $(t_1–t_2)$	Second Study $(t_1–t_2)$	Second Study (t_3)
conducted	2007/2008	2012/2013	2015
published	2010	2015	2017
countries	7	9	7
confirmands	19445	28070	5373 ǀ 3149*
workers	2386	4172	-
units / groups	943	1635	-
parents	6909	-	-

* Total sample ǀ number of respondents that filled in all three questionnaires (t_1, t_2, t_3).

It is not the intention here just to report central results of these studies. Instead, the focus lies on the aforementioned core elements of non-formal education and, by that, on the question how the international studies on confirmation work contribute to an empirical understanding of non-formal education. The analysis will not include the element of volunteerism which is addressed in a separate article (Schweitzer in this volume).

3.2 Researching non-compulsory education

As already stated in the introduction, the non-mandatory character of confirmation work has far-reaching implications for empirical research. First, unlike school education, *attendance data* requires specific attention. Figure 1 presents the participation rates in terms of percentages of the whole population of the age group in eight European countries.

On the one hand, the figure shows that confirmation work is a central field of non-formal education on a European scale. Currently, almost half a million young people between the age of 14 and 16 are confirmed each year in these eight countries. On the other hand, participation rates are visibly declining. There are, though,

Figure 1: Participation rates in confirmation work in percent of the whole population of the age group in the respective country

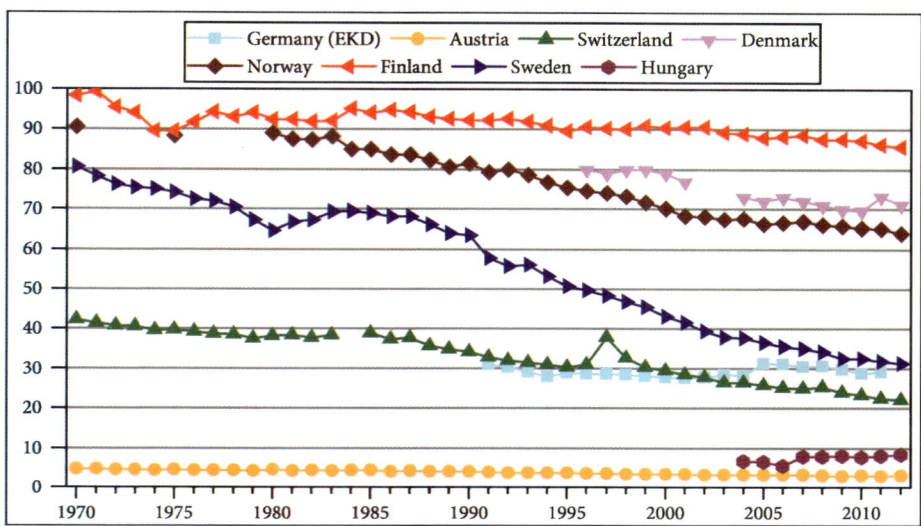

Taken from Simojoki et al. 2015, 307. The information for Poland was not available.

notable differences between the countries. In Sweden and Norway, the decline is particularly strong while in other countries, like Finland, Germany, Austria and Hungary, the participation rate stays relatively stable. With such striking differences even between countries that are regionally, culturally and religiously close like Finland and Sweden, one is tempted to attribute these differences to the respective quality of confirmation work. However, the empirical findings clearly refute this assumption. The most satisfied confirmands come from the country where the number of participants has fallen the most: In 2013, 9 out of 10 Swedish confirmands expressed overall satisfaction with their confirmation work (Maaß and Simojoki 2015, 127). Obviously, declining participation is not primarily due to existing deficits in practice. It is embedded in comprehensive processes of social, cultural and religious transformation (individualization, pluralization, de-institutionalization of religion, etc.), which have specific effects in different national and regional contexts.

Because non-formal education is voluntary, it is particularly important in this field that educational activities are geared to the needs and expectations of the target group. In the two studies on confirmation work in Europe, more than 45000 confirmands were asked about their motives for signing up (I take part in confirmation time *because…*). Additionally, their expectations were explored (I take part in confirmation time *to…*). The response options included personal, social factors on the one hand (influence of family, friends, social conventions and expectations), and theological, pedagogical, biographical, social and personal-pragmatic motives on the other hand. Figure 2 presents the answers in ascending order.

Figure 2: Expectations and motives for attending confirmation in 2007 and 2012

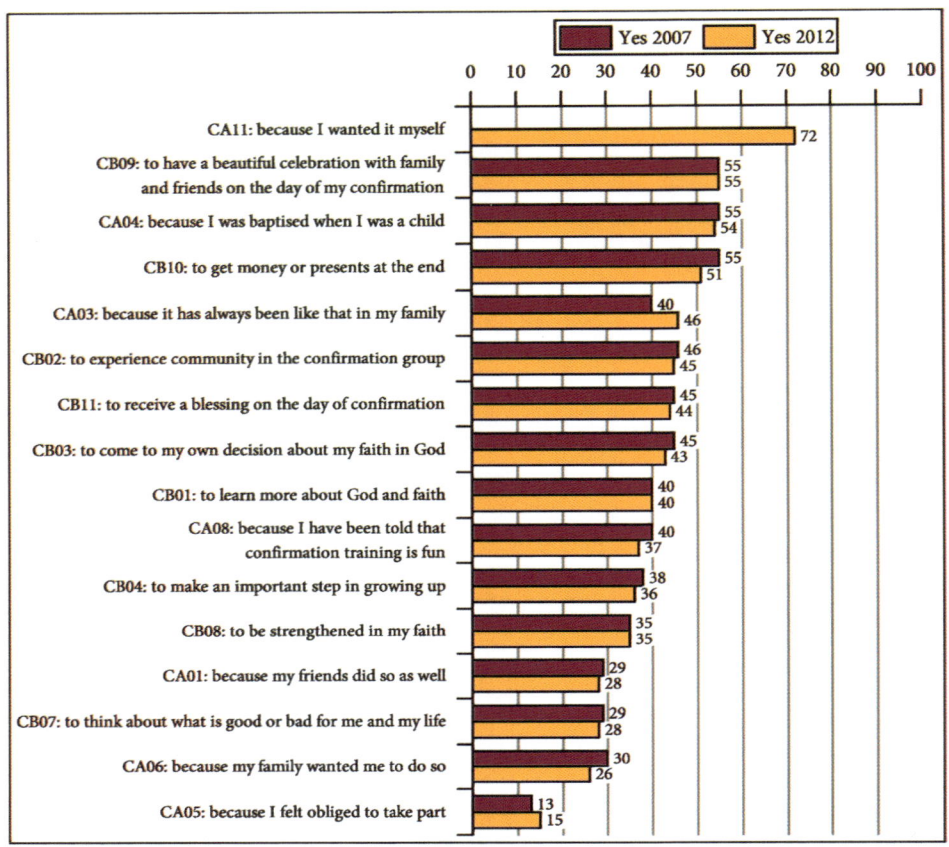

Taken from Hardecker and Bromander 2015, 60. N = 1989–19208 (2007), N = 25950–26023 (2012); scale: 1 = not applicable at all; 7 = totally applicable; the share of those with a positive response (5, 6, 7). CA 11 was not asked in 2007.

Given the rather short span of five years, it may not be surprising that there are almost no significant changes between the first and the second study. If one looks at the highest and lowest scoring items, it becomes clear that a vast majority of confirmands see their decision to register for confirmation as an act of self-determination. Seven out of ten respondents state that they take part in confirmation time because they wanted it themselves. Items that indicate external pressure or social influence by the family or friends achieve the lowest values.

Beyond this dominant aspect, the answers do not give a clear picture. On the contrary, the next most popular factors are remarkably heterogeneous. The prospect of a big family celebration, the faith-based reference to baptism and the "material blessings" (money and presents) are all of similar importance, closely followed by family tradition, group experiences and two central objectives of the Protestant tradition (blessing and religious autonomy). Overall, the statements of the young

people do not validate the frequently expressed assumption that young people attend confirmation time primarily for non-religious and non-theological motives. In
the light of the empirical findings, there seems to be little sense in playing off one
factor against another. Faith and fun, family tradition and church tradition, community and autonomy, material and spiritual blessings should not be seen in isolation.
For the young people, the combination of these elements makes confirmation work
attractive.

3.3 Researching programmatic aims

As already stated, non-formal education is often guided by programmatic aims that
are distinctive for the providing institution, organization or social movement. For
workers in the field of confirmation work it is of central importance that the confirmands are "strengthened in their faith" (Niemelä 2010, 245). Therefore, both
studies on confirmation work had a strong focus on the faith of the confirmands
and its development during and after confirmation time.

One of the advantages of international comparative research is that it captures
similarities and differences on the macro-level of countries. To improve the validity of interpretations, several faith-related indexes were computed, measuring
faith-based motives and experiences as well as Christian beliefs and interest in the
Christian tradition in the beginning and at the end of confirmation time (cf. Ilg,
Maaß and Schweitzer 2015, 345–349). Figure 3 shows the mean scores on the index "Christian beliefs 1" that is based on selected items of the t_1-questionnaire of
the second study.

The status of Christian beliefs among confirmands is visibly dependent on the
national, cultural and religious contexts in which they live. The approval to Christian beliefs is strongest among the Lutheran confirmands in Poland, the Reformed
and Lutheran confirmands in Hungary and the Methodist confirmands in Germany.
In the Nordic countries where the clear majority of the population belongs to the
Lutheran church the approval to core beliefs of the Christian faiths is notably lower,
especially in Finland, Sweden and Norway (cf. Christensen et al. 2015, 34–35).
The low approval to institutionalised belief systems concurs with the findings of
current values studies which show that the general degree of individualization is
much higher in Scandinavia than in the countries of East-Central Europe (cf. Bréchon 2017, 238–241). The values of the German speaking confirmands seem to lie
somewhere in between these poles. The comparatively lower scores for Switzerland
are partly due to age. Swiss confirmands are in average one year older than those of
the other European countries.

If the belief of the confirmands is shaped by the religious matrix of cultures
on the macro-level, it is on the micro-level linked to the religious dispositions and
backgrounds of the individuals. The studies clearly show that faith-related attitudes
in the beginning and at the end of confirmation time are strongly connected to the

Figure 3: Mean scores on "Christian beliefs" index at the beginning of confirmation time (2012)

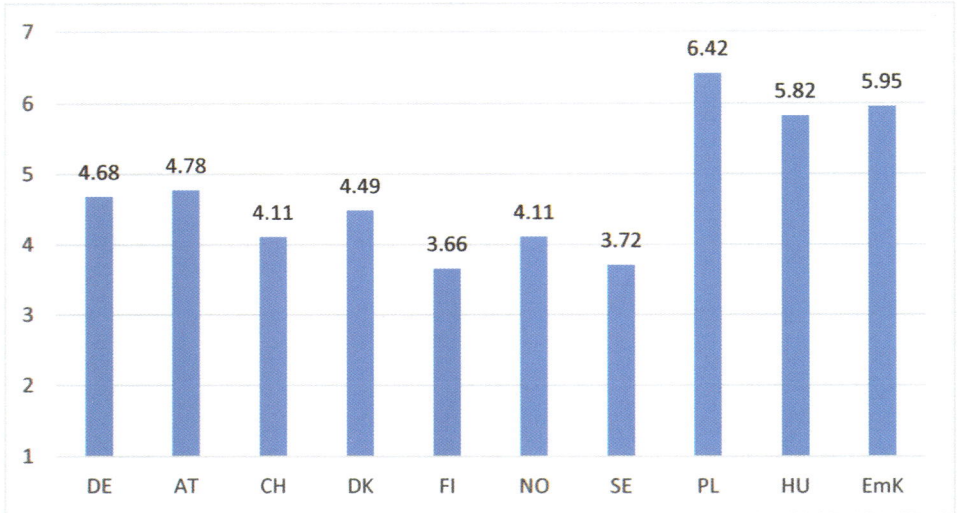

Taken from Bromander and Hardecker 2015, 39. N (countries) = 358–10024; scale: 1 = not applicable at all; 7 = totally applicable.

religious background in terms of religious practice in childhood and childhood experiences in the church (cf. Krupka, Ilg and Schweitzer 2015, 121–122).

Such findings are important because they give protection from exaggerated expectations that are sometimes placed on non-formal education. Compared to societal influences and family socialization, confirmation work has only limited influence on faith development of Protestant adolescents. However, it does make a difference. In the second study, 35% of the respondents stated in the beginning of confirmation time that they take part to be strengthened in their faith. At the end as many as 55% stated that they actually had been strengthened in their faith (Hardecker and Bromander 2015, 62). Furthermore, multi-level analyses on the basis of the t_3-survey carried out two years after confirmation revealed that positive experiences during confirmation time have long-term effects: "Confirmands who enjoy their confirmation time are more likely to maintain the attachment to Christian faith" (Ilg, Tervo-Niemelä and Maaß 2017, 127).

3.4 Researching institutional embeddedness

It was noted that non-formal education, unlike informal learning, is characterised by a certain degree of social, organizational or institutional embeddedness. Even if it is mostly not the main aim, non-formal education is expected to reinforce the identification of the participating individuals with the providing organization, institution or social movement. For the European churches engaged in confirmation work, this specific dimension of non-formal education poses a considerable challenge: On the one hand, they are interested in strengthening the church commitment of the young people attending confirmation time as sustainably as possible. On the other hand, weakening attachment to religious institutions is widely regarded as one of the characteristic features of both societal change and adolescent development in Central and Northern Europe.

Consequently, in the studies on confirmation work in Europe much attention was paid to the question of how attachment to church changes during and after confirmation time. For the second study, four types of church commitment were distinguished via cluster analysis (Tervo-Niemelä, Schlag and Koch 2017, 64–65):

1. *Believing and belonging* (strong belief in God and a strong sense of belonging to the church both on the level of identification and of practice)
2. *Believing but not belonging* (strong belief, but a low sense of belonging)
3. *Moderate belief, moderate belonging*
4. *Distanced* (little if any belief and no sense of belonging).

The designations of the first two types are inspired by Grace Davie's studies on individualized religion in Western societies (Davie 1994; 2000). However, one difference has to be kept in mind: In Davie's work, "believing without belong-

Figure 4: Average importance of church membership among the four groups of belonging and believing: t₁ (2012), t₂ (2013), t₃ (2015)

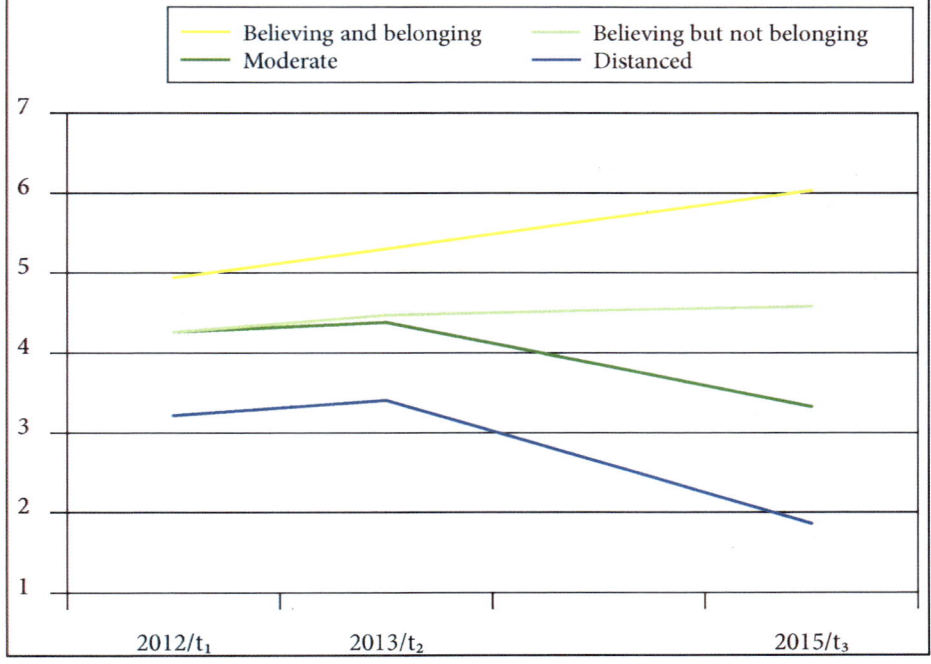

Taken from Tervo-Niemelä, Schlag and Koch 2017, 70. N = 2907; mean values on a scale 1 to 7 (1 = not applicable at all; 7 = totally applicable)

ing" points especially to persons who live their religious convictions outside the churches. Here, the phrase refers to adolescent church members to whom their church membership is not personally important.

How is the importance of church membership perceived among these four groups in the beginning and at the end of confirmation time and two years later? In their analysis, Tervo-Niemelä, Schlag and Koch came across a striking pattern (see Figure 4): "the differences between the groups are strengthened after confirmation".

Whereas church membership becomes slightly more important in all groups during confirmation time, the curves diverge, once the time together is over. The ones who both believe and belong value their church membership significantly higher two years after confirmation. With those who believe but do not belong, a slight increase can be observed. By contrast, the significance of church membership decreases strongly among the other groups. On the long haul, confirmation work seems to give the most to those who already have – and least to those who are distanced from the beginning (cf. Krupka, Ilg and Schweitzer 2015).

3.5 Researching educational spaces and learning environments

Traditionally, Protestant instruction in preparation for confirmation was not shaped by a participatory learning culture that is instructive for contemporary concepts of non-formal education. For many centuries it consisted almost exclusively in the unidirectional transmission of catechetical knowledge. Consequently, rote learning used to be its main characteristic. This understanding corresponded to the view of the church as an institution into which the adolescents had to be incorporated. Far from being a team-player, the pastor was seen as an authority whose teaching was not to be questioned. In the most European countries, this traditional shape has been replaced by more subject-oriented, activating and creative ways of teaching and learning: "The term 'confirmation work' itself is expressive of the new ways of working with confirmands. Today's confirmation work is often much closer to youth work than to traditional kinds of teaching at school." (Schweitzer, Ilg and Simojoki 2010b, 279)

In a way, this development culminates in the confirmation camps. Originally introduced in Finland during the 1950s, the camp form has become more and more popular in many European churches. In Finland and Sweden, the whole confirmation time is typically centered around such camps which usually last for about a week or even longer. In Austria, Germany, Norway and Switzerland, the camps are shorter, but also well established. In the studies on confirmation work in Europe, the number of days in a camp proved to be a particularly strong indicator of successful confirmation work. The camp period contributes positively to overall satisfaction, to a positive group experience, to involvement and participation, to faith development and even to the satisfaction with church services (Niemelä 2010, 252; Niemelä and Ilg 2015, 115–116). Additionally, it is an important predictor for volunteering in the church after confirmation (Ilg, Tervo-Niemelä and Maaß 2017, 122–123). However, the impact of a longer camp period is not limited to positive experiences during confirmation time. The camp setting clearly affects the learning culture of confirmation work: "The longer the camp period, the more participatory methods are used while the amount of teacher-centered methods declines." (Niemelä and Ilg 2015, 116) The effects of this shift are particularly evident on the level of meaningfulness. The more days confirmands spend together in the experience-oriented learning environments of camps, the more relevant they tend to find what they have learned during confirmation time (Maaß and Simojoki 2015, 132–133). Obviously, camps are not only about fun. They are also about learning.

4. Conclusion and perspectives for further research

The findings presented in this article support the basic assumptions that empirical research on confirmation work contributes to a better understanding of non-formal education. However, they disclose some desiderata that need to be addressed in further research on this Protestant field of non-formal education. At the end of this article, four research questions are posed that deserve more attention in the future – one for each dimension of non-formal education that were explored in this article.

1. Regarding *non-compulsoriness*, the presented insights into the subjective reasons for taking part in confirmation work capture only one side of the coin. Taking into account that the participation among Protestant adolescents is declining in many contexts, they should be complemented by empirical research on those *Protestant adolescents who decide not to attend. What are their motives for not participating in confirmation work?*
2. With respect to the *programmatic objective* of supporting the confirmands in their faith development, the *confirmands with no prior religious socialization* need to be focused on more. *How do they look back to their experiences with faith and their faith development during confirmation time?* Here, obviously, qualitative interviews come into play.
3. Concerning *institutional embeddedness*, a striking imbalance can be detected in current research on confirmation work. Whereas the church commitment among Protestant adolescents has been intensively researched, little if any empirical attention has been paid to the question *how committed the church is to young people*. Interviews with church leaders or parish councils could shed some light on the *guiding perspectives of the providers* of this Protestant field of non-formal education: *Is confirmation work about ecclesial integration of young people or about a youth-driven church?*
4. Pertaining to *learning environments* the educational dynamics during the camp period should be captured more broadly. In this article, the camps were analysed as a setting of non-formal education. That is, however, only one facet of the com-

plex learning experiences in camps. Confirmation camps are also, maybe even foremost, *physical spaces of informal learning* which "happens" more or less unintentionally, when young people, for example, sit and sing around the bonfire, have deep conversations or just enjoy life together. Ethnographic research methods could provide a valuable tool for approaching *the complex interrelations between non-formal education and informal learning in confirmation camps.*

References

Bréchon, P. (2017). Individualization and Individualism in European Societies. In: P. Bréchon and F. Gonthier (eds.). *European Values: Trends and Divides Over Thirty Years.* Leiden: Brill, 232–253.

Christensen, H.R., Høeg, I.M., Lagger, D., and Schweitzer, F. (2015). What the adolescents believe. In: F. Schweitzer, K. Niemelä, T. Schlag and H. Simojoki (eds.). *Youth, religion and confirmation work in Europe: The second study.* Gütersloh: Gütersloher Verlagshaus, 32–44.

Coombs, P.H., and Ahmed, M. (1974). *Attacking rural poverty: How non-formal education can help.* Baltimore: John Hopkins University Press.

Davie, G. (1994). *Religion in Britain since 1945: Believing without belonging.* Hoboken: John Wiley & Sons.

Davie, G. (2000). *Religion in modern Europe: A memory mutates.* Oxford/Cambridge: Oxford University Press.

European Commission and Council of Europe (2004). *Pathways towards validation and recognition of education, training and learning in the youth field.* Strasbourg and Brussels. https://pjp-eu.coe.int/documents/1017981/1668227/Pathways_towards_validati.pdf [14.06.2018].

Hardecker, G., and Bromander, J. (2015). Expectations, Motivations and Experiences of the Confirmands. In: F. Schweitzer, K. Niemelä, T. Schlag and H. Simojoki (eds.). *Youth, religion and confirmation work in Europe: The second study.* Gütersloh: Gütersloher Verlagshaus, 59–70.

Ilg, W., Maaß, C.H., and Schweitzer, F. (2015). Methodology. In: F. Schweitzer, K. Niemelä, T. Schlag and H. Simojoki (eds.). *Youth, religion and confirmation work in Europe: The second study.* Gütersloh: Gütersloher Verlagshaus, 328–349.

Ilg, W., Tervo-Niemelä, K., and Maaß, C.H. (2017). Believing, belonging and volunteerism in adolescence: Predictive factors from childhood and confirmation time in a multi-level framework. In: F. Schweitzer, T. Schlag, H. Simojoki, K. Tervo-Niemelä and W. Ilg (eds.). *Confirmation work, faith, and volunteerism: A longitudinal study on Protestant adolescents in the transition towards adulthood.* Gütersloh: Gütersloher Verlagshaus, 114–127.

Krupka, B., Ilg, W., and Schweitzer, F. (2015). Giving least to those who need it most? How gender, social and religious background influence the attendance and experience of confirmation time. In: F. Schweitzer, K. Niemelä, T. Schlag and H. Simojoki (eds.). *Youth, religion and confirmation work in Europe: The second study.* Gütersloh: Gütersloher Verlagshaus, 117–124.

Lafraya, S. (2011). *Intercultural learning in non-formal education: Theoretical frameworks and starting points.* Straßburg: Council of Europe Publishing.

Maaß, C.H., and Simojoki, H. (2015). Minding the gap: Overall satisfaction and perceived daily life relevance of confirmation work. In: F. Schweitzer, K. Niemelä, T. Schlag and H. Simojoki (eds.). *Youth, religion and confirmation work in Europe: The second study.* Gütersloh: Gütersloher Verlagshaus, 125–134.

Niemelä, K. (2010). Religious change during confirmation time. In: F. Schweitzer, W. Ilg and H. Simojoki (eds.). *Confirmation work in Europe: Empirical results, experiences and challenges. A comparative study in seven countries.* Gütersloh: Gütersloher Verlagshaus, 106–116.

Niemelä, K., and Ilg, W. (2015). From classrooms to camps? Effects of different physical learning spaces and teaching methods in confirmation work. In: F. Schweitzer, K. Niemelä, T. Schlag and H. Simojoki (eds.). *Youth, religion and confirmation work in Europe: The second study.* Gütersloh: Gütersloher Verlagshaus, 59–70.

Schweitzer, F., Ilg, W., and Simojoki, H. (eds.) (2010a). *Confirmation work in Europe: Empirical results, experiences and challenges. A comparative study in seven countries.* Gütersloh: Gütersloher Verlagshaus.

Schweitzer, F., Ilg, W., and Simojoki, H. (2010b). Summary of the results – perspectives for the future. In: F. Schweitzer, W. Ilg and H. Simojoki (eds.). *Confirmation work in Europe: Empirical results, experiences and challenges. A comparative study in seven countries.* Gütersloh: Gütersloher Verlagshaus, 276–303.

Schweitzer, F., Niemelä, K., Schlag, T., and Simojoki, H. (eds.) (2015). *Youth, religion and confirmation work in Europe: The second study.* Gütersloh: Gütersloher Verlagshaus.

Schweitzer, F., Schlag, T., Simojoki, H., Tervo-Niemelä, K., and Ilg, W. (eds.) (2017). *Confirmation work, faith, and volunteerism: A longitudinal study on Protestant adolescents in the transition towards adulthood. European perspectives.* Gütersloh: Gütersloher Verlagshaus.

Simojoki, H., Schweitzer, F., Schlag, T., and Niemelä, K. (2015). Summary of the results – perspectives and challenges. In: F. Schweitzer, K. Niemelä, T. Schlag and H. Simojoki (eds.). *Youth, religion and confirmation work in Europe: The second study.* Gütersloh: Gütersloher Verlagshaus, 294–315.

Tervo-Niemelä, K., Schlag, T., and Koch, M. (2017). Changes and trends in church commitment after confirmation. In: F. Schweitzer, T. Schlag, H. Simojoki, K. Tervo-Niemelä and W. Ilg (eds.). *Confirmation work, faith, and volunteerism: A longitudinal study on Protestant adolescents in the transition towards adulthood.* Gütersloh: Gütersloher Verlagshaus, 61–76.

V
Young Volunteers

Researching voluntary commitment after confirmation and long-term effects of confirmation work

Perspectives from Germany

Friedrich Schweitzer

1. Research topics and questions

The title of this chapter refers not only to one topic but actually contains two topics which are of special interest in terms of researching non-formal religious education, although in different respects: voluntary commitment on the one hand and long-term effects of non-formal religious education on the other. Moreover, it also refers to the question of researching these two topics and to the methodological challenges which arise in this context.

Concerning the first topic – voluntary commitment in general –, there clearly has been a new appreciation of this kind of commitment in many countries during the last years or even decades (cf. for example, BMFSFJ 2016; Arnesen et al. 2013; Hustinx et al. 2015). The so-called refugee crisis of the year 2015 probably can be seen as exemplary in this respect. Among others in Germany, it would have been impossible to welcome the many refugees without the help of the numerous volunteers who became active in this situation. Voluntary work has therefore been appreciated as indispensable for a humane society and, in addition to this, as part and parcel of a strong civil society which, in turn, is interpreted as a presupposition for flourishing democracies. Moreover, and even more important in the context of education, there has been something like a process of discovering the special role of young volunteers (cf. from different countries Ilg et al. 2018; Bundesministerium 2015; Freitag et al. 2016; Center For Frivilligt Socialt Arbejde 2014). To again use Germany as an example, young people between the ages of 14 and 19 years are the group in society with the highest percentage of volunteers (cf. Ilg et al. 2018, 17–26). At the same time, however, the traditional assumption that volunteers typically are people in early retirement still seems to dominate public opinion, in society at large as well as in the church. Consequently, giving more attention to young volunteers is of special interest in several respects, especially for doing justice to the young people whose commitment deserves much more attention and appreciation.

Another context for discovering the importance of young volunteers was the recent research on confirmation work in Europe. Between 2007 and 2015 two major research projects on confirmation work were carried out in nine European countries, with questionnaires for the confirmands, for the ministers as well as for the volunteers who are active in this field (cf. Schweitzer et al. 2010 and 2015; cf. Simojoki in this volume). In many of the countries participating in these research projects, young volunteers play an important role for confirmation work. In Germany alone, there are 62000 volunteers per year involved in confirmation work, many of them still in their adolescence. Finland, however, is the country with the longest tradition of having teams of young volunteers as part of confirmation work, and the percentage of young people being trained as young leaders after their confirmation is even higher than in Germany (cf. Niemelä and Porkka 2015).

Young people's commitment to voluntary work is related to non-formal religious education in a number of ways. Concerning volunteers in confirmation work, their voluntary commitment is part of a non-formal educational program offered by the church. In this sense, the volunteers are acting as religious educators in the non-formal sector, although their tasks are not always explicitly related to what traditionally is seen as religious education but often are more practical, for example, planning and organising games with the confirmands. Moreover, the work carried out by the volunteers also implies educational experiences related to the volunteers themselves (cf. Schweitzer et al. 2016). As described below, the volunteers express that, through their commitment, they have acquired new skills and competences and they often report that they have matured in a number of important respects due to their voluntary commitment, for example, concerning leadership skills. Consequently, it makes sense to view voluntary work as non-formal religious education. Calling it "religious" is at least justified in the context of the church where faith-related motives and questions play an implicit and often even explicit role which is not to say that religious aspects do not also play a role in other contexts of voluntary work and commitment.

The second research question concerns possible long-term effects of non-formal religious education, in this case of confirmation work. Increasingly, the question of long-term effects is raised by church leaders who are concerned about losing members and who are wondering how the educational programs offered by the church could be used for stabilising church membership. Yet the question of long-term effects is also of interest in terms of general educational research because so little is known about such effects in the area of non-formal education. Can the sometimes enthusiastic reports about educational effects of non-formal education be backed by empirical evidence?

Both research topics raise complex methodological issues. By definition, voluntary work is characterised by its low degrees of institutionalization and regulation. Consequently, research procedures must be suitable and sensitive to different forms of voluntary commitment and their organizational contexts which distinguishes this research from studies on Religious Education at school. Moreover, reaching a sample of respondents is much more demanding than in school-type settings where pupils can be reached in their classrooms. In most cases, the volunteers are not organised in well-defined groups or formal associations that can be used for contacting them but must be identified as individuals.

Asking about long-term effects of confirmation work raises additional questions. It is always difficult to clearly distinguish effects of confirmation work from other possible influences, for example, from the family or from Religious Education at school. With long-term approaches, it becomes even more difficult to control such additional influences – a difficulty which increases over time since possible influences and respective effects may multiply. The longer the time span in question, the more other influences can make themselves felt. This is the main reason for the need for multiple perspectives and research approaches in this case as well as for the importance of statistical approaches controlling for different influences instead of relying on simple correlations.

Another question refers to how long-term effects can be identified. In other words, what are the indicators of such effects and what are the reasons for choosing these indicators? In the studies which form the basis of this chapter, a number of indicators of long-term effects of confirmation work were identified (cf. especially Ilg et al. 2018): (1) voluntary commitment after confirmation, (2) the relationship to the church, (3) the relationship to the Christian faith. It would, of course, be possible to use different or additional indicators but these three can be considered broad enough for capturing different orientations and attitudes of young people. Moreover, a number of research designs were developed with the idea that making use of a number of approaches could also contribute to securing valid results.

It must also be mentioned at this point that the German studies on which this chapter draws in the first place, were inspired by the work of Kati Tervo-Niemelä and Jouko Porkka in Finland (cf. Niemelä 2008; Niemelä and Porkka 2015 with additional references). These colleagues can be considered true pioneers in researching voluntary work in the context of confirmation work as well as long-term effects of confirmation work.

2. Research designs

Given the complex nature of the research questions relating to both voluntary commitment and long-term effects of non-formal religious education as well as the methodological difficulties ensuing from this, the present chapter draws not only on a single study but on five related studies which were conducted in Germany. These studies approach the two research topics from different perspectives. In brief, these studies can be described in the following manner:

1. A qualitative study with young volunteers in confirmation work at the age of 16 to 18 years in a number of selected locations in different regions in Germany (group interviews; N=48) (Schweitzer et al. 2016, 122–254). The aim of this study was to find out in depth about the motives and experiences of this particular group of volunteers who, after their own confirmation, continued as young leaders in this field. The qualitative approach allows for contextual and individualised insights into the biographies of the volunteers and the experiences connected to them.

2. A qualitative study with adolescents and young adults – volunteers as well as non-volunteers at the age of 18 to 26 years in a number of selected locations in different regions in Germany (individual interviews; N=30) (Ilg et al. 2018, 91–154). The study had its focus on subjective views of long-term effects of confirmation work and of its meaning for motivating young people for voluntary commitment. Like with the first study, this investigation also had a focus on contextual insights.

3. A quantitative-representative study with 18- to 26-year-olds (N=2714; representative for the whole age group and with an additional sub-sample of Protestant volunteers) (Ilg et al. 2018, 31–90). The study was designed such that comparisons between different groups in society (especially Protestants, Roman Catholics, non-affiliated respondents who together comprise more than 80% of the population in Germany) would be possible. Since only Protestants take part in confirmation work, this design allows for clear comparisons of young people with and without the respective experience. In this case, the emphasis had to be on representative results in order to make the comparisons possible methodologically.

4. A quantitative study with a questionnaire for former confirmands two years after their confirmation (N=1937; non-representative longitudinal data) (Schweitzer et al. 2016, 34–121). This study was aimed at long-term effects mostly in terms of attitudes towards the Christian faith and the church. It only included a small number of volunteers but the responses of the non-volunteers concerning their reasons for not volunteering have a broader base in this study. The special value of this approach lies in the insights based on truly longitudinal results which are quite rare in the context of research on youth and religion.

5. A quantitative study with a questionnaire for former confirmands four years after their confirmation (N=509; non-representative longitudinal data) (Ilg et al. 2018, 155–228). The aims of this study were identical with those of study 4. In addition, the results are of special interest because of the relatively long time-span they cover (2012, the beginning of the confirmation time of these respondents, to 2017). Again the main interest of this approach is in truly longitudinal results.

The different samples of these studies imply that results have become available for both, volunteers and non-volunteers which allows for interesting comparisons. Moreover, the studies include a focus on volunteers in confirmation work but also on other fields within and without the church.

Together the results from these different studies promise a somewhat robust basis for gaining insights into the situation and the presuppositions of volunteerism in adolescence and young adulthood as well as the long-term effects of confirmation work. It should be emphasized, however, that these studies were the first of their kind which excludes, among others, cross-references to earlier results for comparative evaluation, and that the results certainly do not cover all pertinent questions (for further discussion of this limitation see below, pp. 261–263). In the long run, if additional studies of this kind should become available (which would, of course, be most desirable) more comprehensive interpretations will become possible.

Also, the relationship between the different studies deserves special considerations. It must be clear from the beginning that the results from the different studies cannot just be combined in a direct manner – like pieces of a puzzle which yield a complete picture. Instead, the different studies are based on different methodologies and work with different samples. However, it makes sense to consider these studies as different spotlights shedding light on certain aspects which show up in all or at least in some of the studies. Another way of putting it would be that the studies allow for a conversation between the different results. In this sense, both is possible that results can be seen as mutually confirming certain interpretations and views but also as raising additional questions.

3. Selected results

In the following, the focus will be on voluntary commitment as long-term effect of confirmation work because this commitment can be viewed as a core indicator of such effects. This focus implies, however, that other important perspectives will not be pursued here to the same degree, for example, the experiences of being a volunteer which were also investigated in the different studies, with interesting results that can only be briefly mentioned here (for these results see Schweitzer et al. 2015). Moreover, other long-term effects of confirmation work concerning the relationship to church and faith will also not be presented (for results and discussions of these effects see Ilg et al. 2018). This does not mean that these aspects are less important. Yet in terms of the present discussion with its focus on methodological questions it is sufficient to concentrate on the example of voluntary commitment. In many ways, the results and methodological considerations presented in this chapter are parallel to those concerning attitudes towards the church and the Christian faith.

The studies used both quantitative and qualitative approaches. Since the different methodologies also lead to different results, they will be presented separately before discussing them in connection to each other.

Selected quantitative results

The guiding question concerning young people becoming volunteers after their confirmation was related to the predictors for this decision. A number of such predictors could be identified in the different studies, among others, based on regression analysis.

In general, experiences during confirmation time turned out to be a strong predictor of voluntary commitment after confirmation. The confirmands who were satisfied with their confirmation time were clearly more likely to become volunteers after their confirmation than those who were not satisfied with their confirmation time. This general result could be specified in a number of concrete respects concerning good experiences with confirmation work. Yet one element of confirmation work turned out to be of special importance: the chance to try out voluntary work (cf. Schweitzer et al. 2016, 91–108). In many cases, although not in all parishes in Germany, the confirmands have the opportunity to work as volunteers in one or several fields of their choice during confirmation time. Often they can do so for limited periods of time. It seems that this experience has a powerful effect on young people's interest in becoming a volunteer on a more long-term basis after confirmation.

From a different perspective, the answers of those who did not become volunteers after their confirmation, also shed light on the presuppositions for becoming a volunteer. Among others they show the need for being asked and being invited personally to become involved with some kind of voluntary activity. Figure 1 presents the reasons for not volunteering in church or Christian youth work indicated by the former confirmands two years after their confirmation.

According to these responses, lacking time seems to be the most important obstacle for becoming a volunteer. Given the increasingly long hours adolescents in Germany have to spend in school this explanation appears quite plausible. Yet the data indicate that competing interests also play a role for the young people, be it in

Figure 1: Reasons for not being active as a volunteer

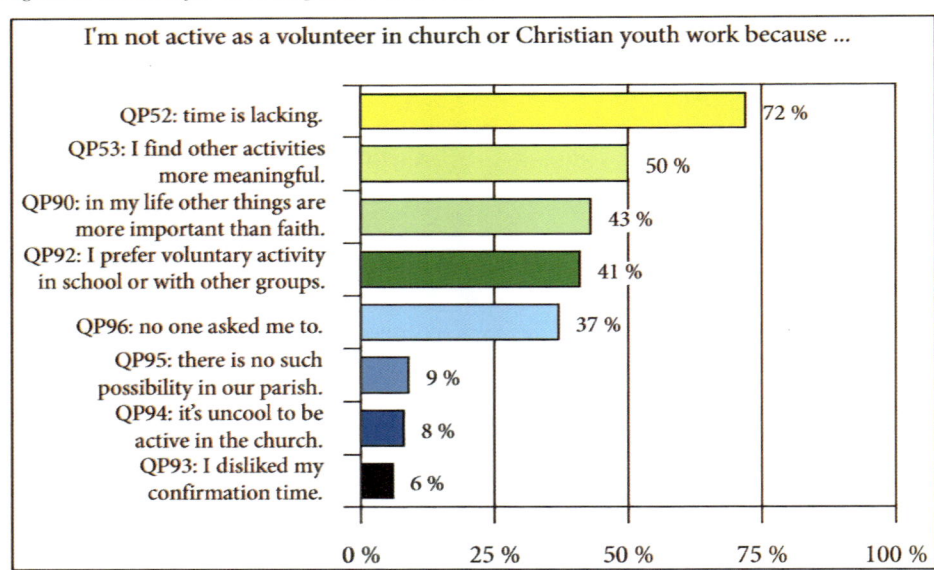

N = 1529-1544; the share of those with a positive response (5, 6, 7) on a scale 1 to 7 (1 = not applicable at all; 7 = totally applicable).

From: Schweitzer et al. 2017, 137

terms of the choice of the field where they want to be involved or be it in terms of their religious orientations. In this case, it must be acknowledged that naturally, not everyone is equally interested in the Christian faith.

However, the fact that 37 % of the respondents say that they have not been asked to become a volunteer is more troublesome. It raises the question if there is a selective process involved through which only certain people are approached while others are not taken into consideration from the beginning. Most likely, ministers or other workers only approach those adolescents who appear to be motivated and who, because of their personal presuppositions, present themselves as potentially good voluntary workers. Those adolescents who appear to be more difficult to handle and less promising are then left out. Further analysis of background data shows that it is the adolescents who are more distant from the church and who have not experienced stronger forms of religious socialization during childhood, who are the least likely to become volunteers. Consequently, the selective process involved in approaching or not approaching young people as potential volunteers works against giving more distanced adolescents a chance for new experiences with the church. It is easy to see that this result should be alarming to the ministers and workers responsible for organising voluntary work and for giving access to this kind of commitment. It seems that chances for attracting more young people as volunteers are missed, especially with those who could benefit most from more involvement with the church which would be a new experience for them.

Concerning the motivation for being a volunteer, the quantitative study with the 18 to 26 years old adolescents and young adults (representative for the whole age group) yields interesting results. Table 1 presents the results for Protestant respondents.

Table 1: Motivation for being a volunteer
Reasons for voluntary commitment (18 to 26 years old Protestant respondents, N=1449–1466)

I am active as a volunteer because, …

EP32: it is fun	83 %
EP66: I like doing things with other people	76 %
EP67: I want to contribute to a better society	77 %
EP69: I want to learn something which will be of use to me in later life	69 %
EP73: doing something for others is part of my faith	49 %
EP91: it looks good on my CV	45 %

adapted from Ilg et al. (2018), 46.

The response "because it is fun" receives by far the strongest approval. This response which is familiar from other studies should not be understood to mean that young volunteers are only interested in having fun. It would be mistaken to think of today's adolescents only in terms of a hedonistic so-called "fun generation". Instead the results show that for the adolescents and young adults, serious commitment and having fun are not opposites but must, in fact, go together for them.

Similarly, the next two items with high approval rates indicate that the motive of "being with other people" and "to contribute to a better society" belong together in the eyes of the young people. Again, positive personal experiences are important but they clearly go hand in hand with the commitment to others and to the common good of society. Opposed to this, other motives which could be called extrinsic ("it looks good on my CV") are present but play a smaller role than other motivations. This is also true, however, for explicit connections to the Christian faith ("doing something for others is part of my faith"). It seems that this motive does not fit with ways in which many of the young volunteers perceive themselves, although it should not be overlooked that half of the respondents answer this question affirmatively. Many young people probably have different ways of seeing themselves and the connection between faith and action may well turn out to be a typical adult interpretation.

The representative study also showed that early familiarity with voluntary work is another strong predictor of later commitment (cf. Ilg et al. 2018, 35–40). Adolescents and young adults with parents who were active as volunteers when their children were young, are clearly more likely to become volunteers themselves when they are old enough. That this familiarity occurs more often with Protestants in Germany than, for example, with people without religious affiliation explains why German Protestants are among the most active groups in the field of voluntary work. Voluntary commitment is, as it were, hereditary. The influence of experiences during childhood can be interpreted as an asset of Protestantism. At the same time, however, the issue of selective processes and of the exclusion of potential young volunteers repeats itself in this respect. It seems to be easier to motivate young people as volunteers if they are already familiar with voluntary work and have been convinced of its importance from early on. Ministers and other workers will probably be intuitively thinking of these adolescents first when they are looking for new candidates for a certain task. Yet just following this apparently well-founded intuition will not lead them to those more distanced adolescents who might also be willing to become volunteers, provided that they are asked. Since they have not been familiarized with the benefits of volunteerism by their parents, it is most likely harder to motivate them – and it may also be more demanding for the ministers to work with them. Yet there would be a clear chance to attract new people to this field of work, and voluntary commitment should not be restricted to those who have a strongly Christian background from the beginning and whose parents were able to pass on their experiences as volunteers.

In sum, according to the results from the different studies, there are indeed long-term influences from childhood as well as more recent effects related to confirmation work and to being able to try out voluntary work during confirmation time. The influences from the family remain important but so are experiences from later educational programs offered by the Protestant church. Results from other studies most of all carried out in Finland even indicate that there is a point at which the influence of voluntary commitment outweighs the effects from childhood socialization. This point, however, is only reached after several years of being a volunteer in confirmation work (Porkka and Tervo-Niemelä 2017, 178–179) – an interesting development which, in the future, should also be investigated in Germany. Such a study would require a design which allows for comparisons between different groups of young volunteers, for example, one-time volunteers on the one hand and volunteers who have continued their commitment over several years on the other.

Selected qualitative results

The qualitative results provided by the studies presented here are also of special interest concerning the question of how young people become volunteers (cf. especially Schweitzer et al. 2016, 122–254; Ilg et al. 2018, 91–154). They allow for more detailed and multi-faceted insights into the sometimes complex processes involved in terms of the individual biographies and the views described by the respondents. This is the natural strength of qualitative approaches which, in this sense, must complement the quantitative approaches with their more general and, in part, representative results.

In many cases, the qualitative results confirm that experiences during confirmation time can indeed be an important starting point for voluntary commitment. To quote one of the respondents who, looking back to the time of confirmation, describes the effects of encountering volunteers (Ilg et al. 2018, 98):

> "*The [volunteers] go there and somehow they do it for a week during vacation time. I want to do this as well. The other children [who come] after me also deserve this, so to speak. This was the beginning. Everything that has happened since in the last 10 years, I can say, had its base in having experienced [voluntary] work*" (23-year-old female interviewee)

Yet the results also show that viewing confirmation work as a starting point should not be understood in the sense of a one-time decision with linear consequences. Many of the interviewees refer to continued formative processes which entailed new experiences as well as ups and downs concerning their motivation for being a volunteer. It also becomes obvious that this process is often influenced by encounters with adults – ministers and other workers – and that motivation for voluntary work needs to be carefully supported over time. In any case, there is a need for additional experiences after confirmation if such motivations are to be upheld over time. The influence of confirmation time is clearly not enough to keep the motivation for becoming – and staying – a volunteer alive over possibly several years. For this reason, it is important that there are programs offered by the church for young people after confirmation and that such programs make it possible to sustain one's commitment to voluntary work in the context of the church.

The qualitative studies also allow for insights into the reasons for not becoming a volunteer. Typically and interestingly in terms of confirmation work and the church, these reasons have nothing to do with being critical of volunteerism in general or with questioning its meaning and importance for the common good. Instead, just like in the quantitative questionnaires, the issue of time plays a pivotal role in the qualitative material. Yet the interviews reveal more clearly that the availability of time also has to do with personal priorities and with choices made by the young people themselves. Time appears to be a general problem for many adolescents and young adults who, in addition to following their personal interests in their free time, are struggling to find enough time-slots for their many school-related obligations and other tasks or interests, for example, in connection with their training for a profession or studying at a university. Yet some of them do find time for voluntary work while others do not. Consequently, the issue of time and of time constraints clearly deserves deeper scrutiny. Time cannot be interpreted as an exclusively objective limitation. This does not mean that the objective time constraints should be neglected – the many hours spent at school will naturally not allow for other activities outside of school, but the objective limitations are not the whole story. Subjective experiences and personal decisions also are of influence, in general as well as with finding time for voluntary commitment.

The emphasis on personal and subjective factors influencing the possible commitment to voluntary work is further corroborated by the fact that distance to the church as a general experience also seems to be a reason which explains why young people do not want to become volunteers. According to the interviews, this distance does not only refer to personal attitudes towards the church but also and more concretely to a lack of contact with the church after confirmation.

Concerning the motivation for being a volunteer, many interviewees explain how their initial personal motivation was reinforced through positive experiences with the group of volunteers to which they belonged or, in some cases, still belonged at the time of the interviews. It seems very important to them that there is a group of volunteers and that they are part of this group, not only sharing their work with their peers but also sharing many other things in terms of friendship. In many cases, young volunteers appear to experience their voluntary commitment as a basis for new friendships and for a sense of belonging which is dear to them. The following statement from a young volunteer shows this (Schweitzer et al. 2016, 98):

> *"It's just like that there are the friends as well who are active there anyway, and then one thinks: yes, one does something with them or one does something which is good, so to say, and in addition, with the friends, that's really fun [laughs], and this is really important for me"*. (16-year-old male interviewee)

Another important theme in the interview material refers to competences which young people say they have acquired in the context of voluntary work – social competences and educational competences, for example, as well as experiences with leadership skills. More specifically, they speak of the process of gaining and exercising competences by putting such competences to practical use, for example, in teaching situations with confirmands (the following statement comes from Schweitzer et al. 2016, 225).

> *"That one knows how long approximately I have to give them time for it. That one has a better feeling for this. That one does not think: okay, here is a verse from the Bible, all of you have to have read it in five minutes, have worked through everything, have interpreted everything as much as possible. That five minutes are not enough here, for example"*. (17-year-old female interviewee)

In this context it is of special importance to many of the young people that their voluntary activities include and allow for a responsibility of their own. The young people obviously do not just want to take over tasks defined by others, for example, by a minister or a senior worker. They demand leeway for defining their own tasks themselves, for trying out new ways and of gathering insights with how they work.

In sum, the qualitative material demonstrates that young volunteers are willing to take over tasks and serious responsibilities but that they also want to be allowed to make decisions of their own concerning the ways in which they carry out their tasks. In some cases, the adolescents and young adults also have more far-reaching visions of how the church could become more attractive to young people in general – an asset which, according to the interviewees, has not been put to use in most parishes by taking up the young people's ideas and putting them to practice. This observation shows that much remains to be done in terms of making the most of having young volunteers involved in confirmation work and other fields of work in church or society.

The results from the qualitative studies are quite rich and detailed which implies that it is not possible to do justice to them here. Readers who are interested in a more comprehensive presentation of these results should consult the publications from these research projects themselves (Schweitzer et al. 2016, 122–254; Ilg et al. 2018, 91–154). In the following, the focus will be on methodological questions.

4. Methodological considerations

Researching voluntary commitment after confirmation and long-term effects of confirmation work does indeed hold special methodological challenges. In the studies on which this chapter is based, voluntary commitment after confirmation was used as an indicator of long-term effects. It is clear that this is not the only possible indicator of such effects – other indicators would be, for example, personal faith-related convictions or the relationship to the church which were in fact also used in the projects but are not included in this chapter. Yet the example of voluntary commitment shows that there are a number of ways in which confirmation work and later voluntary commitment are in fact connected. Several features of confirmation work, especially the chance to have first experiences with voluntary work during confirmation time, can be considered important predictors of later voluntary commitment. Methodologically, the identification of such predictors shows that it is indeed possible to reach reliable results concerning long-term effects of confirmation work

Especially the qualitative results also show that long-term effects should not be understood as only related to confirmation time itself. While experiences during confirmation time can be considered an important beginning, there are additional factors after confirmation which also need to be taken into consideration, like opportunities for meaningful contact with the church after confirmation and, even more importantly, experiences with voluntary work itself. These additional factors can be considered as necessary reinforcements of motives initially developed during confirmation time. They are necessary in the sense that in their absence, the initial motives would probably not have survived and definitely will not survive in the longer run.

This observation can also serve as an example of how quantitative and qualitative results can be connected. First of all, however, as mentioned in the beginning of this chapter, it must be clear that the results from the different studies described above cannot just be combined with each other by using them interchangeably. The quantitative and the qualitative studies worked with different samples and they employed different methodologies, including the actual research instruments (set questionnaires on the one hand and open interviews using only brief guidelines on the other). Moreover, the different studies were not part of an integrated consecutive research process in which quantitative and qualitative steps or phases could have built upon each other, for example, by developing hypotheses in qualitative studies and then testing the hypotheses quantitatively by using representative samples. Since this was not the case, it seemed most appropriate to view the different studies as different spotlights, each of them shedding light on certain aspects while leaving other aspects in the dark. This allowed for bringing the different results into conversation with each other without claiming to have achieved true triangulation. The resulting interpretations are richer and more reliable than understandings which are based on single studies or methodologies. Yet it is also obvious that, at least in certain respects, they remain hypothetical. For example, in future research the qualitative results concerning the need for additional experiences with the church after confirmation and for support, for example, from ministers in order to keep alive the motivation for being a volunteer could be tested quantitatively. This would require another major study with a design that is able to reliably capture different situations and experiences of volunteers, of their contacts with ministers and other senior workers, in terms of the duration of their commitment, of their tasks, etc. It is easy to see that the results which have become available so far, can be called a good beginning in most of these respects but that there is much space for future research as well.

There can be no doubt that making use of quantitative as well as qualitative methodologies proved to be useful because both research approaches allow for finding answers to different questions. This applies, of course, in general but is of special importance in the present context. In a field like voluntary work, inevitably both objective and subjective factors play an important role. As the results indicate, voluntary commitment is closely related to experiences in young people's families of origin which can be called an objective factor since the impact of such experiences is not premised on young people being aware of this interrelationship (although this awareness can also be there and then be of influence as well). It is a relationship which was identified from the quantitative data and by statistical analysis. At the same time, the young volunteers' experiences – their thoughts and feelings connected to voluntary work – also are of influence. Such experiences can be captured more aptly by qualitative studies than by predefined questionnaires because, as the interviews show, they can be highly individual and personal.

Compared to formal educational settings like school, voluntary work in the context of the church or of other institutions in society is much more volatile. By definition, there are no predefined general regulations for how voluntary work is to be carried out, for example, in terms of the amount of time to be invested or of the responsibilities that a volunteer should have. This flexibility and openness makes empirical research much more difficult than in the case of school-related research. In the case of the research projects described in this chapter, the attempt was made to develop a number of different research designs, each of them in correspondence with the respective research questions and the situations or contexts addressed. Volunteers in confirmation work at the age of 16 to 18 years, for example, could be reached for group interviews by contacting systematically selected parishes in which their work takes place. The older age group in these studies, the 18- to 26-year-olds, could not be reached in this manner. This is why a professional research institute (Kantar EMNID) had to be contracted for this task. Altogether, the projects show that it was indeed possible to find viable research designs and samples which were suitable for investigating voluntary work, in itself as well as in the perspective of long-term effects of confirmation work.

Yet what ultimately counts in terms of empirical research will always and rightfully be valid research results. To some degree, the combination of the different studies can be considered a first step towards cross-validation between the studies and the different approaches. Another step was comparing results from the present studies with results from other research projects – parallel projects from other countries, general research on youth and religion, general surveys on volunteers, etc. In addition to this, adherence to the criteria of empirical research in the social sciences was mandatory for all of the present studies. Especially in the survey conducted by the Kantar EMNID Institute but also with the two national studies on confirmation work in Germany, it was possible to make use of fully representative samples, due to the continuing support from another professional social science institution (GESIS – Leibniz Institute for the Social Sciences, Mannheim).

5. Conclusions

The major conclusion from the various studies on confirmation work and on its long-term effects certainly must be that voluntary commitment after confirmation is an increasingly important type of non-formal religious education. In addition to its beneficial effects for the people who are addressed by this work, for example, the confirmands, it allows for experiences which are of special value for the development of the people doing this work themselves. It gives them access to a community of (young) voluntary workers, allows for experiencing one's abilities as well as for developing or acquiring new competences. All of these observations show that it is important to find out more about voluntary work and its presuppositions. Research findings of this kind can lead to more effective ways of supporting this field of non-formal religious education with an age group which tends to be hard to reach, for example, through programs offered by the church. The results which have become available so far also indicate that there is in fact a need for further improvements, among others concerning the selective and potentially exclusivist processes identified in the studies in relationship to recruiting potential new volunteers. More young people could and should be motivated to become volunteers – possibly they are even already in fact motivated but they have not been asked to become volunteers

In this sense, research on young volunteers is meaningful in itself because it can contribute to further developing the field. Yet from a different point of view, it also makes sense to view voluntary commitment after confirmation as one of the important long-term effects of confirmation work. Most of all, this way of considering and researching voluntary work shows that there are indeed palpable effects of confirmation work which can be traced even several years after confirmation.

In the context of research and discussing methodological questions, it is also important to state that the research reported in this chapter clearly adds to the general evidence of the feasibility of gaining valid research results on non-formal religious education. While it remains true that such research can be carried out more easily in the context of schools (which is probably one of the reasons why most existing studies were carried out there), it is not true that valid results cannot be reached in the non-formal sector of religious education. This should be considered a good reason for further research on non-formal religious education. It does not hold true that reliable research results cannot be reached here.

Taken together, the observations concerning the meaning of voluntary work and the possibility of interpreting the motivation for it as a long-term effect of confirmation work on the one hand and the feasibility of researching it on the other, the final conclusion must be that churches and other stakeholders in this field, including the state with its interest in a strong civil society, should feel encouraged and required to invest more resources into this field and also into research related to it. Clearly the studies described in this chapter can be viewed as an important beginning which, at the same time, implies that they are just a beginning. Much more should be known about the different fields of voluntary work and about the motivation that makes young people enter such a commitment, in the context of the church but also in society at large.

References

Arnesen, S., Folkestad, B., and Gjerde, S. (2013). *Frivillig deltakelse i Norden – et komparativt perspektiv 2*. Bergen: Senter for forskning på sivilsamfunn og frivillig sektor.

BMFSFJ 2016 = Bundesministerium für Familie, Senioren, Frauen und Jugend (ed.) (2016). *Freiwilliges Engagement in Deutschland. Der deutsche Freiwilligensurvey 2014*. Berlin: BMFSFJ.

Bundesministerium für Arbeit, Soziales und Konsumentenschutz (ed.) (2015). *Bericht zu der Lage und zu den Perspektiven des Freiwilligen Engagements in Österreich. 2. Freiwilligenbericht*. Wien: Bundesministerium für Arbeit, Soziales und Konsumentenschutz. www.sozialministerium.at/cms/site/attachments/1/4/3/CH3434/CMS1451900458557/soziale-themen_freiwilliges-engagement_bericht-zur-lage-und-zu-den-perspektiven-des-freiwilligen-engagements-in-oesterreich.pdf [04.12.2017].

Center For Frivilligt Socialt Arbejde (ed.) (2014). *Frivillige Rapport 2012. Den Frivillige Sociale Indsats*. Silkeborg: Center for Frivilligt Socialt Arbejde.

Freitag, M., Manatschal, A., Ackermann, K., and Ackermann, M. (2016). *Freiwilligen-Monitor Schweiz 2016*. Zürich: Schweizerische Gemeinnützige Gesellschaft.

Hustinx, L., von Essen, J., Haers, J., and Mels, S. (eds.) (2015). *Religion and Volunteering. Complex, Contested and Ambiguous Relationships*. Cham u. a.: Springer.

Ilg, W., Pohlers, M., Gräbs Santiago, A., and Schweitzer, F. (2018). *Jung – Evangelisch – Engagiert. Langzeiteffekte der Konfirmandenarbeit und Übergänge in ehrenamtliches Engagement. Empirische Studien im biografischen Horizont*. Gütersloh: Gütersloher Verlagshaus.

Niemelä, K. (2008). *Does Confirmation Training Really Matter? A Longitudinal Study of the Quality and Effectiveness of Confirmation Training in Finland*. Tampere: Church Research Institute.

Niemelä, K., and Porkka, J. (2015). Confirmation Work in Finland. In: F. Schweitzer, K. Niemelä, T. Schlag and H. Simojoki (eds.). *Youth, Religion and Confirmation Work in Europe. The Second Study*. Gütersloh: Gütersloher Verlagshaus, 223–232.

Porkka, J., and Tervo-Niemelä, K. (2017). After Confirmation: Results for Finland. In: F. Schweitzer, T. Schlag, H. Simojoki, K. Tervo-Niemelä and W. Ilg (eds.). *Confirmation, Faith, and Volunteerism. A Longitudinal Study on Protestant Adolescents in the Transition towards Adulthood. European Perspectives*. Gütersloh: Gütersloher Verlagshaus, 172–183.

Schweitzer, F., Ilg, W., and Simojoki, H. (eds.) (2010). *Confirmation Work in Europe. Empirical Results, Experiences and Challenges. A Comparative Study in Seven Countries*. Gütersloh: Gütersloher Verlagshaus.

Schweitzer, F., Niemelä, K., Schlag, T., and Simojoki, H. (eds.) (2015). *Youth, Religion and Confirmation Work in Europe. The Second Study*. Gütersloh: Gütersloher Verlagshaus.

Schweitzer, F., Schlag, T., Simojoki, H., Tervo-Niemelä, K., and Ilg, W. (eds.) (2017). *Confirmation, Faith, and Volunteerism. A Longitudinal Study on Protestant Adolescents in the Transition towards Adulthood. European Perspectives*. Gütersloh: Gütersloher Verlagshaus.

What happens after volunteering?

10-Year longitudinal research on young volunteers in Finland

Kati Tervo-Niemelä

1. Background

> *I grew in faith especially during voluntary training and those activities.*
>
> *I started voluntary activity after confirmation. That led me to other church youth activities in my church. I did not really regard faith as important during confirmation time, but this changed when I was active in volunteer work.*
>
> *When I was 18 or 20, I realised that there were no more activities for me in the church and our group of volunteers just fell apart. Step by step, I drifted away from faith issues and I no longer felt like I was welcome in the church.*

The comments above show the importance of church voluntary activity for the youth as well the different developmental patterns that may take place during and after volunteering. Earlier studies show that volunteering seems to function in many ways to help make young people committed to the church. Young volunteers are much more likely to have a positive attitude towards the church two years after confirmation time than those who did not volunteer (Porkka et al. 2017, 108) and are more likely to believe and have a strong sense of belonging to the church (Tervo-Niemelä et al. 2017, 72). However, interest in volunteering and the active step to volunteer seems to need many supporting factors. During confirmation time, contacts with those working as volunteers and opportunities to try out volunteer work are important factors in making young people willing to volunteer in the church as well as somebody asking them to volunteer (Ilg et al. 2017, 122; Porkka et al. 2017, 104). Those who volunteer are more likely to come from homes where religion was present at least to some extent in their childhood than those who do not end up volunteering (Ilg et al. 2017, 122, 125). Friends often play an important part in volunteering as well; typically, friends make the decision to begin the activity together, and the same applies for quitting the activity (Porkka 2004, 93–94). This is especially true for those whose motives to volunteer are mostly social and external (Porkka 2009). Socially motivated volunteers' spiritual motives are typically lower than other volunteers' motives (Niemelä 2002, 118). These young volunteers are more likely to volunteer only for a shorter period while those who are spiritually motivated are likely to remain volunteers for a longer period (Niemelä 2008, 117–118). However, the biggest drop out tends to already take place before voluntary activity: only about half of those who plan to volunteer actually end up taking part in volunteer training (Niemelä 2008, 152).

Confirmation time as such often marks a turning point in the lives of young people. About half of young people experience that their faith has been strengthened during confirmation time (Hardecker and Bromander 2015, 63; Niemelä 2006). It is clear in many ways that experiences related to confirmation time are the key factor in getting interested in volunteer activity (Niemelä 2008, 149–153). For example, satisfaction with confirmation time predicts voluntary activity in the future (Ilg et al. 2017, 122). Satisfaction with confirmation time tends to predict the interest in joining volunteer training more than actual attendance (Niemelä 2008, 153). However, it is obvious that without positive experiences related to church and its faith during confirmation time, such interest does not emerge. The most important motive to volunteer is the perception that it is fun (95%): half of the volunteers join because they want to go to a camp and more than half also want to learn more about God and faith (Porkka et al. 2017, 93). However, after confirmation time and when reaching early adulthood, young people in general tend to distance themselves from the church and the likelihood to leave the church increases (Niemelä 2008; Niemelä 2015). Especially those already distant during the confirmation time tend to become more distant, while the pattern among those closer to the church during confirmation time seem to take multiple paths after confirmation time (Tervo-Niemelä et al. 2017).

In this article, the interest is in long-term developmental trends among those young people who actually volunteer and those who do not. What kind of changes take place over a 10-year perspective among volunteers and non-volunteers in youth and early adulthood in relation to church and faith?

The data was collected among young people who were confirmed in the Evangelical Lutheran Church of Finland. In Finland, 70.7% of the population belong to the Evangelical Lutheran Church of Finland (January 1, 2018). Annually about 50000 young people are confirmed which corresponds to 85.8% of those 15-year-olds (in 2016). Confirmation work is by far the largest form of non-formal religious education in the Evangelical Lutheran Church of Finland and in the whole country. At the same time, annually about 22000 young people attend volunteer education after confirmation time to become YCVs, young confirmed volunteers. This volunteer education typically follows immediately after the confirmation time and may last one or more years. About 15000 work as volunteers per year; this figure corresponds to one third of the confirmands (36% in 2016). Volunteers are mostly one to three years older than confirmands, some of them are first-time volunteers and some of them more experienced volunteers. This means that volunteer activity is very popular among young people; it can be estimated that about one in four young confirmands per age-group end up volunteering after confirmation time. This activity is by far the largest form of volunteer education in the whole county, not only in terms of religious volunteer education, but also if all the forms of volunteer education within all sectors including both formal education and the civil sector. In addition, it is one of the next largest forms of non-formal religious education (after confirmation work) in the Evangelical Lutheran Church of Finland and in the whole country. Only children's day clubs attract more participants, in this case 3- to 5-year-old children (38000 in 2016). However, if one takes into account the number of children per single year-cohort, it can be estimated that there are more young people in each year-cohort in YCV-training than there are in church children's clubs (20.9% of those 3–5 years attend day clubs).

2. Design and method

This chapter is based on a longitudinal data set collected during a ten-year period from 2002 to 2011 among young Finns aged 14/15 to 25 years old, starting from the time they started their confirmation time until they were about 25. It is a 10-year follow-up study of young people who went through confirmation preparation and were confirmed in 2002 in the parish of Tampere[1] in the Evangelical Lutheran Church of Finland. The study contains four sets of questionnaires: a questionnaire (A) at the beginning of confirmation time in 2001 (at the age of 14/15) (N=1322; 90% of all confirmands in Tampere); a questionnaire (B) at the end of confirmation time in 2001 (at the age of 15) (N=1159; 79% confirmands); a questionnaire (C) distributed to the subjects five years later, in the spring of 2006 (at the age of 20) (N=416; response rate 30%), and a questionnaire (D) that was completed ten years later, in the fall of 2011 (at the age of 25) (N=276; response rate 21%). As can be expected, the response rate from the participants has declined from the age of 14 to the age of 25. While the response rate at the beginning of confirmation was as high as 90%, it has declined to 21% ten years later. However, when comparing those who responded to the fourth questionnaire compared to those who did not answer, only one clear difference emerges: women are overrepresented among those who replied to the fourth survey round (68% are women, while women amounted to 50% in the first and second survey round). No other notable differences between the two groups could be found. For example, they were almost equal in their relation to Christianity at the beginning of and after confirmation time.

In this article, the focus is on the last data set (collected when the respondents were at the age of 25) and on the differences between those who have volunteered in the church after confirmation and those who have not. By comparing these groups in the light of the 10-year longitudinal data, the aim is to find out what kind of changes are likely to take place later in early adulthood among those young people who volunteered after confirmation time and those who did not. This data only consists of young people in one Protestant context, in the Evangelical Lutheran Church in Finland and, therefore, the results cannot be generalized to other Protestant countries. With this data, the aim is to illustrate the possible trends that may take place in youth and emerging adulthood among those persons who were confirmed and later volunteered or not in the Protestant church and also to help to predict future pat-

---

1 Tampere is the third largest city in Finland with 200000 inhabitants. The parish of Tampere includes primarily urban areas, along with some smaller rural population centers.

terns among the youth who volunteer and who do not volunteer in early adulthood also in other churches.

In the analysis, short-time and long-time volunteers are separated. Short-time volunteers refer to those who volunteer only for a year or less and long-time volunteers are those who volunteered for a longer period.

3. Changes among volunteers and non-volunteers in emerging adulthood – the case of Finland

The earlier studies among young Protestants show that there seems to be a trend between the age of 13/14 to the age of 16/17 years among the Protestant youth that those who are distant get more distant after confirmation, while those with a close relationship to the church tend to be strengthened in their relationship (Tervo-Niemelä et al. 2017). One important factor behind different developmental patterns seems to be volunteering: whether young people have been active after confirmation in church volunteer work or not.

Looking at the Finnish 10-year longitudinal data and the changes that take place after confirmation in a 10-year perspective, the first notion from the data shows that the question of belonging to or leaving the church becomes vital during one's emerging adulthood. The data from young adults who were confirmed ten years earlier show that at the age of 20, as many as 7 % had left the church and five years later as many as 22 % (24 % of men and 20 % of women) had left. This corresponds with the estimates that can be drawn from the church statistics. The longitudinal data also shows that the general attitude towards church membership has turned notably more critical and also more decisive after the age of 20. At the age of 25, only 6 % of those who were confirmed 10 years earlier thought that they could not think of leaving the church under any circumstances. However, while the share of those who think that they could not think of leaving the church had declined and the share of those who had already left had increased, the share of those who had thought of leaving but decided to stay as members had also increased (from 11 to 21). At the same time, the share of those who had not thought of leaving at all or were unsure had declined. This means that between the ages of 20 and 25, these young adults had increasingly taken clear stands and decided on their church membership status: staying or leaving.

However, there are noteworthy differences among volunteers and non-volunteers, and more precisely among long-time volunteers and other young people. Volunteering does not necessarily make young people stay in the church, but the likelihood is much higher. This especially applies to long-term volunteering. On the other hand, the influences of short-term volunteering seem to be much more limited. At the age of 25, less than one in ten of long-term volunteers had left the church while one in four of non-volunteers and short-term volunteers had left the church (see Figure 1). In addition, the attitude towards church membership dif-

Figure 1: Attitude towards church membership among Finnish short- and long-term volunteers and non-volunteers 10 years after confirmation at the age of 25.

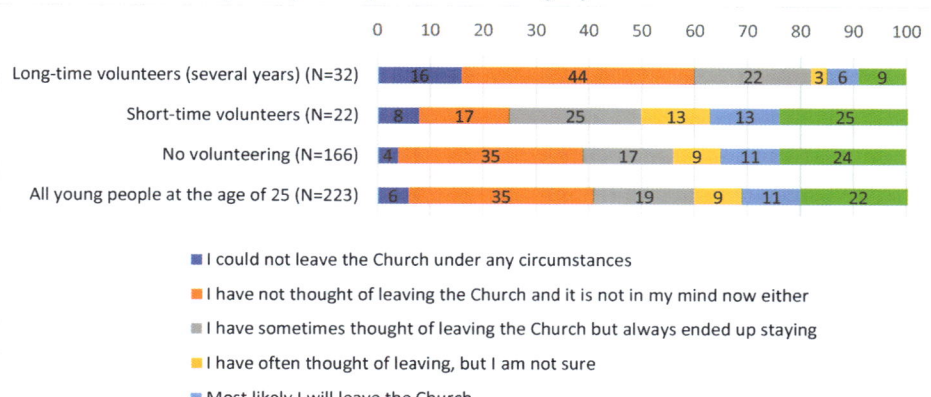

I could not leave the Church under any circumstances

I have not thought of leaving the Church and it is not in my mind now either

I have sometimes thought of leaving the Church but always ended up staying

I have often thought of leaving, but I am not sure

Most likely I will leave the Church

I have already left the Church

fers among volunteers and non-volunteers. Of the long-term volunteers, 82% either could not think of leaving the church under any circumstances or have not ever thought of church leaving or if they have thought of it, have always ended up staying, while for the short-term volunteers the respective figure is 50% and for the non-volunteers 56%.

The data show that voluntary activity is a meaningful factor predicting patterns in religious change in youth and early adulthood, also more generally. Changes in belief follow the same trend as the changes in church membership. In Figure 2, changes in belief in God are presented among those who have volunteered (either short- or long-term) and among those who did not volunteer, and the self-estimation of the change in belief is also shown.

The results show that confirmation time has typically a positive influence for belief in God among young people; both for those who later volunteer and those who do not volunteer. However, the positive changes are more common among those who later volunteer. There are also notable changes after confirmation time: long-term volunteers are typically strengthened in their belief also after confirmation while short-term volunteers and non-volunteers tend to become distanced from faith after confirmation. At the age of 25, almost two out of three (63%) of long-term volunteers say that they believe in God while only 36–38% of short-term volunteers and non-volunteers agree. Both among short-term volunteers and non-volunteers, the share of non-believers has risen clearly after confirmation, but among short-term volunteers this rise has taken place between the years 20 and 25 while among non-volunteers earlier. This means that volunteering activity seems to have kept the short-term volunteers closer to church and its faith for a few years, but this influence has not lasted. Non-believing has also increased among long-time volunteers between the age of 20 to 25, from 4% to 12%, while the rise among

Figure 2: Belief in God among Finnish volunteers and non-volunteers at the beginning of confirmation time, in the end of it and 5 years later and 10 years later

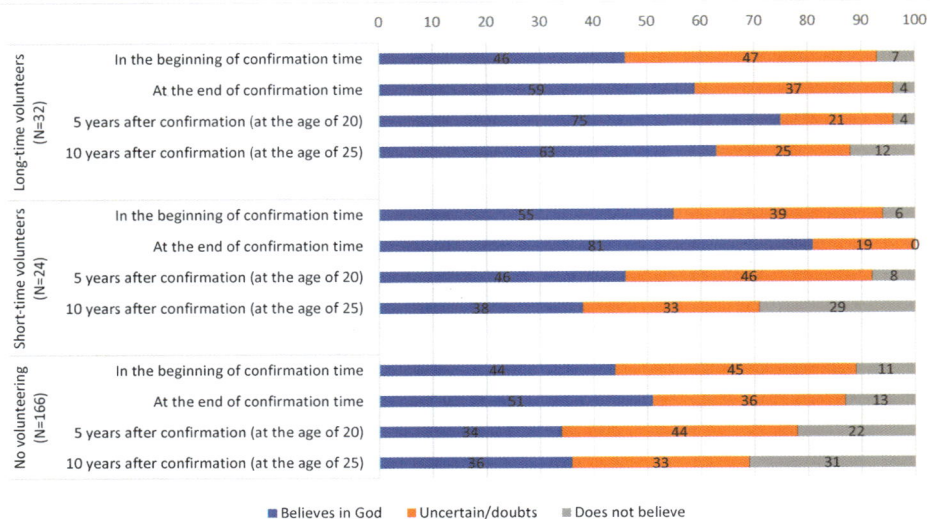

short-time volunteers has been from 8% to 29% and among non-volunteers from 22 to 31%.

Personal experiences of the changes in belief among the young people support the results shown above. When young people were asked 10 years after confirmation how their faith in God and relation to faith had changed after their confirmation, almost half (44%) of the long-term volunteers said that God and faith are closer to them at the age of 25 than at the time of confirmation and one fifth (22%) say that they have become more distant (see Figure 3). Of the short-term volunteers only 13% stated that God and faith are closer at the age of 25 and one third say that they are more distant.

Answers to open-ended questions reveal a bit more of these changes. The following comments from the short-term volunteers open up the process of distancing among them:

When growing up and life getting busy, I have not thought of faith as much as during confirmation time. During confirmation time, we are at a vulnerable age and easily influenced by others. This is the reason why many become believers during that time. Now I am considering leaving the church. The gay-issue is the main reason; I feel that everybody should have the right to a church wedding (short-term volunteer at the age of 25)

God and faith do not belong to my daily life any longer. During confirmation time I thought of these issues more and when I attended church activities (short-term volunteer at the age of 25)

I feel that I have grown apart from the church. I feel that I was naïve when I was young, but when growing up, I have started to think differently and question these issues. I feel

Figure 3: Perceptions of changes in faith in God and relation to faith after confirmation time among non-volunteers, short-term and long-term volunteers at the age of 25.

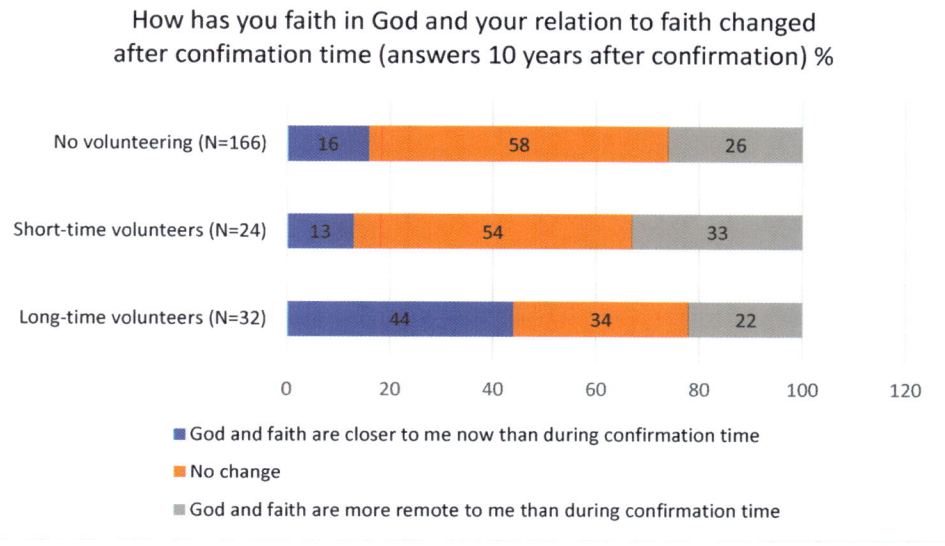

How has you faith in God and your relation to faith changed after confimation time (answers 10 years after confirmation) %

- God and faith are closer to me now than during confirmation time
- No change
- God and faith are more remote to me than during confirmation time

that I am paying church taxes in vain since those faith issues are not close to me any longer. I have remained as a member mostly just because that is a tradition (short-term volunteer at the age of 25)

During confirmation time I had not yet questioned my faith. However, after that I started to question it, which at least so far has led to denying God (short-term volunteer at the age of 25)

These comments reveal increasing distancing from the church and increasing questioning related to faith among short-term volunteers when moving towards emerging adulthood. This distancing and questioning may make them end up fully leaving the church. Responses reveal that young people tend to start questioning their faith in emerging adulthood, and what was learned in childhood and during confirmation time may not any longer seem plausible. In early adulthood young people may also start to interpret her or his earlier beliefs and attitude as naïve, as something that reflects lack of reasoning. At the same time, church and its stands and actions may also be one key reason for distancing, especially the same-sex issue was mentioned. Moreover, several short-term volunteers reveal that questioning faith was already there during confirmation time, at least to some extent.

During confirmation time, I still believed at least to some extent in God and that the Bible is true. The more I thought of it and the more I read literature related to the topic, the more I started to realise that it is only a product of imagination. Nowadays, I do not regard myself as a Christian and, therefore, I do not want to belong to a Christian community (short-term volunteer at the age of 25)

During confirmation time, it is easy to go with the flow and with the group pressure. There is no space for your own thoughts. When the group-pressure started to ease, my interest in faith also started to loosen, since there was after all no personal interest at all. Now I am planning to leave the church since I never use its service. Price-quality balance; by far too expensive (short-term volunteer at the age of 25)

The comments above show that some short-term volunteers were already sceptical towards faith in the beginning of volunteer activity (and during confirmation time) but just felt that they went "with the flow" and followed their friends. This supports the notions of earlier research that short-term volunteering is often linked to social or extrinsic motives (Niemelä 2002, 117–118; Porkka 2009).

Opposed to this, long-time volunteers point out strongly the importance of volunteer activity to both bringing them closer to faith as well as keeping them close. These young adults spoke of the importance of both voluntary activity and church youth work in general. In addition, confirmation time as such was often mentioned as a meaningful experience.

I started voluntary activity after confirmation. That led me to other church youth activities in my church. I did not really regard faith as important during confirmation time, but this changed when I was active in volunteer work (long-term volunteer at the age of 25)

It was not until during confirmation time that I started to think of faith and to reflect whether He would be the right road. When I attended church youth activities after confirmation, I got an answer and my faith was strengthened. Those church youth activities were most meaningful (long-term volunteer at the age of 25)

My confirmation time was a positive surprise. I got many new friends and after that I volunteered for a few years. My local parish supported us young people very well and the pastors and other people in the church understood us young people very well (long-term volunteer at the age of 25)

Some of the long-term volunteers even, when reporting moving away from the church, at the same time mention the importance of volunteering and say:

Faith has got more distant and been buried under the daily rush and hassle after those years when I attended church youth activities. I miss those times, church and like-mindedness which united us friends. Currently I feel that there is nothing interesting going on in the church or parish (long-term volunteer at the age of 25)

However, in all cases the closeness that may have started during confirmation time does not stay in adulthood and leaving the church becomes an option also among the long-term volunteers. Sometimes it is linked to active reasoning and reflection.

After confirmation time I was active in church and I studied Lutheran faith very thoroughly. At some point I started to question many things and finally ended up resigning from the church, since the church no longer corresponded with my world. I do not believe in the Lutheran God and many narrowminded thoughts and apparent and fake friendliness/openness disturbed me (long-term volunteer at the age of 25)

There are also stories in which volunteer activity results in disappointment. Other factors may have anyhow kept the young adult as a member and close to faith. However, bad experiences may result in losing the connectedness to the parish and church.

> *I came to believe more strongly and to feel closer to God as I grew older. However, I almost lost the connection to my parish because of bad experiences in church voluntary work after confirmation* (long-term volunteer at the age of 25)

Some former long-term volunteers may also consider leaving the church or at least feel disappointed with the church and its standpoints even though they feel close to faith, but they are disappointed with the church and its decisions.

> *I do not really think of leaving the church, but the secularization of the church and the watering down of its message has made me wonder how long could this really continue until I no longer recognise this community and feel it as my own. At the same time faith has become more active and a clearer part of my daily life. Through my own reflections I feel that I have started to understand better the relation between faith and other areas of life* (long-term volunteer at the age of 25)

4. Discussion

In this chapter, changes in the relationship to church and faith have been presented among short- and long-term volunteers and non-volunteers in a longitudinal research perspective, based on ten-year longitudinal data collected among confirmands in Finland. The results show that emerging adulthood is in many ways critical for the relationship to faith and church – and this applies to both volunteers and non-volunteers. It is far more likely for long-term volunteers to remain close to faith and God during these years, but they are not fully protected from distancing either. Distancing may be linked to active reasoning, disappointing experiences, feelings that the church and its standpoints do not correspond with one's worldview or it may be just a slow drifting away when the contacts with the church and parish activities are loosening. The results show that, especially among short-term volunteers, the distancing process typically takes place in early adulthood, among non-volunteers this process typically began already earlier, soon or immediately after confirmation, if there had ever even been a closeness to faith. Long-time volunteering is typically an indicator of a close relationship to church and faith, but even that is not always enough.

The results call strongly for activities among young adults. Even after long-time volunteering, young people may feel that there is no place for them or any activities for them in the church. This accompanied with life changes in emerging adulthood increases the likelihood to drift away from the church.

The results also show that active membership and closeness to church and faith typically needs continuous positive experiences on both the institutional level and on the individual level. This means that one needs to feel both the church and its faith as meaningful and important on a personal level and at the same time, also to feel that the church as an institution and with its activities has something to offer or that the church as an institution corresponds with one's own worldview and values. If the connectedness either on an individual or on an institutional level is weak, the likelihood to leave the church rises especially in the midst of changes in emerging adulthood. Even a strong personal level meaningfulness may not be enough if the church as an institution fails to meet the needs of a young adult.

The chapter is based on longitudinal data. Using such data gives a possibility to follow developmental patterns on an individual level in a unique way. However, there are also weaknesses when using longitudinal data sets, especially when the follow-up period is long. The biggest one is related to the loss of participants. The longer the follow-up period, the greater the loss typically is. Here, we have been following the same young people for 10 years from the age of 14/15 to the age of 25. During those years, many changes tend to take place in the lives of the partici-pants. It is possible that young people with certain developmental patterns are lost in the follow-up study. In this case, boys are more often lost, but the comparison of religious attitudes in the beginning and the end of confirmation time among those who responded and who did not respond to the last round of questionnaire shows no clear differences in attitudes.

The study and its results also call for further longitudinal studies among young people which would go beyond emerging adulthood. What changes are likely to take place when the same young people, former confirmands grow older, establish their families, have children of their own or face losses and disappointments in life and how do they value their confirmation time in a lifelong perspective? Since the loss of the data is most likely vast when the follow-up period is very long, such a study would require a large sample of young people, preferably in an international, comparative form.

References

Hardecker, G., and Bromander, J. (2015). Expectations, Motivations and Experiences of the Confirmands. In: F. Schweitzer, K. Niemelä, T. Schlag and H. Simojoki (eds.). *Youth, Religion and Confirmation Work in Europe*. Gütersloh: Gütersloher Verlagshaus, 59–70.

Ilg, W., Tervo-Niemelä, K., and Maaß, C. (2017). Believing, belonging and volunteerism in adolescence. Predictive factors from childhood and confirmation time in a multi-level framework. In: F. Schweitzer, T. Schlag, H. Simojoki and K. Tervo-Niemelä (eds.). *Confirmation work, Faith and Volunteerism. A Longitudinal Study on Protestant Adolescents in the Transition towards Adulthood – European perspectives*. Gütersloh: Gütersloher Verlagshaus, 114–129.

Niemelä, K. (2002). *Hyvä rippikoulu – Rippikoulun laatu ja vaikuttavuus*, Tampere: Kirkon tutkimuskeskus.

Niemelä, K. (2006). The quality and effectiveness of confirmation classes in Finland. In: *Journal of Beliefs & Values* 27(2), 2006, 177–190.

Niemelä, K. (2008). *Does Confirmation Training Really Matter? A Longitudinal Study of the Quality and Effectiveness of Confirmation Training in Finland.* Tampere: Church Research Institute.

Niemelä, K. (2015). "No longer believing in belonging" – A longitudinal study of Generation Y from confirmation experience to church leaving. In: *Social Compass* 62(2), 172–186.

Porkka, J. (2004). *On kunnia olla isonen. Suomen evankelis-luterilaisen kirkon isostoiminta 2000-luvun alussa.* Helsinki: Kirkkohallitus.

Porkka, J. (2009). Rippikoulusta seurakunnan vapaaehtoistyöhön – isoseksi hakemisen motiivit ja odotukset. In: T. Innanen and K. Niemelä (eds.). *Rippikoulun todellisuus.* Tampere: Kirkon tutkimuskeskus.

Porkka J., Schweitzer F., and Simojoki H. (2017). How Confirmands become volunteers. In: F. Schweitzer, T. Schlag, H. Simojoki and K. Tervo-Niemelä (eds.). *Confirmation work, Faith and Volunteerism. A Longitudinal Study on Protestant Adolescents in the Transition towards Adulthood – European perspectives.* Gütersloh: Gütersloher Verlagshaus, 84–113.

Tervo-Niemelä, K., Schlag, T., and Koch, M. (2017). Changes and Trends in Church Commitment after Confirmation. In: F. Schweitzer, T. Schlag, H. Simojoki and K. Tervo-Niemelä (eds.). *Confirmation work, Faith and Volunteerism. A Longitudinal Study on Protestant Adolescents in the Transition towards Adulthood – European perspectives.* Gütersloh: Gütersloher Verlagshaus, 61–76.

VI
Observations and conclusions

Conclusions

Friedrich Schweitzer, Wolfgang Ilg, Peter Schreiner

The present volume is the first international publication with a clear focus on research concerning non-formal religious education. While not excluding other methodologies, the emphasis is on empirical approaches to this field of work. The volume offers a forum for summarising the state of the art of research on non-formal religious education in eight European countries and provides a critical review of existing research as well as of current research projects.

The fields covered in the different chapters are the following: Christian youth work (cf. Ilg; Wolking), Catholic religious education with an emphasis on youth work and altar service (cf. Könemann and Sajak), First Communion Catechesis (Altmeyer and Boschki), kindergarten (Wörn et al.; Rothgangel and Jäggle), Sunday School (Danilovich; Schreiner), confirmation work and young volunteers (cf. Christensen; Simojoki; Tervo-Niemelä; Petterson; Schweitzer). The breadth of these fields shows the rich variety of non-formal religious education. More general reports come from different national contexts or non-Christian perspectives (Leganger-Krogstad on Norway; Schlag and Voirol-Sturzenegger on Switzerland; Danilovich on Belarus; Ulfat on Islamic contexts).

In many of the chapters the three types of education – formal, non-formal and informal – are discussed with an emphasis on how they differ but also with an eye on overlapping concerns and common challenges. Furthermore, the authors describe the research methods used in different projects and suggest perspectives for future research in the non-formal field. In doing so, they bring together insights on educating, teaching and learning in religious education that might be valid beyond particular national contexts. In this respect, there also is a comparative dimension which plays a role in most of the chapters, referring to already existing comparative research but also stressing the need to further develop comparative approaches in new ways.

The main aim of the volume is to bring together experiences and results of empirical research in the field of non-formal religious education in different European countries. There also is the hope that this endeavor can help to generate new research projects which could be carried out in international cooperation. In this concluding chapter the articles and insights will be discussed in light of four questions:

– What do the results say about the meaning and functioning of non-formal learning in the religious sphere?
– Which methodological approaches seem to be promising for this kind of educational settings?

- What are the implications of the central results of the different studies concerning the future development of non-formal religious education?
- What directions can be derived from these studies for future research?

1. Formal, non-formal and informal learning: A critical review

1.1 Definitions, distinctions, overlaps

Most chapters include a definition or at least an approach to what non-formal (religious) education means and how it differs from formal and informal education or learning. At the end of the volume it appears helpful to review the different definitions and concepts of non-formal education.

First of all, in most cases the understanding of non-formal education is based on its distinction from informal and formal education. Consequently, the definition of non-formal education presupposes a clear understanding of formal and informal education. Concerning the field of *formal (religious) education* there is much agreement among the authors of the different chapters. This concept refers to institutionalized forms of education that follow a syllabus and provide formal qualification and exams. Moreover, formal education especially in the context of school is compulsory, although in many cases pupils are allowed to decide if they want to participate in Religious Education or not. (Religious Education with capital letters refers to the school subject that exists in most European countries, in different forms and based on different organizational models, sometimes related to churches or other religious bodies; in some cases Religious Education currently is subject to fundamental changes as the reports from Norway and Switzerland show; cf. Leganger-Krogstad; Schlag and Voirol-Sturzenegger in this volume). Several chapters in this volume include an analysis or evaluation of the relationship between formal religious education on the one hand and non-formal religious education as well as informal religious education on the other. These different forms of education should not be viewed in isolation from each other but as complementary modes of education and learning. Moreover, the different forms of education clearly seem to influence each other at various levels by shaping the presuppositions for the respective other forms of education. Religious education or nurture in the family, for example, appears to remain influential in formal and non-formal educational contexts even in adolescence and adulthood.

There also is far-reaching agreement between the authors of the different chapters in this volume concerning the delineation of non-formal education in relationship to formal education. Accordingly, non-formal (religious) education can be characterized by the following aspects (cf. Simojoki in this volume).

Non-formal religious education:

- is non-compulsory,
- takes place outside the formal educational system in schools, training institutions and universities, in a broad range of learning fields from sports activities to education in churches,
- is not related to scholastic certificates,
- is situated in experience-oriented (sometimes outdoor) learning environments which are less restricted in time and space than school, providing opportunities for participatory learning based on activating teaching methods,
- is less professionalized in a formal sense and open for voluntary activities,
- is particular and partial, i.e. non-formal education often pursues particular programmatic aims (e.g. in the case of environmental associations or human rights groups) and specific interests (e.g. in the case of sport activities) or is connected to a particular ethos (e.g. in the case of Christian youth work).

The third form of education, i.e. *informal religious education* is a topic which would deserve further analysis as well. There is a similar lack of research concerning the informal sector, just like in the case of non-formal religious education. Yet it has not been the intention of the present volume to cover research on informal religious education. The different chapters only address the informal sector in its relationship to non-formal religious education, in order to reach a clearer understanding of the meaning of the different concepts. In this perspective, non-formal religious education is distinguished from informal forms which are:

- unplanned,
- exclusively part of everyday life,
- not connected to any educational setting,
- unpredictable and spontaneous,
- without defined aims.

Although some educational processes, for example in youth work, are rather similar to informal learning, especially an institutional setting and defined educational aims are typical attributes of non-formal learning which distinguish it from informal educational processes.

This attempt of summarising the different definitions provided in the chapters of this volume should not lead to the misunderstanding that the three concepts or the aspects and sectors they refer to are clearly separate. In many ways, the understanding of the different forms of education also depends on the perspective chosen. When the perspective of the active role of the learner, for example, is made the starting point, it can be argued that formal education should also include non-formal and informal elements because they are important for both, the needs of individuals as well as of society. Another aspect concerning the interplay between the different forms of education has been highlighted, for example, by Rauschenbach (Rauschenbach 2009): Young people's success in the formal realm of education, especially in school, depends to a high degree on competences which can be acquired in non-formal educational settings. This is especially true for the field of personal and social competences, like team-work, time-planning or the ability for self-directed work. Thus non-formal learning may be organized independently from formal learning but it nevertheless can prepare young people for succeeding in terms of formal education.

As shown by many of the chapters from the different countries in this volume, there also is much overlap between the programs used for formal and non-formal religious education. Only rarely do these programs correspond to the ideal-type distinctions offered in the literature. Instead, in many cases the characteristics of all three forms of education seem to apply at the same time. Participation in confirmation, for example, is of course voluntary but it is nevertheless the presupposition for certain rights within some churches. Participation in early childhood religious education programs is not compulsory but in some cases, admission to confirmation is based on it. Attending kindergarten or not is a decision which parents are allowed to make but once the decision has been made, the consequences in terms of expected presence are similar to school attendance. In such and similar cases one could almost speak of a continuum between the different forms of education. Moreover, as already described in a number of respects, there often is an interplay between the different forms of education which again speaks against viewing the distinctions between the three forms of education as set in stone.

In the end it makes most sense to understand the three forms of religious education and the concepts related to them as different perspectives which allow for different points of view. This implies that they are less useful for clearly delineating different sectors than discussing different needs in education. Thus the emphasis on non-formal and informal education is important to avoid the ever-threatening educational monopoly of school and to strengthen programs outside of school which are still suffering from not being valued as truly educational in many places. The emphasis on non-formal education can also be critically directed against state-sponsored education as the only type of education available. Non-formal education usually does not rely on the state as its sponsor but on associations and institutions which are part of civil society. In this sense, non-formal education is based on democratic principles in society at large. Most of all, however, non-formal education should be appreciated as an opportunity for young people to assume responsibilities of their own and to independently plan educational opportunities, for themselves or for others, instead of just passively adapting to the parameters of education at school. This understanding also is the reason why the actual awareness of the importance of non-formal education in different countries must be addressed.

1.2 Growing awareness for non-formal education in the different countries

Based on the reports from the different countries represented in this volume there seems to be a general tendency towards growing awareness of the importance of non-formal education in general as well as of non-formal religious education in particular. At the same time, there also appears to be a need to further strengthen this awareness.

The growing awareness for educational fields outside the formalized sector is also confirmed by contemporary political debates. The concept of non-formal education receives political validation and recognition especially from European institutions, mainly as part of the concept of lifelong learning where different ways of learning and education are recognized on an equal level. An early example is the final Declaration of the 5th Conference of Ministers responsible for Youth within the Council of Europe from 1998. Here the ministers encouraged the member states to promote equal opportunities by recognising training and skills acquired by young people through non-formal education/learning, and by identifying various ways to certify experiences and qualifications acquired in this framework.

Furthermore, the Parliamentary Assembly of the Council of Europe addressed in a Recommendation on non-formal education in 2000 all those who shape educational policies, and promotes the following perspective: "Non-formal education is an integral part of a lifelong learning concept that allows young people and adults to acquire and maintain the skills, abilities and outlook needed to adapt to a continuously changing environment. [...] An important part of non-formal education is carried out by non-governmental organisations involved in community and youth work." (Council of Europe 2000)

This was also confirmed in the European Qualifications Framework EQF (2008) as a tool for making the national education systems and the respective required qualifications more understandable and comparable across the different countries and systems. The EQF promotes equal recognition of formal and non-formal education as well as of informal education (cf. Schreiner 2012, 252–255). As a further step a recommendation on validating non-formal and informal learning was launched in 2012 (cf. Cedefop 2015). For example, universities are now obliged to acknowledge competences that students have acquired outside the academic institutions and to recognize them in terms of credit points for their university studies. In practice this can mean that a person who has worked as a youth leader on a voluntary basis can have certain requirements waived in the course of his or her studies.

1.3 Questions concerning principles for successful non-formal education

What are the presuppositions for successful non-formal education? And which criteria should be applied in evaluating this success? Once the importance of non-formal religious education has been established, such questions must also be addressed in more detail. Judging from the chapters in this volume it seems fair to say that the discussion on these questions has just begun. The empirical results reported from the different countries can be interpreted as first steps in this direction but much work still remains to be done.

For example, a number of characteristics of non-formal (religious) education are mentioned in a number of the chapters which can be understood as hypotheses concerning successful non-formal education. Im sum, they emphasize:

- voluntary and self-organized forms of learning,
- intrinsic motivation of participants,
- close connection to young people's aspirations and interests,
- participatory and learner-centered approaches,
- open character and structure of respective programs,
- transparency and flexibility of curricular guidelines,
- evaluation of success and failure in a collective process and without judgement on individual success or failure (the 'right to make mistakes'),
- supportive learning environment,
- chances for voluntary commitment (also fostering the idea of learning in teams),
- preparation and staging of activities with a professional attitude, regardless of whether the activity is run by professionals or voluntary workers,
- sharing of results with the interested public and a planned follow up.

The identification of these principles is mostly derived from self-reports of practitioners who have been asked to describe their experiences with non-formal education from an actor perspective. This implies that the expertise behind these principles is most of all practical. It may also be informed by theoretical work but there is no empirical evidence concerning non-formal religious education in relationship to the effects of applying these principles. As far as the principles have been tested in other fields, it may be assumed that the respective results also apply to religious education. Yet such assumptions should be tested in further research.

2. Methodologies and research approaches

One of the main questions guiding this volume from the beginning has been if it is possible to do serious research in the non-formal sector or if the open structure of this field excludes reliable research designs and valid results. The different research projects described in this volume may be taken as evidence that it is indeed possible to do this kind of research and that reliable results can in fact be achieved. Sampling remains more of a challenge in the non-formal sector than in formal contexts. Yet many of the research projects actually worked with robust samples and plausible research designs.

The contributions document a rich picture of methodologies and research approaches. In most of the projects a combination of quantitative and qualitative methods was used. The quantitative methods provide reliable statistical data mainly using questionnaires, whereas the qualitative methods provide findings on the basis of interviews and case studies. In both respects, advanced procedures were applied in the different research projects.

2.1 Qualitative research

In the field of qualitative approaches a number of methods were used to analyse interviews:

- Multi-step method developed by Schmidt (2012) based on a five-step process, starting with creating categories for the interpretation of transcribed interviews, then organized in an analysing guide, which was used and then revised. On this basis, the interviews are coded and the data encrypted. On the basis of the codes an overview of the different cases becomes possible and finally this creates the basis for selecting cases for more in-depth analysis.
- Personal interview procedure according to Inghard Langer (2000) as unstructured open interviews focused on personal dialogue.
- Structured qualitative content analysis (Kuckartz 2014), focused on categories that contain the substance of the investigation. They become tools of the analysis and also elements of a theory. This method is directed by a research question, sometimes also by a hypothesis or a theory. It can be used to describe social phenomena, centered on the meaning of the content but does not follow a set procedure for interpretation such as the so-called objective hermeneutics (Oevermann et al. 1979).
- Content analysis (Mayring 2014), an approach of systematic, rule guided qualitative text analysis which tries to preserve some methodological strengths of quantitative content analysis but to also make it fit with qualitative procedures.
- Intervention studies that are considered to yield reliable insights on possible effects of educational approaches in teaching units.
- Ethnographic approaches.
- Grounded Theory.
- Thematic coding (Flick 2012) as a form of qualitative analysis which involves recording or identifying passages of text or images that are linked to a common theme or idea, allowing to index the text with categories. A framework of thematic ideas can then be created on that basis.
- Scientific evaluation of existing programs or best-practice models.

2.2 Quantitative research

In the field of quantitative approaches questionnaire-based surveys are normally used for the acquisition of data. Especially in fields that used to be blind spots of empirical research, the studies presented in this volume had to start out by collecting data about the framework and the general situation in a given non-formal field of work. The respective chapters describe youth work (Ilg), Orthodox Sunday Schools (Danilovich), Protestant Sunday Schools (Schreiner) or the mini-confirmands program (Christensen). Evidently, the researchers felt the need of generating basic reports on the reality of these offers as a starting point for deeper research endeavours. In contrast to the much studied area of school learning, the non-formal learning world still has continents lacking even basic descriptions. In this case, quantitative survey studies have the task to describe the landscape of a certain non-formal field, giving an overview of its size and characteristics. Thus, readers can become aware, for example, of how often a certain offer takes place, how many children take part in it, what role paid and voluntary workers play, etc. The example of the long-term international research project on confirmation work which also started out with basic descriptions of this kind, shows how in-depth analysis becomes possible once such a descriptive basis has been secured (cf. Simojoki).

Beyond mere descriptions of the situation, quantitative methods can provide further insights by using inferential statistics (correlations, regression analysis, analysis of variance, etc.). The claim of presenting an overall picture of a research field presupposes a representative collection of data points (for example, parishes, groups or individuals) and a large enough sample size. Again, the international studies on confirmation work with more than 30000 young people involved in the surveys show the potential of large-scale studies also in the non-formal field. In studies of this size, also multi-level methods can be applied, offering insights into individual as well as group effects of educational activities.

Other than many common studies which only ask young people involved in a certain program, the complex study of First Communion Catechesis in the Catholic Church (Altmeyer and Boschki) works not only with several surveys over time, but also includes the comparison with a control group, thus identifying specific effects of a non-formal "treatment". This procedure allows for testing hypothetical assumptions: The method of structural-equation models develops theories of the interdependency between different variables and tests these models with research data.

A special approach to the effectiveness of certain educational activities is applied in intervention studies. Here, two or more groups receive a different treatment. If the groups differ in the outcome of the criteria variable, it can be assumed that the intervention has had a specific effect. In the present volume, only the research project presented by Wörn et al. uses intervention studies. To be precise, this intervention study is actually located in a field of formal learning, e.g. the training of kindergarten teachers. It is no surprise that intervention studies are much more common in school settings than, for example, in youth work. As soon as the participants have a decisive role in deciding on group activities it is hardly possible to conduct different intervention schemes planned by an external research team. Nevertheless, given the need for finding out more about the actual effects of certain educational programs, possibilities for capturing such effects empirically are also important in the field of non-formal religious education.

In some studies in the non-formal sector, preference is given to action research which provides the opportunity for developing interactive shared research, allowing the research object to participate in a more active role in the research itself. Naturally, certain research tasks, such as the actual data collection (e.g. in guideline interviews), are exempt from this specific methodology.

2.3 Combining qualitative and quantitative results

One of the main questions which remains is how to combine the outcomes of different research approaches and methodologies. There can be no doubt that making use of quantitative as well as qualitative methodologies proves to be useful because both research approaches allow for finding answers to different questions. This applies, of course, in general but is of special importance in the context of non-formal religious education, for example, in doing research on young volunteers (Schweitzer in this volume).

In some projects quantitative and qualitative types of research were combined. As long as they are not part of an integrated consecutive research process in which quantitative and qualitative steps or phases can build upon each other, however, the results can not just be put together. It may be different when the different methodologies and approaches become integrated, e.g. by developing hypotheses in qualitative studies and then testing the hypotheses quantitatively by using representative samples. In most cases presented in this volume it seems most appropriate to view the different approaches as different spotlights, each of them shedding light on certain aspects while leaving other aspects in the dark. This allows for bringing the different results into conversation with each other without claiming to have achieved true triangulation. The resulting interpretations are richer and more reliable than understandings which are based on single studies or methodologies (cf. Wörn et al.; Schweitzer in this volume).

2.4 Characteristics of research in the religious area

Regarding the special character and aims of non-formal *religious* education the reports in this volume show that only few studies focus on the religious content or the theological questions connected to it – an observation which is explicitly mentioned in the Norwegian contribution (Leganger-Krogstad in this volume) but can be made in many of the research projects presented. One could provocatively ask how meaningful the content taken up in non-formal religious settings really is if content tends to be neglected when it comes to empirical studies. Yet this would probably be too simple, at least in certain respects. Content-related and theological perspectives are often involved in empirical work, even if this is not always made explicit. Using again the example of the studies on confirmation work in Europe it can not only be said that the results of this research are highly pertinent in terms of theology but that these results are also based on theological criteria and decisions (cf. Simojoki et al. 2018).

Another observation relates to further research lacunae. Considering the studies described in this volume it also becomes clear that especially studies with a broader approach and basis, for example long-term observations of a field or systematic co-operation in an international network, are lacking so far. One promising experience has been the cooperation within the "International Network for Research and Development of Confirmation and Christian Youth Work" (http://www.confirmation-youthwork.eu) which was founded in 2007 and has coordinated different studies on a European level, especially the studies on confirmation work (cf. Simojoki in this volume). Interestingly enough, these studies have not only gained a lot of attention in the nine participating European countries but also triggered parallel studies in other countries like Belarus (cf. Danilovich in this volume) or in the United States of America (Osmer and Douglass 2018).

3. Observations concerning the future development of non-formal religious education

It is not possible to sum up the 17 chapters presented in this volume in a few lines. Yet some observations concerning the future development of non-formal religious education emerging from these contributions can be stated. The observations may help to highlight the potentials and promises of non-formal religious education in additional ways.

A first observation sounds fairly simple: Non-formal educational settings often are associated with a lot of fun by the (usually young) people who participate in such programs. In contrast to school, providing opportunities for having fun and a framework for good relationships can be seen as a fundamental presupposition for successful offers in this area. As participation is voluntary, an offer that is not promising and attractive for the target group will soon disappear. "Fun" in this sense is related to intense experiences, time for friendship and relevance for daily life. This is why it should not be confused with superficial entertainment.

The workers in the non-formal area seem to be of special importance for the participants and their number is often much larger than the number of paid workers (cf. Ilg in this volume). In contrast to school teachers they can take on the role of "older friends". Moreover, participation in a non-formal program often leads one to become a volunteer in this field or related fields later on. At the same time, the professionalization needed for attractive programs spurs developments towards a larger number of paid workers, as it is described for the Faith Education Reform in Norway (cf. Leganger-Krogstad in this volume) or the school-related youth work in Germany (cf. Wolking in this volume). As the contribution of Schweitzer (in this volume) shows, successful non-formal education promotes young people's motivation for voluntary commitment. Thus non-formal education is not only the result of voluntary work but at the same time is one of its roots. When non-formal fields become professionalized, it is important to maintain a basic feeling of voluntary commitment even if some parts of the work are organized by professionals. In other words, professionalization does not necessarily mean that paid staff is taking tasks over from volunteers but rather pave the way for improved opportunities for volunteerism supported by full-time workers.

When one asks about how new developments in the non-formal field come about, it can often be observed that changes in the sector of formal education trigger major initiatives outside of school. This can be clearly observed with the changes concerning Religious Education in school in Norway and Switzerland, which in both cases were a decisive factor for the development of new youth work and confirmation schemes in the respective Churches (cf. Leganger-Krogstad; Schlag and Voirol-Sturzenegger in this volume; cf. also the effects of Danish school reform described by Christensen in this volume). These examples are especially noteworthy as they also show the sometimes rapid rates of changes which can affect even settings of formal religious education with a long tradition. Regarding the discussions on the future of Religious Education as a school subject, for example, in Germany it seems striking that the idea of strengthening non-formal approaches as a complementary strategy has not yet been discussed more thoroughly – although Norway and Switzerland show the options for possible compensatory approaches in religious learning by strengthening non-formal religious education.

When comparing formal and non-formal settings in religious education, one striking difference lies in the innovative potential which non-formal education includes. The remarkable examples from Swedish confirmation work (Petterson in this volume) show the flexibility with which a Church has reacted to problems in the participation rates of confirmation work. Made possible by open framework regulations and the willingness of the Swedish Church to invest money in this field, new forms of confirmation work have been established which have the potential of giving confirmation work a completely new image, be it connected with hunting, football or a film profile. Looking at these innovative examples, one wonders why experimental changes are not also tried out in other fields more often.

Looking at the contributions dealing with Islamic religion (cf. Ulfat; Rothgangel and Jäggle in this volume), it becomes obvious how controversial not only educational programs in this field can be but also the research referring to such programs.

It is also significant – and in fact deplorable – that, for the most part, approaches to interreligious education are still lacking in the non-formal field. The importance of research in respect to interreligious issues may be seen from the results of current investigations in the field of kindergarten (cf. Wörn et al. in this volume).

Taken together these observations clearly speak for giving non-formal religious education more emphasis, be it in church or in society. This field of education appears to be very vital and full of additional potentials that should no longer be underestimated. Non-formal religious education can include unique learning experiences which are not available anywhere else, neither in the formal nor in the informal sector.

4. Perspectives for future research

The one statement which can be found in almost all of the chapters in this book is that "more research is needed". On the one hand, the compilation of different studies concerning non-formal religious education in this book shows some impressive results. On the other hand, this compilation makes it very clear that many questions remain open and that much more needs to be investigated and discovered in this field.

Taking the studies in the present book as the starting point, especially the following approaches deserve more attention in future research:

– One important wish concerns international cooperation of researchers jointly researching a comparable field in different countries with methods or questionnaires which are as similar as possible. As the research project on confirmation work shows, this kind of international cooperation seems to be much easier on the basis of quantitative than of qualitative research. Nevertheless, qualitative research with joint international approaches would be interesting for future research as well.

– In an increasingly globalized world, international cooperation should not be limited to European countries. Future projects should also involve research on non-formal education in other parts of the world. As first successful examples of transatlantic research cooperation show (Osmer and Douglass 2018), a broader view can be enriching for research as well as for the praxis of non-formal education.

– Long-term studies are still too rare. It seems promising to learn about effects over time by following a certain group of (young) people over years – also after they have no more contact with their former involvement with non-formal education.

– If more studies with a control group or intervention studies could be implemented, this would help to identify learning effects from Religious Education in school as well as from non-formal religious education. Which kind of learning has what effects for the young people?

– As the project from Finland shows (Tervo-Niemelä in this volume), churches should become more interested in research on people who drop out of religious institutions, for example, on people leaving the church. In this respect, future research should also include possible positive of negative effects of formal and non-formal education at different stages of people's biographies concerning dropping out of the church at a later point of their lives.

– How can different denominations learn from each other in respect to non-formal education? The most well-known example of such ecumenical learning has been the idea of having camps as part of confirmation work which were first developed in Finland, at least in Europe (for earlier camp approaches in the United States of America cf. Osmer and Douglass 2018). One may also wonder, for example, if Protestant programs with confirmation work for children imply that there have been influences from the Catholic Church and the First Communion Preparation there, although the Danish mini-confirmand program (Christensen in this volume) developed in a context without much Catholic presence.

– One challenging task for researchers might also be to make their research re-sults more accessible for practitioners. Even more, if practitioners are enabled to have access to reliable data of their own, for example, from easy to use eval-uation tools, their willingness to support research projects and the interest in evidence-based work in the non-formal area might increase significantly. Ap-proaches of this kind are documented in the chapter on mapping Christian youth work (Ilg in this volume) but could be extended to many other fields as well.

5. Outlook

The idea for this book goes back to an international consultation in Tübingen/Ger-many in March 2018 which also explains the high share of reports from Germany. One clear understanding among the researchers of the conference was that more exchange as well as more international cooperation in this field is needed. In this respect the volume documents first steps in this direction that should be followed by more structured exchange and comparative research initiatives. The aim must be to build a structured research network with vivid exchange and tools for collaboration. This step could also contribute to the further appreciation of non-formal religious education and its effects on strengthening civil society.

   The more non-formal education receives attention in the course of a biograph-ical learning history, the more important it will also be to have reliable scientific accounts of what is going on in the non-formal settings. Non-formal education of-ten operates on the basis of voluntary commitment. In contexts where not even the leaders of a program are paid, it is difficult to convey that money should be spent on research activities. So the institutions can hardly be expected to raise funding for appropriate studies. Therefore, research on non-formal education is in need of funding from central agencies or actors like the state or – in the context of religious education – from churches, mosques or other religious bodies.

At a time when, in the educational as well as in the political field, there are more and more demands for evidence-based approaches, the non-formal sector would necessarily be put at a serious disadvantage if the research there remained on a low level. Strengthening research on non-formal religious education appears to be key strategy for strengthening the field of non-formal activities on the long run.

References

Cedefop (2015). *European guidelines for validating non-formal and informal learning.* Luxembourg: Publications Office. Cedefop reference series; No 104. http://dx.doi.org/10. 2801/008370

Council of Europe (Parliamentary Assembly) (2000). Non-formal education. Recommendation 1437(2000). http://assembly.coe.int/nw/xml/XRef/Xref-XML2HTML-EN.asp? fileid=16762&lang=en [08.03.2019].

Flick, U. (2012). *Qualitative Sozialforschung. Eine Einführung.* Reinbek bei Hamburg: Rowohlt.

Kuckartz, U. (2014). *Qualitative Inhaltsanalyse. Methoden, Praxis, Computerunterstützung.* Weinheim/Basel: Beltz Juventa.

Langer, I. (2000). *Das persönliche Gespräch als Weg in der psychologischen Forschung.* Köln: GwG-Verlag.

Mayring, Ph. (2014). *Qualitative content analysis: theoretical foundation, basic procedures and software solution.* Klagenfurt. http://nbn-resolving.de/urn:nbn:de:0168-ssoar-395173 [08.03.2019].

Oevermann, U., Allert, T., Konau, E., Krambeck, J. (1979). Die Methodologie einer "objektiven Hermeneutik" und ihre allgemeine forschungslogische Bedeutung in den Sozialwissenschaften. In: *Interpretative Verfahren in den Sozial- und Textwissenschaften,* ed. H.-G. Soeffner. Stuttgart: Metzler, 352–434.

Osmer, R. R., and Douglass, K. M. (eds.) (2018). *Cultivating teen faith. Insights from the confirmation project.* Grand Rapids: Eerdmans.

Rauschenbach, T. (2009). *Zukunftschance Bildung. Familie, Jugendhilfe und Schule in neuer Allianz.* Weinheim/München: Juventa.

Schmidt, C. (^{9}2012). Analyse von Leitfadeninterviews. In: *Qualitative Forschung. Ein Handbuch,* ed. U. Flick, E. von Kardorff and I. Steinke. Reinbek: Rowohlt, 447–456.

Schreiner, P. (2012). *Religion im Kontext einer Europäisierung von Bildung. Eine Rekonstruktion europäischer Diskurse aus protestantischer Perspektive.* Waxmann: Münster.

Schweitzer, F. (2017). Researching Non-Formal Religious Education: The example of the European Study on Conformation Work. In: *HTS Teologiese Studies/Theological Studies* 73(4), a4613 https://doi.org/10.4102/hts.v73i4.4613

Simojoki, H., Ilg, W., Schlag, T., and Schweitzer, F. (2018). *Zukunftsfähige Konfirmandenarbeit. Empirische Erträge – theologische Orientierungen – Perspektiven für die Praxis.* Gütersloh: Gütersloher Verlagshaus.

Authors

Dr. *Stefan Altmeyer*, professor of Religious Education at the Catholic Faculty of Theology, Johannes Gutenberg University Mainz, Germany

Dr. *Reinhold Boschki*, professor of Religious Education at the Catholic Faculty of Theology, University of Tübingen, Germany

Dr. *Leise Christensen*, pastor and external lecturer of the Research and Development Center, Church of Denmark, Denmark

Dr. *Yauheniya Danilovich*, researcher at the Faculty of Protestant Theology, WWU Münster, Germany

Dr. *Wolfgang Ilg*, professor of Youth Work and Congregational Education, University of Applied Sciences Ludwigsburg, Germany

Dr. *Martin Jäggle*, professor em. of Religious Education and Catechetics at the Catholic Faculty of Theology, University of Vienna, Austria

Dr. *Judith Könemann*, professor of Practical Theology, Religious Education and Gender research at the Faculty of Catholic Theology, WWU Münster, Germany

Dr. *Heid Leganger-Krogstad*, professor em. for Religious Education at MF Norwegian School of Theology, Religion and Society in Oslo, Norway

Rebecca Nowack M.A., researcher at the Catholic Faculty of Theology, University of Tübingen, Germany

Dr. *Per Pettersson*, professor of Sociology of Religion at CTF, Service Research Center, Karlstad University, Sweden

Dr. *Martin Rothgangel*, professor of Religious Education at the Protestant Faculty of Theology, University of Vienna, Austria

Dr. *Clauß Peter Sajak*, professor of Practical Theology and Religious Education at the Faculty of Catholic Theology, WWU Münster, Germany

Dr. *Thomas Schlag*, professor of Practical Theology and Religious Education at the Faculty of Theology, University of Zürich, Switzerland

Dr. *Peter Schreiner*, director of the Comenius Institute/Protestant Center for Research and Development of Education, Münster, Germany

Dr. Dr. h. c. *Friedrich Schweitzer*, professor of Practical Theology and Religious Education at the Protestant Faculty of Theology, University of Tübingen, Germany

Dr. *Henrik Simojoki*, professor of Protestant Theology / Religious Education at the Institute for Protestant Theology, University of Bamberg, Germany

Dr. *Kati Tervo-Niemelä*, professor of Practical Theology at the University of Eastern Finland, Joensuu, Finland

Dr. *Fahimah Ulfat*, junior-professor for Islamic Religious Education at the Center for Islamic Theology, University of Tübingen, Germany

Dr. *Rahel Voirol-Sturzenegger*, lecturer for Religious Education at RefModula (theological formation in the Reformed Churches of Bern-Jura-Solothurn), Bern, Switzerland

Golde Wissner, Dipl. psych., Dipl. theol., researcher at the Protestant Faculty of Theology, University of Tübingen, Germany

Dr. *Alexandra Wörn*, researcher at the Protestant Faculty of Theology, University of Tübingen, Germany

Lena Wolking, Dipl. theol., researcher at the Protestant Faculty of Theology, University of Tübingen, Germany